RECREATION PLANNING AND MANAGEMENT

RECREATION PLANNING AND MANAGEMENT

Edited by Stanley R. Lieber and Daniel R. Fesenmaier

Venture Publishing
State College, Pennsylvania

Design by Marilyn Shobaken
Technical Illustrations by William W. Porter

First published in the USA in 1983
by Venture Publications
1640 Oxford Circle, State College, PA 16801

First published in the UK in 1983
by E. & F. N. Spon Ltd,
11 New Fetter Lane, London EC4P 4EE

© 1983 Venture Publications
Printed in the United States of America

ISBN 0 910251 03 7

Library of Congress Card Number 82-050955

Contents

Foreword

The purpose of this book is to provide undergraduate students with basic information about the provision of outdoor recreation services. Although the Outdoor Recreation Resources Review Commission stimulated interest in recreation research in the 1960's, no coordinated research agenda at the national, regional, state, or local level existed until 1979. The first National Agenda for Recreation Research was prepared by the U.S. Department of Interior's Heritage Conservation and Recreation Service and the National Recreation and Parks Association. Ten tasks were identified as having the highest priority among professional, employer, and expertise groups. These were: 1) Fuel Shortages and Fuel Costs, 2) Integrating Recreation with other Recreation Management Activities, 3) The Value of Resource Use for Recreation compared with other uses, 4) Comprehensive Recreation Plans, 5) Fostering Cooperation among Providers of Recreation, 6) Increased Recreation Opportunities for the Elderly, 7) Vandalism, 8) Media Influence on Recreation and Leisure Interests and Choices, 9) Estimating the Economic Value of Outdoor Recreation, and 10) Survey Research Techniques.

In approving the National Agenda for Recreation Research for public distribution, Cecil Andrus, U.S. Secretary of the Interior, wholeheartedly agreed with the central conclusion of the agenda: "The prevailing research need for recreation in the 1980's will be to document, with precision, the contribution of recreation to the physical, mental, emotional, social, economic, and political health and well-being of individuals in their homes, neighborhoods, cities, states, and nations (p. 26)." Although no book can definitively address all ten points of the national agenda, the five sections comprising this book were developed so that students will better understand: 1) the value of public outdoor recreation, 2) some of the basic recreation demand forecasting methods, 3) how the preferences of recreationists are identified with regard to the recreation potential of land and future participation, and 4) the roles of people concerned with and responsible for the provision of public outdoor recreation.

To this end, the first section of this book contains chapters identifying the benefits of leisure participation, the estimation of demand for recreation, the economic contributions of leisure and recreation facilities, the willingness of the public to pay for such facilities and one way in which recreation businesses can be located. The second section of the book constitutes an overview and guide to the major forecasting methods currently in use. Trend extrapolation, delphi forecasting, structural forecasting and dynamic forecasting are reviewed. The third section of this book addresses the problem of defining the information needed for recreation planning. This section includes an overview of procedures for evaluating the recreational potential of land as well as the scenic beauty of areas and the means by which data may be gathered to determine the current and future demand for recreation. The fourth section of this book focuses upon management considerations which can effect the quality of recreation provision. The fifth and concluding section of this book is entitled Recreation Planning

Issues. The contrasting viewpoints in this section illustrate the different viewpoints of educators, state and regional planners, and national policy makers with regard to the future of outdoor recreation planning.

It is our hope that this book will provide the reader with a more integrated perspective on the value of leisure participation and outdoor recreation and some of the major components of the planning process. In organizing this book, we have solicited the opinions of many individuals; the errors of omission and commission are our own. Nevertheless, we wish to thank the contributors who have labored extensively to improve the readability and presentation of the material.

Stanley R. Lieber
Daniel R. Fesenmaier

Section One:
The Value of Leisure and Outdoor Recreation

1

Social Benefits of Outdoor Recreation: An Introduction

John R. Kelly

Is it important for public agencies to provide resources for outdoor recreation? In a condition of abundance in public resources, provision of access and opportunities for recreation at lakes and rivers, mountains and forests, deserts and beaches is self-evidently desirable. In 1981 on over a billion occasions, individuals or groups invested time and money to get to such public recreation sites for a day or longer. Over half the adult population went fishing in 1981 and 35 percent camped in a developed site at least once (Kelly 1980). There is no lack of evidence that people use outdoor recreation resources when they are available.

However, we are not in a condition of abundance, but of relative scarcity. The financial resources of cities, counties, states, and the federal government are limited. Everything desired by citizens, even by majorities, will not be provided. Further, the extent of support raises the issue of relative value. Just how important is resource-based outdoor recreation? Are its benefits significant for society? And to what extent can those benefits be measured and compared to other goods and services?

Recreation and the Quality of Life

There is now considerable evidence that rising incomes and standards of living are not inevitably accompanied by greater life satisfaction and sense of well-being (Campbell 1981). Rather, economic changes since the Industrial Revolution have come at the cost of such social changes as urbanization. According to Angus Campbell, late director of the Institute for Social Research of the University of Michigan:

> What appears to have happened is that an increasing number of people have achieved a degree of economic security that has liberated them from an obsessive concern with income, with a consequent increase in the importance of nonmaterial needs--the need

for a sensitive and responsive marital relationship, for challenging and significant work, for the respect and approval of friends, for identification with the community, and for a stimulating and fulfilling life.

Campbell goes on to write that "for the most part these people are talking about values that cannot be counted in dollars." From years of investigating what makes people satisfied with their lives, Campbell became convinced that economic factors are important as a base, rather than as a focus of concern. Strong first-hand relationships, especially those of the family, are the primary factor in life satisfaction. Relationships of trust, communication, stability, and enjoyment come first. Whatever supports and enhances such relationships, provides places and times for being together and interacting in enriching ways, contributes to the very center of life's quality.

Evidence from national surveys indicates that leisure is one major element in life satisfaction, in one case accounting for more variance than marriage, work, or finances (Kelly 1977), and in another having about the same influence as work satisfaction (London et al. 1977). However, such indicators do not specify outdoor recreation's contribution nor do they tell us just why leisure and recreation are that important.

One indication is that recreation is found to be enjoyable. Life consists of more than obligations and accomplishments; there is the enrichment of activity and interaction chosen because it is enjoyed. Time-use research reports that enjoyment is important (Robinson 1977) even though difficult to quantify.

A second indication is in that relationship between recreation and the human community. If the primary relationships of family and friends are the major factor in well-being, then opportunities to build, maintain, and enjoy those relationships are central to our lives (Kelly 1982). Leisure is not left over or peripheral, but is significant for its contribution to our primary relationships.

A third indication is the consistency with which persons at all levels of income, education, and occupation status develop plans and priorities for recreation.

However, such indications provide only the starting-point for this chapter. There are two isues that we will address together:

1. What are the dimensions of the benefits of outdoor recreation?

2. Are the kinds of opportunities provided by public programs an important component of outdoor recreation participation?

Recreation Benefits: A Multidimensional Matter

The complexity of assessing recreation benefits begins with the phenomenon itself. To begin with, there are the perceived benefits—the reasons why people decide to participate. These vary with the kind of activity, companions, environment, and factors specific to the situation (Kelly 1982). The anticipation of definite outcomes is a major impetus in attracting participation.

There are, however, other types of benefits as well. These might include behavioral changes such as improved health or job productivity, the preservation of the resource from more destructive uses, secondary or "spin-off" benefits such as increasing the tax base for community services or enhanced family solidarity, and economic benefits that increase regional income or add to the economy in some measurable way.

Benefits can be classified for convenience as one of three types. The three types are not entirely discrete. There is some overlap and fuzziness reflecting the inter-relationship of the differentiating dimensions.

1. *Personal benefits:* Outcomes from recreation that begin with the individual may be termed *personal.* They include enjoyment and all the other experiential components of participation. As will be analyzed more fully, personal or ex-periential benefits include excitement and relaxation, escape from and intimate association with other people, environmental appreciation and immersion, learn-ing and testing competence, familiarity and exploring what is new, tranquility and stimulation. Further, from these experiences are perceived more long-term benefits such as self enhancement through improved mental health, the develop-ment of self-reliance and competence, inaugurating and building relationships of trust and communication, and a renewal in both mind and body. Personal benefits include both the immediate experience and the developmental conse-quences for the self that endure, at least for a limited time.

2. *Societal benefits:* Outcomes from recreation that are related to social groups or collectivities may be termed *societal.* First of all, they refer to the support and enhancement of intimate communities, those family and friendship groups that are central to life. However, there are other kinds of societal benefits as well, in-cluding possible contributions to the development of larger communities, increas-ed productivity in the economy, and a higher level of public health. Such benefits are partly the extension of the longer term personal benefits. However, their im-pact is on the society or on some level or type of social organization. Benefits to social institutions—the family, government, school, and community—are societal rather than personal. Further, such benefits may also be long-term, such as supporting conservation of the ecological basis for human life and contributing to the basis for social cohesion.

3. *Economic benefits:* Outcomes that add to some level of the economy are *economic.* Such benefits include the contribution of resources to the market, pro-viding employment in the production of goods and services, or some addition to economic development. These economic benefits may be primary, such as income-producing employment, or secondary, such as the demand for goods and services in communities with a significant recreation-related employment compo-nent. Like other benefits, economic outcomes may exist in both short and long-term time frames.

Placing an economic value on the three kinds of benefits is quite different from categorizing the values themselves. It may be difficult to place a dollar valuation on some long-term secondary economic benefits, but feasible to measure just what the experience of a week of camping is worth to an individual.

Here only two types of social benefits will be addressed: the personal and societal. The value of recreation's contribution to the economy has been analyzed in a number of ways and has resulted in increasingly complex formulations. Whatever their validity, they do not directly measure the social benefits being considered here.

Social Benefits and Economic Valuation

When specific programs or projects are contemplated, it may be useful or even mandated that an economic benefit-cost assessment be completed. When recreation is one of the benefits anticipated, then a dollar valuation consistent with the other values employed is required. There have been a number of methods developed for approximating such values for the good, recreation opportunity, that does not have a market price (Dwyer, Kelly, and Bowes 1977). Most have been based on the concept of "willingness to pay" (Clawson and Knetsch 1966). The question is ascertaining what users would pay were the opportunity supplied in a price-elastic market. Since there is no such market, the valuation should include not only what is actually paid, but also the "consumer's surplus" or the worth of the opportunity above the cost.

Such willingness to pay may be measured by several methods or combinations of methods (Bishop and Heberlein 1980, Johnson 1981). The total cost of travel is one proxy of willingness to pay, but undervalues proximate resources and does not incorporate what is often the greatest investment in the experience, the scarce resource of time. Various survey approaches directly and indirectly measure what participants believe they would be willing to pay for use or not to lose the opportunity. Survey results have been found to vary according to methodology--direct questions, bidding, etc.--and in relation to perceived alternatives and their costs. Further, neither method is likely to assess either long-term values that might be lost were the resource turned to other uses or secondary social benefits beyond the experience and enjoyment of use.

On the one hand, economic valuation methods overlap with the social benefits being examined here. For example, a willingness to pay for travel or entry is one indication of the anticipated personal experience. On the other hand, such dimensions as the contribution to well-being through support of family cohesion are not likely to be amenable to dollar measurement by any approach. For the most part, individuals find themselves unable to put a price on just those elements of life that are most important to them. What is the economic value of a rich family life, integration into accepting social groups, the experience of productivity, development of social competence and positive self-definitions, or new insight into oneself? Social values are much more basic to life than the more familiar question of "How do you place a dollar value on a sunset?"

The Basis of Public Recreation Provisions

Historically, public entrance into providing recreation opportunity has been based on two issues: equity and resource scarcity (Kelly 1982). In industrial cities, public recreation was a response to acute deprivation of both children and adults. Poverty combined with crowding in the cities of the late 19th century to cut off access to areas for play. At about the same time, the first national and urban parks were opened in an effort to preserve unique and special areas and develop them for recreation use. Equity was the basis of urban public recreation and resource scarcity determined the areas designated for outdoor recreation and appreciation by multi-level public programs.

Related to the equity and resource scarcity bases for public provisions is the issue of efficiency. For the most part, those who swim in public pools, use public beaches, picnic and camp in public parks, and play softball at public playing fields could not afford to own or rent the land required for their activity. The costs of urban land of any kind, water access, and other high cost resources would be prohibitive for all but a few. However, even in circumstances where users could own or rent such opportunities, it would be inefficient. Scarce resources used only for limited periods can be made available to the widest range of users at lowest total cost by public management.

There are two parallel problems if one depends entirely on the marketplace for such recreation resource provisions. The first is equity: some potential users, such as children, will be priced out of access. If recreation is a public good, then market suppliers will tend to bias access toward those with the greatest alternative resources. The second limitation is that of long-term conservation. Suppliers who seek investment return will tend to manage the resource in ways that maximize present use, even at the cost of the future quality of the resource. Therefore, the traditional bases of public recreation, equity and resource scarcity, continue to provide the main arguments for continuing a balance between public and market provisions for recreation.

The main issue is that of benefits. Just what are the outcomes of public opportunities for outdoor recreation? Do the resources developed and managed by government agencies yield benefits of particular significance? The economic benefits are not incorporated in this introduction. There has already been considerable attention to the economic side of recreation. Here we will attempt to summarize the state of the art in assessing the social outcomes of resource-based outdoor recreation.

Further, there is no attempt to address the question of relative efficiency. Alternative resources, access costs and barriers, and the pressures of potential users for resource development by public and commercial providers are, for the most part, regional and local issues. Equity and resource scarcity will continue to require public action to meet even minimal demand and to provide for the long-term care of many resources. Public recreation would be forsaken only at the cost of mortgaging the opportunities of future generations. Since costs continue to rise, recovery of resources would be at incalculably high costs later.

SOCIAL BENEFITS

In 1981, a summary of social benefits of outdoor recreation was developed for the U. S. Forest Service (Kelly 1981). The following analysis is based on sections of that report. In some areas, it is possible to make quite direct statements of the kind of benefits under consideration, to analyse data providing evidence for the realization of the benefits, and to discuss the implications of the analysis. For example, there has been enough research on the range of psychological outcomes to present them in a relatively straightforward manner.

On the other hand, some benefits can be approached only in an inferential format. An argument is developed as follows: It is established that certain matters are significant to individuals or groups in our society or to the society itself. Further, there is evidence that outdoor recreation fosters and facilitates those outcomes. Therefore, outdoor recreation contributes social benefits even though they cannot be separated from other contexts making complementary contributions. For example, the demonstrated interaction potential of outdoor recreation settings for families enhances the communication, coherence, and enjoyment of this institution basic to our social system. Such a result is perceived by participants as a valued outcome of camping, visiting seashores, sightseeing, and other resource-requiring activities. However, we cannot separate out the contribution of such occasions from other interaction that also supports familial relationships.

The dilemma is that those benefits that are most important and most profoundly contribute to well-being may be those least amenable to measurement. Some of the social and developmental benefits outlined in the sub-reports take place in forest and water environments in enriched and enhanced ways. But they do not occur uniquely in such resources, and the precise benefit of a day of resource use cannot be measured. Whether or not the importance of the benefit is directly proportional to its incommensurability, any attempt to present benefits must include inferential argument as well as empirical analysis.

PERSONAL BENEFITS

Personal benefits are based in the immediate experience of participation in a resource-based activity. Such activity varies widely from relaxed and immobile contemplation to strenuous and demanding climbing. Most, but not all, is done in the company of other people. Further, the environments vary as widely as the activities—from crowded beaches to isolated mountain lakes, from desert valleys to mountain peaks. The experiences are related to both the activities and the environments, but are wholly determined by neither. For the most part, the data on experiential outcomes are probabalistic and identify those outcomes most commonly experienced.

The immediate experience, however, is not the end of the outcomes. What happens to persons and groups has both immediate and cumulative impacts. We return from a set of experiences somewhat different in how we define ourselves and relate to other people. A group such as a family unit emerges from a week together with some changes in communication and interaction patterns. Therefore, the immediate experiences are the bases for more long-term changes that may be perceived as benefits.

Psychological Benefits

From an extensive data base compiled primarily by Forest Service research, a high degree of consistency has been found as to the general benefits and those related to particular activities made possible by the resource. These outcomes are defined as indicators of psychological outcomes that lead to changes in behavior, personal development, and a sense of well-being (Brown 1981).

Common to all outdoor recreation are relationships with nature, escape from social pressure, and contact with the recreation group. Common to all activities except ORV use are escape from physical pressures and learning/exploring. The benefits of physical fitness and exercise and family togetherness are reported for most activities. In general, there are four types of psychological benefits reported: (1) Environmental: experiencing natural surroundings and being separated from back-home pressures; (2) Social: enjoying companions and building relationships, expecially with family; (3) Developmental: learning and exploration with longer-term skill and self-definition consequences; and (4) Health: fitness benefits from involvement in the outdoor environment as well as rest and relaxation.

These outcomes are found across regional lines and generally among all who engage in such outdoor recreation. Further, they are consistently valued highly. Although there are differences, as for those who come in family groups rather than friendship groups, these benefits are experienced on rivers and in the wilderness, in winter as well as in summer. They are resource-dependent in being based on the experience of being in the environment or engaging in activity that requires the special outdoor resource (Driver and Brown 1975, Brown and Haas 1980).

Such experiential benefits are not one-to-one with the environmental context. Rather, multiple benefits are found in the various resource and activity contexts. The immediate feeling of satisfaction is the basis for inferences about longer-term results. The preferences for such outcomes are relatively consistent in similar settings (Harris 1981). The type of resource does make a difference in psychological results (Rossman and Ulehla 1977). There is no generic and undifferentiated "outdoor" category of activity. Rather, the different settings provide direct experiences related to the environments as well as necessary resources for the variety of activities. Therefore, those seeking particular satisfactions from their outdoor recreation investments provide a demand for many different kinds of water and forest opportunities which cannot be readily substituted for each other. The resource and its management are major factors in the kinds of benefits anticipated and experienced (Hautaluoma and Brown 1978).

Mental Health Benefits

There is ample evidence that participants in outdoor recreation believe that both mental and physical health are enhanced by such activity (Buchanan 1981). The psychosomatic relationship between mental and physical health is well documented. However, whether the relationship with outdoor recreation is "real" or only a perceived feeling requires further analysis. Among the ranks of mental health problems are types of stress related to urbanization and the pressures of involvement with urbanized social and economic institutions (Glass and Singer, 1972; Kirmeyer, 1978). The problem of stress with its emotional and physical components is related to such pressures. Then the dimensions of outdoor recreation outcomes provide a reprieve from such pressures and lead to psychological outcomes of relief and renewal (Grubb 1975, Cicchetti and Smith 1973). The importance of the outdoor environment to the outcomes is reinforced.

Outdoor Recreation in the Community

Community public recreation programs have been investigated to measure the salient benefits for participants (Rossman 1981). A comparison of programs that take place indoors and outdoors reveals a significant difference in outcomes. Both have major satisfactions related to social interaction and physical health improvement. The difference comes between the indoor programs' major skill-learning component and the importance of the environment in the outdoor programs. Relating and responding to the natural setting is the third major dimension of programs in outdoor settings, even when they involve strenuous exercise and measurement of outcomes. Being outdoors is different, not only in the forest setting but close to home. Small local provisions are complemented by larger forest resources, and local programs often use state and federal forests for their special outdoor events.

Child Development

Developmental social psychologists have identified a number of major tasks that must be accomplished in human development through the life span (Erikson 1963). Those in childhood and youth are especially critical because they are the basis for development and fulfillment throughout life. The personal characteristics of trust, autonomy, initiative, industry, and identity are central and partly sequential in earlier years (Kleiber and Rickards 1981). The environmental context of outdoor recreation can be a facilitating element in human development. Combined with the crucial social relationships, especially familial in childhood, the special world of the outdoors provides the opportunity for the child to deepen intimate relationships, participate in maintenance tasks, try new activities and skills not possible at home, and develop confidence in coping with a new environment (Shephard 1979). The social and environmental contexts combine to give enhanced opportunities for human growth and identity development. These opportunities may be especially valuable for those with physical or mental limitations and handicaps (Byers 1979).

Human development does not halt in childhood or the teen years, but is a lifelong process. The special opportunities of outdoor recreation facilitate development that may be constrained in the more routinized contexts of the daily round.

SOCIETAL BENEFITS

Societal benefits are those that pertain primarily to groups rather than to individuals. Some such benefits are directed toward the society itself in its functional maintenance. Other benefits are identified more with smaller groups, the family, or the local community. Some are related to particular social values, such as environmental awareness and concern.

However, such distinctions are not always clear. Benefits to the family also yield benefits for the entire social system. Purely economic results, not included in this chapter, have secondary consequences for social institutions and for individuals. The focus here is on those ways in which outdoor resource-based recreation produces benefits for social groups.

Family Benefits

Family interaction is itself a major element in leisure and central to the leisure and life satisfaction of most adults (Kelly 1978). The outdoor context provides special opportunities for interaction freed from many of the routines and obligations of at-home interaction. As a consequence, communication is enhanced by both the separation from home and by the joint activities made possible by the environment. There is evidence of increased marital satisfaction and familial coherence from such joint recreation (Orthner 1975, 1976). Leisure has been found to contribute to the development of familial intimacy, trust, communication, and stability. Outdoor environments provide a special set of opportunities for such development (West and Merriam 1970).

Social Cohesion

The outcomes of outdoor recreation participation are far more profound than escape and feeling better (Cheek 1981). Outdoor recreation research shows evidence of the high levels of satisfaction obtained and the significance of social relationships (Bultena and Klessing 1969). Outdoor recreation, for the most part, involves getting away from pressures and other people *with* selected companions. Those companions, family and intimate friends, are the primary relationships in which we find security, express ourselves, and are integrated with the social world. The outdoor resource provides a context for the development and enhancement of those primary relationships in ways that make the experience especially valued (Field and O'Leary 1973). Further, that experience of intimacy is the basis for the network of relationships outward to the social institutions that hold the society together. This benefit of outdoor recreation is not only to the individual and the family, but is societal. It is a contribution to social integration that individuals report is important and different from interaction at home and in the community (Burch 1965, Cheek and Burch 1976).

Rural Community Benefits

Benefits to rural communities relatively near outdoor recreation resources are twofold: The first benefits result from the recreation opportunities provided and their use by community members. Not only individual and small-group usage, but occasional use for community events provides for reinforcement of traditional rural values and of community solidarity (England, Gibbons, and Johnson 1979). The second set are those secondary benefits that stem from the use of the recreation resources by others (England 1981). Community institutions and services may be supported by the increased incomes, tax base, employment for indigenous young people, and a variety of service businesses. It must be recognized, however, that large-scale recreation development may be so overwhelming as to transform the rural community into a special-use town with quite different values and institutions (Smith, Hogg, and Regan 1971).

Environmental Benefits

The management of land for recreation use may preserve it from serious degradation by other uses. However, a further environmental benefit is based on the experience of being in the natural setting. Outdoor recreation participation may produce an awareness of the ecological interdependence of existence. More specifically, resource-based outdoor recreation provides a context for behavior that takes account of and is directed toward the natural environment with the potential of altering future attitudes and behavior (Dunlap and Heffernan 1975, Geisler, Martinson, and Wilkening 1977). Evidence of the relationships of environmental attitudes and outdoor recreation participation indicates that such resource use is one factor in attitudes favoring concern with long-term effects of human interventions (Gale 1981).

OVERVIEW OF SOCIAL BENEFITS

There is considerable documentation of the values derived from the special experiences associated with resource-based outdoor recreation. Participants believe their lives have been enhanced in many ways by the resource-related experiences. They value such opportunities highly and report high levels of satisfaction. This valuation is substantiated by the considerable efforts made to secure time for such activity, travel to the sites, acquire the equipment required for participation, and plan for the experience. Further, foregone opportunities in the use of time and income indicate the importance of such experiences to participants.

As previously outlined, outdoor recreation has been found to be a multidimensional experience with components related to the environment, social interaction, and personal engagement with activity. Such experiences are also more than immediate. Satisfaction involves anticipation and recollection, as well as the period of participation. Participants report consequences that endure past the time of the experience itself. Benefits of psychological and physical well-being, solidarity with family and friends, and the development of competence and self-reliance, as well as the intrinsic excitement and involvement of the moment, remain significant to the participant.

It would be possible to argue that there are three levels of outcomes. The first are the immediate experiences of involvement. The second are mid-range, the anticipations and recollections of the immediate experience that yield satisfaction for what may often be quite long periods of time. The third are those outcomes that are long-term and stable and make an enduring difference in the lives of participants. Such enduring outcomes may be personal as they contribute to attributes and characteristics important to development. Whenever persons experience greater ability to take initiative, relate in depth to another person, or meet a challenge, then they become somewhat different persons. They define themselves more positively and subsequently cope with the world in enhanced ways.

Enduring outcomes of a social nature involve the full range of human relationships. The initiation, building, and maintenance of intimate relationships is the foundation of human life. Nothing is more important to the self or society. It is in such relationships that we find the core meaning of our lives and develop as human beings. Further, it is from such primary relationships outward that we relate to the institutions of our society. Damage or lack of development in intimate communities of family and friendships has twofold consequences. First, we fail to develop the confidence and competence of human selfhood. Personal development is truncated. Further, we fail to develop an adequate basis for relating to others, for learning the intricacies of social interaction in the multiple settings and situations of our social worlds.

Evidence that outdoor recreation opportunities are special in the experience of participants is not to be dismissed simply as insignificant "fun." Rather, it is in such experiences that enhanced realization of personal and social development have been documented. Outdoor recreation environments are demonstrably special, and the experiences made possible by those environments are highly valued because of their contributions to the lives of participants.

References

Bishop, R. C., and Heberlein, T. A. "Simulated Markets, Hypothetical Markets, and Travel Cost Analysis: Alternative Methods of Estimating Outdoor Recreation." Agricultural Economics Staff Paper Series No. 197. Madison: University of Wisconsin, 1980.

Brown, P. J., and Haas, G. E. "Wilderness Recreation Experiences: The Rawah Case." *Journal of Leisure Research* 12(1980):229-241.

Bultana, G. L., and Klessing, L. Satisfaction in Camping. *Journal of Leisure Research* 1(1969):348.

Burch, W. R., Jr. "The Play World of Camping: Research Into the Meaning of Outdoor Recreation." *American Journal of Sociology* 70(1965):604-612.

Byers, E. S. "Wilderness Camping as a Therapy for Emotionally Disturbed Children: A Critical Review." *Exceptional Children,* 1979, pp. 628-635.

Campbell, A. *The Sense of Well-Being in America: Recent Patterns and Trends.* New York: McGraw-Hill, 1981.

Cheek, N. H., Jr., and Burch, W. R., Jr. *The Social Organization of Leisure in Human Society.* New York: Harper and Row, 1976, Chap. 7.

Cicchetti, C. J., and Smith, V. K. "Congestion, Quality Deterioration, and Optimal Use: Wilderness Recreation in the Spanish Peaks Primitive Area." *Social Science Research* 2(1973):15-30.

Clawson, M., and Knetsch, J. L. *Economics of Outdoor Recreation.* Baltimore: Johns Hopkins Press, 1966.

Driver, B. L., and Brown, P. J. "A Social-Psychological Definition of Recreation Demand, with Implications for Recreation Resource Planning." In *Assessing Demand for Outdoor Recreation,* pp. 63-88. Washington, D.C.: National Academy of Sciences, 1975.

Dunlap, R. E., and Heffernan, W. B. "Outdoor Recration and Environmental Concern: An Empirical Examination." *Rural Sociology* 40(1975):18-30.

Dwyer, J.; Kelly, J.R.; and Bowes, M. "Improved Procedure for Valuation of the Contributions of Recreation to National Economic Development." Urbana, Illinois: Water Resources Center, University of Illinois, 1977.

England, L.; Gibbons, W.; and Johnson, B. "The Impact of a Rural Environment on Values." *Rural Sociology* 44(1979):119-136.

Erikson, E. *Childhood and Society.* New York: Norton, 1963.

Field, D. R., and O'Leary, J. T. "Social Groups as a Basis for Assessing Participation in Selected Water Activities." *Journal of Leisure Research* 5(1973):16-25.

Geisler, C. C.; Martinson, O. B; and Wilkening, E. A. "Outdoor Recreation and Environmental Concern: A Restudy." *Rural Sociology* 42(1977):241-49.

Glass, D. C., and Singer, J. E. *Urban Stress.* New York: Academic Press, 1972.

Grubb, E. A. "Assembly Line Boredom and Individual Differences in Recreation Participation." *Journal of Leisure Research* 7(1975):245-269.

Hautaluoma, J. E., and Brown, P. J. "Attributes of the Deer Hunting Experience: A Cluster-Analytic Technique." *Journal of Leisure Research* 10(1978):271-287.

Kelly, J. R. "Social Position and Leisure Participation as Factors in Leisure and Life Satisfaction." Paper at the National Recreation and Parks Association, Las Vegas, 1977.

Kelly, J. R. "Family Leisure in Three Communities." *Journal of Leisure Research* 10(1978):46-60.

Kelly, J. R. "Outdoor Recreation Participation: A Comparative Analysis." *Leisure Sciences* 3(1980):129-154.

Kelly, J. R. "Social Benefits of Outdoor Recreation." Champaign: Leisure Behavior Research Laboratory, University of Illinois, 1981.

Kelly, J. R. *Leisure.* Englewood Cliffs, N.J.: Prentice-Hall, 1982.

Kirmeyer, S. L. "Urban Density and Pathology." *Environment and Behavior* 10(1978):247-269.

London, M.; Crandall, R.; and Seals, G. "The Contribution of Leisure and Job Satisfaction to Quality of Life." *Journal of Applied Psychology* 62(1977):328-344.

Orthner, D. "Leisure Activity Patterns and Marital Satisfaction Over the Marital Career." *Journal of Marriage and the Family* 37(1975):91-102.

Orthner, D. "Patterns of Leisure and Marital Interaction." *Journal of Leisure Research* 8(1976):98-111.

Robinson, J. *How Americans Use Time.* New York: Praeger, 1977.

Rossman, B. B., and Ulehla, Z. J. "Psychological Reward Values Associated with Wilderness Use: A Functional-Reinforcement Approach." *Environment and Behavior* 9(1977):41-66.

Shephard, P. "Place and Human Development." In *Children, Nature and the Urban Environment* (USDA Forest Service General Technical Report (NE-30). Washington, D.C.: U.S. Government Printing Office, 1977.

Smith, C.; Hogg, T.; and Regan, M. "Economic Development: Panacea or Perplexity for Rural Areas." *Rural Sociology* 36(1971):173-186.

West, P. E., and Merriam, L. "Outdoor Recreation and Family Cohesiveness." *Journal of Leisure Research* 2(1970):251-259.

2

The Economic Value of Cultural Facilities: Tourism in Toronto

Geoffrey Wall

Thoughts of tourism conjure up pictures of the four "S's" in the minds of many people: sea, sun, sand, and sex. Palm-fringed, tropical islands bordered with white beaches and brown bodies represent an image of an ideal tourist destination for many people and such images are created and promoted by marketers from many parts of the world including the Caribbean, the Mediterranean, South Africa, the Pacific, and Australia. However, while tourism is highly visible in such locations and may dominate the economies of many coastal areas in the tropics, not all tourism is of this type. In fact, although the cosmopolitan character of many urban areas may make tourism less evident to the casual observer, the major cities of the world are some of the most prominent tourist attractions.

A number of factors combine to make cities centers of tourism. These include the wide variety of attractions, the availability of a sophisticated supporting infrastructure, and the ability of cities to cater to multi-purpose visits. Each of these factors will be considered briefly.

Many tourist facilities have high thresholds and ranges (Haggett 1979, p.136). This means that it requires a large number of people to make the provision of such facilities viable, but that people are willing to travel long distances, on occasion, to patronize such facilities. Cities, by definition, are the homes of large numbers of permanent residents, whose demands combine with those of regional residents and tourists from greater distances, to sustain a wide variety of high order functions (Wall and Sinnott 1980). Such functions include major museums and art galleries, concerts by prominent groups and artists, theatrical productions, professional sports events, specialist shops and restaurants, and educational establishments with well-established reputations. Many of these facilities are located in close proximity to each other so that the range of choice of activities available to both residents and visitors is unusually large. The theatre district of Broadway in New York City, and the West End in London, are examples of areas in cities devoted to and renowned for their provision of recreational opportunities. Forty-second Street and Times Square in New York City, and Soho in London, are other areas which have become noted for recreation of a different type. The ethnic communities which have become concentrated in parts of many cities have contributed to the landscape, cuisine, and cultural diversity of our urban areas. The Chinatowns of New York City, San Francisco, Toronto, and Vancouver are cases in point.

High order functions, including specialized recreational opportunities, could not exist if they were not readily accessible. Our major cities are blessed with well-developed transportation systems which include underground railways, bus and tram services, taxis, and a dense road network. Although it is fashionable to complain about traffic congestion, parking problems, and deficiencies of public transportation in cities, it is worth noting that large numbers of people, sometimes numbering millions, move around in cities and successfully reach their destinations every day. Furthermore, cities are the foci of national and international road, rail, and air networks so that communication systems channel travellers to our cities.

In addition, cities are the location of much commercial accommodation provision. In fact, hotels have come increasingly to dominate the central core of many large cities, as well as areas adjacent to transportation terminals (Hutchinson 1980). They have ceased to be purveyors of overnight accommodation alone, but have diversified their functions to include restaurants, bars, pools, saunas, live entertainment, meeting rooms, boutiques, and even babysitting services. The modern hotel has ceased to be solely a place where the out-of-town traveller stays overnight while he conducts his business or enjoys himself elsewhere. Hotels now provide recreational opportunities for both local residents and visitors from further afield. As well as being part of the infrastructure, they have become tourist attractions in their own right, and today's hotel proprietors do all they can to satisfy as many of the needs of their patrons as possible so that they do not have to leave the hotel to spend their money elsewhere.

Although it is sometimes convenient for the collection of statistics or to simplify description to classify reasons for travel as either business or pleasure, many visits to cities are multi-purpose in nature. The concentration of offices and business concerns in and around our cities generates large volumes of travel, but the traveller often elects to combine business with pleasure and take advantage of the recreational opportunities which may not be available in the home community. Furthermore, as centers of population, cities are likely to be residences of friends and relatives who provide an excuse for a visit, inexpensive accommodations, and often are knowledgeable guides. A surprisingly large proportion of visitors to cities resides at the homes of friends and relatives during their stay. For example, Vaughan (1976b) found that staying with friends and relatives was the largest accommodation category for vacationers in Edinburgh, Scotland, accounting for 28 percent of bednights occupied by visitors to that city.

The Roles of Cultural and Recreational Facilities

Urban cultural and recreational facilities are not simply tourist attractions. They are multi-purpose facilities. Many museums and art galleries have a conservationist objective in that they attempt to conserve and display artifacts which are a part of our heritage. In doing this they also perform an educational role as the significance of their displays is interpreted to their visitors. If the experience is an enjoyable one, they are also fulfilling a recreational function. Unfortunately there are often conflicts between these objectives. The preservation of artifacts may conflict with the entertainment role. Conversely, the heat, humidity, and vibration created by numerous visitors may threaten the safety of fragile exhibits. Visitor numbers and behavior may have to be controlled in the interests of preservation, but this may compromise the educational or recreational role of tourist facilities. In much the same way, theatre groups, dance companies, orchestras, and other types of performing arts may sometimes have to select between programs which are innovative, challenging, or have restricted appeal and those that attract a mass audience. Clear statements of objectives and priorities in guiding decisions on programming face decision-makers who also must have a thorough understanding of their potential clientele.

These potentially conflicting functions of cultural facilities also have important economic consequences. While it would be wrong to evaluate culture in solely economic terms, it would be equally inappropriate to ignore economics altogether, particularly in times of financial stringency. Devotees of the arts have been reluctant, traditionally, to undertake economic analyses of their operations, but the situation is changing, partly out of necessity, and partly because it is becoming realized that support for cultural facilities can be gained from knowing the economics underlying cultural facilities, as well as how such facilities impinge upon the community (Wall 1981). Weiner (Kreisburg 1979, p. 13) has described the situation as follows:

> To substitute the economic value of the arts for their creative and spiritual value would be a severe distortion. However, to ignore their economic importance and especially their usefulness in promoting balanced economic growth would also be a serious mistake.

The importance of knowing one's audience, visitor profile, or market is well understood by many operators of privately-owned recreational facilities such as theme parks, because this information has important planning, management, and advertising implications. Consider this statement by the general manager of a prominent Ontario lion safari (Platiel 1978) concerning the value of visitor surveys:

> We spend a great deal of time gathering statistics. Many of the publicly-owned attractions in Ontario don't have this or can't give it to me when I call, but you have to have this whether your business is pumping gas or selling shoes. . . You have to have your visitor profile at any given time; you have to know how they are changing.

There is a lesson here for many publicly-owned attractions which do not always survey their visitors on a regular basis. However, the situation is changing slowly as more recreational and cultural institutions recognize the value of knowing who their visitors are and how their clientele is changing.

The Study

The purpose of this chapter is to document the role of recreational and cultural facilities in urban areas, with particular emphasis being devoted to the economic aspects of their operation and impact. The present author was responsible for identifying the visitor profiles of five recreational and cultural institutions in the city of Toronto in 1978 (Wall and Sinnott 1981). The study sites which were examined were the Art Gallery of Ontario, the Metro Toronto Zoo, Ontario Place (which may be described as a publicly-owned and operated waterside theme park), the Ontario Science Centre, and the Royal Ontario Museum. The study was unusual in that it was a coordinated investigation and similar questions were asked at the same time at all five sites so that direct comparisons could be made between clienteles.

This was the first time such information had been available in a comparable form and, in the case of one of the sites, it was the first visitor survey which had been undertaken. Four main objectives were established at the outset of the study: (1) to describe the socio-economic characteristics of visitors; (2) to identify the origins of the visitors to each site and to ascertain the extent to which the facilities were satisfying local, regional, and tourist markets; (3) to identify the proportions of first-time and return visitors, and to determine whether there were differences in the on-site activity patterns of these two groups; and (4) to assess the extent to which the attractions were complementary or competitive from a user standpoint. The ultimate goal, of course, was to derive specific implications for site management, as well as more general guidelines for the planning and management of similar facilities, both in Toronto and elsewhere.

Results

To illustrate the utility of such surveys, selected information will be presented along with a brief discussion of some of the implications.

Visitor profiles   The audiences of all five facilities can be broadly described as young and from well-educated, white collar, upper income backgrounds. This is important because all five facilities are funded partially from public funds, but at present, they are failing to attract the less prosperous segments of society. Thus public funding of such facilities can be interpreted as a subsidy to the rich. In order to counter such criticism it is desirable that a broader cross-section of society be attracted. This can be done by subsidising less privileged groups, directing advertising in their direction, modifying programs and exhibitions, arranging special events, and improving accessibility by public transit.

Visitor Origins   With respect to visitor origins, in the cases of the Art Gallery of Ontario, the Toronto Zoo, Ontario Place, and the Royal Ontario Museum, most customers came from Toronto or the surrounding area which constitute the primary trade area of these facilities (Table 1). Visitors from the United States constituted an almost identical share of attendance at each of these sites. The situation at the Ontario Science Centre was somewhat different for a larger proportion of its customers came from the United States, particularly the border states, than from all of Ontario, including Toronto. Subsequent surveys have indicated that although the proportion of American visitors always remains high, the visitor mix at the Science Centre varies somewhat at different times of the year (Sinnott 1980).

These results indicate that the Science Centre has been particularly successful in marketing its wares, partly because it has an active publicity program and touring exhibitions, and partly because it has a conscious policy of placing recreation above conservation. The "hands-on", interactive displays are particularly attractive to visitors (Gillies 1981). The Science Centre is also helped by the fact that whereas most large cities have art galleries, museums, and fun fairs, few have a science and technology centre that is comparable in scope. Given the goals of each institution, it may be desirable to design on-site activities and promotional campaigns tailored specifically for each of the local, regional, and tourist markets. The origins of visitors also has important implications for spending patterns.

Table 1

Visitor Origins

	AGO[a]	ZOO[b]	OP[c]	OSC[d]	ROM[e]
Metro Toronto	53.0%	35.5%	56.1%	20.5%	47.6%
Ontario, within 100 km	5.6	21.3	12.6	6.8	9.0
Ontario, 101 - 200 km	3.0	4.3	2.5	4.6	3.8
Ontario, beyond 200 km	5.1	5.0	3.0	9.1	5.2
Other Canada	6.6	9.9	4.0	10.3	7.6
U.S., Border States (N.Y., Mich., Pa., Ohio)	13.6	13.5	11.1	31.2	13.8
U.S., Other States	7.1	7.1	2.5	11.0	7.6
Other Countries	6.1	3.5	8.1	6.5	5.2

[a]Art Gallery of Ontario   [c]Ontario Place   [e]Royal Ontario Museum

[b]Metro Toronto Zoo   [d]Ontario Science Centre

Return Visits Just as manufacturers of soap powder try to create "brand loyalty," the managers of recreational and cultural facilities want to get their visitors to return and, if possible, bring others with them. The Art Gallery of Ontario, Ontario Place, and the Royal Ontario Museum enjoy a higher volume of repeat customer business and a shorter "turnaround" time between return trips than either the Zoo or the Science Centre (Table 2). At each attraction with the exception of the Zoo, the great majority of visitors from Metropolitan Toronto was on a return trip. Each of the facilities under examination is in fact a series of

Table 2

Time Profile of Visitation

	AGO	ZOO	OP	OSC	ROM
Frequency of Past Visits					
None	36.5%	65.2%	24.5%	56.1%	28.4%
1 - 2	14.2	19.9	10.7	23.3	19.1
3 - 4	7.1	10.6	14.3	11.1	14.7
5 or More	42.1	4.3	50.5	9.5	37.7
Time of Most Recent Visit					
Within Last--					
Month	35.2%	16.3%	32.5%	6.9%	20.0%
Six Months	28.1	12.2	6.0	8.6	15.2
Year	19.5	44.9	41.1	23.3	23.4
Five Years	12.5	26.5	19.2	47.4	22.1
More than Five Years Ago	4.7	--	1.3	13.8	19.3
Expectations re Next Visit					
Expect to Return--					
This Year	57.8%	19.3%	69.2%	31.6%	47.4%
Next Year	5.5	13.8	6.6	22.1	8.6
Unspecified Future	22.6	51.0	16.7	38.0	34.4
Do Not Expect to Return	14.1	15.9	7.5	8.3	9.6

linked exhibitions and activity centres. There is a tendency for first-time visitors to "do" the facility, viewing a large number of exhibits and participating in more activities than return visitors. Repeat visitors often have more awareness of the offerings and more selectivity in choice of what to do. It follows that if the mix of first-time and return visitors changes, this will lead to alterations in the internal distribution and circulation of visitors, creating new and intensifying old areas of congestion and alleviating others.

In order to keep visitors coming back, many cultural facilities adhere to the maxims of "ever changing" and "ever bigger" displays as new attractions are sought and introduced. For example, the Art Gallery of Ontario followed up the Tutankhamun exhibition with a display of Turner watercolours and an exhibition entitled "Van Gogh and the Birth of Cloisonism." It is a great challenge to continually acquire noteworthy and prominent attractions and this may require considerable forethought, usually measured in years rather than months. For example, the exhibition of El Greco paintings at the National Gallery of Art in Washington, D.C. scheduled for 1982 was threatened by political changes in Spain, and funding difficulties which exacerbated escalating transportation and insurance costs. Weintraub (1982, p. 50) stated that:

> the exhibition was in the making more than four years and it involved huge amounts of time and man power, and international phone calls, travel and personal communication rivaling any diplomatic effort in recent decades. Putting together any major loan exhibition is a herculean task.

Competition and Complementary   The extent to which facilities are competitive or complementary is an important question with great economic significance. For example, it was feared by some that the opening of a theme park on the outskirts of Toronto would attract visitors from Ontario Place and threaten the viability of the Canadian National Exhibition, an annual fair. Others argued that the new theme park would attract tourists who would also patronize other facilities in the community. The competitive and complementary nature of facilities is likely to impact differing segments of the clientele differently. For example, the local resident of Toronto who has a Saturday or Sunday afternoon to spare, may decide to go to a particular facility and that decision may exclude him from others on that occasion. In the short term, the facilities are competitive in the local market. On the other hand, distant potential visitors may view the city and be impressed by the number and diversity of recreational opportunities. In the tourist market the facilities may be complementary. The variety and combination of facilities may attract visitors where a single facility would fail to do so because they may be able to visit several in a sequence or because they do not have to worry about overcrowding at one facility spoiling their visit.

In an attempt to get some idea of recreational preferences, visitors to each of our study sites were asked to rank the five study sites with respect to their attractiveness. The results are summarized in Table 3. In all cases but the Zoo, the site, at which the interview took place was usually ranked first. Perhaps surprisingly, the Zoo achieved only third spot among its own audience. The Science Centre and Ontario Place appeared to appeal to the widest range of interests. Either the Art Gallery or the Zoo was selected as the least desirable attraction by respondents at

Table 3

Summary of Expressed Site Preferences

	AGO	ZOO	OP	OSC	ROM
First Choice	AGO	OP	OP	OSC	ROM
Second Choice	ROM	OSC	OSC	OP	OSC
Third Choice	OSC	ZOO	ZOO	ROM	AGO
Fourth Choice	OP	ROM	ROM	ZOO	OP
Fifth Choice	ZOO	AGO	AGO	AGO	ZOO

all sites. Visitors to the Zoo, Ontario Place, and the Science Centre on the one hand, and to the Art Gallery and the Royal Ontario Museum on the other, shared similar preferences. Knowledge of such relationships can be used to establish joint exhibitions, package deals, and passport (single price) admissions to exploit or encourage complementary site interrelationships.

Although the main objective of cultural facilities may not be to make money, it is just as vital that they do their economic homework. The research techniques are the same and the lack of financial stability may be just as threatening to public facilities as private facilities, even if the economic goal is merely to break even or to lose as little as possible. The arts may be contributing to their own image as a drain on the economy by their failure to consider their role in society in the broadest possible terms. They attract visitors who spend money in the community and they do this as a normal course of their operations. This role should be documented rather than spurned. When the accounting is done the balance sheet may be much more favourable than many devotees might fear.

Fortunately, such documentation is beginning to appear. The economic impact of tourism on Victoria, British Columbia has been examined (Capital Regional District 1979) and Vaughan (1977b) has calculated the economic impact of the Edinburgh Festival in Scotland. The economic impact of the Quebec winter carnival has been described (Hulbert 1971) and the National Endowment for the Arts (1981) has published a volume of examples in the United States. A recent study in Kansas City has suggested that non-profit performing arts groups are a major contributor to the economy. By themselves, these performing arts groups are responsible for more than 1,500 full-time and part-time jobs and generate more than $4 million in other direct local expenditures. As these expenditures reverberated through the Kansas City economy they made an economic impact of at least $25 million and possibly, according to some estimates, as much as $46 million during the 1978 to 1979 season (Midwest Research Institute 1980). That's big business!

Beyond this, smaller communities are trying to get a part of the action as they

Table 4

Conservative Estimates of Expenditures in Toronto Made by
Visitors to the Tutankhamun Exhibition

Visitor Origins	Proportion of All Visitors	Expenses (To Nearest $ Million)
Out-of-town overnight	18.6	11 Million*
Out-of-town day	37.5	6 Million*
Toronto residents	43.9	3 Million
Total		20 Million

*Excludes transportation

set up their own maple syrup, apple butter, or bean festivals and the number of festivals and other special events has expanded rapidly in recent years.

Special events are particularly attractive to tourists and can be used to highlight the economic role of culture. One such event was the recent exhibition of artifacts from the tomb of the Egyptian King Tutankhamun which toured North America and included a two-month sojourn at the Art Gallery of Ontario in November and December 1979 (Wall and Knapper 1981). During that time approximately 800,000 people visited the exhibition, including 100,000 children who came on school tours. The origins and expenditures of the remaining 700,000 visitors are summarized in Table 4. Almost half the visitors were from Metropolitan Toronto and they spent at least $3 million dollars in the city in connection with their visit. A little over a third of the visitors were out-of-town day visitors, but they spent considerably more money. This was largely due to their greater expenditures on transportation and food, for differences in spending on souvenirs was less marked. Furthermore, unlike the expenditures of Toronto residents, which represented the circulation of money which was already in the city and would likely have been spent there anyway, the expenditures of out-of-town visitors was a transfer of money into the city from outside. Visitors who stayed overnight in the city comprised less than one fifth of all visitors to the Tutankhamun Exhibition. However, because of their length of stay and food and accommodation requirements, they had a disproportionately large impact on Toronto. The expenditures of overnight visitors were almost twice as large as those of the out-of-town day visitor group and four times that of the much larger group of Toronto residents. In excess of 30,000 hotel room-nights were taken up by visitors to the exhibition.

The gross expenditures of visitors to an exhibition are only a partial indicator of economic impact because they do not include the costs of staging the exhibition, including the costs of crowding and congestion imposed on the local community. Many of the direct costs of hosting the exhibition, such as the hiring of security guards, and the manufacture and sale of souvenirs, can be regarded as a benefit to the community. No attempt was made to trace the expenditures of visitors as they were respent in the local economy for insufficient data were available on the spending patterns of local businesses to calculate reliable economic multipliers. Nevertheless, the sales tax received by the provincial government probably exceeded the annual subsidy given to the Art Gallery of Ontario.

Discussion

The distinction which is often made between privately owned and operated and publicly owned and operated economic activities is often a false dichotomy with respect to urban recreational facilities. It is true that many hotels and restaurants, movie theatres, and theme parks are owned by individuals, chains, or multinational corporations and are operated primarily to produce a profit. On the other hand, many of the recreational and cultural attractions are owned and operated by governmental agencies and operate with deficits. However, transport systems, which are so vital to the operation of the private sector, are usually public facilities, and publicly owned recreational facilities may be the drawing cards which attract visitors to the city who then patronize facilities, such as hotels and restaurants, owned by the private sector. Performers may receive direct public subsidies, as in the case of many ballet companies or symphony orchestras, or may be financially independent, like many rock stars, although the latter may perform in public concert halls. Conversely, the arts may receive patronage from corporations. Although some may frown at this with the fear that commercial interests may pollute artistic integrity, this need not be the case for prominent artists have worked for centuries under the patronage of royalty or the wealthy of their time. The modern corporation does not patronize the arts for solely altruistic motivations. It uses tax-deductable dollars to enhance the corporate image. At the same time, it should be acknowledged that anything which moves people, be it a ballet or a ball game, is likely to be of benefit to the travel trade including gasoline companies, hotel chains, the brewing industries, and purveyors of travellers' cheques and credit cards.

This study has argued that the large cities of the world are major tourist attractions and, as such, they deserve more attention than they have been given. They attract tourists because of the number and diversity of high order attractions, because of the availability of supporting infrastructure, and because of their proclivity to draw multi-purpose trips. Many of the attractions are cultural facilities which have not always regarded themselves as being part of the tourist business. It is argued that these facilities should undertake visitor surveys to identify their clienteles with some precision so that their products can be marketed more successfully. Furthermore, the contributions which such facilities make to the community should be documented in the broadest sense, including the business which they attract for other sectors of the economy. If this is done, such facilities may not always prove to be the financial liabilities which initially they may appear.

The techniques and goals of this chapter are not the only ones that deserve attention. Other useful methodologies include broad based household surveys of leisure time activities (although these will usually be beyond the resources of individual facilities); local household surveys to gauge the degree of, and reasons for, failure to support specific facilities; on-site tracking studies in which visitors are followed and their behavior is observed; and time-lapse photography. The latter two research methods are particularly useful for ascertaining the extent to which particular exhibits are able to sustain interest. Lastly, much can be gained by mingling with the crowds, participating and observing with open eyes and ears. For example, the casual comment which is overheard may alert the manager to signs which are difficult to follow, exhibits which are hard to understand, and aspects of the facility which are particularly appreciated. In short, paying attention to the demographics of visitors and the reasons for tourism can lead to the successful marketing of cultural events and affect the way such facilities are valued when resource allocations are made. To quote a popular television commercial, "the arts are good for business."

References

Capital Regional District. *The Impact of Tourism on the Capital Region Economy.* Victoria, B.C.: Regional Planning Department, 1979.

Gillies, P. *Participatory Science Exhibits in Action: The Evaluation of the Visit of the Ontario 'Science Circus' to the Science Museum, London.* London: Science Museum, 1981.

Haggett, P. *Geography: A Modern Synthesis.* 3d. ed. New York: Harper & Row, 1979.

Hulbert, F. "La Rayonnement et L'impact Economique du Carnival de Quebec. 34(1971):77-104.

Hutchinson, J. M. "Analysis of Changing Tourist Accommodation Distribution in Toronto Using Point Pattern Techniques." M. A. thesis, University of Waterloo, Ontario, 1980.

Hutchinson, J. M., and Wall, G. "Community Festivals in Canada and the Anatomy of One of The Most Popular: Oktoberfest." *Recreation Canada* 6(1978):20-25.

Kreisburg, L. *Local Government and the Arts.* New York: American Council for the Arts, 1979.

Midwest Research Institute. "Economic Impact of the Performing Arts on Kansas City." Kansas City: unpublished report to the Hallmark Educational Foundation, 1980.

National Endowment for the Arts. *Economic Impact of Arts and Cultural Institutions.* Washington, D.C.: 1981.

Platiel, R. "Big-Time Family Fun: Child's Play it's Not." Toronto: *Globe and Mail,* 10 August 1978.

Sinnott, J. "Visitor Profile: March Break 1979." Unpublished report prepared for the Ontario Science Centre, Toronto, 1980.

Vaughan, R. *The Economic Impact of the Edinburgh Festival, 1976.* Edinburgh: Tourism and Recreation Research Unit, University of Edinburgh, 1977a.

Vaughan, R. *The Economic Impact of Tourism in Edinburgh and the Lothian Region, 1976.* Edinburgh: Tourism and Recreation Research Unit, University of Edinburgh, 1977b.

Wall, G. "A comment concerning some economic issues facing Canadian cultural institutions." *Leisure Studies Association Quarterly* 2(1)(1981):8-9.

Wall, G., and Knapper, C. *Tutankhamum in Toronto:* Waterloo: Department of Geography: University of Waterloo, 1981.

Wall, G., and Sinnott, J. "Urban Recreational and Cultural Facilities as Tourist Attractions." *Canadian Geographer* 24(1981):50-59.

Weintraub, B. "El Greco: The making of an exhibition." *Museum* 3(1982):50-55.

3

Recreation Benefits for Benefit-Cost Analysis

John F. Dwyer

Management of public recreation resources involves important decisions concerning the allocation of funds, as well as changes in the output of recreation and other goods and services. Public and private scrutiny of these decisions continues to grow as public recreation opportunities increase in importance and public funds become scarce. Important questions are asked about the return on investment of public funds and changes in the value of recreation and other outputs expected from management options. With a proposal to construct a forest campground, the important issues may involve the relative value of the camping experiences to be provided against the cost of constructing and operating the campground and foregoing the opportunities for timber harvest and noncamping recreation that will no longer be available if the campground is built. These, and other questions concerning the desirability of reallocating scarce public resources, are increasingly evaluated from the standpoint of benefit-cost analysis. This chapter outlines methodology appropriate for estimating recreation benefits for benefit-cost analysis. To set the stage for that discussion, the economic theory and concepts of value for benefit-cost analysis are summarized.

BENEFIT-COST ANALYSIS

Benefit-cost analysis assesses changes in the value of goods and services that are expected to result from undertaking a management option. Benefits represent the additional value of goods and services produced, while costs are the value of goods and services that could have been produced had the needed resources remained in their most likely alternative use. The difference between benefits and costs is termed net benefits and is a measure of the gain in national social welfare from undertaking the management option.

The definition of benefits is best understood if the motivation behind benefit-cost analysis is examined. The benefit-cost is a <u>potential Pareto</u> criterion. With a true <u>Pareto</u> criterion, a management option is considered worthwhile if the re-allocation of resources that it initiates makes no one worse off and at least some-one better off. In order to pass such a test, it would be necessary for those who gain from an option to actually make payments to compensate those who lose. Under the benefit-cost test, however, an option is considered worthwhile if such compensation could be made even though it may not actually be made. Clearly, if the sum of gains and losses is positive, actual monetary transfers between gainers and losers could be made and overall welfare would still be increased above the initial level. This approach has been outlined for public projects that concern water and related land resources (U.S. Water Resources Council 1973).

With benefit-cost analysis, the concern is with the total or aggregate change in benefits for all affected users, not with the gain or loss of any particular in-dividual. Benefits and costs are ordinarily measured by the sum of each individual recipient's valuations. Thus a dollar of benefits enters with the same weight regardless of who derives the benefits. In order to evaluate the distribution of benefits and costs among the population, some consensus of the weights to be at-tached to the gains and losses of each individual would be required. In the absence of such a consensus, the distributional impacts of a management option should be considered separately as a part of the comprehensive analysis that would also include benefit-cost analysis and other criteria for public investment. This is the approach taken by Clawson (1975), Marty (1975), U.S. Water Resource Council (1973), and Worrell (1970). It should be recognized that benefit-cost analysis is one among several important criteria for public decision-making that are outlined in the works cited above. For an introduction to benefit-cost analysis, see Freeman (1979), Howe (1971), Little (1957), Mishan (1976), and Peskin and Seskin (1976).

Willingness of Users to Pay

Positive benefits arising from increases in the output of recreation and any other goods and services influenced by a management option are appropriately measured by the willingness of users to pay for each unit of output provided. The concept of willingness to pay for recreation is payment by participants specifically for the use of opportunities created by the management option being evaluated. In this usage, willingness to pay includes entry and use fees (if any) actually paid plus the estimated maximum monetary amount (if any) in excess of these charges that users could be induced to pay (the consumers' surplus). It is not appropriate to include payment for equipment, food, travel, or lodging that may be made in conjunction with the trip or recreation activity, since these payments are not specifically for use of the site and associated opportunities. These associated ex-penditures by users during a recreation outing are ordinarily considered a con-tribution to regional economic development under the framework of the com-prehensive analysis of an option.

With some goods and services, such as scenic beauty and certain dispersed recreation opportunities, most or all of the benefits will be in the form of the amounts users would be willing to pay, but are not required to pay under present institutional arrangements. With goods sold in a competitive market, such as timber, minerals, and livestock forage, a larger portion of the benefits are likely to be in the form of market expenditures. With all outputs, the appropriate concept of value for increases in production is the willingness of users to pay, which includes actual payments plus the maximum monetary amount (if any) in excess of these charges that users could be induced to pay. With benefit-cost analysis, it does not matter what portion of the willingness of users to pay for a good or service is actually paid, as the total is considered as benefits. It is this ability of benefit-cost analysis to reflect user benefits for a wide range of goods and services on a comparable basis that makes it a powerful tool for analysis of public management options.

Compensation Required

For evaluation of benefits lost by elimination of existing resources (e.g., fishing experiences lost or degraded when a river becomes severely polluted), it is appropriate to measure the lost benefits as the minimum compensation required to ensure that present users would be neither better nor worse off after receiving this compensation than they would be without the option being undertaken (in this case, a reduction in water quality). If this amount were paid to them by those who gain from the option, the remainder of the willingness of users to pay would be net benefits—a measure of the increase in national social welfare. Compensation required, like willingness to pay, may be approximated by an area under the demand curve for the resource. As with willingness to pay, explicit bounds may be set on the approximation using the procedures presented by Willig (1976).

Empirical evidence obtained from direct questioning of recreationists (Hammack and Brown 1974; Randall, Ives, and Eastman 1974; Brookshire et al. 1977) indicates that willingness to accept compensation exceeds willingness to pay by amounts far in excess of the expected differences. The precise explanation for the wide difference is not yet known, but weakness in the approaches for direct estimates of the willingness to accept compensation seems likely. While accurate measurement of willingness to accept compensation presents numerous difficulties, there is no question that it is the appropriate measure of lost benefits. From a practical standpoint, at present it is best to present willingness of users to pay as the lower bound estimate of lost benefits, with the recognition that with especially desirable or unique resources this may be a significant underestimate of the lost value. For a further discussion of valuation concepts, see Dwyer and Bowes (1978a, 1978b) and Gordon and Knetsch (1979).

Management Options

Before evaluating specific approaches and models for recreation benefit estimation, careful attention must be given to the kinds of management options that are to be evaluated, and the changes in the attributes of recreation sites they are expected to generate. The recreation site may be viewed as having physical, biological, social, and managerial attributes. In evaluating management options, it is important to consider the expected changes in these attributes and the resulting influence on benefits.

Management-induced changes in site attributes may be physical: additional roads into a wildlife management area, construction of a new campground, or building a new reservoir; biological: stocking fish and game, planting trees or shrubs; social: changes in the level of use and characteristics of users; and managerial: new rules and regulations, changes in the amount of information provided to users, involvement of users in management efforts. Changes in these attributes may have a significant impact on the willingness of users to pay for recreation sites. For example, some individuals may be willing to pay more for campgrounds that offer special features such as heated swimming pools, square dancing, or beautiful scenery. Thus, in estimating the willingness of users to pay for recreation opportunities, it is important to take into consideration the characteristics of those opportunities.

In addition to depending heavily on site attributes, the willingness of users to pay for use of a recreation site is strongly influenced by its proximity to users and substitute sites. For example, the value of a new campground may depend heavily on the availability of other campgrounds. If the new site is closer to users than existing campgrounds, but offers similar experiences, large numbers of users may choose to use the new campground and may be willing to pay higher fees for its use over the more distant campgrounds. This is similar to the willingness of individuals to pay more for milk at the neighborhood grocery store than at a more distant supermarket because of the savings in time and in travel costs. At the same time, users may be unwilling to pay high fees for a new campground when there are numerous similar campgrounds located like distances from their homes.

Since public recreation opportunities have a wide range of site attributes and vary significantly with respect to proximity to other sites and user populations, the value of the recreation they provide varies considerably. Furthermore, public resource management options typically involve a site, or a set of sites, in a specified area, rather than opportunities over widespread areas. Consequently, it is not appropriate to estimate average values over a large geographic area, but rather to estimate values of the recreation associated with the particular site or area influenced by the management option being evaluated.

In sum, the values of recreation opportunities influenced by public resource management options are likely to vary markedly with their attributes and location with respect to other opportunities and users. Consequently, it is not appropriate to estimate average values for a large area, an activity, or set of activities, but rather to develop models that will take into account the important determinants of recreation values and estimate the values of the particular opportunities influenced by management options. Those models will now be discussed.

Benefit Estimation Models

In the absence of sufficient market price information to derive the demand for public recreation experiences, models to predict the willingness of users to pay are developed from user behavior (the travel-cost-based approach) or their responses to questions (the direct-questioning-based approach). Dwyer, Kelly, and Bowes (1977) provide detailed guidelines for use of these approaches. The values derived through application of modern versions of these procedures are appropriate for benefit-cost analysis and are sufficiently precise to guide decisionmaking. With either approach, the basic procedures is to: (1) develop models on the basis of existing behavior or user responses to questions concerning actual or possible opportunities, and (2) use these models to predict the willingness of users to pay for recreation opportunities that are expected to be available under alternative management options. The first step is ordinarily carried out by researchers, the second, by managers and planners, although a cooperative effort may be highly productive. It should be emphasized that it is not necessary to estimate a new model for each application, since existing models may be applied to a new situation. Managers can use models developed by researchers to estimate benefits that can be expected from management options without actually implementing those options.

The Travel-Cost-Based Method

The travel-cost-based method makes use of a model for predicting trips to a site from alternative destinations. That model, in its most elaborate form, can be summarized by:

$$V_{ij} = f(C_{ij}, T_{ij}, P_j, o_i, D_i, Q_j, C_{ik}, Q_k) \tag{1}$$

where
V_{ij} the number of trips from origin i to site j
C_{ij} travel cost for a trip between origin i and site j
T_{ij} travel time for a trip from origin i to site j
P_j the entry fee for use of site j
0_i the population of origin i
D_i characteristics of individuals at origin i
Q_j the attributes or characteristics of site j
C_{ik} the vector of travel costs to substitute sites (k = j) available to users from origin i
Q_k the vectors of quality characteristics of substitute areas (k = j)

The complexity of the travel-cost-based models developed to provide estimates of the willingness of users to pay for recreation opportunities depends on the character of the management options being evaluated, the resources available to build the model, and the resources available to managers and planners who will use the model. As a minimum, information must be available on (1) the origin of visits to the site, (2) travel cost from each origin to the site, and (3) site attributes that are expected to be altered by the management options. Information on substitute sites becomes critical when their availability varies considerably among origins. Ordinarily, only similar sites are considered as substitutes (i.e., campsites in a model for predicting trips to a campsite).

Estimates of the parameters are based on trips from various origins (i) to a site (j). The wide range of travel costs and substitute sites facing individuals at origins found at different distances from a site, as well as varying populations at each origin, provides considerable information about the influence of these variables on participation. In order to estimate the influence of the quality characteristics (Q_j) it is necessary to estimate the model jointly for a number of sites that have different levels of Q. The model can be used to estimate the number of trips expected under new or modified conditions, provided the manager or planner has estimates of the relevant variables to enter into the model.

The model is used to estimate the number of trips that will be made at various entry fees. These estimates are points on the aggregate demand curve for a site. The area under that demand curve is an estimate of the willingness of users to pay for use of the site. The site demand curve is estimated in the following way. By solving for the number of trips from each origin to the site under existing conditions and summing the visits from all origins, an estimate of use under current fees is obtained. To obtain estimates of use at a higher fee, the travel cost (C_{ij}) is incremented by the specified increase in fees, the number of visits from each origin calculated, and the number of visits from all origins summed to estimate use at that fee. The procedure is repeated with successive increments in travel cost (hence the name travel-cost-based method) to sketch out the aggregate demand curve for the site. This procedure assumes that individuals will react to increasing user fees as they do to increases in travel costs. For example, it is assumed that if the fee for using a site is increased by five dollars, individuals at each origin will reduce their use to the level of similar individuals who have the same set of substitutes, but face a five dollar higher travel cost to the site.

For a discussion of the theoretical base of the travel-cost-based method, see Maler (1974) and Knetsch (1974). Illustrative studies include the evaluation of a new ski facility (Cicchetti, Fisher, and Smith 1976); state parks (Cesario and Knetsch 1976); urban parks (U.S. Army Corps of Engineers 1976); reservoir recreation (Knetsch, Brown, and Hansen 1977; Burt and Brewer 1971); and water pollution abatement (Feenburg and Mills 1980). Recent models incorporate regional estimation procedures that provide analytical frameworks which take explicit account of alternative sites. That is, they jointly estimate the demand for existing sites of various quality, thus allowing the prediction model to account for interaction among areas in attracting visitors.

The Direct-Questioning-Based Method

The direct-questioning-based method makes use of a model that estimates the value of a recreation experience from responses to a questionnaire or a personal interview. It is helpful to view the method as having two stages. An initial effort is aimed at developing a model to predict an individual's willingness to pay for use of a site. As with the travel-cost-based method, explanatory variables must include those attributes that are expected to be altered by the management options that will be evaluated. Individuals might be given a description of a site and asked how much they would be willing to pay to use that site. Alternatively, a bidding game approach may be used where an individual is given a description of a site and asked if he would use it if a specified fee was charged. Depending on the individual's response, the fee would be raised or lowered until the individual's maximum willingness to pay for use of the site was determined. These efforts would generate a model such as the following:

$$WTP = g(Q_j, D_j) \tag{2}$$

where
WTP an individual's willingness to pay for a visit or season of use
Q_j the quality or characteristics of recreation experiences available at site j
D_j the characteristics of the users of site j

The availability of alternative destinations, ordinarily included in the travel-cost-based model, is not included in the model developed through direct questioning. It is assumed that the influence of alternatives is reflected in the individual responses.

To estimate the value of recreation provided by an existing area, a second survey is aimed at a larger sample in order to identify the users and values of the explanatory variables. Using the results of this survey and the equation which explains individual willingness to pay, the valuation of each user or group of users is calculated and summed to estimate total willingness to pay. In estimating the willingness of users to pay for a proposed site, estimates of the characteristics of users are required. These can be based on the population of the likely market area. Unlike the travel-cost-based method, a demand curve is not estimated as an intermediate step in estimating the willingness of users to pay.

For a discussion of the theoretical base of the direct-questioning-based method, see Bradford (1970). In past applications of this method to recreation, researchers (Cicchetti and Smith 1973; Cocheba and Langford 1978; Davis 1963, 1964; Hammack and Brown 1974; and McConnell 1977) developed equations to predict an individual's willingness to pay for a visit or season of use that are in the form of equation (2).

Choice of a Method

Both the travel-cost-based and the direct-questioning-based methods can produce acceptable estimates of the willingness of users to pay for the use of recreation sites under various management options. When data on the origin of users is readily available, such as with user registration or permit forms, it may be easier to estimate a travel-cost-based model. However, if origin-destination information is not available, or is available for a range of sites that are not sufficiently diverse to include the management options to be evaluated, the direct-questioning-based approach may be appropriate. For these reasons, many applications of the travel-cost-based method have involved reservoirs, campgrounds, state parks, and ski areas where information on the addresses of visitors is ordinarily recorded. Similarly, use of the direct-questioning-based approach has concentrated on the evaluation of a range of site conditions such as different levels of congestion, number of fish caught, waterfowl bagged, expected encounters with elk, and conditions of hunting environment.

It is important to note that it is the model, not its results, that is to be applied to management options. That is to say, the equation, in the form of equations 1 and 2, is to be applied to the management options under consideration.

Regardless of the method chosen, its appropriate use will produce estimates of recreation benefits that are far superior to estimates by managers and planners (Dwyer, Kelly, and Bowes 1979). When important decisions concerning the allocation of public resources are being made that involve tradeoffs between important goods and services, those tradeoffs should be made in light of the best available estimates of the willingness of users to make those trades.

Conclusion

The increasing significance of the recreation outputs of public resource management options, mounting attention to benefit-cost analysis, and improvements in recreation benefit estimation methodology argue strongly for increased efforts to estimate recreation benefits. Useful estimates of recreation benefits can be derived from models based on user behavior (travel-cost-based approach) or user responses to questions (the direct-questioning-based approach). Models developed using these approaches can be used to estimate the recreation benefits associated with management options. Those estimates of recreation benefits are fully comparable to the estimates of benefits for other market and non-market priced goods and services included in benefit-cost analysis, thereby facilitating the evaluation of tradeoffs between recreation and other goods and services produced by public projects. Use of these procedures to estimate recreation benefits will contribute significantly to the effectiveness of public decisionmaking concerning recreation resources.

References

Bradford, D. F. "Benefit-Cost Analysis and Demand Curves for Public Goods." *Kyklos* 23(1970):775-791.

Brookshire, D. C. et al. "Economic Valuation of Wildlife." Final report for U.S. Fish and Wildlife Service, Phase I, Resource and Environmental Economics Laboratory. University of Wyoming, Laramie, 1977.

Burt, O. R., and Brewer, D. "Estimating Net Social Benefits From Outdoor Recreation." *Econometrica* 39(1971):813-27.

Cesario, F. J., and Knetsch, J. L. "A Recreation Site Demand and Benefit Estimation Model." *Regional Studies* 10(1976):97-104.

Cicchetti, C. J.; Fisher, A. C.; and Smith, V. K. "An Econometric Evaluation of a Generalized Consumer Surplus Measure: The Mineral King Controversy." *Econometrica* 44(1976):1259-1275.

Cicchetti, C. J., and Smith, V. K. "Congestion, Quality Deterioration, and Optimal Use: Wilderness Recreation in the Spanish Peaks Primitive Area." *Social Science Research* 2(1973):15-30.

Clawson, M. *Forests for Whom and for What.* Baltimore: The Johns Hopkins University Press, 1975.

Cocheba, D. J., and W. A. Langford. "Wildlife Valuation: The Collective Good Aspects of Hunting." *Land Econ.* 54(1978):490-504.

Davis, R. K. "The Value of Big Game Hunting in a Private Forest." 20th Conference North American Wildlife National Resource Trans, p. 393-403. Washington, D.C.: Wildlife Management Institute, 1964.

Davis, R. K. "The Value of Outdoor Recreation: An Economic Study of the Maine Woods." Ph. D. thesis, Harvard University, 1963.

Dwyer, J. F.; Kelly, J. R.; Bowes, M. D.; and Bowes, M. "Needed Improvements in Recreation Benefit Estimation." *Journal of Leisure Research* 11(1979):327-332.

Dwyer, J. F., and M. D. Bowes. "Benefit-Cost Analysis for Appraisal of Recreation Alternatives." *Journal of Forestry* 77(3)(1979):145-147.

Dwyer, J. F., and Bowes, M. D. "Concepts of Value for Water-Based Recreation Opportunities." *Water International* 3(1978a):11-15.

Dwyer, J. F., and Bowes, M. D. "Concepts of Value for Marine Recreational Fishing." *American Journal of Agriculture Economics* 60(1978b):1008-1012.

Dwyer, J. D.; Kelly, J. R.; and Bowes, M. D. "Improved Procedures for Valuation of the Contribution of Recreation to National Economic Development." Water Resources Center, University of Illinois at Urbana-Champaign, 1977.

Feenburg, D., and Mills, E. S. *Measuring the Benefits of Water Pollution Abatement.* New York: Academic Press, 1980.

Freeman, A. M. III *The Benefits of Environmental Improvements: Theory and Practice.* Baltimore: The Johns Hopkins University Press, 1979.

Gordon, I. M., and Knetsch, J. L. "Consumer's Surplus Measures and the Evaluation of Resources." *Land Economics* 55(1979):1-27.

Hammack, J., and Brown, G. M. *Waterfowl and Wetlands: Toward Bioeconomic Analysis.* Baltimore: The Johns Hopkins University Press, 1974.

Howe, C. W. "Benefit-Cost Analysis for Water System Planning." Water Resource Monograph 2. Washington, D.C.: American Geophysical Union, 1971.

Knetsch, J. L.; Brown, R. E.; and Hansen, W. J. "Estimating Expected Use and Value of Recreation Sites." In *Planning for Tourism Development: Quantitative Approaches,* edited by C. Gearing; W. Swart; and T. Var. New York: Praeger, 1977.

Knetsch, J. L. "Outdoor Recreation and Water Resources Planning." *Water Resources Monograph 2.* Washington, D.C.: American Geophysical Union, 1974.

Little, I. M. D. *A Critique of Welfare Economics.* New York: Oxford University Press, 1957.

McConnell, K. E. "Congestion and Willingness to Pay: A Study of Beach Use." *Land Economics* 53(1977):185-195.

Maler, K. *Environmental Economics: A Theoretical Inquiry.* Baltimore: The Johns Hopkins University Press, 1974.

Marty, R. "Comprehensive Analysis of Public Forestry Project and Program Alternatives." *Journal Forestry* 73(1975):701-704.

Mishan, E. S. *Cost Benefit Analysis.* New York: Praeger, 1976.

Peskin, H. M., and Seskin, E. P., eds. *Cost-Benefit Analysis and Water Pollution Policy.* Washington, D.C.: The Urban Institute, 1976.

Randall, A.; Ives, B.; and Eastman, C. "Bidding Games for Valuation of Aesthetic Environmental Improvements." *Journal of Environmental Economics and Management* 1(1974):132-149.

U. S. Army Corps of Engineers. "Analysis of Supply and Demand of Urban Oriented Nonreservoir Recreation." IWR Research Report 76-R2. Fort Belvoir, Virginia: U. S. Army Engineer Institute For Water Resources, 1976.

U. S. Water Resources Council. "Water and Related Land Resources, Establishment of Principles and Standards For Planning." Federal Register 38:Part III. No. 174, 1973.

Willig, R. D. "Consumer's Surplus Without Apology." *American Economic Review* 66(1976):589-97.

Worrell, A. C. *Principles of Forest Policy.* New York: McGraw-Hill, 1970.

4

Visitor Expenditures and the Economic Impact of Public Recreation Facilities in Illinois

Stanley R. Lieber
David J. Allton

Local governments have often claimed that the siting of conservation and recreation facilities have negative economic impacts on their local areas. The main reason for this is the loss of property tax revenues from lands owned by the state which formerly were income producing. By examining property taxes only, local governments have failed to recognize the full range of impacts generated by conservation and recreation properties, including their intangible benefits (Millard and Fisher 1979, Dean et al. 1978, Stoevener et al. 1974).

Public facilities have a variety of impacts on visitors (primary impacts, e.g., experiencing nature) and on the area in which they are located (secondary impacts). Secondary impacts are typically referred to as local economic impacts. They occur because the existence of a facility in the local area generates benefits (positive impacts) and imposes costs (negative impacts) to local residents, local businesses, and local governments. These positive and negative impacts take the form of gains and losses in sales, income, employment, taxes, and local government costs. An example of a positive impact is the salaries and wages paid to employees working at state parks. A negative impact would be the lost farm income from land previously in private ownership.

These impacts are caused by the acquisition, development, operation, and use of state parks and properties. These different causes can result in impacts that occur at one time, periodically, and continuously. Impacts take place in the local area (defined as the local community, township, county, or other local jurisdiction), but also occur in the region, state, and nation. Lastly, one can define impacts as direct (due to initial expenditures) or as indirect (due to local responding to the initial expenditures). A thorough analysis of local economic impacts would require examining the effect of the impacts through time, the directness of the impacts, and the locality (extensiveness) of the impacts (Crompton and Van Doren 1978, Kalter and Lord 1968).

Obviously, state agencies and local governments can benefit from the availability of accurate, statewide data for assessing local economic impacts. Since visitor expenditures generally comprise the largest component of local economic impact after the initial acquisition and development of land are completed, the collection of statewide data on visitor expenditures is important. Accurate data on visitor expenditures, therefore, can contribute to accurate local economic impact assessments and are complementary to other categories of information. Information on the acquisition development and maintenance costs of state properties that effect local economic impact can generally and more easily be obtained from state agencies or local governments. The purpose of this chapter, therefore, is to present information on visitor expenditures for publicly owned conservation and recreation properties in Illinois so that we may examine the significance of the siting of such properties as they impact local areas. Once these initial expenditures are known, a variety of methods for evaluating indirect impacts already exist (Badger, Schreiner, and Presley, 1977).

Visitor Expenditures

For use in assessing local economic impacts, visitor expenditures must be made in local areas by non-local visitors only. The local area is defined as the county (or counties) in which a Department of Conservation (DOC) facility or property is located. It is assumed that only local expenditures by visitors impact the local economy although expenditures made outside the local area may have an impact on the local area due to interactions within the region, state, or nation. Furthermore, it is assumed that expenditures made by county residents, in conjunction with visiting a DOC area, do not impact the local economy. Local expenditures made by residents from within the county in which the conservation or recreation property is located may have an impact on the local area only if these visitors would have made expenditures outside the county as an alternative to visiting their local DOC property.

For visitor expenditure data to be most useful in estimating local economic impacts, the expenditures must be representative of visitor expenditures during the course of a year; they must be per person, per day (pppd) averages; they must be available by type of expenditures, length of visitor stay, and type of DOC property. Data gathered according to these criteria can be applied to monthly and yearly attendance figures gathered by the Department of Conservation and similar agencies in other states and, along with other information, can be used to estimate economic impacts of state properties on local areas. Length of visitor stay refers to visitor use as either day use or overnight (one or more nights). Data gathered in this format for different regions or states can be compared and used to evaluate public investments in outdoor recreation.

The Illinois Department of Conservation manages three major types of properties: (1) state parks, (2) state historic sites, and (3) state conservation areas. For the purposes of this research, we will define type of expenditure as:

a. food (including purchases of groceries and purchases at restaurants)

b. transportation (including purchases of gasoline, oil, etc., and commercial carrier services, e.g., buses)

c. lodging (including motel, cabin, etc., accommodations)

d. governmental fees (including camping fees and hunting and fishing licenses)

e. other purchases (including souvenirs, etc.)

Study Design

In order to obtain a sufficient quantity and variety of household data for non-local visitor expenditures, 26 DOC facilities were visited on-site. Table 1 presents the name of the facilities and the date of the on-site interviews and Figure 1 portrays the major urban areas of the state as well as the locations of the on-site surveys. A total of 657 non-local interviews were obtained as well as 137 interviews with local residents of the county in which the facility was located. Table 1 also presents the acreages of each of the facilities as well as average annual attendance figures for each facility for the 1976-1980 period.

It is worth noting that the properties upon which on-site interviewing was conducted occupy 23 percent of the total property acreage administered by the Department of Conservation. Slightly over 40 percent (40.8%) of total annual average attendance (1976-1980) took place at the 26 sites visited between March of 1981 and February of 1982. However, if 4 sites visited during special events (Starved Rock State Park, Rock Cut State Park) or hunting seasons (Iroquois Conservation Area, Horseshoe Lake Conservation Area) were excluded as well as 2 unique historical sites (Grant's Home, Cahokia Mounds), the remaining facilities accounted for 29.9 percent of the annual average attendance at all state facilities. These remaining facilities, which generally tend to have less unique physical or cultural features and activity opportunities will be considered as baseline sites for analysis purposes. Illinois does not develop its properties into resort-parks as do states such as Kentucky. In essence, then, these 20 facilities represent developed state parks, but without special developments or national tourist features.

Interview Procedures On-site interviews were conducted for different days of the week and at different times of the year (Table 1). Although on-site interviews are considerably more expensive than a random digit dialing telephone survey or even a mailed questionnaire, a reasonable body of evidence indicates that visitor expenditure estimates obtained from on-site interviews are more accurate than those obtained by other methods (Mak, Moncur, and Yonamine 1974, Badger et al. 1977). No interview was conducted with a minor and most often interviews were conducted with the head of a household when a family was being interviewed. The average interview took less than five minutes. Interviews began as early as 4:30 a.m. (at hunting sites) and continued to as late as sundown.

The procedure for the on-site survey work was as follows. First, two interviewers would visit the site superintendent for the facility in order to obtain infor-

Table 1

Acreage and Average Annual Attendance at DOC Facilities

Facility	On-Site Interview Date(s)	Total Acreage	Average Annual Attendance in 1976-1980 (in 1,000's)
Kickapoo State Park	May 30, 1981	1,685	990
Washington County State Conservation Area	May 31, 1981	1,377	204
Cahokia Mounds State Historic Site	June 13, 1981	998	274
Silver Springs State Park	June 27, 1981	1,314	226
Marshall County Rice Lake State Conservation Areas	June 28, 1981	6,000	66
Wayne Fitzgerell State Park	July 2, 1981	3,300	327
Red Hills State Park	July 3, 1981	948	374
Illinois Beach State Park	July 10, 1981	2,332	1,507
Chain O'Lakes State Park	July 11, 1981	6,500	844
Moraine Hills State Park	July 11, 1981	1,668	420
Fox Ridge State Park	July 24 and Aug. 9, 1981	781	235
Vandalia Statehouse State Historic Site	July 25, 26, & Aug. 9, 1981	2	20
Weldon Springs State Park	Aug. 1, 1981	370	586
Moraine View State Park	Aug. 1, 1981	1,687	419
White Pines State Park	Aug. 8, 1981	385	484
Grant's Home State Historic Site	Aug. 8, 1981	7	139
Siloam Springs State Park	Aug. 22, 1981	3,183	265
Pere Marquette State Park	Aug. 29, 1981	7,800	867
Lincoln's New Salem State Park	Aug. 29, 1981	520	316
Ferne Clyffe State Park	Aug. 30, 1981	1,073	295
Starved Rock State Park	Sep. 19, 1981	2,524	1,395
Iroquois County State Conservation Area	Nov. 7, 1981	1,920	11
Horseshose Lake State Conservation Area	Nov. 14, 1981	6,111	209
Rock Cut State Park	Feb. 6, 1982	2,700	1,482
Argyle Lake State Park	Feb. 7, 1982	1,052	547
Sample Total		58,855	12,590
Statewide Total		246,199	30,835

mation on the number and location of tent and recreational vehicle campers. After acquainting themselves with the major areas of the facility, the interviewers made a thorough "sweep" of the entire facility by automobile. In all cases where

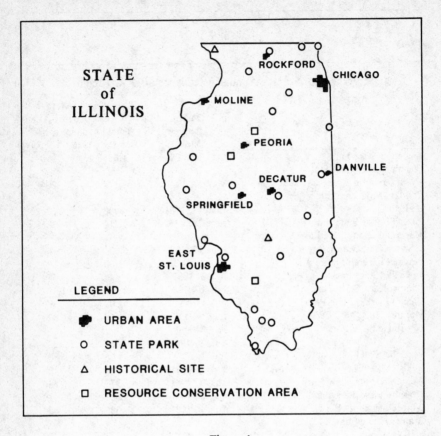

Figure 1

Sites For The Visitor Expenditure Survey

interviews began in the morning, camping areas were the first to be visited. The interviewers proceeded around all the tent and recreational vehicle campgrounds (on foot) until a maximum of fifteen non-local interviews were obtained from all types of campers. Then, sweeps of the day use areas, such as picnicking and fishing areas, were undertaken by the interviewers until at least an equal number of interviews were obtained. When this occurred, a second sweep of camping and day use areas began. A time limit of one hour was put on visits to either a day use area or a camping area in any one sweep through a facility. This time limit was particularly important for facilities where sample sizes of 25, in terms of an adequate mix of campers and day use visitors, were hard to obtain because of inclement weather. The only exceptions to these procedures occurred at Horseshoe Lake and Iroquois County Conservation Areas. Because of the nature of the hunting season and the DOC's procedures by which hunters enter these areas, all interviews in the hunting areas were obtained at the site superintendent's hunting checkpoint just before hunters entered the state facilities, usually between 4:30 a.m. and 6:30 a.m.

Analysis

Table 2 shows the pppd expenditures by category for each facility. The standard error of estimate is shown in parentheses for each type of expenditure, as well as the average number of people per interview ($\bar{x}$) and the standard deviation of group size (∞). Next to the name of each area is the number of non-local interviews obtained for local visitor expenditures. One facility, Siloam Springs State Park, was located on the boundary of two counties, and for this one facility, an operational distance of fifteen miles was substituted for the distinction between local and non-local origins of visitor expenditures. Line 17a of Table 2 portrays the estimates of expenditures for thirty-four households that resided more than fifteen miles from the park. Line 17b of the table portrays expenditure estimates for nine households that lived outside of the two counties whose common border passed through Siloam Springs State Park.

From a simple overview of the data, one can note several points. First, a large proportion of the sampled sites have pppd total expenditures (less government fees, which do not contribute to the local economy) in the $4.00-$5.00 range and relatively small standard errors of estimate. Second, a smaller group of sites had substantially larger pppd total expenditures, but these sites were sampled during special events conducted at the site, or during hunting season, or at highly significant and well known historic areas. Nevertheless, it appears that special events, such as those held at Starved Rock State Park and Rock Cut State Park, do generate substantially greater visitor expenditures than would otherwise be expected. Third, average group size per interview was substantially larger than expected at Fox Ridge State Park and Fern Clyffe State Park because of unusual group and family reunion picnics as well as Labor Day celebrations (Ferne Clyffe State Park). The pppd estimates of expenditures are not out of range of most of the other typical state properties. Fourth, Iroquois County Conservation Area ($3.39) and Horseshoe Lake Conservation Area ($5.15) have the highest pppd travel expenses of all the facilities, thereby indicating the unusual drawing power of hunting areas (in season). Fifth, expenditures for lodging were greatest for the following three facilities: Grant's Home, Horseshoe Lake Conservation Area, and Cahokia Mounds. Grant's Home is located in a recreation resort region focusing upon Galena, Illinois; Cahokia Mounds is located near the metropolitan St. Louis Area, thereby encouraging side trips to the facility; and Horseshoe Lake provides a unique geese hunting opportunity which attracts non-local visitors from both Chicago and St. Louis. In contrast, Iroquois County Conservation Area had low lodging expenditures, probably because of its proximity to metropolitan Chicago. Sixth, although a few state parks have government fees averaging more than $1.00 pppd, none of the facilities compare to Iroquois County Conservation Area's estimates of $9.40 pppd and the Horseshoe Lake Conservation Area estimate of $14.70 pppd.

Table 2

Per Person Per Day Expenditures by Out-of-County Recreators
(All Figures in Dollars and Cents)

Site Number- Name of Area	Group Size		Expenditure				Total (Minus Gov't) (SE)	GOV'T FEES (SE)
	$\bar{x}$	$\bar{e}$	FOOD (SE)	TRANSPOR- TATION (SE)	LODGING (SE)	OTHER (SE)		
1. Kickapoo State Park (27)	4.37	4.12	3.14(1.18)	0.89(0.29)	0.00(0.00)	0.46(0.20)	4.49(1.51)	0.58(0.13)
2. Washington County Lake (42)	5.10	4.07	1.63(0.30)	0.79(0.21)	0.00(0.00)	0.46(0.14)	2.88(0.42)	0.87(0.12)
3. Cahokia Mounds (18)	3.89	1.45	5.28(1.65)	2.42(0.60)	3.34(2.27)	0.80(0.26)	11.85(3.62)	0.05(0.05)
4. Silver Springs State Park (35)	3.76	2.52	3.06(0.67)	2.38(0.78)	0.07(0.05)	0.55(0.19)	6.06(1.32)	0.09(0.08)
5. Marshall County & Rice Lake (16)	3.63	1.36	3.10(0.98)	0.91(0.34)	0.00(0.00)	0.28(0.13)	4.29(1.29)	0.76(0.15)
6. Red Hills State Park (20)	2.75	1.16	3.10(0.84)	0.88(0.26)	0.00(0.00)	0.47(0.31)	4.45(1.21)	1.59(0.16)
7. Chain O' Lakes State Park (34)	4.12	2.11	3.12(0.55)	1.14(0.22)	0.00(0.00)	0.90(0.39)	5.16(0.90)	0.86(0.12)

8. Moraine Hills State Park (28)	4.89	2.94	2.75(0.61)	0.89(0.31)	0.00(0.00)	0.55(0.20)	4.19(0.81)	0.14(0.10)
9. Illinois Beach State Park (32)	3.38	1.72	3.06(0.51)	2.34(0.98)	1.85(1.50)	0.83(0.26)	8.08(1.86)	0.82(0.15)
10. Wayne Fitzgerrell State Park (28)	3.29	1.56	2.08(0.35)	1.87(0.42)	0.00(0.00)	0.87(0.18)	4.82(0.59)	1.48(0.15)
11. Fox Ridge State Park (21)	9.43	16.30	2.03(0.63)	2.53(0.97)	0.00(0.00)	0.05(0.03)	4.61(1.16)	0.15(0.05)
12. Vandalia Statehouse (25)	2.76	1.30	2.31(0.52)	1.79(0.72)	0.00(0.00)	0.00(0.00)	4.10(1.08)	0.00(0.00)
13. Weldon Springs State Park (26)	2.88	1.42	2.17(0.51)	1.31(0.38)	0.00(0.00)	0.69(0.24)	4.17(0.88)	1.42(0.15)
15. Moraine View State Park (28)	2.79	1.20	2.73(0.47)	1.06(0.29)	0.00(0.00)	0.61(0.16)	4.40(0.74)	0.97(0.14)
15. White Pines State Park (26)	5.12	5.81	2.88(0.66)	0.98(0.42)	0.62(0.39)	0.20(0.10)	4.68(0.88)	0.29(0.06)
16. Grant's Home (30)	4.30	6.84	9.35(1.40)	2.00(0.45)	4.83(1.50)	2.27(0.82)	18.45(3.12)	0.11(0.06)
17a. Siloam Springs State Park (34)	3.15	1.56	1.08(0.33)	0.49(0.20)	0.00(0.00)	0.30(0.11)	1.87(0.41)	0.76(0.12)
17b. Siloam Springs State Park (9)	3.44	1.88	2.02(1.07)	0.45(0.23)	0.00(0.00)	0.22(0.12)	2.69(1.07)	0.66(0.27)
18. Pere Marquette State Park (30)	4.07	2.65	2.80(0.58)	0.40(0.19)	1.00(0.57)	0.34(0.18)	4.54(0.94)	0.49(0.13)

Table 2

Per Person Per Day Expenditures by Out-of-County Recreators
(All Figures in Dollars and Cents)

| Site Number Name of Area | Group Size | | Expenditure | | | | | |
	$\bar{x}$	ℓ	FOOD (SE)	TRANSPOR-TATION (SE)	LODGING (SE)	OTHER (SE)	Total (Minus Gov't) (SE)	GOV'T FEES (SE)
19. Lincoln's New Salem State Park (35)	4.91	4.25	2.30(0.40)	1.02(0.29)	0.00(0.00)	0.98(0.19)	4.30(.66)	0.21(0.08)
20. Ferne Clyffe State Park (30)	8.90	10.80	1.15(0.30)	0.69(0.22)	0.00(0.00)	0.11(0.06)	1.95(0.49)	0.32(0.11)
21. Starved Rock State Park (40)	3.93	3.57	5.24(0.78)	1.38(0.25)	1.46(0.64)	1.54(0.30)	9.62(1.37)	0.90(0.12)
22. Iroquois County Conservation Area (25)	2.80	1.71	5.32(0.85)	3.39(0.95)	0.40(0.40)	0.11(0.10)	9.22(1.49)	9.40(.54)
23. Horseshoe Lake Conservation Area (19)	3.16	1.74	11.62(1.49)	5.15(1.24)	5.78(1.52)	0.72(0.45)	23.27(3.35)	14.70(0.22)
24. Rock Cut State Park (29)	3.24	1.62	6.85(0.93)	2.47(0.59)	1.77(1.03)	2.18(1.03)	13.27(2.76)	0.00(0.00)
25. Argyle Lake State Park (5)	2.20	.84	1.23(0.78)	0.00(0.00)	0.00(0.00)	0.00(0.00)	1.23(0.78)	0.00(0.00)

Table 3

Per Person Per Day Visitor Expenditures

Amt.	Local Residents Item	(n = 137) (SE)	Amt.	Non-Local Residents Item	(n = 657) (SE)
$2.25	Food	(.22)	$3.62	Food	(.18)
.87	Trans.	(.11)	1.57	Trans.	(.11)
.36	Misc.	(.08)	.72	Misc.	(.08)
.11	Lodge	(.01)	.83	Lodge	(.08)
3.59	Subtotal		6.74	Subtotal	
.55	Gov.		1.32	Gov.	
$4.14	Total		$8.06	Total	

Table 3 portrays the average pppd expenditures for two groups of respondents. Portrayed in the table are the pppd expenditures by type of expenditure for 137 local households visiting DOC properties and the data for 657 non-local visitors. Every category of expenditure is larger for the non-local visitors than for the local visitors to state properties. In terms of total expenditures in the local area, out-of-county visitors outspent local residents by $6.74 to $3.59. All categories of expenditure by non-local visitors were almost twice as large as that of local county residents. In a sense, the difference between $6.74 and $3.59 or $3.15 pppd (excluding government fees) constitutes money spent by non-local visitors near or at DOC properties that would not have been spent at local facilities in their home counties. This amount of money ($3.15) represents additional expenditures in the visited area allocated from household budgets above and beyond at-home recreation expenditures. One might say that the $3.15 pppd expenditure figure is a representation of the unique value of state recreation facilities in Illinois. Given the data, the state of Illinois received about $1.32 pppd in government fees from non-local visitors as compared to $0.55 from local county residents. Additionally, since many local establishments receive a nominal fee or percentage of sales receipts of hunting and fishing licenses, etc., a sizable amount of money can be accrued locally due to purchases under the government fees category.

Factors Effecting Expenditures Beyond these descriptive differences in pppd expenditures, several features were hypothesized to contribute to variation in pppd expenditures. The site and visitation characteristics expected to relate to variation in the level of visitor expenditures were: (1) the type of DOC site, (2) the significance of the resource at the facility, (3) the degree of urbanization surrounding the area, (4) the length of visitors' stay, (5) interviewing during a DOC-sponsored special event, (6) interviewing during a hunting season, and (7) the distance travelled to the site.

Table 4

Results from Multiple Regression on Visitors' Expenditures
20 sites, (n = 485)

	With Distance in the Analysis		Without Distance in the Analysis	
	b	F-Ratio	b	F-Ratio
County (Dist.)	1.58	12.20		
State Park	.82	.82	.18	.04
Cons. Area	.50	.16	− .56	.21
Day Use	− .69	1.91	− .92	3.82
Near Town	.99	.49	.85	.35
Sig. Resource	− .83	2.41	− .99	3.40
In Town	1.78	10.70	1.73	9.83
Constant	2.47		4.13	

Multiple R = .235   Multiple R = .177
R^2 = .055 R^2 = .031
R^2 = .042 (adj) R^2 = .019 (adj)
F = 4.00   F = 2.58

These independent variables were operationalized as dichotomous variables in the following manner. For the type of site, each interview was characterized as to whether or not the interview took place at a state park or whether or not the interview was obtained at a conservation area (two dichotomous variables); for the significance of the physical or cultural resource base, the researchers were supplied with a dichotomous and subjective scale as to whether or not the resource base was significant by members of the DOC's Division of Planning; for the degree of urbanization, a dichotomous variable was constructed to indicate whether or not a large urban area was nearby (in the local area); the length of stay was operationalized as being either day use or longer; whether or not interviewing took place during a special event sponsored by the Department of Conservation and whether or not an interview was obtained at a hunting site where two more dichotomous variables; distance was operationalized as being the location of one's residence in either an adjacent county (to the one in which a site was located) or in one that was further away from the DOC property. In all the analyses, the pppd expenditure for each interview constituted the dependent variable and was assigned values of either zero or one.

Table 4 and 5 portray the multiple regression analysis for the 20 baseline sites

Table 5

Results from Multiple Regression on Visitors' Expenditures
26 sites, (n = 643)

	With Distance in the Analysis		Without Distance in the Analysis	
	b	F-Ratio	b	F-Ratio
County (Dist.)	1.94	7.3		
State Park	1.33	.7	.55	.1
Cons. Area	2.33	1.3	1.03	.3
Day Use	−2.62	14.3	2.94	18.3
Near Town	9.62	29.3	9.63	28.9
Special Event	6.61	36.1	7.22	44.7
Hunting Season	10.64	38.2	11.99	52.4
Sig. Resource	1.34	3.5	1.25	3.00
In Town	2.15	7.6	1.97	6.4
Constant	(1.04)		(3.07)	

Multiple R = .467	Multiple R = .457
R^2 = .218	R^2 = .209
R^2 = .207 (adj)	R^2 = .199 (adj)
F = 19.64	F = 20.97

(Table 4) and all 26 sites (Table 5). Each table contains the regression coefficients of the independent variables and the F-ratio of each independent variable. Also shown are the multiple correlation coefficients (R), the multiple coefficient of determination (R^2), the multiple coefficient of determination adjusted for degrees of freedom and the F-ratio for the overall equation. All variables were "forced" to enter the regression equation simultaneously. The second analysis excluded (for both Tables 4 and 5) a distance variable for the origin of the individual or persons who were interviewed, indicating whether the non-local visitor was from an adjacent county or from further away. Because of the dichotomous nature of each independent variable, the F statistic and the regression coefficients have significant interpretive value. If a variable accounts for significant variation in pppd expenditures, then the regression coefficient indicates the amount of money which is contributed by the presence of an attribute or variable to the value of expected visitor expenditures.

For the information shown in Table 4, the F statistic must exceed 3.68, at the .05 level with 6,478 degrees of freedom, for an independent variable to be considered as significantly contributing to the explanation of variations in pppd expenditures. When distance was excluded from the analysis of the 20 baseline DOC properties, only whether or not the visit was one day or longer and whether or not the DOC property was actually within the boundaries of a town were of any consequence in accounting for differences among visitors' expenditures. Nevertheless, all of the independent variables in this analysis might be discarded when taken as a group because of the statistically nonsignificant F-ratio obtained for the entire equation (2.58) and the very low multiple coefficient of determination (R^2 = .031, adjusted R^2 - .019). Very little predictive power existed among the variables hypothesized to influence visitor expenditures at the baseline facilities. Even with the inclusion of the distance variable in the analysis, the explanatory power of the variables only increased by making the entire equation significant at the .05 level (the equation's F-ratio of 4.00 is greater than 3.68) although not at the .01 level (the equation's associated F-ratio of 4.00 is less than 6.90) given the appropriate degrees of freedom. The locality of the origin (distance) and whether or not the facility is located within a town's boundaries become statistically significant and relate to pppd visitor expenditures at these 20 recreation areas. Put another way, variations in pppd expenditures appear to be related to the social or demographic characteristics of the group that was interviewed and the availability of opportunities for nearby shopping, rather than any of the supply features of DOC properties. Although state agencies cannot manipulate peoples' travel behavior to these baseline facilities, siting DOC properties within the jurisdiction of towns could significantly increase visitor expenditures.

Table 5 portrays information which is similar to that just discussed, but substantially more reliable in accounting for variations in pppd visitor expenditures in local areas because of much larger predictive levels (multiple correlation coefficients). Once again the type of DOC property visited does not account for significant variations in pppd expenditures. However, all the other variables do account for statistically significant variations in expenditures at the .05 probability level (F = 2.71). In addition, all variables, except for the significance of the physical or cultural resource base, are statistically significant at the .01 probability level (F = 4.31).

For the two analyses presented in Table 5, the regression coefficients are strikingly similar, with or without travel distance, as a predictor variable. The regression coefficients (for the statistically significant variables) do not change by more than a few percent when the distance variable is included, indicating that distance is an independent variable not confounding visitation characteristics. For these visitation characteristics, one can make a significant interpretation of the dollar value that each of these independent variable represents. For example, if one travelled from a non-adjacent county to a site, stayed overnight, used the facility during hunting season, and the facility was not near a town, one would obtain an expected pppd expenditure of $1.94 - $2.63 + $10.64 + $1.04 or $11.00. This description might characterize Chicago area residents utilizing the Iroquois County Conservation Area during hunting season ($\overline{x}$ = $9.42, σ = $1.49).

In essence, one can construct a variety of user profiles for DOC facilities with these coefficients and predict the pppd expenditures of these users because of the significance of the multiple correlation coefficient of the equation. Furthermore, one can estimate the total impact of a mix of user profiles by non-local visitors by applying estimates of pppd expenditures to hypothetical visitation rates for each separate user profile and by multiplying these dollar values by estimates of activity or visitor days for individual facilities. Statewide estimates of the economic impact of visitor expenditures can be generated by applying dollar values generated for user profiles to statewide attendance figures.

Discussion

First and foremost, most DOC properties do not exhibit significant variations in pppd expenditures that are related to site characteristics. There are, however, significant differences in pppd expenditures which are related to a facility's relative location (i.e., in a town) and as travel distances increase for non-local visitors. Second, significant increases in pppd expenditures are related to hunting, special events scheduled at regular DOC properties, and nationally significant historic sites. The results from the multiple regressions shown in Table 5 portray the evidence supporting this conclusion. Third, the predictive utility of the multiple regression equations was 46 percent as good as perfect when the full range of DOC properties and recreation activities were taken into account.

Depending upon whether non-local hunters are from adjacent counties or from further away, expenditures increased by $11.99 or $10.64 pppd, respectively. Special events scheduled at DOC properties added $7.23 to pppd expenditures for non-local visitors residing in adjacent counties and $6.61 pppd for those visitors who travelled further. Travel distance does not appear to affect the level of expenditures associated with whether or not a DOC property is within a town's jurisdiction. When a DOC property is within a town, non-local expenditures by residents from adjacent counties increased the value of total pppd expenditures by $9.61. Those non-local visitors, who travelled from non-adjacent counties, spent an extra $9.62 pppd in local areas. Depending upon the location of the origin of non-local visitors, either $1.97 pppd (adjacent county residents) or $2.15 pppd (non-adjacent county residents) was added to our "best guess" estimate of visitor expenditures. The length of stay decreased local economic impacts on a pppd basis more for non-local visitors from adjacent counties ($2.94) than for those travelling from farther away ($2.62). The significance of the resource base of DOC properties added only $1.34 pppd to local economic impacts when non-local visitors from adjacent counties ($2.94) than for those travelling from farther away ($2.62). The significance of the resource base of DOC properties added only $1.34 pppd to local economic impacts when non-local visitors came from non-adjacent counties and $1.25 was added to pppd expenditures when the non-local visitors originated from adjacent counties. Lastly, non-local visitors who came from counties which were not adjacent to those of the local economic impact area added about $1.94 pppd to their expenditure patterns.

This figure ($1.94) indicates the magnitude of both discretionary travel and the interaction effects of the other independent variables with distance. The interaction effects however, are slight, as illustrated by the correlation coefficients between travel distance and the other independent variables. The largest simple correlation coefficient between travel distance and any other independent variable was 0.209 (interviewed during hunting season). The next three largest travel distance correlations were 0.189 (DOC property within a town), −0.157 (near a town), and 0.154 (interviewed during a DOC sponsored special event). In total, about 14 percent of the variation in travel distances systematically co-varied with the other independent variables.

Statewide Visitor Expenditures

What do these data signify with regard to the net economic impact of public conservation and recreation properties on local governments in Illinois? Table 6 portrays the value of non-local visitor expenditures. Columns one and three are copied from Table One. The figures used in column two come from state traffic surveys made at the entrance to the study areas and from the office of the site superintendent at each property. Column five was copied from Table Two. Column four was obtained by multiplying columns one and two together. The information in columns seven and eight represents purchases made locally by the state recreation or conservation area, the percentage of total sales expenditures and the salaries paid to conservation or recreation property employees living in the local area, and the percentage of salaries paid to local personnel.[1]

There are several ways to interpret these figures as well as those pppd averages described in Table 3. First, for the entire state, let us estimate the maximum and minimum visitor expenditures one would obtain based on the average yearly attendance estimates. If every visitor to a DOC property went to a local facility, instead of an alternative facility across county lines, then the value of direct visitor expenditures would be ($3.59 x 30,835,000) $110,698,000. In addition, the state would collect ($0.55 x 30,835,000) approximately $16,959,000 in government fees of all types related to recreation trips. If all conservation and recreation property visitors were non-local visitors, expenditures would total ($6.74 x 30,835,000) $207,828,000 and ($0.32 x 30,835,000) $40,702,000 in government fees, respectively. Obviously, visitors to DOC properties originate in both local and non-local areas and the true estimates of their expenditures lies somewhere in between these extremes.

To better pinpoint this figure and the value of relatively typical state park systems without special events and without hunting facilities or special historical sites, we estimated the non-local activity days that occurred at the 20 baseline sites (5,476,000) and the total visitor days which occurred at these 20 sites (9,070,000). Then, we calculated the percentage of these visitor days at baseline facilities, 60.4

---

[1]These data were made available for the 1981 fiscal year by the DOC's Division of Planning and Analysis.

percent, which were non-local in origin. Logically, 39.6 percent of the visitor days at the survey facilities were local in origin. Given the standard error of proportions (about 2%), these figures compare favorably to the pattern for the total sample of 26 sites; 7,639,000 visitors of 12,590,000 were non-local in origin (60.8%) and 39.2 percent were local in origin.

If we apply these figures to the statewide annual average attendance values for the 1976 to 1980 period (30,835,000) and to total visitor expenditures and government fees made by non-local and local visitors, we obtain a more realistic estimate of total statewide expenditures for a relatively low service level park system. For Illinois, these figures are (30,835,000 x 60.4% x $6.74) $125.50 million for non-local visitor generated retail sales, (30,835,000 x 39.6% x $3.59) $43.8 million of expenditures by local visitors, (30,835,000 x 60.4% x $1.32) $24.6 million dollars in government fees by non-local visitors, and (3,835,000 x 39.6% x $.55) $6.7 million in government fees of all kinds from local visitors. By adding these figures, direct retail impacts in Illinois (for 1981) are about $169.3 million and government revenues should have been in excess of $31.3 million. State government retail service expenditures (local and non-local) and payroll (local and non-local personnel) expenditures made by the state government approximated $4.9 million for these 26 survey sites and about $20.0 million statewide for fiscal 1981 (81.7% of these expenditures were in local areas). In total then, our "best guess" estimate of direct local impacts from visitor expenditures approximates $185.6 million and government fees from all sources related to recreation trips ($31.3 million) more than offset the maintenance and personnel costs ($20.0 million) of all facilities statewide.

Furthermore, most studies dealing with direct and indirect economic impacts indicate that the economic multipliers associated with the total expenditures (indirect as well as direct expenditures) range between 1.50 and 2.00 and often are as high as 3.0 (see Badger, et al. 1977, Gamble, 1964). With conservative multipliers of between 1.5 and 2.0 for total expenditures, one would approximate total expenditures to be between $278.4 million and $371.2 million annually in Illinois.

To date, the most extensive acquisition and development of property in Illinois has occurred at Illinois Beach State Park, north of Chicago on Lake Michigan, although the Illinois park system was more than 90 percent in place by the early 1960's and had been formally established for more than 20 years (Trotter 1962). Less than $20 million has been spent by the Department of Conservation to acquire and develop the park's acreage, notwithstanding the fact that this acreage constitutes some of the most expensive lakeshore acreage in the state. If one were to assume that all of the other state parks and conservation properties were equally costly, no more than $2.0 billion would have been spent to acquire the entire inventory of the state's total properties at current prices. In fact, most of the state's acquired lands have been of marginal agricultural value or were given to the state after limited stripmine reclamation. It is almost inconceivable that the cost of acquisition, development, and amortization over the past 30 years and until the year 2000 would have resulted in higher costs than direct and indirect visitor expenditures over the same period, no matter what the interest rate on comparable investments would have been for the same period of time. Revenues generated in the local economics of Illinois by recreation in the next 20 years should greatly exceed $6 billion when one considers only current expenditures (direct and indirect) and the time period and excludes inflationary pressure on the dollar that will

Table 6

Value of Non-Local Visitor Expenditures

(1) Atten-dance 1976-1980 (000's) (Yearly) Average)	(2) Percent NonLocal	(3) Facility	(4) Atten-dance NonLocal (000's)	(5) Total Visitor Expendi-tures (pppd)
990	30	Kickapoo	297	$4.49
204	85	Washington County	173	2.88
274	90	Cahokia	247	11.84
226	65	Silver Springs	147	6.06
66	70	Marshall County	46	4.29
88	50	Rice Lake	44	2.39
374	45	Red Hills	168	4.45
844	60	Chain O'Lakes	506	5.16
420	65	Morain Hills	273	4.19
1507	65	Illinois Beach	980	8.08
327	30	W. Fitzgerell	98	4.82
235	40	Fox Ridge	94	4.60
20	85	Vandalia	17	4.10
586	50	Weldon Springs	293	4.17
419	55	Moraine Views	230	4.40
484	85	White Pines	411	4.68
139	95	Grant's Home	132	18.45
265	40	Siloam Springs	106	1.87
867	90	Pere Marequette	780	4.54
316	98	Lincolns New Salem	310	4.30
295	65	Feryne Cliff	192	1.95
1395	60	Starved Rock	837	9.62
11	98	Iroquois C.A.	11	18.84
209	85	Horseshoe Lake	178	23.27
1482	50	Rock Cut	741	13.27
547	60	Argyle Lake	328	1.23
12590			7639	

result in greater total revenues. The value of the local revenues generated in the past by recreation facilities can only be guessed at because the best comparative index of monetary value (the Consumer Price Index) only originated in 1967. For these last fifteen years, however, the estimated value of expenditures in terms of today's dollar value exceeds more than $3.1 billion. Beyond the unpriced primary

(6)	(7)	(8)	(9)	(10)
$ Non-local Retail Exp (000's)	$ Local Sales (000's)	% Local Sales	$ Personnel Local Exp (000's)	% Local Personnel
1,334	47	62	152	100
498	17	33	48	55
2,924	44	86	110	100
891	11	29	67	100
386	11	50	21	39
286	47	87	64	80
748	14	34	67	100
2,611	73	80	164	100
1,144	27	41	129	100
7,918	120	93	308	100
472	9	17	130	80
432	25	69	33	50
70	7	58	40	100
1,222	30	62	68	100
1,012	44	65	107	100
1,923	18	36	102	100
2,435	17	44	116	100
198	36	60	54	100
3,541	35	20	213	85
1,333	69	79	282	85
374	26	67	108	100
8,052	102	74	253	100
207	4	46	32	100
4,412	53	83	97	100
9,833	72	87	185	93
403	44	72	89	100
	1002		3039	

impacts of recreation on the visitor, it would be highly unlikely that recreation and conservation properties in Illinois could ever by considered as having low economic value and substantial negative economic impacts not offset by visitor expenditures.

References

Badger, D. D.; Schreiner, D. F.; and Presley, P. W. "Analysis of Expenditures for Outdoor Recreation at the McClellan-Kerr Arkansas River Navigation System." IWR Contract Report 77-4. Fort Belvoir, Virginia: U.S. Army Engineer Institute for Water Resources, December 1977.

Crompton, J. L., and Van Doren, C. S. "Changes in the Financial Status of Leisure Services in 30 major U.S. Cities, 1964-1974." *Journal of Leisure Research* 10:(1978): 76-89.

Dean, G.; Geta, M.; Nelson, and Siegfired, J. "The Local Economic Impact of State Parks." *Journal of Leisure Research* 10(1978):98-112.

Frick, G. E., and Ching, C. T. K. "Generation of Local Income from Users of a Rural Public Park." *Journal of Leisure Research* 2(1970):260-263.

Gamble, H. B. *The Economic Structure of Sullivan County Pennsylvania.* University Park, Pennsylvania: The Pennsylvania State University, Agricultural Experiment Station Bulletin 743, June 1967.

Kalter, R. J., and Lord, W. B. "Measurement of the Impact of Recreation Investments on a Local Economy." *American Journal of Agricultural Economics* 50(1968):243-256.

Mak, J. J. Moncur, and Yonamine, D. "How or How Not to Measure Visitor Expenditures." *Journal of Travel Research* 16(1977):1-5.

Millerd, F. W., and Fisher, D. W. "The Local Economic Impact of Outdoor Recreation Facilities." In *Land and Leisure,* edited by C. S. VanDoren; G. B. Priddle; and J. E. Lewis, pp. 244-258. Chicago, Illinois: Maaroufa Press, 1979.

Stoevener, H. S.; Pelting, R. B.; and Reiling, S. D. "Economic Impact of Outdoor Recreation: What Have We Learned?" In *Water and Community Development: Social and Economic Perspectives,* edited by D. R. Field; J. C. Barron; and B. F. Long. Ann Arbor, Michigan: Ann Arbor Science Publishers, 1974.

Trotter, J. E. *State Park System in Illinois.* Chicago, Illinois: University of Chicago, Department of Geography Research Paper No. 74, 1962.

Wagner, F. W., and Washington, V. R. "An Analysis of Personal Consumption Expenditures as Related to Recreation, 1946-1976." *Journal of Leisure Research* 14(1982):37-46.

5

Pricing Policies in Outdoor Recreation: A Study of State Park Financing in Oklahoma

Timothy D. Schroeder
Daniel R. Fesenmaier

Traditionally, outdoor recreation at low or no cost has been considered a public right, and therefore much of the costs of providing outdoor recreation resources have been met through general taxation. As a response to increased demand and little or no growth in state resources, however, many state planning agencies have attempted to develop ways to directly charge the recreator for the provision of facilities and services. Thus, recreation administrators have argued for a more laissez faire perspective in supplying the public with outdoor recreation facilities. Following these trends, the state of Oklahoma has recently begun to examine the prospect of increasing user fees to more accurately reflect the costs of providing recreation opportunities. This chapter presents the principal findings of a recent study where alternative pricing policies for Oklahoma state parks were investigated.

Arguments For and Against the Use of Tax Revenues to Support Outdoor Recreation Opportunities

The provision of public outdoor recreation, although traditionally considered free of direct charge, is not without costs. These costs basically have taken two forms: fixed costs consist mainly of land acquisition and physical improvements such as access roads, water supplies, camping grounds, and equipment; variable costs include those costs needed to manage and maintain these facilities. Nationwide, general revenue taxes are the principle means by which these costs have been met. Bond issues and special taxes, such as those commonly imposed on liquor or cigarettes, constitute other ways which local or state governments have indirectly charged residents for the provision of public recreation facilities. In addition, user fees such as admission, rental, and permit fees have become an increasingly popular method of supporting recreation facilities and services.

Historically, the rationale for the special role of government in financially supporting recreation opportunity followed a number of arguments ranging from the concept of collective utility (i.e., public outdoor recreation resources benefits all citizens), to the belief that flaws in the private market systems (i.e., a free market system) adversely affect the range of opportunities that might be offered. The collective utility argument is based upon the concept that everyone benefits in some way from recreation areas, and thus, the cost of provision should be shared. Direct benefits to those who participate include psychological benefits such as relaxation or escape and improvement in physical well-being and social skills (Chubb and Chubb 1981). Collective utility also takes into account those increased benefits that are gained indirectly from recreation participation (i.e., third party benefits). These benefits include social benefits, such as the reduction of crime and increased productivity in the work force and economic benefits, such as jobs generated by recreational spending. Examples of services that provide collective utility and are supported by public funds include the national defense and roadway systems.

Another commonly cited argument supporting public provision of outdoor recreation is based on the belief that the free market system is inappropriate for goods that exist to serve public interests. More specifically, it is argued that the commercial market may not respond adequately to consumer preferences. For example, a private entrepreneur might overlook important but costly educational or aesthetic aspects of recreation in pursuit of increased profits. It also has been suggested that significant historical or religious artifacts might be allowed to deteriorate if direct charges to the public were unable to maintain a sufficient return on investment. Finally, it is argued that few, if any, private individuals or corporations are capable of obtaining the investment capital required to build, let alone maintain, extensive outdoor recreation facilities such as the national park system (Clawson and Knetsch 1966).

In recent years doubts concerning the equity of public provision of recreation facilities have been raised by the results of a number of studies (Knudson 1980; HCRS 1979; Peacock and Godfrey 1975). Most importantly, studies have shown that participation in outdoor recreation is highly variable among the population (Fesenmaier 1982, Lieber 1979). Low income groups and the handicapped, for example, have very limited access to most of the publicly provided outdoor recreation facilities of this nation; similarly, participation varies substantially among various age groups. Many have argued that because the benefits of public recreation are enjoyed by a relatively small segment of society, public funding of recreation ought to be limited to those facilities with a broad appeal.

Many people have argued for the use of entrance fees and similar charges, suggesting that besides providing needed income, pricing policies can be effectively employed to allocate scarce natural resources. Experience has demonstrated that significant funding can be raised through user fees. Federal recreation agencies, for example, have reported offsetting six to ten percent of their operations and maintenance (O&M) budgets through user fees. Similarly, states, counties, and cities have used pricing to provide up to twenty-five percent of their O&M

budgets (U.S. Department of Interior 1979, p. 221). More recent analyses by Howard and Crompton (1980) showed that many cities in the United States are becoming increasingly more reliant upon user fees as a source of revenues. Beyond this, Howard and Crompton's analyses indicated that many of the older communities, which are experiencing inflows of poorer people, are experiencing a substantial decrease in income generated through user fees.

Charges for the use of recreation resources can also be employed as effective management tools, particularly with regard to rationing (Manning and Baker 1981). For example, higher fees have been charged during peak times such as weekends or holidays to discourage overcrowding. Similarly, lower fees are often charged during hours of traditionally low visitation to promote the use of facilities. This form of pricing policy, it is argued, makes better use of available resources by directing the public into a more consistent pattern of use.

Finally, pricing policies may be used to stimulate growth and development of private sector recreation. A study completed for the Heritage Conservation and Recreation Service found that user fees at federal recreation areas were consistently lower than their private counterparts; camping fees averaged between $1.42 and $2.40 at federally owned facilities and between $4.00 and $7.75 at privately run campgrounds (HCRS, 1979). The differences between the costs for the use of private and federal facilities, then, reflect the level of subsidy that is currently provided by the government. This discrepency may also explain why so few private campgrounds exist in America today. Essentially, this heavy public subsidy may prevent private companies from offering the kinds of facilities desired by the public (the "state park" type camp site) and thus, may discourage the campground development that could alleviate current pressures on public camping facilities.

Pricing Issues in Oklahoma

The arguments for the use of general revenues as the principal means of supporting recreation have long been accepted in Oklahoma and are currently reflected in low user fees. With recent cutbacks in federal assistance and growing demand for high quality facilities, however, the arguments supporting pricing policies are becoming more acceptable to park administrators who desire to maintain current service levels for visitors. During the summer of 1981, the state of Oklahoma began investigating the feasibility of generating more income through recreational fees. In order to accomplish this task, a study was conducted which, in part, attempted to identify three factors that are considered essential in implementing a pricing policy: (1) the public's perception of the importance of recreation; this allows one to estimate the size of the outdoor recreation market prior to gauging the effects of a recreation pricing policy; (2) the public's acceptance of the concept of paying user fees at public recreation areas; and (3) the level of monetary support that the public is willing to provide for current recreation opportunities; this information can be used to estimate the potential economic value of user fees to the state.

The Sample

The most recent Statewide Comprehensive Outdoor Recreation Plan (SCORP) was completed by the Oklahoma Department of Tourism and Recreation during the summer of 1981. An important component of this project was a citizen survey which provided, among other information, data needed by the state to investigate recreation pricing policies and whom they impact. The SCORP survey consisted of telephone interviews with 1801 randomly selected residents of Oklahoma. During the interviews, representatives of each household (a member of the household exceeding 18 years of age) were asked their opinions about outdoor recreation and conservation issues, recreation participation patterns in 38 different activities, and about the general characteristics of their families.

Results

The Importance of Outdoor Recreation

Nationally, outdoor recreation has traditionally been considered an important factor affecting an individual's quality of life and residents of Oklahoma are, apparently, no exception. Of the households interviewed, over 95 percent had engaged in some form of outdoor recreation during the previous year. The results of the survey also indicated that passive activities such as walking for pleasure and visiting a zoo were among the most popular activities; physical activities such as boating, were not as common. In addition, more than one third (37 percent) of Oklahoma residents reported visiting a state park during the preceding twelve months.

This high level of participation indicates that Oklahoma residents are actively involved in outdoor recreation and suggests that recreation is an important element in their lives. The results of subsequent questions verify that not only do residents of Oklahoma consider recreation opportunities important but that they are highly satisfied with the current level of offerings within the state (see Tables 1 and 2). As Table 1 shows, over 90 percent of those interviewed considered outdoor recreation important in maintaining a high quality lifestyle; this attitude was consistent throughout the state. Moreover, approximately 92 percent of those interviewed indicated that they were at least "somewhat to very satisfied" with outdoor recreation facilities in Oklahoma (see Table 2).

Public Acceptance of Fees

When public recreation agencies have considered the adoption of user fee programs in the past, objections to the fees have been sometimes voiced by the general public and by special interest groups. The Heritage Conservation and Recreation Service (1979) identified several major concerns about user fees. Two of these concerns might be anticipated as major political problems in Oklahoma: (1) a perception by some citizens that user fees are double taxation; and (2) the possibility that user fees might inhibit recreation participation by those who need it most, such as the poor and the elderly. A national study of the public's will-

Table 1

Importance of Recreation Faciliites to Residents of Oklahoma

Planning Region	Not Very Important	Somewhat Important	Very Important
1	22.8%	32.2%	45.0%
2	13.3%	37.8%	48.9%
3	25.4%	33.6%	41.0%
4	28.3%	39.0%	32.7%
5	25.2%	43.7%	31.1%
6	28.9%	36.2%	34.9%
7	19.5%	42.0%	38.5%
8	18.0%	41.3%	40.7%
9	29.8%	42.7%	36.5%
10	20.8%	45.0%	34.2%
11	13.4%	45.4%	41.2%
State	18.4%	41.9%	39.7%

ingness to pay user fees for outdoor recreation services indicated strong general support for fees (Economic Research Associates 1976). Response differed, however, among demographic groups. For example, a lower percentage of young people than older people thought that outdoor recreation should be more pay-as-you-go. Low income people, on the other hand, were more likely than high income people to agree that public facilities should be supported through user fees. Overall, 60 percent of those interviewed nationwide indicated that outdoor recreation should be supported through increased user fees.

Various studies conducted at state and local levels also show that people generally support an increased role for user fees. Manning and Baker (1981), for example, evaluated the possibilities for the implementation of an entrance fee for Oakledge Park on Lake Champlain in Vermont and found that 60 percent of the park visitors supported a $1.00 per car admission fee, both before and after the fee was implemented. Contrary to what might have been anticipated, senior citizen use of the park increased ten-fold. Manning and Baker concluded that park visitors are receptive to reasonable user fees and that a well-designed fee program does not necessarily discriminate against older people.

The opinions of Oklahomans about recreation user fees were also examined by Badger et al. (1977) through 1600 on-site interviews completed at Oklahoma state

Table 2

Level of Satisfaction with Recreation Opportunities in Oklahoma

Planning Region	Not Very Important	Somewhat Important	Very Important
1	11.6%	41.8%	46.6%
2	5.9%	39.3%	54.8%
3	11.8%	43.7%	44.5%
4	5.7%	43.3%	51.0%
5	8.5%	55.6%	35.9%
6	7.5%	46.5%	46.0%
7	8.0%	51.5%	40.5%
8	9.2%	55.1%	35.7%
9	8.0%	50.5%	41.5%
10	6.7%	44.1%	49.2%
11	8.5%	59.3%	32.2%
State	8.3%	48.7%	43.0%

parks and cultural attractions. Seventy percent of the park visitors said they would be willing to pay a $10.00 annual fee to use the state parks. Of those who were camping at non-fee campsites, 54 percent reported that they would be willing to pay a $3.00 per night camping fee. Most visitors who supported the use of fees cited the inability of tax funds to cover needed services as their reason for support. Thirty percent of those opposed to an entrance fee felt that they could not afford a permit or that a fee would constitute double taxation.

Analysis of the 1982 Oklahoma SCORP data also revealed that the public supports the user fee concept (see Tables 3 and 4). Respondents were asked to indicate their preference about how the costs of operating state parks should be obtained in the future: (1) solely through state support, (2) state support supplemented by user fees, or (3) through user fees only. Sixty-five percent of those interviewed indicated that state support supplemented by user fees was the best way to finance the state park system. Thirty-two percent thought the parks should be totally state supported, while only three percent indicated that parks should be totally fee supported. Respondents were also asked if a fee should be charged for reserved camping space. More than three-fourths (76 percent) said that a fee should be charged. With regard to age and income groupings, the 18 to 24 year old age group was less supportive of fees. There were no clear relation-

Table 3

Percent of Respondents in Favor of Fee for Reserved Camping

Age Groupings	Percent in Favor	Education Levels	Percent in Favor
18 to 24 year olds	63.6	Did not complete high school	73.8
24 to 34 year olds	74.5	High school graduate	74.6
35 to 54 year olds	76.9	College graduate	74.7
55 years and older	75.5		

Ethnic Background	Percent in Favor	Income Level	Percent in Favor
White	74.8	Less than $8,000	71.0
Black	73.6	$8,000 - $10,000	77.9
American Indian	63.3	$10,000 - $15,000	74.9
Hispanic	75.0	$15,000 - $20,000	75.4
		$20,000 - $30,000	75.1
		$30,000 - $50,000	78.4
		$50,000 & greater	78.6

Satisfaction with State Parks	Percent in Favor	Attendance at State Parks	Percent in Favor
Satisfied	75.3	Visited State Park during past year	76.2
Not Satisfied	60.5	Did not visit State Park during past year	73.5

SOURCE: Oklahoma SCORP Interviews, 1982.

ships between income and the fee variables, except that the extremely low income group (less than $8,000) was less supportive of fees than other income groups.

In general, Oklahomans are supportive of instituting user fees to finance the development of recreation facilities and discrimination against socioeconomic groups appears to be an unfounded concern with regard to user fees. In fact, it appears that the groups against whom discrimination was anticipated are more supportive of user fees than the general population.

Table 4

Respondents' Opinions on Future Financing of State Parks
(Percentages)

Age Groupings	Full State Support	Partial State Part. Fee Sup.	No State Support
18 to 24 year olds	42.4	55.5	2.1
25 to 34 year olds	30.6	66.6	2.8
35 to 54 year olds	30.9	66.8	2.3
55 years and older	32.4	63.7	3.8
Educational Levels			
Did Not Complete High School	39.1	55.4	5.4
High School Graduate	31.2	66.6	2.2
College Graduate	29.8	68.1	2.0
Ethnic Background			
White	32.7	64.7	2.6
Black	36.0	58.1	5.8
American Indian	29.3	65.5	5.2
Hispanic	26.7	73.3	0.0
Income Level			
Less than $8,000	42.5	53.0	4.5
$8,000 - $10,000	30.8	65.0	4.2
$10,000 - $15,000	33.1	64.9	2.0
$15,000 - $20,000	34.9	62.5	2.6
$20,000 - $30,000	31.7	67.0	1.3
$30,000 - $50,000	29.3	70.2	0.5
$50,000 & greater	25.5	72.5	2.0
Satisfaction with State Parks			
Satisfied	31.8	65.8	2.4
Not Satisfied	40.3	51.2	8.5
Attendance at State Parks			
Visited State Park Past Year	32.9	65.3	1.8
Did Not Visit State Park Past Year	32.5	64.1	3.4

SOURCE: Oklahoma SCORP Interviews, 1982.

Recreational Spending

The leisure and recreation market is a large and rapidly expanding segment of the U.S. economy. It has been estimated that $244 billion was expended during 1981 by Americans for leisure goods and services. The average American spends one dollar out of eight on the enjoyment of leisure time. During the period from 1965 to 1981 leisure spending increased 321 percent; adjusted for inflation, this represents a real increase of 47 percent (U.S. News 1981, p. 62). Recreation and leisure are also components in the economy of Oklahoma. Tourism and recreation spending was estimated at $2.5 billion in 1981 and is the third largest industry in Oklahoma, behind agriculture and oil. A number of recent studies, however, show that this level of expenditure can be substantially increased through more effective marketing practices and changes in pricing policies. Economic Research Associates (1976) found that recreators were willing to spend almost double their current level for outdoor recreation activities. Similarly in Oklahoma, the results of the SCORP study indicate that recreators are willing to pay substantially more for their recreational outings.

Perhaps a more important consideration than how much people are willing to spend, however, is the relationships between the cost of providing an outdoor recreation service and the amount people are willing to expend to participate. According to the SCORP survey, those families who visited the state parks and lodges during the previous year reported a medium expenditure of $75.04 per year in the vicinity of a state park.[1] Extrapolating this value for the approximately 565,200 households that visited a state park during the previous year (37 percent of all Oklahoma residents) yields $42,441,352 or about 2.5 times the state's operation and maintenance budget.[2]

The data provided some additional insight into the recreational spending per person per day for participation in a variety of outdoor recreation activities. The per day expenditures reported in the SCORP study included backpacking, $5.18; motorized boating, $7.79; sailing, $13.95; tent camping, $8.48; vehicle camping, $8.09; canoeing, $6.64; hiking, $1.11; fishing, $7.32; hunting, $5.45; and off-road vehicle riding, $3.49. The amount expended to participate in outdoor recreation varies considerably among activities. Of course, the costs to the public of providing facilities would vary among the types of activities. In addition, it is worth noting that not all recreational services would be cost effective to operate

---

[1] This level of family expenditure reflects the high level of use of the state's cabin and lodging facilities as well as the high cost of boating. The median value of $75.04 was used to represent the most likely level of expenditure because the distribution of expenditure values was severely positively skewed. Extrapolation using the mean value, $211.52, yields an estimated $119,552,370 being spent at or near state parks in Oklahoma.

[2] The amount appropriated for the operation of the state park system in Oklahoma, was approximately $16.5 million for FY 1983. These funds operate a system of 37 state parks, 27 recreation areas, 14 monuments and memorials and 7 resort hotels.

Table 5

Cost Effectiveness of Selected Outdoor Recreation Services

Outdoor Recreation Service	Expenditure[1] Per Visitor	Cost Per[2] Visitor	Expenditure/[3] Cost Ratio
Motorized Boating	$7.79	$3.24	$2.40
Family Camping	8.31	2.56	3.25
Day Hiking	1.11	4.58	0.24
Backpacking	5.18	12.06	0.43
Canoeing	6.64	0.26	25.54

[1]Based on data from Oklahoma SCORP interviews, 1982.

[2]Based on 1970 costs reported by Tyre (1975). Doubled to account for inflation.

[3]Expenditures divided by costs.

on a fee supported basis. For instance, the cost of providing wilderness areas is very high on a per user basis and a user fee which would reflect this cost would prohibit wilderness recreation for most people. By combining data from the SCORP interviews with information on the costs of forest recreation in the southern United States (Tyre 1975) some cost effectiveness comparisons can be made among outdoor recreation services. The results of analysis for five different activities indicate that while canoeing may be a very cost effective activity to provide, hiking and backpacking have very low cost effectiveness (see Table 5).

The household survey shows that outdoor recreation in Oklahoma has considerable economic value and reasonable user fees are supported by the public. The comparisons of cost effectiveness, however, indicate that the economic value of individual activities varies substantially. In many circumstances, the actual costs of provision can easily be recovered, while others, such as backpacking or dayhiking, require that the state carry most of the financial burden.

Summary

This chapter has demonstrated that an effective pricing policy can be successfully implemented to support the cost of quality outdoor recreation in Oklahoma. More specifically, the results indicate that there is a substantial demand for recreation within Oklahoma and, perhaps more importantly, the public is willing to bear a substantial portion of the actual costs of recreation through increased entrance and user fees. Finally, consumers are indeed capable of providing a significant portion of the cost for the state's outdoor recreation facilities, although some activities fees must be used to support other activities that require substantial resources and costs.

In order to implement a successful pricing policy at outdoor recreation facilities a number of important steps must be taken. Most importantly, planning agencies must develop policies which act to stimulate private enterprise while acknowledging the special role of the public sector in providing recreation opportunities. Furthermore, planners must adapt a strong marketing approach to insure the public that the price of participating in an activity accurately reflects the benefits, as well as the cost, of recreation activity.

References

Badger, D. D.; Parks, L.; Quinlan, C. A.; and Lenard, V. K. *Impact of Travel Related Leisure time Activities in Oklahoma - 1977 Survey Data.* Stillwater, Oklahoma: Dept. of Agricultureal Economics, Oklahoma State University, 1980.

Clawson, M., and Knetsch, J. L. *Economics of Outdoor Recreation.* Baltimore: The Johns Hopkins Press, 1966.

Chubb, M., and Chubb, H. *One Third of Our Time?* New York: John Wiley & Sons, 1981.

Economic Research Associates. *Evaluation of Public Willingness to Pay User Charges for Use of Outdoor Recreation Areas and Facilities.* Washington: U.S. Department of Interior, 1976.

Fesenmaier, D. R. "Outdoor Recreation Study in Oklahoma, 1981-82." Technical Report, Statewide Comprehensive Outdoor Recreation Plan, Oklahoma Department of Tourism and Recreation, Oklahoma City, Oklahoma, 1982.

Heritage Conservation and Recreation Service. *Fees and Changes Handbook.* Washington: U.S. Department of Interior, 1979.

Howard, D. R. and Crompton, J. L. *Financing, Managing, and Marketing Recreation and Park Resources.* Dubuque, Iowa: William C. Brown Company, 1981.

Knudson, D. M. *Outdoor Recreation,* New York: MacMillan Publishing Co., 1981.

Lieber, S. R. "Outdoor Recreation Behavior in Illinois," Technical Report, Statewide Comprehensive Outdoor Recreation Plan, Illinois Department of Conservation, Springfield, Illinois, 1979.

Manning, R. E., and Baker, S. C. "Discrimination Through User Fees: Fact or Fiction?" *Parks and Recreation,* September 1981, pp. 70-74.

Peacock, A., and Godfrey, C. "Public Provision of Museums and Galleries: The Economic Issues." In *Recreational Economics and Analysis,* edited by GAC Searle. New York: Longman, 1975.

Tyre, G. L. "Average Costs of Recreation on National Forests in the South." *Journal of Leisure Research* 7(1975):114-120.

U.S. Department of the Interior. *The Third Nationwide Outdoor Recreation Plan: The Assessment.* Washington: U.S. Department of the Interior, 1979.

6

Assessment of Regional Potentials for Rural Recreation Businesses

Stephen L. J. Smith
D. Christopher Thomas

Much of the scientific thought in Western civilization is shaped by the tension of opposites: the universal versus the particular, understanding versus experience, theory versus fact, reason versus desire, rules versus values (Unger 1975). The results of this intellectual tug-of-war can be seen in much of the literature in resource planning and management, including the body of literature that has developed around locational decision-making. The purposes of this chapter are to review two basic and opposing perspectives on locational decision-making and to present a method that combines some of the characteristics of both perspectives.

The first half of this chapter is devoted to a critical look at the two perspectives on location: (1) locational theory and (2) site selection methods. The former tends to be abstract, general, mathematical, and formal; the latter tends to be concrete, specific, empirically simple, and often dependent on personal judgement.

In the second half of the chapter, a method is developed and illustrated using data from Southern Ontario. The method is designed to identify regions where future business expansion for recreational enterprises might be most feasible. It is intended for use for a specific but common class of business: private enterprises that depend predominantly on local customers (individuals living within 25 miles or so of the business) and that do not have any special resource requirements. Examples of this class of business include drive-in theatres, restaurants, pay fishing lakes, equestrian facilities, trap and skeet ranges, and golf courses.

LOCATIONAL PERSPECTIVES

Locational Theories

The earliest locational theory that has made a lasting contribution is von Thunen's "isolated state" model. Beginning with a hypothetical isolated market place surrounded by an isotropic plane, von Thunen (1875) sought a theory that would predict where certain types of agricultural crops would be grown. His approach was to examine the relationship between transportation costs for different types of crops when grown at different locations and the market value of those crops. The pattern his model eventually predicted was a series of concentric circles with intensively farmed, high value crops grown close to the centre and extensively farmed, low value crops grown further out. Because of the central role of transportation costs in this work, von Thunen's model and the models of other researchers who followed his lead (e.g. Weber 1909, 1911, Hoover 1948) is commonly referred to as the transportation cost approach.

Although von Thunen's assumptions make his model quite simplistic, he has provided the inspiration for a number of recent models for planning tourism regions (Yokeno 1974, Miossec 1977) and for explaining patterns of intra-urban recreational businesses (Vickerman 1975).

During the first decades of the twentieth century, some economists and geographers became interested in the locational forces and interrelationships between industries and between urban places. Initially this work began with a simple modification of von Thunen's model (Ohlin 1935) whereby the central market place was replaced with a localized resource used by some industry. However, subsequent models grew in complexity and scope until the formal statements of locational interrelationships among towns and cities made by Christaller (1933) and among industries and economic regions (Losch 1944). This literature is known variously as central place theory or as the locational interdependence approach. It continues today as a major part of economic and urban geographic theory. Among the many contributions made by central place theory were formalizations of the concepts of:

1. *Threshold Populations:* the minimum population size necessary to support different types of industries.

2. *Hinterlands:* geographic areas, varying in size depending on the type of good or service produced, that contain the threshold population.

3. *Hierarchies:* different central places (towns and cities) will be of different but predictable sizes; a few large towns will offer everything a larger number of smaller towns do, plus additional goods and services.

Christaller elaborated these concepts into his theory describing the patterns and spacing of towns in response to transportation costs and the demand for goods and services. Losch further generalized this work by applying it to an analysis of the shape of market hinterlands in an area with a non-uniform population distribution, variable transportation costs, and irregular resource patterns.

Central place theory, per se, has had little application in the study of recreation industries and resorts. Indeed, when Christaller (1964) turned his attention to tourism, he observed that tourism and resort patterns appeared to obey laws that were in direct contrast to central place forces. However, some of the concepts of central place theory, such as the notions of uniform spacing, threshold populations, and hierarchical centers can be found in recreation geography, especially in the context of early analyses of urban services (e.g. Rolfe 1964, Mitchell 1969).

Despite the success and power of central place theory, it was probably inevitable that some researchers would grow dissatisfied with it. A nagging concern was that there were still a large number of alternative models that emphasized different variables and relationships--and each one appeared to work some times and not at others. This dissatisfaction eventually grew into the third and most recent approach to locational theory, the generalized market approach. This approach is an attempt to combine previous models into a more general model under which the earlier work would appear as special cases.

Two different strategies were employed to develop a general model. The first was that outlined by Isard (1956). Isard's strategy was essentially "technical" (to borrow a term from stock market analysis). He looked for certain regularities and common features in all models and then combined them into one comprehensive model, without making any new detailed structural analysis or major structural modifications.

Greenhut (1956), in contrast, might be described as a "fundamentalist" in his treatment of previous locational concepts. He felt there were inherent weaknesses in earlier models that could not be rectified by simply combining them. Instead, he argued that it was necessary to identify fundamental components of location decisions made by firms and then rebuild these components into a more powerful general model. One of the more important contributions by Greenhut was his addition of risk and uncertainty to models of locational decision-making. Unlike the "Isard school of regional economics", Greenhut was not willing to make the implicit assumption that individual firms would behave as spatial monopolists in selecting sites. Greenhut's firms operate in a world that is actually a spatial oligopoly--a world characterized by the relatively close spacing of a small number of competing firms who do not know what each other will do in the future. This world is neither perfectly monopolistic nor perfectly competitive. Greenhut's model is still abstract, but it is more realistic than many others proposed by locational theorists.

The corpus of locational theory provides a powerful theoretical base for much regional scientific analysis of industrial and urban settlement patterns. In practice, though, it is not always useful for the planning of individual firms. Too many variables are assumed away. The models require a relatively high degree of mathematical proficiency; and they tend to be designed for the analysis of entire systems rather than of individual units. Nonetheless, locational theories have made contributions to practical site selection. These contributions can be summarized as a series of generalities or "laws" that bear on the success of a firm:

1. Location is a critical element in the potential success of a business.

2. The choice of the best location of a business involves making tradeoffs between transportation costs, production costs, resource availability, access to market, and the cost of land.

3. Certain types of businesses do better if they are located in clusters; others do better if they are spread as far apart as possible from each other; still others are indifferent to the location of competitors.

4. The available market and the number of existing firms limit the potential for development.

5. Businesses that have high costs for shipping resources or that are tied strongly to a particular resource base will tend to locate close to that resource. Businesses that have high costs for shipping their final product or who depend on customers travelling to acquire their product will tend to locate close to the market.

These observations, derived from theory and supported by experience, are a lead-in to the second approach to locational decision-making: the site selection tradition.

Site Selection

In the broadest sense, site selection includes assessment of the market and sales potential of particular sites; their physical suitability for development (including the presence of or potential for utilities); surrounding land uses, both current and proposed, and the availability of each potential site, including cost, terms of sale or lease, and the presence of zoning or deed restrictions. Evaluation of each of these matters involves the skills of separate specialists. For the purposes of this chapter, we limit ourselves to an examination of the first one: market and sales potential. Three general methods have been commonly used for assessing this potential: (1) scaling, (2) regression, and (3) "customer behaviour."

Scaling   Scaling involves the comparison and ranking of potential sites on the basis of some previously developed list of important site characteristics. Fishbein (1963, 1967) developed the most formal expression of scaling—the multi-attribute, multi-brand method. In its initial formulation, scaling was used to estimate the market share of different competing brands, but the same logic can be applied to estimating the relative desirability of different sites or regions for development. The steps involved are:

1. Identify variables related to the attractiveness or potential success of sites for the business in question. This might be based on a survey of existing literature, previous experience, or on a survey of experts.

2. Weigh each variable by assigning points in approximate proportion to their relative importance as site characteristics. Again, this can be based on ex-

perience or on the opinions of knowledgable persons in the field. At the simplest level, the weight might be a scale with only two levels: "Essential" and "Desirable But Not Essential." More sophisticated, precise scales can be developed if adequate research exists to support them. However, there is little value in being spuriously precise.

3. Evaluate each potential site on the basis of the degree to which it has each characteristic identified in Step 1. If any site fails to have any essential qualities, it should be dropped from further consideration. For the remaining sites, assign points proportional to the degree they have each characteristic.

4. Multiply the points for each characteristic at each site by the weight for that characteristic. Total the weighted points for each site. The sum represents the relative ranking of that site.

Examples of this approach can be found in a variety of contexts: Brick (1959) and Applebaum (1968) used scaling for general retail sales. Taylor (1965) used it for land-extensive outdoor recreation activities and sites. Gearing, Swart, and Var (1974) and Var, Beck, and Loftus (1977) have applied scaling to regional tourism planning and development. Despite its relatively wide use, there are a few problems with scaling that should be mentioned.

Perhaps the most serious is the need to rely on an ultimately subjective choice of important site characteristics and on the evaluaton of each site. Experienced planners, developers, and researchers can often identify characteristics that appear to have been important in past circumstances, but the development of the list is no better than their judgment.

The mathematical manipulation of the weights and scores can also be suspect. Weights and scores developed in this method are treated as if they had interval scale properties. Although it is possible, under some circumstances, to develop an interval scale for site selection, most scales are merely ordinal. In practice, the results of arithmetic operations such as multiplication or addition of ordinal scales can result in statistical nonsense. One can make some serious errors of judgment if too much is read into the differences between ranks.

Scaling also does not indicate whether a particular site can be successful, or, indeed, if any of the alternatives being considered have the potential to be successful. Scaling merely provides a relative ranking of sites. Finally, sites to be assessed must first be chosen on the basis of availability, intuition, or some other criterion external to the scaling method; and the sites can be assessed only one at a time. Simultaneous comparisons are not possible; this can be a slight disadvantage if one has a large number of individual sites to look at.

Regression   Like scaling, regression techniques compare a set of independent site characteristics to some measure of site success. There are certain differences, such as statistical sophistication, that will become apparent. The basic steps are as follows:

1. Identify key site characteristics in the same way that one might for scaling. Only those characteristics for which data are available at both existing and potential sites should be used.

2. Choose an appropriate measure of site success. Reliable quantitative measures are preferrable to a subjective expert evaluation, although the latter might sometimes be necessary. Measures of success might include percentage profit, sales volume, number of customers, or cash flow.

3. Collect data for each of the independent and dependent variables from established business locations.

4. Regress the independent variables against the dependent variable. The choice of a multiple regression algorithm--stepwise, curvilinear, ridge--depends on the quality and characteristics of the data and availability of electronic data processing systems.

5. The resulting model will typically be of the form (for a linear regression):

$$Y = A + B X + B X + \ldots B_n X_n$$

where:
Y = measure of site success
A = regression constant
B_n = regression coefficients
X_n = site characteristics

To use this model for site assessment, insert appropriate values from each potential sites in place of X_n, multiply by the associated value of B_n, and sum to obtain an estimate of site success.

Although regression is statistically more sophisticated than scaling, it has many of the same limitations. The model is only as good as the initial variable selection, and that means that model is limited by the researcher's ability to understand the situation, to selection appropriate variables and model structure, and by the availability of data.

The regression approach is based on an assumption of the Box-Jenkins type, essentially that past relationships will continue. This assumption is necessary because regression models, even those based on the wisest choice of variables and best data sources, are not causal models at all but statistical descriptions of past situations which can be extrapolated.

A number of technical issues can also influence the validity of regression results. Independent variables that are too highly correlated with each other (a condition called multicollinearity) will spuriously raise the level of explained variance and will create incorrect and unstable estimates of the regression coefficients. Least squares regression (the most common type used) is based on the assumption that the error associated with estimated values of the dependent variable is independent of the observed value of that variable (a condition called homoscedasticity). For example, this means that the error associated with sales predictions for a small business should have the same expected size and distribution as the error associated with predictions for larger businesses. In many cases, needless to say, this assumption is not met and the model performs poorly.

Lastly, the power of a regression model, measured by explained variance, is dependent on the level of aggregation. As a rule, the higher the level of aggregation, the higher the level of explained variance (Young and Smith 1979). Because the level of aggregation in site selection is low—individual sites are the unit of analysis—many regression models explain only small amounts of the total variance.

Despite these problems, regression is still widely used in recreation research for forecasting future levels of consumption or "demands." They are most common in site-specific forecasts of user levels for recreational travel. A few examples and critical discussion can be found in the work of Cesario and Knetsch (1976), Cheung (1972), Burby, Donnelly, and Weiss (1972), and Ewing (1980, 1982).

"Customer Behavior" In 1966, Gruen and Gruen proposed a method to estimate probable sales levels of businesses at different locations on the basis of customer profiles. Although their full procedure is rather lengthy, it can be adequately summarized by the following steps:

1. Develop a customer profile (age, sex, income, and so on) on the basis of customer surveys at existing businesses.
2. For existing sites and their surrounding market areas, calculate two ratios:

   i. <u>Number of people who fit profile and are customers</u>
       Total number of people who fit profile

   ii. <u>Number of people who do not fit profile but are customers</u>
       Total number of people who do not fit profile

3. Estimate probable shape, size, and population of market areas around the proposed sites on basis of willingness-to-travel studies conducted at other sites. Use the ratios obtained from *i* to *ii* (above) to estimate the total number of customers to be expected.

4. Estimate the impact of competition in the new area on the total market volume by assuming customers will go to nearest store.

5. If possible, adjust the estimates to reflect the effects of surrounding land uses and other local characteristics on customer behavior.

6. Calculate the ratio of cash to charge customers at existing stores. Estimate the average purchase for each type of customer. Assuming ratios and sales volumes will remain constant, estimate the number of charge and cash customers in new market area and the total volume of their purchases. Sum cash and charge sales to get total sales.

7. Subtract the estimated sales from estimated costs at each site to identify the site with the highest estimated net profits.

The Gruens' method requires, obviously, a market survey and experience in established market areas to be able to assess customer reactions to land uses and other factors that the Gruens suggest be included. This information, if available, makes for a rather useful model; but if it is not available, the method cannot be used.

Another, but lesser problem is the assumption that competing firms will proportionally divide the market area between themselves on geographic lines. This is not often the case. Real market areas have complex shapes and can show substantial overlap. To complicate the matter further, some businesses, such as automobile dealers and fast food franchises, actually benefit from clustering.

Finally, by defining the optimal site on the basis of net profitability, one must also obtain estimates of site costs. Certainly this is a matter that any developer will have to consider sooner or later, but it does complicate initial site selection by introducing it right from the start.

Every one of these three basic techniques has strengths and weaknesses. Each is appropriate in different circumstances, depending on the availability of data and previous experience of the researcher and developer. One common characteristic is that each of these methods requires the definition of specific sites before analysis can begin. If a developer already owns or has options on several pieces of property and merely wishes to choose the best alternative, a site-specific study may be desirable at the outset. On the other hand, if a developer is looking at a rather large geographical area, perhaps an entire state or province, a site-by-site evaluation procedure is inefficient. A more feasible strategy would be to narrow the search for future business locations to a relatively small number of possible regions. Once a few likely regions have been identified, more detailed site specific studies can be undertaken.

What is being described here is a need for a method of the middle ground (to paraphrase Robert Merton), a method that is more tied to empirical reality and problem-solving than locational theories, but broader in scope than site-specific studies. The balance of this chapter presents such a method.

ASSESSMENT OF REGIONAL POTENTIALS

A model designed to assess regional potentials, belonging midway between locational theories and site selection, should combine elements of both. It should be based, in part, on the concept of "economic regions," or at least be capable of assessing regional characteristics. It should recognize the facts of spatial competition and market place equilibrium, and should be based on an objective analysis of available data sources. The method outlined below was designed with these criteria in mind. Its basic logic might be described as follows.

The total number of firms in a particular business operating in a region is not only a function of the available market, but a function of entrepreneurs' perceptions of that market, the tenacity and skill of existing business managers to stay in operation, the availability of venture capital to start new businesses, and other factors. The result is that at any given time the number of businesses operating in a region does not necessarily reflect equilibrium conditions. Because of uncertainty and the factors mentioned above, the optimal number of firms may be different than the current number. Over time, however, there will be some movement towards equilibrium.

Business decisions, however, cannot be made on the same time scale needed to test for whether a particular market is in equilibrium. Further, if the population or its economic characteristics are changing at the same time the number of businesses is changing, equilibrium may never really be reached. What is needed is an alternative to a time-consuming longitudinal study to estimate what the optimal number of businesses in any region might be. Such an alternative may be a latitudinal study. In other words, one might assume (with a certain degree of risk) that equilibrium conditions can be identified by looking synoptically at a large number of regions and the relationship between market variables and the number of businesses.

The Assessment Method

Given these preliminary comments, there are six basic steps to assess regional potentials for some business:

1. Identify a measure of business success (the dependent variable) and a set of regional economic and social variables (the independent variables) that can reasonably be considered to influence the volume of business in the region.

2. Define a set of regions and collect data for those regions.

3. Regress the independent variables against the dependent variable and obtain estimated values of the dependent variable for each region.

4. Compare the estimated and observed values of the dependent variable to obtain residuals. Because some degree of error between the observed and expected is highly likely, a tolerance interval should be specified to define "equilibrium." In this example, any residual within plus or minus one standard deviation is considered small enough to be defined as "equilibrium."

5. Convert the residuals to standardized scores and note which regions have residuals greater than plus or minus three standard deviations, if any. These are outliers, and they can have a disproportionate effect on the estimation of the regression equation.

6. Rerun the stepwise regression with the outliers temporarily removed and calculate residuals as before. Then calculate the expected numbers of firms and the residuals for the outliers, using the coefficients from the regression equation. Note those regions with residuals greater than plus or minus one standard deviation. These regions are those that have more or fewer businesses than one would expect, given general market conditions; thus they represent regions in which a "shake-out" of inefficient businesses is to be expected (if there are "too many" firms) or in which there is room for new firms to enter (if there are "too few" firms). Other regions are probably in "equilibrium" and may not be capable of supporting new business growth.

Empirical Example

This method can be illustrated by considering the county-level patterns of development of golf courses in Southern Ontario. Golf courses in Southern Ontario are not especially tied to any particular resource base. With only certain local exceptions, such as the presence of swamps, bogs, and environmentally sensitive areas, golf courses can be located anywhere there is sufficient open space. Further, they are relatively easily identified; reliable inventories of the number of courses are available.

Because the basic question this method is designed to answer is whether a particular region can support any more golf courses, the absolute number of courses in each county was chosen as the dependent variable. Some measure of profitability might have been desirable, but such information is usually not available for any private firms. All data were obtained for the year 1977.

A lengthy list of independent variables was developed on the basis of existing census and market survey information for the counties in Southern Ontario (see Figure 1). This list was then shortened by retaining only those variables previously identified in outdoor sports and recreation literature as relevant to participation rates. Table 1 is a list of the independent variables finally chosen for analysis.

To further shorten this list, and to minimize any potential problems from multicollinearity, a principal components analysis was run on the independent variables. Several analyses were run to find an optimal balance between a high degree of retained variance and a parsimonious solution. A five component solution explaining 63 percent of the variance provided the best balance. Table 2 is a summary of the higher factor loadings. The five factors were identified as: (1) a *male population* component, (positive loadings for number of males 0-14 years, 15-24 years, 25-34 years, 35-49 years, 50-64 years, 65+ years, and negative loadings for number of females in same age categories); (2) an *urbanness* component, (positive loadings for total tax returns over $30,000, urban/rural population ratio, total disposable income, number of licensed restaurants and private clubs, population density, population, and number of households); (3) an *age-sex balance* component, (negative loadings for percentage of males 0-14 years, 25-34 years, 35-49 years, 50-64 years, 65+ years, and positive loadings for percentage of females in all age groups); (4) a *high income/professional* component, (position loading for percentage of labour force employed in management/administration and negative loading for percentage of labour force employed in farming/forestry/mining); and (5) a *youthfulness* component (negative loadings for percentage of males 15-24 years and for females 15-24 years). Scores for the forty-three counties and these five components were then computed and were used as the dependent variable in a two-stage forward stepwise multiple regression.

The first stage of the regression analysis identified seven counties as outliers. These were temporarily removed from the data set and the regression run again. The second stage produced a model that explained about 92 percent of the variance. Table 3 is a summary of the results of that analysis.

Residuals were then calculated for every region. Because the residuals are

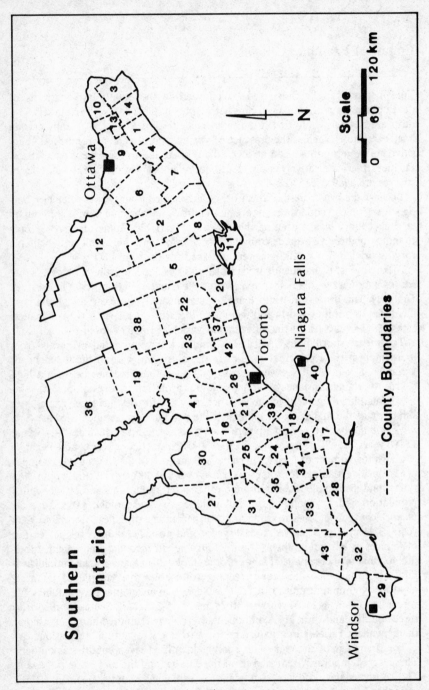

Figure 1

Administrative Areas of Southern Ontario

Key to Figure 1

No.	County				
1.	Dundas	16.	Dufferin	31.	Huron
2.	Frontenac	17.	Haldimand/Norfolk	32.	Kent
3.	Glengarry	18.	Hamilton/Wentworth	33.	Middlesex
4.	Grenville	19.	Muskoka	34.	Oxford
5.	Hastings	20.	Northumberland	35.	Perth
6.	Lanark	21.	Peel	36.	Parry Sound
7.	Leeds	22.	Peterborough	37.	Durham
8.	Lennox/Addington	23.	Victoria	38.	Haliburton
9.	Ottawa	24.	Waterloo	39.	Halton
10.	Prescott	25.	Wellington	40.	Niagara
11.	Prince Edward	26.	York	41.	Simcoe
12.	Renfrew	27.	Bruce	42.	Ontario
13.	Russell	28.	Elgin	43.	Lambton
14.	Stormont	29.	Essex		
15.	Brant	30.	Grey		

defined as the observed value minus the predicted, a large negative residual indicates possible underdevelopment and a large positive residual indicates possible overdevelopment. The estimated number of golf courses and the residuals were calculated for the outliers using the second stage results. In all, ten regions appeared to be seriously overdeveloped and six appeared to have room for further market expansion. Table 4 is a summary of the patterns of residuals.

Discussion

Although this method has utility for estimating potentials for future expansion of rural recreation businesses on a regional level, there are certain limitations and assumptions that should be mentioned. The first major assumption is that the residuals are indeed a reflection of marketplace disequilibrium. Disequilibrium in the Southern Ontario golf course market is probably a fact, but other factors may have contributed to the existence of a few substantial residuals. The model itself may have been improperly specified. All variables were assumed to be linearly and additively related to each other, and this may not necessarily be the case. The relatively high R^2 of 91 percent suggests the model specification is not grossly in error, but other forms of the model might have produced smaller residuals for some counties.

Some key variables may have been omitted from the analysis. Two important variables that could not be included were the availability of investment capital for new golf courses and the presence of zoning restrictions against farmland conversion. Inclusion of these might have helped explain some of the residuals in counties with apparent potential for further growth. It is likely, however, that these issues (capital availability and zoning restrictions) would be identified in subse-

Table 1

Independent Variables Selected for Analysis

Variable
Label

001	Total number of males: 0-14 years
002	15-24 years
003	25-34 years
004	35-49 years
005	50-64 years
006	65 + years
007	Total number of females: 0-14 years
008	15-24 years
009	25-34 years
010	35-49 years
011	50-64 years
012	65 + years
013	Percentage of males between: 0-14 years
014	15-24 years
015	25-34 years
016	35-49 years
017	50-64 years
018	65 + years
019	Percentage of females between: 0-14 years
020	15-24 years
021	25-34 years
022	35-49 years
023	50-64 years
024	65 + years
025	Total number of tax returns showing taxable incomes over $30,000
026	Urban/Rural population ratio
027	Total personal disposable income
028	Number of licensed (alcohol) restaurants
029	Number of licensed (alcohol) private clubs
030	Population density
031	Population
032	Number of households
033	Percentage of labour force employed in: Management/Administration/
034	Farming/Forestry/Mining

quent site-specific studies. Thus, their omission at this stage of the analysis does not mean they are permanently ignored.

This method is based on the further assumption that the variety of golf courses (in terms of size and quality) in each region are approximately the same. One also assumes that the long-term existence of a golf course is an adequate indicator of

Table 2

Principal Component Loadings (Highest Loadings Only)

Variable Label*	Component 1	Component 2	Component 3	Component 4	Component 5
001	.974				
002	.981				
003	.983				
004	.983				
005	.989				
006	.986				
007	− .974				
008	− .983				
009	− .972				
010	− .986				
011	− .988				
012	− .909				
013			− .848		
014					− .891
015			− .760		
016			− .766		
017			− .900		
018			− .727		
019			.802		
020			.802		− .809
021			.815		
022			.888		
023			.948		
024			.779		
025		.902			
026		.954			
027		.969			
028		.973			
029		.889			
030		.937			
031		.973			
032		.974			
033				.750	
034				− .817	

*see Table 1 for interpretation of label numbers

its profitability. Because some golf courses are publicly owned, this is not necessarily true. However, the total number of golf courses in Southern Ontario is still growing, and anecdotal evidence indicates that the industry is reasonably healthy.

Table 3

Summary of Multiple Regression of Five Components with
Number of Golf Courses

Variable	B
Component 1	1.443
Component 2	1.223
Component 3	−0.513
Component 4	0.727
Component 5	−0.175
Constant (A)	6.573
R^2	.916

Additionally, the model does not make any allowance for clever and aggressive management or for bungling, incompetent management. A poor manager can defeat any locational benefits that might be derived from a good location. A skilled manager, on the other hand, can sometimes overcome some of the disadvantages of a bad location.

Finally, it is assumed that the socio-economic characteristics of a particular county affect only the golf courses in that county; similarly, the only population characteristics relevant to a golf course are those of the people living in the same county as the golf course. To the degree that a course draws customers from outside the region, the model's results are less valid.

Summary

There is an adage in many businesses (probably started by a real estate agent) that the three most important factors for success are "location, location, and location." While the degree of importance that site selection actually plays in the success of a business can be debated, most planners, developers, and researchers would agree that it is an important issue. The method illustrated here provides a systematic and objective (within certain limits) means of identifying regions where further development is warranted and in identifying regions where the market may be saturated. Additionally, the model also has application in public policy. Some government agencies are mandated to provide support and incentives for small business development in economically depressed regions. If their support is to be effective, these agencies need to identify that combination of business ac-

Table 4

Number of Golf Courses (Observed and Predicted) for Southern Ontario Counties, 1977

County	Observed	Predicted	Residual	Comment*
Dundas	1	2.3	−1.3	under
Frontenac	5	6.2	−1.2	
Glenqarry	0	2.7	−2.7	under
Grenville	1	3.7	−2.7	under
Hastings	6	4.5	1.5	
Lanark	4	4.9	−0.9	
Leeds	6	3.3	2.7	over
Lennox/Addington	1	2.2	−1.2	
Ottawa	21	16.7	4.3	over
Prescott	2	2.9	−0.9	
Renfrew	1	4.2	−3.2	under
Russell	1	1.2	−0.2	
Stormont	2	3.9	−1.9	
Brant	6	5.2	0.8	
Dufferin	1	1.1	−0.1	
Haldimand/Norfolk	5	3.5	1.5	
Hamilton/Wentworth	13	12.8	0.2	
Muskoka	8	4.5	3.5	over
Northumberland	4	4.6	−0.6	
Peel	11	11.8	−0.8	
Peterborough	7	5.7	1.3	
Victoria	3	4.9	−1.9	
Waterloo	13	9.4	3.6	over
Wellington	5	5.1	−0.1	
York	34	36.2	−2.2	under
Bruce	5	4.1	0.9	
Elgin	3	4.8	−1.8	
Essex	10	10.4	−0.4	
Grey	5	3.6	1.4	
Huron	5	3.3	1.7	
Kent	6	5.0	1.0	
Middlesex	11	10.6	0.4	
Oxford	4	3.6	0.4	
Perth	3	4.8	−1.8	
Parry Sound	1	2.4	−1.4	
**Durham	17	4.7	12.3	over
**Haliburton	1	5.0	−4.0	under
**Halton	16	6.7	9.3	over
**Niagara	21	11.4	8.6	over
**Simcoe	19	7.8	11.2	over
**Ontario	9	25.1	−16.1	under
**Lambton	11	5.4	5.6	over

*indicates probable over or under-development
**indicates outliers removed during second stage of regression

tivities and location that has a high probability of providing the type of economic progress sought. Judicious application of the method discussed in this chapter can provide valuable information in determining whether a particular development proposal has a chance of resulting in a successful business. Certainly the method provides no final answers for either government or private industry, but it can help simplify the complex, expensive, time-consuming, and vital process of site selection.

References

Applebaum, W. "Store Characteristics and Operating Performance." In *Guide to Store Location Research,* edited by C. Kornblau. Reading, Massachusetts: Addison-Wesley, 1968.

Brick, J. C. "Gasoline Service Station Appraisal." In *Encyclopedia of Retail Site Appraisal,* edited by E. Friedman. Englewood Cliffs, New Jersey: Prentice-Hall, 1959.

Burby, R. J.; Donnelly, T. G.; and Weiss, S. F. "Vacation Home Location: a Model for Simulating the Residential Development of Rural Recreation Areas." *Regional Studies* 6(1972):421-439.

Cesario, F. J. and Knetsch, J. L. "A Recreation Site Demand and Benefit Estimation Model." *Regional Studies* 10(1976):97-104.

Cheung, H. K. "A Day Use Visitation Model." *Journal of Leisure Research* 4(1972):139-156.

Christaller, W. *Die Zentralen Orte in Suddent Schland.* Jena, 1933.

Christaller, W. "Some Considerations of Tourism Location in Europe: The Peripheral Regions—Underdeveloped Countries—Recreation Areas." *Papers of the Regional Science Association.* 12(1964):95-105.

Ewing, G. O. "Progress and Problems in the Development of Recreational Trip Generation and Trip Distribution Models. *Leisure Sciences* 3(1980):1-24.

Ewing, G. O. "Modelling Recreation Trip Patterns: Evidence and Problems." *Ontario Geography* 19(1982):29-56.

Fishbein, M. "An Investigation of the Relationships Between Beliefs About an Object and the Attitude Toward That Object. *Human Relations* 16(1963):232-240.

Fishbein, M. "Attitude and the Prediction of Behavior." In *Readings in Attitude Theory and Measurement,* edited by M. Fishbein, pp. 477-492. New York: John Wiley and Sons, 1967.

Gearing, C. E.; Swart, W. W.; and Var, T. "Establishing a Measure of Touristic Attractiveness." *Journal of Travel Research* 12(3)(1974):1-8.

Greenhut, M. L. *Plant Location in Theory and Practice.* Chapel Hill, North Carolina: University of North Carolina Press, 1956.

Gruen, C., and Gruen, N. J. *Store Location and Customer Behavior.* Technical Bulletin 56. Washington, DC: Urban Land Institute, 1966.

Hoover, E. M. *The Location of Economic Activity.* New York: McGraw-Hill, 1948.

Isard, W. *Location and Space Economy.* Cambridge, Massachusetts: MIT Press, 1956.

Losch, A. *Die Raumliche Ordnung der Wirtschaft.* Jena: Gustar Fischer, 1944.

Miossec, J. M. "Un Modele de L'Espace Touristique." *L'Espace Geographique* 6(1977):41-48.

Mitchell, L. S. "Toward a Theory of Public Urban Recreation." *Proceedings of the Association of American Geographics* 1(1969):103-108.

Ohlin, B. *Inter-Regional and International Trade.* Cambridge, Massachusetts: Harvard University Press, 1935.

Rolfe, E. "Analysis of the Spatial Distribution of Neighbourhood Parks in Lansing: 1920-1960." *Papers of the Michigan Academy of Science, Arts, and Letters* 50(1964):479-491.

Taylor, G. D. "An Approach to the Inventory of Recreational Lands." *The Canadian Geographic* 9(1965):84-91.

Unger, R. M. *Knowledge and Politics*. New York: The Free Press, 1975.

Var. T.; Beck, R. A. D.; and Loftus, P. "Determination of Touristic Attractiveness of the Touristic Areas in British Columbia. *Journal of Travel Research* 5(1)(1977):23-29.

Vickerman, R. W. "The Leisure Sector in Urban Areas." Chapter 8 in *The Economics of Leisure and Recreation*. London: The MacMillan Press, 1975.

von Thunen, J. H. *Der Isolierte Stast in Beziehung Auf Landwirtschaft and Nationalokonomie*. 3d ed. Berlin: Schumacher-Zarchlin, 1875.

Weber, A. "Uber den Standard der Industrien: Reine Theorie des Standarts." Tubingen, 1909.

Weber, A. "Die Standortslehre und die Handespolitik." *Archive fur Sozialwissenschaft und Sozialpolitik* 32(1911):667-688.

Yokeno, N. "The General Equilibrium System of Space-Economies for Tourism." *Reports for the Japan Academic Society of Tourism* 8(1974):38-44.

Young, C. W. and Smith, R. V. "Aggregated and Disaggregated Outdoor Recreation Participation Models." *Leisure Sciences* 2(1979):143-154.

Section Two:
Outdoor Recreation Forecasting Methods

1

An Introduction to Recreation Forecasting

Daniel J. Stynes

Forecasting plays an important role in most organizations since virtually all planning and decision-making must rest upon understandings of, or assumptions about, the future. Forecasting models are tools to help us better understand the future, including the role of past and present decisions in shaping it. In this section we introduce four different approaches to forecasting and applications of these methods to outdoor recreation planning and management. This initial chapter introduces forecasting and forecasting methods. Subsequent chapters will present particular methods in greater detail.

To be useful, forecasts and forecasting models must be relevant to decision-making. The purpose of this chapter is to help the reader understand how to select a forecasting method or model suited to a particular decision-making situation. Selecting an appropriate forecasting method requires a clear understanding of one's purposes and situation, as well as a general knowledge of the assumptions and requirements of different methods. The latter is also necessary to properly interpret and apply the results of a forecasting study.

CHOOSING A FORECASTING METHOD

The selection of a particular forecasting method is a complex decision. Most organizations must make a variety of projections as part of planning, management, and decision-making. Each forecast may involve a different set of circumstances and may require distinct forecasting methods. The greater one's familiarity with a variety of both qualitative and quantitative forecasting methods and their strengths and weaknesses, the better one is able to select the appropriate tool for a given situation. There are four factors to consider in selecting a forecasting method.

1. <u>Organizational Environment</u> A forecasting method must be suited to the skills and resources of the organization. Different methods require different levels of ability of the forecast preparer and forecast user. If a method is beyond the stability of the existing situation. Different methods will be required for short range versus long-range forecasts, for highly accurate versus ball park estimates, for detailed versus highly aggregated forecasts, and for stable versus unstable considered. Finally, the forecasting method or methods must fit the existing planning and decision-making structure of the organization.

2. <u>Decision-making Situation</u> The appropriate forecasting technique will depend upon the particular decision-making situation surrounding a forecast. Important factors are: (a) the time horizon of the decision/forecast, (b) the lead time to make the forecast/decision, (c) the level of detail and accuracy needed, and (d) the stability of the existing situation. Different methods will be required for short range versus long range forecasts, for highly accurate versus ball park estimates, for detailed versus highly aggregated forecasts, and for stable versus unstable situations. The time required to prepare a forecast can vary from a few minutes to several years. Organizations desiring more complex forecasting methods must anticipate forecast needs in order to have forecasts available when they are needed.

3. <u>Existing Knowledge (data and theory)</u> All forecasts are extrapolations from our present knowledge base, and therefore depend upon the quality and quantity of past research. Trend extension methods require accurate historical measurements. Analytical forecasting models involve assumptions which should be theoretically based, and parameters which must be empirically estimated. The complexity and detail of a given forecasting method should be matched to the complexity and detail of our understanding of the phenomona being forecasted and the complexity and detail required to make a given decision.

4. <u>Nature of Phenomona Being Forecasted</u> The first three factors are basically constraints imposed upon the forecast preparer or forecast user. Ultimately, the characteristics of the variables being forecasted and the underlying processes which determine the levels of these variables over time must guide the selection of a particular forecasting model. Choices between forecasting models that are linear or nonlinear, stochastic or deterministic, dynamic or static, and single equations or a system of equations, should be based upon knowledge, or assumptions of how the phenomona actually behave.

The above four factors are completely general and apply to forecasting in almost any kind of organization. Outdoor recreation and recreation organizations have certain characteristics which have determined the types of forecasting methods most commonly used. Recreation forecasting methods may be grouped into four general categories; these are introduced in the next section and discussed in more detail in subsequent chapters.

TYPES OF RECREATION FORECASTING TECHNIQUES

Forecasting methods are usually divided into qualitative and quantitative techniques. Although recent advances in qualitative methods have made this distinction less clearcut, there are several features which differentiate these two methods. Qualitative methods directly incorporate human judgment, while quantitative methods generally employ formal mathematical models. Quantitative methods define variables, specify measurement units, and state formal assumptions. The formal requirements of quantitative models usually result in statistical estimates of the errors associated with a forecast. However, quantitative models are difficult to apply to situations where variables are hard to quantify and relationships are poorly understood. Qualitative techniques are often used in these situations, and particularly in long-range forecasting.

The best known and most highly developed qualitative forecasting technique is the Delphi method. Other qualitative forecasting techniques include life cycle analysis, cross impact matrices, relevance trees, and historical analogies. Quantitative forecasting methods that have been applied in recreation may be grouped into three broad categories: (1) time series models, (2) structural models, and (3) systems or simulation models.

The Delphi method and these three general types of quantitative forecasting techniques are briefly introduced below. Within recreation, quantitative models have primarily been applied to forecast some measure of the volume of recreation participation. Recreation participation (or use) is readily quantified and is perhaps the most useful variable in recreation planning. Qualitative methods, like the Delphi technique, have been applied to forecast future rates of recreation participation, as well as a host of other variables and events that are more difficult to quantify.

1. The Delphi technique is a qualitative forecasting method that relies upon expert opinion to forecast likely futures. The method usually involves several rounds of predictions by a panel of experts. Systematic feedback of information to the panel between rounds generally results in the convergence of opinions toward a group consensus. (See the chapter by Moeller and Shafer.)

2. Time series or trend extension models forecast future rates of participation based upon some pattern in historical measures of participation. This pattern may be linear, exponential, logistic, periodic, or seasonal. The basic assumption underlying these methods is that history will repeat itself and therefore historical trends in data series are indicative of likely future patterns. (See the chapter by Stynes.)

3. Structural models forecast future recreation participation by identifying relationships between participation and a set of demographic, socioeconomic, and environmental descriptors. These relationships are usually identified via statistical analyses of cross sectional data and then applied to forecasts of the independent variables to predict future levels of recreation participation.

Structural models may be divided into trip generation and trip distribution

Table 1

Selecting a Recreation Forecasting Method Suited to Your Organization and Objectives

	Forecasting Method			
	Delphi	Time Series	Structural	Systems
Organizational Environment				
forecasting expertise	low-high	low-medium	medium-high	high
planning/decision-structure	rely upon expert opinion, consensus of different groups	on-going planning & data collection to guide decisions	rely on consultants to develop forecasting models; analytical skills to use and interpret them	based upon simulating futures; resources for complex model development and use
Decisionmaking Situation				
time horizon of forecast	long	short - medium	short - medium	short - long
lead time to develop the forecast	medium	short - medium	short - medium	medium - long
detail needed	low - medium	medium - high	medium - high	low - high
stability	low - high	high	medium - high	low - high
Existing Knowledge	informal and experiential	in form of time series data	knowledge of causal forces & relationships	knowledge of dynamics and change processes
Nature of Phenomona Being Forecasted	hard to quantify, complex, multifaceted	stable, cyclic, or seasonal	determined by a set of quantifiable independent variables	complex, dynamic; strong probabilistic elements, feedback effects

models. Trip generation models use linear, polynominal, or logistic equations to estimate and forecast probabilities or frequencies of participation in recreation activities. (See the chapter by Stynes.) Trip distribution models distribute this activity from population centers or origin zones to destination regions or sites. Various formulations of the gravity model account for the majority of recreation trip distribution models. Some of the more complex versions combine trip generation and trip distribution equations into a single forecasting model. (See the chapter by Ewing.)

4. Systems or simulation models generally combine both structural and time series components in a dynamic model of the system for which forecasts are desired. These models are often capable of forecasting a number of different variables under a variety of assumptions. They assume that recreation participation is the result of a complex process involving both historical factors and present circumstances. Dynamic aspects of recreation systems are captured through timelags, interrelationships between variables, and feedback effects. These models generally involve a system of interrelated equations expressing structural relationships between recreation participation and other variables over time. (See the chapters by Levine and Lodwick.)

These four forecasting techniques are based upon different assumptions about the forces that determine future events and how best to predict the future. Time series methods focus upon historical patterns as indicators of the future, while structural models identify how certain independent variables influence recreation patterns. Systems models assume recreation patterns result from complex relationships involving both historical factors and present conditions. Delphi procedures incorporate a variety of implicit or explicit assumptions made by each of the individual panel members.

In selecting a forecasting method or model for a given problem, one must consider the resources at hand and purposes to which the forecast will be put. The method must be matched to the skills and resources of the organization. The costs of developing the forecast should not exceed the anticipated benefits in improved decision-making. Qualitative methods, like the Delphi technique, can be applied to a variety of forecasting problems, but are most commonly used for long-range forecasting. The quantitative methods for recreation forecasting generally increase in complexity and lead time to develop a forecast as one moves from time series to structural to systems models. The increasing complexity and cost must be weighed against the wider range of uses of the more complex models.

Table 1 is an attempt to summarize the features of each general class of recreation forecasting methods. Since the specific models within each category may vary significantly in complexity and detail, the table should be interpreted as a general guide to those formulations most commonly used in recreation at this time. More specific characteristics of particular forecasting models are summarized by Wheelwright and Makridakis (1980).

GENERAL STEPS IN APPLYING A GIVEN FORECASTING METHOD

If a quantitative forecasting model has been selected, there are seven basic steps for applying the method to a problem. These steps must generally be considered as part of the model selection process since the availability of appropriate data and estimation procedures will often dictate what type of model must be chosen.

1. Selecting the units of analysis   An early decision is the choice of the aggregation level for the model, since this decision will determine the data requirements. Forecasting models may use the individual as the unit of analysis or may forecast from data about population aggregates. This decision is often based upon which type of data is most readily available; however, there are also technical reasons for selecting a micro- or macro-level forecasting model in a given situation (Fesenmaier et al. 1980, Brown and Nawas 1973).

2. Selecting the dependent variable   It is important to precisely specify the variable to be forecasted and how it will be measured. In models that predict individual recreation behavior the dependent variable is typically a probability or frequency of participation. Aggregate recreation forecasting models usually predict the number of participants, the population participation rate, or number of participant or visitor days. Inconsistency in the definition of the units of recreation participation has been a problem in past studies. Most commonly participation is defined as participation in a given activity at least once during the previous twelve months. Some studies have estimated participation on a seasonal basis. There are several ways of defining a recreation visitor day and many different ways of defining recreation activities. Analytical models require that all of these delimiting factors be precisely specified in order to properly define the dependent variable.

3. Selecting the independent variables   Most forecasting models include a set of independent variables that will be used to predict the dependent variable. Selection of these variables should be based upon their ease of measurement, the availability of data, and the utility of each independent variable in predicting the dependent variable. In models requiring forecasts of the independent variables, it is important to select variables that are easily forecasted, or for which forecasts are available.

4. Selecting a particular model   Particular assumptions about the behavior of the dependent variable and its relationships to the independent variables are established in the selection of a given model specification. It is important to choose a model whose assumptions match the behavior of the phenomonon being forecasted. The model must be based upon some theory or explanation of this phenomonon. If a particular event is viewed as the outcome of a sequence of decisions, a stepwise sequence of equations or systems model might be selected. The form of any particular relationship in the forecasting model might be linear, exponential, multiplicative, logistic, polynomial, or any number of mathematical

functions. Linear models dominate the recreation forecasting literature because of their simplicity, general applicability, and ease of estimation. In many cases non-linear forms can be argued on theoretical or logical grounds (Casetti 1969, Zeleny 1976).

5. Selecting an estimation procedure   Once the model form has been chosen there are usually alternative methods for estimating the parameters of the model. The estimation procedures "fit" the model to existing data by means of statistical techniques. Ordinary least squares or linear regression is one of the most popular and simplist methods of estimating a linear model. Often the particular form of the model chosen in step 4 must be based upon the cost and availability of estimation procedures. Non-linear models are generally more difficult to estimate than linear models. Smith and Munley (1978) discuss estimation techniques for recreation participation models. Schechter and Lucas (1978) is a good introduction to procedures for estimating simulation models of recreation behavior.

6. Application of the model   After a model has been identified and the parameters estimated, it is ready to be applied to the problem of forecasting for some future time period. This involves substituting appropriate values of the independent variables into the model and calculating the corresponding value of the forecast (dependent) variable. Structural models often require forecasts of some of the independent variables, which must be made through some other forecasting procedure. In more complex systems models, such forecasts are sometimes generated internally instead of being treated exogenously. Since forecasting involves extrapolating beyond past observations, it is recommended that the predictive ability of a forecasting model be tested on data that were not used in the model estimation procedures. This can be done by estimating the model with a sample of the observations and then using the unused observations to evaluate the model's predictive abilities.

7. Monitoring, validation, and model updating   The best test of any model is an evaluation of how well it performs. Forecasting models must be evaluated based upon their performance over time. A forecasting model should not be evaluated in terms of the accuracy of its predictions, but more importantly, in terms of its utility in decision-making (Martino 1973). Is the model used and is it useful? Models that are used on a continuing basis must be periodically adjusted or re-estimated to reflect changing conditions or new information. Some forecasting methods have monitoring and updating procedures built into the model (e.g., smoothing and filtering techniques). More commonly the user's judgment determines when and how a forecasting model should be modified or replaced.

FORECASTING IN RECREATION

The forecasting methods reviewed in the following chapters represent the current state-of-the-art of recreation forecasting, not what might be encountered in a typical state or municipal recreation agency or a commercial recreation enterprise. Only the larger and more advanced organizations employ these forecasting methods.

Applications of Delphi methods, time series techniques, and structural or systems models have been primarily limited to major state and national recreation planning studies. These have often been one-shot efforts and have not been clearly linked to decision-making.

The reasons for a general lack of forecasting in recreation organizations, and especially the dearth of applications of more formal and complex methods, are tied to the stage of development and characteristics of recreation and recreation organizations. The scientific study of recreation is relatively recent, leaving forecast developers with a limited body of knowledge, theory, methods, and data from which to draw. Little data collection or research has been targeted specifically at the needs of recreation forecasters. Data collected for other purposes is often poorly suited for forecasting. The lack of time series data and reliance primarily upon cross sectional research techniques has limited our knowledge of the dynamics of recreation systems.

Recreation organizations are typically small, with limited time and resources to develop or apply forecasts. More complex models are usually developed by outside consultants, who often do not fully understand the abilities and constraints of recreation organizations to interpret or apply them. Few recreation organizations have personnel trained in the development, interpretation, or application of forecasts.

To date, forecasting has simply not been recognized as a useful or high priority activity within many recreation organizations. Recreation forecasts are generally developed when a need arises, rather than as an ongoing and important function of the organization. Unless forecasting needs are anticipated and planned for, forecasts must be produced under unrealistic time frames with inadequate resources. Such forecasts must be content with low levels of detail, simple methods, and poor quality. Often the necessary data to support forecasting has not been collected systematically over time.

Recreation has made great strides over the past two decades in the advancement of forecasting methods. The next two decades should witness improvements in the applications of these methods to decision-making within recreation organizations. This will require greater attention to the needs of forecasting, and more managers, administrators, planners, and researchers trained in the development, interpretation, and application of forecasting methods.

Suggestions for further reading

Introductions to business forecasting and technological forecasting are presented in Wheelwright and Makridakis (1980) and Martino (1972), respectively. Recreation forecasting techniques are surveyed in Moeller and Echelberger (1974), and Stynes, Bevins, and Brown (1980). The three volume *Proceedings of the 1980 National Outdoor Recreation Trends Symposium* includes a good selection of papers on trend measurement and forecasting in recreation. A comparable Canadian study, *Park and Recreation Futures In Canada,* is also recommended. Ascher (1978) is a good evaluation of forecasting methods from the perspective of forecast users.

References

Ascher, W. *Forecasting: An Appraisal for Policy-Makers and Planners*. Baltimore: The Johns Hopkins University Press, 1978.

Brown, W. G., and Nawas, F. "Impact of Aggregation on the Estimation of Outdoor Recreation Demand Functions." *American Journal of Agricultural Economics* 55(1973):246-249.

Canadian Outdoor Recreation Research Committee. "Park and Recreation Futures in Canada: Issues and Options." Toronto, Canada: Ontario Research Council on Leisure, 1976.

Cassetti, E. "Why Do Diffusion Processes Conform to Logistic Trends?" *Geographical Analysis* 1(1969):101-114.

Clawson, M., and Knetsch, J. L. *Economics of Outdoor Recreation*. Baltimore: The Johns Hopkins University Press, 1966.

Clemson University Department of Recreation and Park Administration. *1980 National Outdoor Recreation Trends Symposium*. Appendix. Extension/Research Paper RPA 1980-5. Clemson, South Carolina: Clemson University, 1980.

Fesenmaier, D. R.; Goodchild, M. F.; and Lieber, S. R. "Correlates of Day Hiking Travel: The Effects of Aggregation." *Journal of Leisure Research* 12(1980):213-228.

Martino, J. P. *Technological Forecasting for Decision-Making*. New York: American Elsevier, 1972.

Moeller, G. H., and Echelberger, H. E. "Approaches to Forecasting Recreation Consumption." In *Outdoor Recreation Research: Applying the Results*. St. Paul, Minnesota: USDA Forest Service General Technical Report NC-9, 1974.

Schechter, M., and Lucas, R. C. *Simulation of Recreational Use for Park and Wilderness Management*. Baltimore: The Johns Hopkins University Press, 1978.

Smith, V. K. "The Estimation and Use of Models of the Demand for Outdoor Recreation." In *Assessing the Demand for Outdoor Recreation*. Appendix B. Washington, D.C.: USDI, Bureau of Outdoor Recreation, 1975.

Smith, V. K., and Munley, V. G. "The Relative Performance of Various Estimators of Recreation Participation Equations." *Journal of Leisure Research* 10(1978):165-176.

USDA Forest Service. *Proceedings 1980 National Outdoor Recreation Trends Symposium* vols. 1 and 2. General Technical Report NE-57. Broomall, Pennsylvania: Northeastern Forest Experiment Station, 1980.

Wheelwright, S. C., and Makridakis, S. *Forecasting Methods for Management*. 3d ed. New York: John Wiley and Sons, 1980.

Zeleny, M. "On the Inadequacy of the Regression Paradigm Used in the Study of Human Judgment" *Theory and Decision* 7(1976):57-65.

2

The Use and Misuse of Delphi Forecasting

George H. Moeller
Elwood L. Shafer

In 1902, the British writer H. G. Wells suggested that there might be a science of the future which would enable us to accurately estimate events in the years and decades ahead. Futurists of today do not believe that the study of the future is an exact science that will allow people to know precisely what is going to happen. But they do believe that we are all active participants in the creation of the future, and that future forecasting provides a way to help shape a more desirable future.

The use of forecasting has increased in all areas of human activity. Forecasting is being used to evaluate economic futures, trends in science and technology, demography, and in sociopolitical and military planning. There is no major industrial, business, or government organization that does not have a long-range planning group at the highest levels of management. This need for forecasting various aspects of the future has been brought about by the explosion in technology and resulting change. Events are occurring rapidly. In effect, time is speeding up. Social, political, and economic institutions simply cannot adopt to this rapid change without, somehow, forecasting relevent trends and interpreting resulting impacts.

One of the most popular of all forecasting methods, the Delphi technique, was developed in the early years of the cold war in response to the need to rapidly evaluate future military contingencies. The purpose of this chapter is to review and take a critical look at the Delphi technique. Its potential for use in forecasting futures that influence natural resources management will also be assessed.

THE DELPHI TECHNIQUE

Description of Delphi

The Delphi technique systematically combines expert knowledge and opinion to arrive at an informed group consensus about the likely occurrence of future events. The technique derives its importance from the realization that projections of future events, on which today's decisions must be based, can be made through the insight of knowledgeable individuals, rather than through predictions derived from well-established theory (Helmer and Rescher 1964).

The Delphi technique is based on the assumption that although the future is uncertain, its probabilities can be approximated by knowledgeable individuals who are able to make judgments about future contingencies. It is intended to provide a general perspective on the future rather than a sharp picture.

Instead of the traditional approach to achieve consensus of opinion through face-to-face discussion, the Delphi technique "eliminates committee activity altogether, thus . . . reducing the influence of certain psychological factors, such as specious persuasion, unwillingness to abandon publicly expressed opinions, and the bandwagon effect of majority opinion" (Helmer and Rescher 1960). In short, the Delphi is a way to develop concensus opinions among groups of experts, without direct confrontation or group pressure.

Individual input is encouraged by maintaining anonymity among those who take part in the Delphi process. Information relevant to encouraging consensus is systematically fed back to participants by the Delphi study director. Several rounds of rethinking the problem, with information feedback provided after each round, usually result in a convergence of group opinion (Dalkey 1967).

Conducting a Delphi Study

The Delphi technique replaces direct open debate with a series of questionnaires sent to a selected panel of experts. The general procedures used to conduct a Delphi investigation are outlined in Table 1.

Like any other study, a Delphi investigation begins with a definable need. A decision must be made today based on some unknown or assumed future condition. For example, an outdoor recreation planner may be developing a campground to meet the design needs of camping vehicles to the year 2000. If today's design criteria were used, it is likely that this goal would not be achieved. The planner needs to make some assumptions about what site and conditions camping vehicles are likely to require in the year 2000, and develop plans accordingly. Because there is no well established theory on which to base this prediction, we

Table 1

Conducting a Delphi Study

Step	Procedure	
Identify events	Determine events from theoretical models, futures scenarios, or literature. Panel members may also suggest events in preliminary questionnaire.	
Write event statements	Clear and precise statements are required to avoid ambiguous interpretations.	
Select and establish panel of experts	Select panelists from area of expertise suggested by the problem. Expertise based on contributions to the literature, peer recognition, etc.	
Mail Delphi questionnaires	Questions asked of panel members	Summary information returned to panel
Round 1 questionnaire	Assign probabilities and dates to events	Edit event statements
	Add events to list	Prepare response summary distributions showing individual responses
	Rate expertise or certainty Solicit information on ambiguous statements	
Round 2 questionnaire	Reevaluate first round responses based on summary distributions	Prepare interquartile response summaries for second round questionnaire
	Provide reasons for changing or not changing responses, if they remain outside interquartile range	Edit reasons given by those outside interquartile range
Round 3 questionnaire	Reevaluate second round responses based on summary information	Prepare summaries of interquartile distribution of third round questionnaire responses
	Provide reasons for changing or not changing responses, if they remain outside interquartile range	Edit reasons given by those outside interquartile range

Round 4 questionnaire	Give individuals final chance to reevaluaste their third round responses based on summary information
	As needed, ask panelists to rate their expertise, evaluate desirability of each event, evaluate interactions between events and evaluate social impact of each event

Data analysis	Prepare event summaries showing event distributions, probabilities, impacts, desirabilities, and interactions
	Use medium prediction as most probable year or event occurrence
	Prepare summaries of interquartile distributions
	Prepare futures scenarios

must turn to the experts in the field of camping vehicles and ask questions like, "What kinds of camping vehicles will be produced in the year 2000?" and "What campground design standards will be necessary to meet camping vehicle needs?" The Delphi technique is one approach to answering these questions.

Once the need for a study is clearly defined, the events and information needed to solve the future-oriented problem must be determined. Each event or item must be clearly defined in an unambiguous, precise statement. People must understand the statements and they must mean the same thing to everyone involved. Based on size and equipment design trends as determined from the literature, the campground designer may specify a list of equipment and size specifications needed to accommodate the camping vehicle of the year 2000.

Next, a panel of experts must be identified and invited to participate in the study. Panelists should be selected for their demonstrated expertise in the particular problem area of concern. There may be few "experts" and they may be easily defined. More often, however, considerable effort will be required to identify experts. This can be done through literature reviews, working with associations or professional organizations, or through a variety of other methods. In the case of recreation vehicles, manufacturer associations may be the best source to identify experts. Once the list of experts is assembled, a letter or phone call will be needed to invite their participation in the study.

Delphi then proceeds through several successive rounds of questionnaires. Each questionnaire contains feedback information from previous panel responses (Weaver 1969). The information returned through each round of questionnaires will vary from study to study. Generally, the first-round questionnaire invites panelists to assign probabilities of occurrence to events, add events that should be included, and edit/comment on events that are ambiguous. When summarized, this information serves to stimulate further thought about points that other panel members may have overlooked and allows them the opportunity to consider arguments they may have at first thought to be unimportant.

The number of questionnaire rounds depends on the particular study and on the degree of concensus that emerges among panel members. Typically, four rounds are required. "Concensus" simply means the point at which the distribution of responses begins to stabilize; additional questionnaire mailings at this point will usually not promote additional concensus, and may, indeed, lead to panel fatigue and mortality.

Through various rounds of questionnaires, results are summarized graphically to show the interquartile range of predictions. The median prediction is used as the most probable estimate for the event, because half the predictions fall above and half below this point. The spread of the interquartile range (middle half of the distribution) serves as an indicator of panel concensus; a wide range indicates panel disagreement, a narrow one indicates panel concensus.

In the campground design example, the panel concensus would be used to develop design standards to meet the needs of camping vehicles to the year 2000. These predictions would represent the most expert thinking in this area.

Generally, panel predictions can be used in a number of ways. Independent events are often woven together to form the most probable future scenario. Specific predictions may be used as estimators in analytical models or for developing or formulating programs to meet a future need. Delphi has often been used, for example, to develop education programs needed to train people for an evolving profession.

Delphi, Pros and Cons

Delphi has both strengths and weaknesses. It is no panacea, but it is a method that can provide useful future perspectives or estimates where there simply is no other technique available.

Weaver (1972) has described some of the flaws in the Delphi technique. Identification of panel experts and evaluation of their expertise present problems. Experts are usually busy people, and it is difficult to get them to serve on a Delphi panel for an extended period of time. Attrition can be severe and the effect of panel drop-out on study results has not yet been evaluated.

Salanick et al (1971) has pointed out that the study director can have a strong effect on Delphi results. The events he/she chooses to include in the study and the way in which events are described can easily lead to misinterpretation. The study director can also influence results by editing panel response-feedback information.

The Delphi technique has been criticized because it usually treats events as independent of one another (Kalkey 1968). It does not provide a way to evaluate the interaction between events. Furthermore, an event's probability of occurrence depends largely on the general perspective assumed by panel members when they make their evaluations. If panel members do not share common perspectives, resulting predictions of events will be based on different criteria.

The Delphi technique has not been extensively tested in predicting events other than those related to technological developments. It has been shown to be most accurate in predicting technological events related to space and medical developments and in forecasting political alliances. The technique has had limited application for predicting events that involve human interaction.

The Delphi technique is deceptively simple. In fact, it may require more time, effort, and be more costly than other predictive techniques. A great deal of effort must be devoted to setting up the initial questionnaire and establishing the panel of experts. Also, the time required to send information to panel members, summarize responses, and resubmit the responses can be considerable.

THE DELPHI TECHNIQUE APPLIED TO RECREATION MANAGEMENT AND PLANNING

Although based on many restrictive assumptions, the Delphi technique is useful where decisions have to be made quickly with limited knowledge, for example, the need to make decisions today to meet the needs of a leisure oriented society. The Delphi technique was used in a recent study to probe the future for oncoming social, managerial, and technological events that are likely to shape the future of park and recreation management in the year 2000 (Shafer and Moeller 1974).

Experts in the fields of biology, ecology, conservation, population dynamics, recreation-resource management, and environmental technology took part in the study. The panel consisted of 909 experts who were selected based on their contributions to the current literature on environment and technology.

The experts were first asked to list events that they felt had a fifty-fifty chance of occurring by the year 2000. They were instructed to consider only those events that related to their own areas of expertise. Responses were summarized and resubmitted to the panel through four rounds of questionnaires following the scheme outlined in Table 1. Each time, panel members were given the opportunity to re-evaluate their previous predictions in light of these summaries and to provide reasons why their responses differed significantly from others—normally when their response fell outside the interquartile range of predictions.

Results were summarized by grouping events by the median year of prediction—the year falling at the midpoint of the distribution of panel predictions. Fifty percent of the experts felt that the event would occur on or before the median year, and 50 percent felt it would occur on or after the median year, or never occur. Descriptive information returned to panel members in each round included the median and interquartile distribution of panel responses, and described individual responses for each event.

Events fell into five categories: Natural-Resource Management, Wildland-Recreation Management, Environmental Controls, Population-Workforce-

Leisure, and Urban Environments. Following are some of the events predicted for the year 2000 or beyond. More detailed results of this study have been reported elsewhere (Shafer and Moeller 1974).

Natural-Resource Management   The panel predicted that the federal role in coordinating natural-resource planning will expand from establishing the first land, water, and air-use plan in 1990 to a comprehensive national land-use zoning plan in 2000. By the year 2000, environmental planning will be effectively coordinated among all levels of government and private interests. Also by 2000, land-use patterns will stabilize, and land preempted for one use will be replaced with comparable land. All land resources, including marine and estuarine areas, will be under intensive management.

Wildland-Recreation Management   By the year 2000, wilderness-management policy will change to allow for more intensive recreational development. Permits, used to control all forms of wildland recreation, will also require certification for certain user groups. The wildland recreation area of 2000 will be vastly different from that of today. Only transportation systems that have a minimum physical and visual impact on the natural environment will be allowed, and only recreation vehicles that employ nonpolluting propulsion systems will be permitted in wildland recreation areas. Heavily used areas will be serviced by air, and parks will be aesthetically improved by underground placement of utility lines.

Technology will aid the park manager of 2000. For example, artificial lighting will extend use of recreation facilities, and remote-sensing devices will be used to monitor park use. Waste-disposing bacteria will be incorporated into recreation-area equipment to reduce sanitary disposal problems. Extensive irrigation of arid regions will broaden and enhance recreational opportunities.

Technology will also create challenging management problems. For example, the experts felt that, by 2000, small private recreational submarines, hovercraft, jet-powered backpacks, and one-man helicopters will be in common use.

The wildlife manager will utilize captive rearing to raise endangered species for release. He will monitor wildlife migrations by satellite. Controls will be placed on hunting, and motorized vehicles will be excluded from all public hunting areas during hunting seasons. By 2000, wildlife resources will be used primarily for nonconsumptive purposes such as photography.

Environmental Controls   Strict international pollution-control standards will be established by 2000, and an international environmental monitoring agency will be organized. Although predictions varied considerably among panel members, other events predicted for the turn of the century include: setting exact human tolerance limits for various pollutants; allowing only biodegradable chemicals to be discharged directly into the environment; and restricting federal reserve chartered banks from financing companies that are known polluters.

Population-Workforce-Leisure   By the turn of the century, panel members predicted 500 miles will be a reasonable one-way distance to travel on a weekend recreation trip. Tax incentives will be available to employers who include recreation facilities in the design and construction of new plants. "Weekends" will be distributed throughout the week. With an average retirement age of 50 years, more total leisure time will be available during retirement. In response to this abundant leisure, the role of public schools will expand to serve the recreation needs of the entire community. Middle-income families will vacation as common-ly on other continents as they now vacation in the United States. Panel members also felt that by 2000 the work ethic will have assumed a lesser role in society, and leisure will become an acceptable life style. An attempt will be made to control population growth through tax incentives, but panel members felt that a man-datory population-control program will eventually be established.

Urban Environments   Improved planning and technology will combine to make future urban environments much more enjoyable than they are today. By 2000, only non-air-polluting vehicles will be allowed in downtown urban areas. Com-puters will be used to control the movement of individual transportation vehicles. More urban land will be provided for leisure enjoyment; cemeteries, water reser-voirs, and planned open space will be available for recreation. Facilities like city parks and play fields will be covered with artificial turf to sustain heavy recreation pressure, and some will be covered with transparent domes to allow year-round use. Natural environments will be simulated inside man-made structures to pro-vide urban residents with recreation opportunities now available only in the out-doors.

Summary and Conclusions

Forecasting is not, and never will be, an exact science. Although the literature abounds with methodology and a plethora of approaches, the Delphi technique has become one of the most commonly used and accepted methods to forecast future events. Some of its strengths and weaknesses have been briefly described. The case example illustrates how the technique can be used in developing future perspectives for natural resource recreation management.

Delphi, or some variation of it, is a very useful tool, but its shortcomings must be recognized. It will not provide a sharp picture of the future, only a perspective on what is most likely to happen, given assumptions about future contingencies and the insights of those participating in the Delphi panel. Athough it has many shortcomings, in the final analysis, Delphi can be a useful tool for futures forecasting. It is doubtful, however, that a standard method will ever be developed for futures forecasting because each organization and each problem situation requires a somewhat different technique to suit each special situation.

Studies of future leisure trends can be used to help make reasonable assump-tions about what the future may hold. At the same time, such studies can help identify potential dangers and opportunities, providing a set of perceptions on which to base decisions in response to a rapidly changing world.

Short-term (five year) forecasting, upon which many of today's man-resource management decision are based, has the advantage of being able to extrapolate from existing trends. But in many resource-related problems, long-range forecasts are needed that consider future breakthroughs in technology. The variables and contingencies of most futures beyond five years can only be assessed intuitively. The Delphi technique is the only method now available to systematically condense intuition into concensus.

References

Dalkey, N. C. *Experiments in Group Prediction.* Rand Corp. Paper P-3829. Santa Monica, California, 1967.

Dalkey, N. C. *Predicting the Future.* Rand Corp. Paper P-3948. Santa Monica, California, 1968.

Helmer, O., and Rescher, N. *On the Epistemology of the Exact Sciences.* Rand Corp. Paper R-353. Santa Monica, California, 1960.

Helmer, O., and Rescher, N. *Report of a Long-Range Forecasting Study.* Rand Corp. Paper P-2982. Santa Monica, California, 1964.

Rescher, N. *The Future as an Object of Research.* Rand Corp. Paper P-3593. Santa Monica, California, 1967.

Salanick, J. R.; Wenger, W.; and Helfer, E. "The Construction of Delphi Event Statements." *Technological Forecasting and Social Change* 3(1971):65-73.

Shafer, E. L., Jr., and Moeller, G. H. "Through the Looking Glass in Environmental Management." *Parks and Recreation* 9(1974): 20-23, 48, 49.

Toffler, A. *Future Shock.* New York: Bantam Books, Inc. 1971.

Weaver, T. W. *Delphi as a Method for Studying the Future: Testing Some Underlying Assumptions.* Syracuse University School of Education Educational Policy Research Center, 1969.

Weaver, T. W. Delphi: A Critical Review. Syracuse University School of Education Educational Policy Research Center. Research Report 7, 1972.

3

Time Series and Structural Models for Forecasting Recreation Participation

Daniel J. Stynes

Two of the most widely used recreation forecasting techniques are simple trend extension and structural linear regression models. Both of these methods predominantly have been applied to the problem of forecasting recreation participation rates or park visitation.

Simple trend extension is one of the more elementary time series techniques. Time series methods in general rely upon historical observations of the variable we wish to forecast in order to identify a pattern or trend that may be extended into the future. The method is easily carried out and understood in its graphical form, where a series of data points are plotted over time and extrapolated into the future. Time series methods require systematic and accurate historical measurements. These methods have therefore been applied primarily to recreation activities or facilities for which an historical series of participation or use is available. These include activities that require some kind of licensing or registration (hunting, fishing, boating) and national and state parks with systematic use estimation procedures. Time series methods assume that the pattern of causal forces underlying a trend remain constant over the forecast period.

Structural models rely upon an understanding of these casual forces in order to estimate the effects on recreation participation of changes in a set of independent variables. Structural methods use present or historical data to first identify a relationship between recreation participation and certain social, economic, and environmental variables. Then assuming this relationship will remain stable over the forecast period, future participation is estimated by applying the relationship to forecasts of the independent variables. Structural models are generally identified using cross-sectional recreation survey data. Linear structural models are the easiest to estimate and apply. These models are often developed in conjunction with major national or state recreation surveys. In this chapter we review the application of structural models to forecast recreation participation. Structural trip distribution models are discussed in more detail by Ewing in a subsequent chapter.

TIME SERIES METHODS

Simple Trend Extension

The lack of good time series data in outdoor recreation has restricted the use of time series methods primarily to simple trend extension. In <u>simple trend extension</u> recreation participation or park visitation (V_t) in time period t is estimated as a function of time,

$$\text{i.e., } \overline{V_t} = F(t)$$

The method may be carried out by plotting the data series on graph paper and simply "extending" the historical trend. If a straight edge is used on standard graph paper, the function F is assumed to be linear. Most applications of simple trend extension assume F is linear since linear functions are the easiest to deal with, and over short time intervals most trends can be approximated by a linear function. Alternatively exponential and logistic functions can be used to model growth processes.

Selection of the function F must be based upon an examination of the historical pattern in the data series and assumptions about the growth process. Linear functions assume visits grow at a constant rate over time. Exponential functions assume the rate of growth in visits is directly related to the number of visits. Both exponential and linear functions are unbounded and can lead to absurd results if projections are made too far into the future. For example, Clawson and Knetsch (1966) and Burton (1981) note that extension of trends in United States and Canadian National Park visits implies that ultimately everyone must visit National Parks virtually every day of the year.

Logistic functions conform more closely to growth processes where constraints to growth or saturation effects are encountered. In the logistic model growth starts out slowly, increases to a maximum growth rate, and then slows down again, eventually approaching some upper limit. Product life cycle curves, popular in marketing, follow the logistic trend with an eventual decline at the end of the cycle (Howard and Crompton 1980). We have found that for long-range projections many recreation activities or products follow trends similar to the product life cycle (Stynes and Szcodronski 1980, Stynes and Spotts 1980).

Figure 1 depicts alternative growth curves, illustrating the problem of using simple trend extension when only a few historical data points are available. With only three past estimates of the dependent variable, linear, exponential, logistic, and product life cycle curves perform similarly in fitting the trend, but yield quite different long-range forecasts. While no one should attempt to use trend extension with so few historical observations, even with many observations the form of the long-range growth curve may not be apparent. Notice that the early and later segments of the logistic curve can be approximated fairly well by linear functions, while the middle portion of the curve resembles an exponential growth curve. For this reason, linear and exponential trend should not be extended more than a few

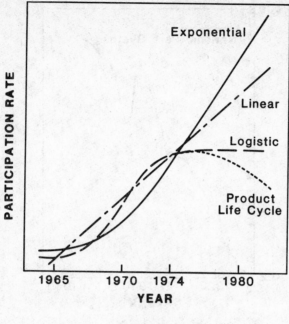

Figure 1

Alternative Time Series Models

years into the future, and changes in the time series pattern should be closely monitored.

An Example   Clawson and Knetsch (1966, p. 118) illustrate the use of informal simple trend extension methods in forecasting National Park System (NPS) visits. They describe their method as follows: "The trend was simply plotted on semi-logarithmic graph paper and extended by using a straight edge" (Figure 2). This procedure results in an exponential growth model. The straight edge approximates a linear function, but use of semi-log paper implies the dependent variable is the logarithm of visits. Thus:

$$\log V = a + bt \quad \text{and} \quad V = 10^{a + bt}$$

where $V =$ NPS visits in a given year t
       $a, b =$ constants
       $\log =$ logarithm base 10
       $t =$ time (in years)

Different projections were developed depending upon which portions of the historical data series were used to orient the straight edge. Pre World War II expansion in the NPS yielded rapid growth in visits during this period. Extension of these trends to 1980 and 2000 yielded quite unrealistic projections. Based upon

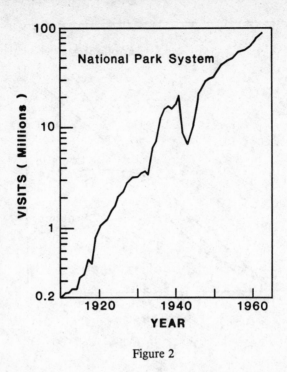

Figure 2

The Pattern of National Park Visitation

the 1953-1960 trend, forecasts to 1980 were 175 million visits, not too far from reported figures of 220 million. If a more formal method is desired, regression techniques can be used to determine the linear or exponential function which "best fits" the historical trend.

Assumptions Regardless of which functional form is selected, simple trend extension methods and time series methods, more generally, assume that historical patterns in the data series are adequate for forecasting. This requires that whatever forces are producing these patterns must not change significantly over the forecast period.

In the above example, changes in the rate of growth of the National Park System and in the population of the United States would violate these assumptions. There are methods for adjusting the simple trend extension procedure to correct these problems. For example, if historical data series on NPS visits were converted to per capita visits (by dividing the visits each year by the United States population in that year), one could then forecast per capita visits to some future year. Multiplying this figure by a corresponding future population estimate yields future visits. This technique separates the effect of population growth from the growth in rates of NPS visitation. Similarly, NPS visits could be divided by some measure of capacity (number of parks, NPS acres, NPS employees) to allow for changes in the size and rate of growth of the NPS over time.

Notice that in simple trend extension the assumption is not that all variables remain constant, but that the pattern of change in the variables (or their influence on park visits) over the forecast period remain the same as it was over the historical period that was used to estimate the forecasting model. Thus, if populations were doubling during a ten year estimation period, they should also be expected to double over a ten year forecast period.

Whenever a significant change occurs in the pattern of any important causal variable or its effect on the dependent variable, one should consider revising or recalibrating the forecasting model. Some of the more sophisticated time series methods have built-in procedures to adjust the model over time based upon comparisons of model forecasts with actual observations. In simple trend extension, the forecaster must use his/her judgment in deciding how far into the future a given forecasting model may accurately project and when to abandon or revise a given model. Simple trend extension is generally not recommended for forecasting more than five years into the future.

We have devoted considerable time to simple trend extension methods since they are the easiest to understand and most commonly used in recreation. There are many other time series methods that are widely applied in business forecasting but seldom used in recreation. In many cases these techniques are more appropriate, simpler, or more powerful than simple trend extension.

Underutilized Time Series Methods

Time series methods, in general, predict future levels of a variable based upon past values. Mathematically, a forecasted value of V in period $t + 1$ ($V_{t + 1}$) is estimated as a functional relationship (F) of n previous values of V and time.

$$\bar{V}_{t+1} = F(V_t, V_{t-1}, \ldots V_{t-n+1}, t)$$

The simple trend extension method described above is the special case where $n = 0$ and V is estimated purely as a function of time.

Moving Averages

Simple moving averages and exponential smoothing techniques estimate future values of V as linear functions of n previous values. In a simple moving average, each previous value is weighted $1/n$. Exponential smoothing permits differential weighting of past values by adjusting a parameter alpha.

Moving Average: $\bar{V}_{t+1} = (V_t + V_{t-1} + \ldots + V_{t-n+1})/n$

Exponential Smoothing: $\bar{V}_{t+1} = \alpha V_t + \alpha(1-\alpha)V_{t-1} + \alpha(1-\alpha)^2 V_{t-2} + \ldots$

$$= \alpha V_t + (1-\alpha)\bar{V}_t$$

Note that the exponential smoothing model can be reduced to two terms, one involving the previous forecast ($\bar{V}_t$) and the other the most recent value of V (V_t).

This makes the technique very simple to apply. Alpha is a parameter assuming values between zero and one. For alpha close to zero the model makes only minor adjustments in the previous forecast, while for alpha near one the model relies more heavily upon the most recent values of V. By selecting alpha appropriately one may develop a model that is very responsive to recent changes in V, or one that relies more heavily on past historical patterns.

As stated above, these models only project one time period into the future, however, by inserting projections back into the model one may forecast ahead several periods. This procedure will lead to the propagation of forecast errors as one projects further into the future.

The advantage of smoothing techniques over simple trend projection is that more recent data is automatically incorporated into the model without having to re-estimate a curve. As their name implies, smoothing techniques smooth out random fluctuations in a data series. The smoothed forecasts, which rely upon several previous observations, generally are more accurate than simply adjusting last year's figure by five or ten percent, especially if last year was atypical. The choice of weights in smoothing formulas is usually subjective and the method can only be used for fairly short-range forecasting.

Smoothing methods are generally used as part of an on-going forecasting pro-

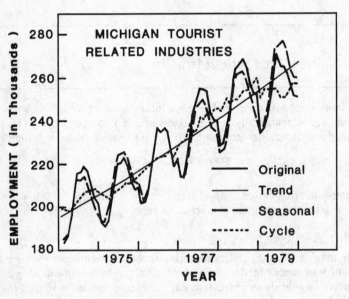

Figure 3

Michigan Tourist Patterns
SOURCE: Michigan Employment Securities Commission, 1980.

gram within an organization, while simple trend extension methods are generally one-shot approaches. Since few recreation organizations have on-going forecasting programs, these simple methods seem largely unknown in recreation.

Seasonal Decomposition Techniques

Another class of time series methods is applicable when the data include an identifiable seasonal or cyclic pattern. A standard method for decomposing time series with regular periodic patterns is to separate the annual trend from seasonal and cyclic patterns. Wheelwright and Makridakis (1980, Chapter 7) describe simple algebraic methods for decomposing such data series. These methods can be used to express recreation participation or park visitation as a product of trend, seasonal, and cyclic components. Alternatively, regression techniques may be used to fit such time series to trigonometric functions (Fourier analysis, harmonic analysis. Figure 3 illustrates the decomposition of tourism-related employment in Michigan into trend, seasonal, and cyclic components. Other applications to tourism are presented by Baron (1975) and Stynes and Pigozzi (1983).

These techniques permit the development of seasonally-adjusted forecasts and open up a range of important decisions in regard to the temporal distribution of recreation use to which the resulting forecasts may be applied. Given the strong seasonality of most recreation activity, it is somewhat surprising that these methods are not more widely used in recreation. The lack of temporally disaggregated time series data seems to be the main obstacle.

More Complex Methods   There are a number of more sophisticated time series forecasting methods that have not received much attention in outdoor recreation. These include autoregressive integrated moving average (ARIMA) models, Box Jenkins techniques, and adaptive filtering methods. The reader is referred to Wheelwright and Makridakis (1980) for an introductory treatment of these techniques.

STRUCTURAL MODELS

Time series methods assume that factors producing a given trend do not change over time. Forecasts can generally be more accurate and more useful if we understand the forces which underlie them. In the structural approach, recreation participation or park visitation in a given year is related to a set of independent variables that might explain or be correlated with use. The general form of these forecasting models is:

$$V_t = F(P_1,...P_n; S_1,...S_m, D_1,...D_q)$$

where V_t is an estimate of participation or visits in period t and the P_i, S_j, and D_k are sets of independent variables also measured in time period t. To forecast for some future time period t', forecasts of each of the independent variables must be made for that period and entered into the structural equation denoted by **F**.

The three sets of independent variables reflect categories of variables that are commonly used in these models. The P's represent variables describing the individual or population in question. A host of variables have been tried with measures of age, gender, and income entering most consistently into these kinds of structural equations. In addition to standard demographic and socioeconomic variables, measures of home ownership, mobility, leisure time, psychological traits, physical ability, skill, and social group membership have been tested in these models. Some of the latter variables are difficult, if not impossible, to forecast and resulting equations are better suited to explaining "what is" than forecasting what "will be."

The S's represent supply variables or measures of the quantity and quality of recreation opportunities. Most models use physical inventory data (e.g., acres of parks, miles of stream, numbers of golf courses), although some recent research is exploring opportunity measures from the consumer's perspective in order to isolate perceived supply or known opportunities. These supply measures may include variables describing the particular park or activity in question, as well as measures of substitute and complementary facilities. How best to measure and incorporate supply variables is a significant area of current research to improve these models.

The D's include various measures of the interrelationship between populations and recreation opportunities. These may be thought of as measures of the distance, cost, or barriers to participation.

The application of structural models to forecasting follows the steps outlined in the introductory chapter. After independent and dependent variables have been clearly defined and quantified, a specific structural equation is estimated from empirical data. The development and estimation of the structural equation is the most difficult part of this forecasting method. Once the specific model has been determined, forecasts of the dependent variable are generated by simply plugging appropriate values of the independent variables into the model. By testing different values of the independent variables one can "simulate" alternative future scenarios. The main difficulty in applying structural models is in forecasting future levels of the independent variables.

The fairly clear division between structural model development and application makes this method well suited to organizations without some of the more technical skills required in model development. Technical consultants can be hired to develop and estimate a model. With proper documentation and instructions, the model can then be used by a recreation organization with minimal technical and analytical skills. While this is true in theory, in practice many structural models go unused because potential clients do not understand them.

Aggregate Structural Models

The early forecasting efforts of the Outdoor Recreation Resources Review Commission include an aggregate structural model for forecasting National Park System visits in the United States (OPRRRC 1962, Study Report #26). The following model was estimated by applying multiple regression techniques to data series from the years 1929-1940 and 1947-1960.

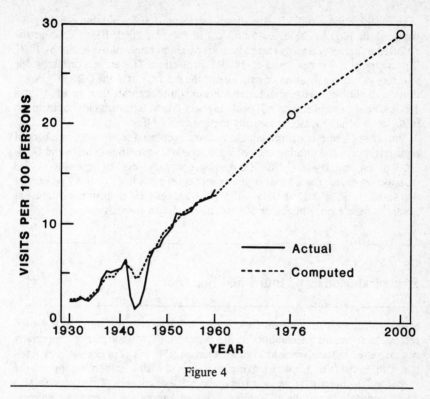

Figure 4

Actual and Computer Visitation

SOURCE: Outdoor Recreation Resources Review Commission, Report 26, p. 8.

$$V = -7.53 + 2.22 \text{ INC} + 1.35 \text{ MOB} + .43 \text{ LT} + .06 \text{ TIME}$$

where

V	=	NPS visits per 100 population
INC	=	real disposable income in thousands of 1960 dollars
MOB	=	mobility measured as thousands of inter-city auto passenger miles per capita
LT	=	hours per week of leisure time per employed person
TIME	=	year, where 1945 = 0, 1946 = 1, 1947 = 2, etc.

The reader should note the selection and operationalization of the dependent and independent variables. In order to fit the model, estimates of each variable were made for the years between 1929 and 1960, omitting 1941-1946. This is a linear model and includes a simple trend component in the final term. Figure 4 compares predicted with actual visits over the model calibration period. The model fits historical trends quite well (coefficient of determination = .9964), but beyond the early sixties it proved to be a poor forecaster.

To predict NPS visits for any year beyond 1960, projections of each of the independent variables have to be made for the year in question and then plugged into the equation. ORRRC developed forecasts to 1976 and 2000.

Using this model, ORRRC predicted per capita NPS visitation would grow from .13 in 1960 to .21 in 1976 and .29 in the year 2000. Based upon actual reported figures, NPS visits reached a level of about one visit per capita by 1976. This is almost five times the 1976 ORRRC projection. This error is primarily due to errors in the specification or structure of the model, not in the ORRRC projections of the independent variables, which were quite accurate (Brown and Hustin 1980). The structural equation is probably non-linear, and variables not included in the model may explain more fully the growth in NPS visits.

Similar aggregate structural equations have been used to estimate numbers of registered boats and hunting and fishing license sales over time (Seneca and Davis 1976, Allen and Dwyer 1978). Depending upon the level of aggregation and variables included, these kinds of linear models explain from 60 to 99 percent of the variation in historical data series. The model's fit to historical data has generally been a poor indicator of its performance in forecasts.

Structural Models of Individual Behavior

Structural models of individual recreation behavior are the most widely used recreation forecasting techniques at the present time. Although one is generally not interested in forecasting individual behavior (if this is even possible), by starting with individual decision-making processes a richer understanding of the forces which underlie recreation trends is usually achieved. These models also avoid some of the pitfalls of highly aggregated approaches. Increasing aggregation levels generally lead to higher correlations between variables and multicollinearity problems in model estimation, but can also lead to spurious correlations and can obscure important relationships (Fesenmaier et al. 1980). Another reason for the prevalence of these models is the lack of good historical time series data. This means that forecasters must generate their own data bases. Cross sectional recreation surveys of households or individuals are already an important part of planning and form a convenient (although not ideal) data base from which to develop forecasting models.

Structural models of individual recreation participation are usually activity specific. The dependent variable is often an indicator (yes or no) of whether or not an individual participated in the recreation activity within a designated time period (usually a year), or a frequency of participation over this period. The same type of model can be used to estimate visitation to a given park or park system.

The ORRRC studies (Report 26, Report 19, Appendix A) also pioneered the development of multivariate regression models for forecasting recreation participation. These techniques were further developed and refined in studies of Kalter and Gosse (1969); Cicchetti, Seneca, and Davidson (1969); and Adams, Lewis, and Drake (1973). The most widely used method today is a two step method detailed in a text by Cicchetti (1973).

The two step method uses cross sectional data from individuals to estimate equations as follows:

The step one equation predicts the probability of participating in a given recreation activity for an individual with a given set of characteristics and opportunities.

$$P = F_1(P_1,...P_n,S_1,...S_m,D_1,...D_1,D_q)$$

The step two equation estimates the frequency of participation in the activity for those individuals who do participate at least once.

$$F = F_2(P_1,...P_n,S_1,...S_m,D_1,...D_1)$$

There are both logical and technical reasons for dividing the participation model into two steps. The independent variables which explain whether or not an individual participates in a recreation activity may be different from those influencing the frequency of participation. Further, the two steps permit us to estimate both the number of participants and the number of activity days. The latter is important to park managers while the former may be more useful to recreation equipment manufacturers.

The technical issues relate to assumptions of statistical parameter estimation procedures. These matters are discussed in Cicchetti (1973) and Smith and Munley (1978). The functional form of these models has traditionally been linear, although more recent applications of these techniques include polynomial, logit, and other model specifications.

These models of individual recreation behavior typically explain from 5 to 15 percent of the variation in participation within the samples that are used to estimate the equations. This is much lower than the aggregate models because of the large amount of "unexplainable" variation in individual behavior. As was the case with aggregate models, these estimates of explained variation are not good indicators of the model's forecasting ability, since forecasting involves extrapolating beyond the sample to future populations.

These models help to identify which variables are presently influencing recreation participation, but do not capture the dynamic underlying recreation participation decisions. The linear models assume constant rates of participation over time within given population subgroups. Research has consistently found this assumption to be in error. Brown and Hustin (1980) clearly identify this assumption as the cause of significant underestimation of 1976 participation rates in the ORRRC forecasts.

Although these models are estimated from data on individuals, in forecasting they are applied to population aggregates. The simplest method is to apply the equations to forecasts of the population means of each independent variable. If the independent variables have been judiciously selected, such forecasts are usually available; but this method relies heavily upon linearity assumptions of the model.

The preferred approach is to subdivide the population based upon the independent variables and apply the model to each subgroup. This method requires forecasts of the average value of each independent variable for each subgroup as well as a forecast of the size of each subgroup. As the number of independent variables exceeds two, the number and complexity of possible subgroupings complicates the forecasting procedures.

The model assumes that the participation rates and frequencies of each subgroup do not change over time. Changes in recreation participation result from changes in the size of each subgroup over time. The model can be useful in examining likely effects of an aging population under the assumption that age groups in the year 2000 will behave like their counterparts today. This assumption can be seriously challenged for forecasts of more than five years into the future.

THE FUTURE OF RECREATION FORECASTING MODELS

While a great deal of progress has been made in the development and application of recreation forecasting models, many problems remain. These may be divided into problems relating to forecasting model development and forecasting model application.

Perhaps the most important problem is the need to upgrade the abilities of recreation organizations to develop, interpret, and apply forecasts. As has been true of planning methods in general within recreation (National Academy of Sciences 1975), forecasting methods are often applied incorrectly. For example, short-range methods like time series and structural models have frequently been used for long-range forecasting. Organizations need to be aware of a wider range of forecasting methods so they may select one that is best suited to a given situation. Some of the underutilized time series methods mentioned above could be particularly useful in directing recreation organizations toward more systematic and ongoing data collection and forecasting programs. An important first step is an increased recognition of the importance and role of forecasting within an organization.

The fact that model development is a task that can be relegated to an outside group of technical consultants is both a blessing and a curse for recreation organizations. Much of the increased awareness and understanding of recreation systems resulting from forecasting stems from being involved in the process of developing forecasts. If recreation managers, administrators, and decision-makers are left out of this process, they lose most of the benefits of a forecasting program. For this reason I strongly recommend internalizing forecasting as much as possible within recreation organizations. This will require appropriate investments in time, resources, and personnel.

Data collection, model development, and decision-making structures that are part of systematic planning within an organization will provide a basis for improvements in forecasting models. Of particular concern to model developers is the sparsity and poor quality of data bases for forecasting. Good time series data, necessary for the development of time series models, are especially lacking.

Both time series and structural models for forecasting recreation are continually being improved. While it will take time for many of these improvements to reach the practicing professional in recreation, present research into forecasting recreation behavior indicates the likely future of recreation forecasting methods. Many of the refinements in time series and structural models are leading to more comprehensive and complex models which take into account additional determinants of change in recreation. These models also have a wider variety of applications.

Prediction of participation in a given activity or visitation to a given site depends upon the quality and quantity of available substitutes. Researchers are exploring how to define and measure substitution and how to incorporate substitution effects in structural models. This often requires a system of inter-related equations.

Participation in recreation activities is dependent upon the supply of available opportunities. One reason for the underestimation in National Park System use forecasts was the failure to consider expansion of the park system. Planners are particularly interested in how much additional recreation activity is stimulated by an increase in supply versus how much use is shifted from one site to another. Both the quality and quantity of opportunities will influence use patterns.

Researchers continue to seek stronger explanatory variables for forecasting recreation patterns. Traditional socio-economic variables explain only a small portion of the variation in recreation participation and have not performed well in forecasting models. In addition to variables measuring supply, substitution, and quality of recreation, researchers are exploring how to include changing value systems, family structures, life styles, status, and knowledge within recreation forecasting models. Variables that are good forecasters of future recreation participation may be different from those that are good estimators of participation today.

Improvements in data bases and theory of recreation behavior go hand in hand with improvements in forecasting models. The development of systematic data collection schemes and comprehensive computerized recreation information systems will provide a valuable resource for future forecasters. As recreation advances as a science, improved theories will guide the structure of forecasting models. Recreation has only begun to examine theories of change such as diffusion, learning, adaptation, product life cycle, and growth models. The application of these more dynamic models to the problems of forecasting recreation behavior should yield considerable improvements in recreation forecasting.

Recreation forecasting models to date have focused either upon the individual or upon entire populations. Using market segmentation techniques, researchers are exploring intermediate levels of aggregation in forecasting models. This should lead to distinct models for different population segments, reflecting differences in consumer choice and change processes. Given the wide variation in recreation activities and tastes, it is unlikely a single model can be uniformly applied across all groups.

Most refinements in forecasting models stem from challenging or revising assumptions of existing models. Ascher (1978) has noted the prevalance of "assumption drag" in forecasting models. This is a tendency to continue to rely upon old assumptions, long after they have been disproven. Assumptions of perfect consumer knowledge, "economic man," linearity, and stable relationships over time have often proven to be invalid in recreation. Yet we continue to include these assumptions in most of our forecasting models. Researchers are exploring different structures for structural forecasting models which relax some of these assumptions.

There is a need to continually update both our forecasts and our forecasting methods and models. Many of the problems noted above require more complex forecasting models. Recreation choices are complex and dynamic and require models with corresponding characteristics if we expect accurate forecasts. Improvements in time series and structural models often result in models which incorporate components of both. These often take the form of combined trip generation-trip distribution models or systems models. These are presented in the following chapters.

References

Adams, R. L., Lewis, R. C., and Drake, B. H. "An Economic Analysis." *Outdoor Recreation, A Legacy for America.* Appendix A. Washington, D.C.: USDI, Bureau of Outdoor Recreation, 1973.

Allen, A. T., and Dwyer, J. F. "A Cross-Sectional Analysis of Hunting, Fishing, and Boating in Illinois." Forestry Research Report 78-8. Urbana, Illinois: University of Illinois Agricultural Experiment Station, 1978.

Ascher, W. *Forecasting: An Appraisal for Policy-Makers and Planners.* Baltimore: The Johns Hopkins University Press, 1978.

Baron, R. R. V. "Seasonality in Tourism--A Guide to the Analysis of Seasonality and Trends for Policy Making." Technical Series Number 2. London: The Economist Intelligence Unit, 1975.

Beaman, J. "Statistical Projections That go Beyond Projections of Past Trends." Canadian Outdoor Recreation Demand Study Technical Note 13. Toronto: Ontario Research Council on Leisure, 1976.

Bevins, M. I., and Wilcox, D. P. "Outdoor Recreation Participation -- Analysis of National Surveys, 1959-1978." Vermont Agricultural Experiment Stations Bulletin 686. Burlington, Vermont: University of Vermont, 1980.

Brown, T. L., and Hustin, D. L. "Evaluation of the 1976 ORRRC Projections." In *1980 National Outdoor Recreation Trends Symposium.* Vol. 3. Extension/Research Paper RPA 1980-5. Clemson, South Carolina: Clemson University, 1980.

Brown, T. L., and Wilkens, B. T. "Methods of Improving Recreation Projections." *Journal of Leisure Research* 7(1975):225-234.

Burton, T. L. "You Can't Get There from Here: A Perspective on Recreation Forecasting in Canada." *Recreation Research Review* 9(1981):38-43.

Canadian Outdoor Recreation Research Committee. "Park and Recreation Futures in Canada: Issues and Options." Toronto, Canada: Ontario Research Council on Leisure, 1976.

Cicchetti, C. J. *Forecasting Recreation in the United States.* Lexington, Massachusetts: Lexington Books, D.C. Heath & Co., 1973.

Cicchetti, C. J.; Seneca, J. J.; and Davidson, P. "The Demand and Supply of Outdoor Recreation." Bureau of Economic Research. New Brunswick, New Jersey: Rutgers, The State University, 1969.

Clawson, M., and Knetsch, J. L. *Economics of Outdoor Recreation.* Baltimore: The Johns Hopkins University Press, 1966.

Fesenmaier, D. R.; Goodchild, M. F.; and Lieber, S.R., "Correlates of Day Hiking Partipation: The Effects of Aggregation." *Journal of Leisure Research* 12(1980):213-228.

Hof, J. G. "Problems in Projecting Recreation Resource Use Through Supply and Demand Analysis." In *Tourism Planning and Development Issues,* edited by Hawkins, Shafer, and Rovelstad, pp. 443-461. Washington, D.C.: George Washington University, 1980.

Howard, D. R., and Crompton, J. L. *Financing, Managing, and Marketing Recreation and Park Resources.* Dubuque, Iowa: William C. Brown, 1980.

Kalter, R. J., and Gosse, L. E. *Outdoor Recreation in New York State.* Ithaca, New York: Cornell University Special Series 5, 1969.

Michigan Employment Securities Commission. "Michigan Tourism Related Employment Study." Research and Statistics Division. Detroit, Michigan: 1980.

National Academy of Sciences. *Assessing Demand for Outdoor Recreation.* Washington, D.C.: USDI, Bureau of Outdoor Recreation, 1975.

Outdoor Recration Resources Review Commission. "Prospective Demand for Outdoor Recreation." Study Report 26. Washington, D.C.: 1962.

Seneca, J. J., and Davis, R. K. "A Cross Section Analysis of State Recreation Activity." *Journal of Leisure Research* 8(1976): 88-97.

Smith, V. K. "The Estimation and Use of Models of the Demand for Outdoor Recreation." In *Assessing the Demand for Outdoor Recreation.* Appendix B. Washington, D.C.: USDI, Bureau of Outdoor Recreation, 1975.

Smith, V. K., and Munley, V. G. "The Relative Performance of Various Estimators of Recreation Participation Equations." *Journal of Leisure Research* 10(1978):165-176.

Stynes, B. W., and Pigozzi, B. W. "A Tool for Investigating Tourism-Related Seasonal Employment." *Journal of Travel Research,* in press.

Stynes, D. J.; Bevins, M. I.; and Brown, T. L. "Trends or Methodological Differences." In *Proceedings 1980 National Outdoor Recreation Trends Symposium* vol. 1. General Technical Report NE-57, pp. 223-232. Broomall, Pennsylvania: USDA Forest Service, Northeastern Forest Experiment Station, 1980.

Stynes, D. J., and Spotts, D. M. "A Simulation Model for Forecasting Downhill Ski Participation." In *Proceedings 1980 National Outdoor Recreation Trends Symposium* vol. 2. General Technical Report NE-57, pp. 55-68. Broomall, Pennsylvania: USDA Forest Service, Northeastern Forest Experiment Station, 1980.

Stynes, D. J., and Szcodronski, K. "Predicting Trends in Michigan Snowmobiler Populations Using Life Cycle and Diffusion of Innovations Theories." In *Proceedings 1980 North American Symposium on Dispersed Winter Recreation,* pp. 148-153. Saint Paul, Minnesota: Office of Special Programs, University of Minnesota, 1980.

USDI, "National Park Statistical Abstract." Denver, Colorado: Statistical Office, National Park Service, 1980.

Wheelwright, S. C., and Makridakis, S. *Forecasting Methods for Management.* New York: John Wiley & Sons, 1980.

4

Forecasting Recreation Trip Distribution Behavior

Gordon O. Ewing

There are two common methods to forecast aggregate behavior patterns. One, called trend forecasting, uses past and present trends to extrapolate into the future; the other, called causal modelling, identifies factors that are believed to underlie variations in the behavior in the past, and then, using assumed values for these factors in the future, predicts the level of future behavior. Trend forecasting generally performs well only when causal factors are stable or are changing at a steady rate. The accuracy of forecasts using causal models depends on the validity of the model, including how fundamental its causal factors really are, and on the accuracy of the estimates of future values of these causal factors. The strength of the causal model over trend forecasting is that if there is an unusual change in values of one or more causal factors it can still make accurate predictions.

CAUSAL MODELS OF RECREATION TRAVEL

The aim in developing causal models of recreation travel is to discover the relative importance of those factors that influence the magnitude of recreation travel. Models of recreation participation, as well as other types of traffic flows, tend to be of two types. There are those called <u>trip generation models</u> which are aimed at explaining why origins (i.e., cities, states, or counties) generate different volumes of trips and discovering those supply and demand factors that influence the participation rate in recreation travel of people from different origins. One might surmise that an origin's participation rate has to do both with characteristics of its population, as well as with its accessibility to and choice of destinations to visit.

In addition, there are <u>trip distribution models</u> which take as given the participation rate and hence the volume of participants from any origin, and attempt to discover why particular proportions of an origin's recreation travellers go to different destinations. The latter are the kind of data analysed in the remainder of this chapter. The data are most easily thought of as a table or matrix of proportions, in which each row of figures represents the proportions of travellers from one origin who go to each of the destinations, which are defined by the columns of the matrix. Hence, for any origin, i, p_j is defined as:

$$P_{ij} = \frac{T_{ij}}{\sum\limits_{k=1}^{n} T_{ik}} \tag{1}$$

where T_{ij} = the number of recreational travellers from i who went to j, and

$\sum\limits_{k=1}^{n} T_{ik}$ = the total number of travellers from i who went to the n destinations being considered.

While origin-to-desination distances account for some of the differences in trip distribution proportions, they do not explain the whole picture. The task in developing models of trip distribution is to discover what other factors play a role. For example, destinations that have large attractive beaches may draw more of an origin's visitors, while destinations surrounded by competitors may draw fewer. In effect, the question addressed by the trip distribution model is "what makes more people from an origin go to one place than another?"

Restating this question at the individual level we can turn to the huge literature on decision-making theory in psychology and economics. (For an overview, see Edwards and Tversky 1967.) While the models described below will be about aggregate volumes of people traveling between various origins and recreation destinations, the literature on individual decision-making provides valuable guidelines for analysing aggregate behavior.

RECREATION TRAVEL AS CHOICE BEHAVIOR

Decision-making theory assumes that many behaviors are the outcome of people making choices between alternative courses of action, and that their choices are guided by the expected benefit accruing from the different alternatives. At any one time, only one alternative can be chosen. The assumption is that the available alternative most likely to be chosen is the one the individual believes will yield the greatest benefit or pleasure.

The most widely used form of this model in the travel demand literature is Luce's choice model (Luce 1959) which says that the probability of an individual choosing any one geographical alternative from a set of alternatives is equal to the benefit perceived to accrue from it relative to the sum of the benefits accruing from all alternatives in the set. Mathematically, this can be expressed as:

$$P_{ij} = \frac{U_{ij}}{\sum\limits_{k=1}^{n} U_{ik}} \qquad j = 1,2,\ldots n \tag{2}$$

where P_{ij} = the probability of the individual at origin i choosing alternative j; and

U_{ij} = the attractiveness or utility that destination j has for the individual at i.

Equation (2)'s probabilistic interpretation of behavior is compatible with the situation where a person chooses one alternative a certain proportion of times and other alternatives other proportions of times. In recreational travel those factors that influence the proportion of times someone goes to one destination are presumably its intrinsic attractiveness, A_j, and some function of its distance from i, $f(D_{ij})$, relative to the attractiveness and distance of other destinations. Thus we can rewrite (2) as:

$$P_{ij} = \frac{A_j/f(D_{ij})}{\sum\limits_{k=1}^{n} A_k/f(D_{ik})} \qquad j = 1,2,\ldots,n \tag{3}$$

The reason for dividing by, rather than subtracting distance in equation (3) and in trip distribution models generally, is a matter of empirical observation. If we plot p_{ij}/A_j against D_{ij} for any origin i, we typically find that the plotted values lie not on a negatively sloping straight line, as subtraction implies, but on a negatively sloping curved line, as division implies.

Using data on the proportion of times, P_{ij}, that each subject at a different location i chooses each of the alternatives, we can estimate the general level of attractiveness, A_j, of each destination to all subjects and the general deterrent effect of distance on the proportion of times destinations at different distances are chosen.

While Luce's choice model describes individual choice behavior, researchers studying aggregate flows of people from an origin to different destinations have found it useful to use a model with the same structure. The term P_{ij} becomes the proportion of travelers from origin i who went to destination j, as defined in equation (1) and U_{ij} in equation (2), is then treated as the average spatial utility of destination j as seen by all travelers from origin i. In fact, we can now combine equations (1) and (3) to give:

$$P_{ij} \equiv \frac{T_{ij}}{\sum\limits_{k=1}^{n} T_{ik}} = \frac{A_j/f(D_{ij})}{\sum\limits_{k=1}^{n} A_k/f(D_{ik})} \qquad j = 1,2,\ldots,n \tag{4}$$

There are many well known examples of the application of this kind of model in the travel demand literature (Huff 1963, Lakshmanan and Hansen 1964, Wilson

1971, Rushton 1981). The critical feature of a model such as equation (4), from the point of view of recreation travel modelling, is that it explicitly acknowledges that the proportion of travellers from an origin who go to a particular destination is affected not only by the attractiveness of a destination's characteristics and by the distance separating them, but also by the attractiveness of, and distances to, all the alternative destinations. A hypothetical example highlights the behavioral realism of this feature. If there are two identical origins at the same distance from a common destination, but one origin is surrounded by attractive alternative destinations and the other is not, it is very likely that the proportion of the former's recreators who go to the destination in question will be smaller than the latter's, because of the greater strength of competition for the first origin's patronage. Note that a simpler model without the competition effect term in the denominator of equation (4) would inevitably estimate identical proportions for both origins. Unfortunately, in the past many models of recreation travel were of that form.

A related weakness of the model without the competition effect in the denominator of equation (4) is that it would produce erroneous forecasts of the proportion of travelers who would go from an origin to any new destinations added to the set (e.g. new parks or other recreation facilities). Imagine we have estimated parameters of an equation with the general form:

$$P_{ij} = A_j/f(D_{ij}) \tag{5}$$

that accurately describes the observed proportion of trips from several origins to various destinations. Now we add a set of new destinations to the system and we want to use equation (5) to forecast the proportion of trips not only to the existing destinations but to the new ones. Equation (5) will forecast no reduction in the proportion of trips to the existing destinations, as well as new trips to the new destinations, the volume of which will depend on their attractiveness, A_j, and distances from each origin. Thus equation (5) implies that the origins have an endlessly elastic demand for recreational travel as new destinations are added to the system. This seems logically indefensible. It would seem more plausible that, while the addition of new destinations might increase an origin's participation rate, some of the trips that previously went to existing destinations will now go to the new centers. This implies some form of implicit competition between destinations, such that the addition of new destinations reduces by varying amounts the proportion of an origin's travelers who go to the existing destinations. This effect is exactly what the competition-effect denominator in equation (4) simulates. A recreation travel model generically equivalent to equation (4) is the focus of the latter part of this chapter.

So far we have skirted the question of how to measure or estimate A_j, the attractiveness of a recreational destination. In recreational travel modelling, the question of what factors influence destination attractiveness is not as easy to answer as it is in modelling travel to shopping centres, where A_j is commonly treated as some function of shopping centre size (Huff 1963, Lakshmanan and Hansen 1965). There are several reasons for this; one being that recreation travel can have different purposes. Thus, the factors that influence where to go on a fishing trip are not necessarily the same that influence where a family goes camping for the weekend, or where to go for day sailing or day hiking. Secondly, the factors that influence the choice of a destination may relate not only to the immediate site of the activity, but also to the environs. For example, a camping destination might be chosen more for the scenery and amenities of the surrounding district than for the amenities of the immediate camp site. And thirdly, amenities such as scenery and "atmosphere" are difficult to quantify.

With the latter two factors in mind, there are two choices open to the modeller. Either he/she must try to identify and measure the variables that are supposed to influence destination attractiveness, or A_j itself can be treated as a parameter to be estimated in equation (4), one for each destination. If A_j is replaced in (4) by a set of amenity variables $\underset{\sim}{X}_j$, the relationship between A_j and the vector of variables $\underset{\sim}{X}_j$ can be written as:

$$A_j = \prod_{k=1}^{q} b_k X_{jk} \tag{5A}$$

where b_k, $k = 1, 2, ..., q$ are parameters to be estimated after inserting (5A) in (5) and which measure the relative influence of each of the amenity variables on the volume of trips to a destination. With no loss of generality (5A) can be rewritten as:

$$A_j = \exp\left(\sum_{k=1}^{q} c_k X_{jk}\right) \tag{6}$$

For any positive value of b_k in (5A), and for each unit increment in X_{jk}, equation (5A) implies that there is a constant increment in the number of trips to destination j, while for any positive value of c_k in (6), equation (6) implies that the number of trips increases at an increasing rate. Empirically-grounded psychophysical theory and the basic propositions of economic utility theory suggest, on the contrary, that marginal utility shrinks with each successive increment of a good or service consumed. This suggests that X_{jk} should be transformed in some manner to allow for the possibility of diminishing marginal utility. Since we do not know the rate of decline in the marginal utility of each of the amenities, a generalized transformation function which allows a variety of rates of decline is appropriate. The Box-Cox family of transformations (1964) satisfied this requirement, and is written as:

$$X_{jk}(\lambda_k) = \begin{cases} \dfrac{X_{jk}^{\lambda_k - 1}}{\lambda_k} & (\lambda \neq 0) \\ \log X_{jk} & (\lambda = 0) \end{cases} \tag{7}$$

Figure 1 shows a range of such transformations for values ranging from -2 to 1, all of which, except $\lambda = 1$, show a diminishing rate of increase in the transformed variable for increasing values of X_{jk}. Gaudry and Wills (1978), in a study of the share of inter-city travel markets capture by four modes of transport, have found that a value of $\lambda = -0.2$ gives an appreciably better fitting model than when no transformation of the amenity variables is made. It should be noted that if A_j, $j = 1,2,...,m$ are treated as parameters to be estimated in equation (4), the issue of transformation does not arise.

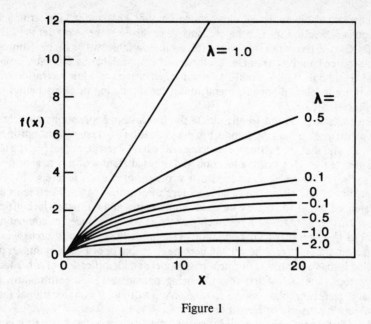

Figure 1

Box-Cox Transformations for Values of Lambda Between −2 and +1

Policy Applications

One of the concerns of those responsible for planning recreation facilities is to be able to forecast the effect of fuel cost increases and of highway improvements on where people choose to take recreation trips. To estimate these would entail adding an out-of-pocket cost variable and a travel-time variable to the definition of U_{ij} in equation (2), the former because we believe people are price-sensitive and the latter because we believe people attach an opportunity cost to the time and effort spent traveling. Assuming distance has no deterrent effect other than those just mentioned with respect to travel time and cost, we might imagine that we could replace the distance function in (4) by travel cost and travel time functions. However, if we assume that most recreation travel is done by car on non-urban highways, then the two variables, travel cost and time, will be almost perfectly colinear. This means that it would be statistically impossible to estimate the separate deterrent effects of travel cost and travel time in a model such as equation (4). It might seem that the solution is to have longitudinal data on recreation trip patterns over a series of years with real fuel cost increases. However, evidence from other fields (Ghoshal 1981, Straszheim 1969) suggests that coterminous changes in such things as disposable income and paid holidays are often more important influences and tend to statistically mask the effect of fuel cost increases. Also, short-term before-and-after surveys to capture the effect of a marked fuel price hike are liable to reveal short-term, but not necessarily long-term, adjustments in recreation travel behavior, such as occurred in the year after the 1974 oil crisis. Only if the parameter on the travel-time variable was available from an external source could a parameter on the travel cost variable be estimated using cross-sectional data with a modified version of equation (4). Thus recreation trip distribution models are not in general useful for estimating price elasticities or travel time elasticities.[1]

These limitations do not wholly vitiate the forecasting applications of recreation trip distribution models. A model such as equation (4), assuming it is properly specified and that the factors influencing utility have been identified, can be used to estimate the effects of the location and other attributes of any new or proposed park, for example, on its level of patronage, provided the levels of these other attributes fall within the domain of levels in existing parks. In effect, one can evaluate alternative possible locations and features and estimate which yields higher patronage, as well as how much patronage will be reduced at competing parks. The question of whether equation (4) is properly specified is discussed in detail later in the chapter, where it will become clear that one of the advantages of modelling is that it permits refinement of a model and identification of other factors previously not suspected of influencing patronage. Such information is essential if recreation planners are to take account of all relevant locational factors influencing the use of recreation facilities.

One general caveat regarding all forecasting models is in order. No matter how well they fit existing recreation trip patterns, their medium-term and longer forecasts will only be reliable if the values of the parameters of the model remain stable over time. Since we know very little about changes over time in the deterrent effect of distance, for example, and about what factors most influence these changes, we cannot say with much certainty yet whether future recreational activity will be more far flung, more concentrated in home regions, or remain about the same as at present. This, in effect, implies that we need to try to identify more fundamental influences on behavior than current models do.

Scales of Data Resolution

In analysing data on the human behavior of a sample, a fundamental decision for the analyst is whether to try to explain the different behavior of each individual in the sample or whether to tackle the simpler task of explaining the distribution of choices made by members of one or more groupings of the sample. A geographical version of this dilemma is to decide what scale of spatial resolution behavioral data should be defined at. At one extreme, one can divide a territory

---

[1]Note that this problem does not arise for trip distribution models used with other types of data. For example in urban areas, varying levels of traffic congestion across a city and the use of different transport modes with different costs or fares per mile result in non-colinear travel cost and travel time values. This enables estimation of separate travel cost and time parameters.

into a set of contiguous origin-destination zones, in which case the datum is a flow volume from one zone to another. The problem with this approach is that there is no natural way to divide a territory into zones and that the parameters estimated by calibrating a model using zonal data will vary depending on where zone boundaries are drawn, or depending on the size and therefore number of zones used. One of the reasons for this variation is that not only do zone-to-zone distance values change with the zoning scheme used, but as the zones are enlarged, the error in distance measurement increases. A single distance measure between two zones, no matter how scientific the measurement, is only an average of a variety of distances actually travelled between the two zones by members of the sample. Hence, there is intrinsic error in the distance measurement, the magnitude of which increases with zone size.

One obvious solution to this problem is to restrict an origin-based sample to very small zones such as towns, villages, and small rural areas which are effectively points if trips of over 20 miles are the norm. Assuming points are the destinations of these trips, they may be so numerous that for any origin town almost every respondent has a different destination, which would produce a trip distribution matrix made up mostly of ones and zeros. There are two responses to this problem. One is to aggregate destinations into zones to increase the size and variance in trip flow values, with the attendant zoning problems already discussed. The other is to restrict the behavior under investigation to only trips to a pre-specified set of destinations, such as state and private parks with camping facilities, for example. In this way there is a unique set of trip volumes and distances with no spatial aggregation error. In practice, unfortunately, many origin-based recreation travel samples tend to use more spatially diffuse sampling schemes, with an insufficient concentration of those participating in a given activity living in the same locality.

Destination-based sampling is an alternative, more cost efficient procedure for collecting point-to-point travel data, since by sampling at destinations, only participants in the relevant activity are surveyed. However, their origins are likely to be spatially diffuse, except for those from larger towns. If the more spatially diffuse rural residents are eliminated to avoid having origin zones, the sample becomes biassed exclusively to the recreation behavior or urban dwellers. However, if they constitute the majority of users of the recreation facilities in question, the bias may be less than that arising from the use of O-D zones. It is point-to-point travel data, referred to here as spatially disaggregated data, that are the focus of the empirical analysis described below.

There is, of course, one further level of disaggregation, where each respondent is treated as a separate observation whose behavior is to be explained (see, for example, Richards and Ben-Akiva 1975). Models of such wholly disaggregated data exist, particularly in urban travel demand analysis, where much of the behavior is habitual, such as someone's consistent use of the same mode of transport for travel to work. To date, however, these models have been much less effective in explaining people's choices of destinations such as places to shop. The reason would seem to be that there is much more event-to-event intra-personal variability in this kind of behavior (Huff and Hanson 1982), a feature shared by recreation travel behavior, and therefore no clear link between one randomly-selected segment of an individual's overall recreation travel behavior and his/her locational and socioeconomic characteristics.

Statistical Estimation of Model Parameters

Over the last decade the literature has strongly emphasized the appropriateness of different methods of estimating the parameters of non-linear travel demand and market share models such as equation (4). The general conclusions reached in three valuable papers by Baxter (1982, 1983) and Wills (1982) are that for certain assumptions about the error distribution of T_{ij} a variety of rearrangements of equation (4) result in either identical maximum likelihood estimates or very similar estimates using weighted least squares regression. For example, Wills demonstrates that identical maximum likelihood estimates result from four different ways of rearranging equation (4) to linearize it. These are two versions of the multinomial logit model due to Theil (1969), a rather more complicated rearrangement due to Nakanishi and Cooper (1974), and the much simpler denominator constants rearrangement due to Cesario (1975). The latter rearrangement is used in the empirical analysis described later in the chapter. Baxter (1982), referring to a proof by Bishop, Fienberg, and Holland (1975), shows that maximum likelihood estimates of the parameters in (4), where P_{ij} is the dependent variable and is assumed to have a multinomial distribution, will give identical parameter estimates to those in an equivalent model where T_{ij} is treated as the dependent variable with a Poisson distribution. Baxter also notes that the entropy maximizing solution to the doubly constrained gravity model (Wilson and Kirkby 1980) produces equivalent estimates to those in the above two cases.

In the analysis described below, T_{ij} is treated as the dependent variable and is assumed to have a Poisson distribution. Maximum likelihood estimates of the parameters in equation (4) are obtained using a linear rearrangement of the equation. Specifically, equation (4) is rewritten by multiplying both sides by T_{ik} as:

$$E(T_{ij}) = \sum T_{ik} \frac{A_j/f(D_{ij})}{\sum A_k/f(D_{ik})} \tag{8}$$

$$= c0_i A_j/f(D_{ij}) \tag{9}$$

where $E(T_{ij})$ = the expected or mean value of T_{ij} for given values of terms on the right-hand side of (8);

A_j, $j = 1,2,...m$ = destination-specific parameters estimated in the model; and

$c,0_i$, $i = 1,2,...,n$ = parameters to be estimated in the model, the values of which can be shown to be identical to $\sum T_{ik}/\sum_k A_k/f(D_{ik})$, $i = 1,2,...,n$, terms which appear in the numerator and denominator of (8)

Hence equation (9) is simply a rearrangement of equation (4) and is easily linearized by taking the logarithm of both sides. This then permits linear estimation methods to be used to estimate the parameters of (9) and hence of (4). The actual form of the distance deterrence function used is $1/\exp \beta D_{ij}$, which can be rewritten as $\exp(-\beta D_{ij})$, a negative exponential function. For simplicity, the sign on β is dropped in algebraic expessions. Thus the right-hand side of the logarithmic estimating equation is written as:

$$\log \hat{c} + \log \hat{U}_i + \log \hat{A}_j + \hat{\beta} D_{ij} \tag{10}$$

where the hatted terms are parameters to be estimated. Equation (10) is treated as a minimal model, i.e., as a base-line model of maximum simplicity against which more sophisticated experimental models can be compared, with a view to improving the fit of the model to the data with a minimum of added complexity.

The actual estimating procedure used is contained in a very powerful and flexible package computer program, Generalised Linear Interactive Modelling (GLIM) written by Baker and Nelder (1978). It uses an iterative estimation procedure for converging on maximum likelihood parameter estimates that allows various assumptions about the error distribution of the dependent variable. The procedure is described in detail in Nelder and Wedderburn (1972), and more briefly and simply in Flowerdev and Aitkin (1982).

GRAVITY MODEL ESTIMATION: AN EXAMPLE OF PROVINCIAL PARKS IN BRITISH COLUMBIA

The Data Set

The data used to estimate parameters of the trip distribution model consist of a 10 percent sample of all parties camping for one night in 40 provincial parks in southern British Columbia during the three summer months of 1976. A record of each respondent's home phone number enabled an origin-destination matrix of party trip volumes to be generated. The object was to analyze the pattern of choices of campers on short (i.e., 2 day), trips from home, since what governs these choices may well differ from what governs destination choice on longer trips. However, since the provincial authorities who collected the data did not have trip modeling in mind when the survey was designed, respondents were not asked whether this was their main destination and whether they had come from home that day. This means that the raw trip distribution matrix is contaminated by data other than pure one-night home-destination-home trips. It contains people at a main destination who took several days to get there and others who are merely using a park as a sleeping stop en route to some other destination.

In order to minimize the presence of such observations in the data, two elimination rules were used. Firstly, all origin-destination pairs more than 300 kilometers apart were eliminated on the assumption that 300 kilometers is about as far as most one-night main destination campers will travel on a two-day trip. Secondly, those parks with separate evidence of having virtually no stops of more than one night were eliminated as being primarily en route stopping places chosen for convenience and not because of the intrinsic utility of the park or surrounding area.

Presumably some en route data have still slipped through the net but, provided they are a small percentage of the total flow volume and are not unduly concentrated on any particular parks or types of O-D pairs, the effect on parameter estimates should be small. The exercise does highlight, however, the kind of difficulties typically encountered when trying to use data not specifically collected for the task in hand. Yet this is a common problem in spatial interaction analysis where the costs to the analyst of collecting original data are prohibitive. The remaining data matrix consisted of a matrix of 24 of the largest origins and 40 parks, with 391 of the 960 possible O-D pairs satisfying the 300 kilometer limit.

Modelling the Data

The right-hand side of the simplest model calibrated against the data, namely equation (9), is shown in Table 1. For reasons of space the O_i and A_j parameter estimates are not shown.[2] Where subscripts are omitted, ij is implied. The variable $R + F$ is road and ferry distance combined, for those routes involving ferry passage to or from Vancouver Island or along the coast north of Vancouver. The deviance statistic shown is asymptotically a X^2 measure of goodness of fit between the observed and estimated T_{ij} values. With 327 degrees of freedom, the deviance statistic is highly significant, i.e., the differences between the observed and expected values are much greater than could be expected to arise by chance. Baker and Nelder (1978) do observe, however, that

> With data on counts or proportions where very large samples are involved the deviance is...likely to be larger than expectation, perhaps much larger, even for models which fit well, as judged by the closeness of the fitted and actual values. This happens because with very large samples very small deviations from the model can be detected, deviations so small as to be of no practical importance, although they produce statistically significant results.

For illustrative purposes only, the coefficient of determination, R^2, between T_{ij} and $\hat{T}_{ij}$ is shown. The 0.90 value for the basic model would, in the absence of the deviance statistic, incline one to accept the basic model as adequate. The reason for the large discrepancy between the high R^2 and the poor deviance statistic is a combination of two facts. Firstly, X^2 is an absolute measure of fit, i.e., it measures the difference between observed and expected values of a variable, whereas R^2 measures that difference _relative_ to the difference between the observed value and the mean value of the variable (in this case, the mean of all the T_{ij}).

This means that R^2 will be high even if there are appreciable differences between the observed and estimated values, provided they are small relative to the differences between the observed values and the mean. Hence X^2, the absolute

---

[2]Since it is ln O_i and ln A_j that are estimated and since each set is unique only up to an additive transformation GLIM automatically sets ln O_i and ln A_l equal to zero, i.e. O_i and A_l are automatically set equal to one.

Table 1

		Deviance $\approx \chi^2$	R^2	D.F.
1. O_iA_j exp	$-.015 (R+F)$	3467	.90	327
2. O_iA_j exp	$-.011(R+3.0F)$	2418	.94	326
3. O_iA_j exp	$-.009(R+3.4F) +.45Q$	2254	.94	325
$=O_iA_j$ exp	$-.009(R+3.4F-48Q)$			
4. O_iA_j exp	$-.009(R+3.3F) +.46Q +.18N$	2232	.94	324
5. O_iA_j exp	$(-.011R4F+.004(R4F-150).N+28Q)$	2205	.94	325
6. O_iA_j exp	$(-.012R4F+.004(R4F-150).N$ $+.27Q+.70SP1-.15SP2)$	2159	.94	323
7. O_iA_j exp	$[(-.009R4F+.005(R4F-150).N).SS1$ $+(-.005R4F+.001(R4F-150).N).SS2$ $+(-.012R4F+.015(R4F-150).N).SS3$ $+.28Q+.83SP1-.21SP2]$	1880	.95	319
8. O_iA_j exp	$[(-.008R4F+.004(R4F-150).N).SS1$ $+(-.004R4F+.000(R4F-150).N).SS2$ $+(-.011R4F+.012(R4F-150).N).SS3$ $+.28Q+.85SP1-.15SP2]$ $SAD^{-.10}$	1828	.95	318
9. O_iA_j exp	$[(-.010R4F+.005(R4F-150).N).SS1$ $+(-.003R4F+.000(R4F-150).N).SS2$ $+(-.011R4F+.012(R4F-150).N).SS3$ $+.27Q+.51SP1-.55SP2$ $+.15NIO]$ $SAD^{-.09}$	1721	.95	317
10. O_iA_j exp	$[(-.008R4F+.004(R4F-150).N).SS1$ $+(-.005R4F+.002(R4F-150).N).SS3$ $+(-.011R4F+.013(R4F-150).N).SS3$ $+.40Q+.56SP1-.93SP2+.15NIO$ $-1.25CH1.N-.26CH2.N+$ $.11CH3.N-.49CH4.N$ $+.12CH5.N+.63CH6.N+.07CH7.N$ $+.56CH8.N]$ $SAD^{-.08}$	1511	.96	309
11. O_iA_j exp	$[(-.008R4F+.004(R4F-150).N).SS1$ $+(-.004R4F+.002(R4F-150).N).SS2$ $+(-.011R4F+.012(R4F-150).N).SS3$ $+.40Q+.61SP1-.93SP2+.16NIO$ $-.43CH1.N+.33CH2.N+.76CH3.N$ $+.28CH4.N+.92CH5.N+1.27CH6.N$ $+.69CH7.N+1.25CH8.N-.009N.PK2]$ $SAD^{-.09}$	1456	.96	308

measure of fit, is a much more demanding test than R^2, the relative measure. Secondly, with a very negatively skewed distribution of T_{ij} values such that the mean is close to the small values and far from the large ones, the total sum of squares, $\sum_{ij} (T_{ij} - \bar{T})^2$, will be greatly inflated by these large values being far from the mean. Consequently, even if the model gives estimates of the large T_{ij} that are significantly far in absolute terms from the observed values, the residual sum of squares $\sum_{ij} (T_{ij} - \hat{T}_{ij})^2$ will still be much smaller than the total sum of squares, resulting in an inflated value for R^2. Thus R^2 is not only a less rigorous measure of fit than X^2, but it is an inappropriate statistic to use when the variable in question is highly skewed, as is the case with virtually all spatial interaction data.

Given that the model does not fit the data well, the remainder of this section discusses attempts to improve the model, as well as the reasoning behind the modifications that were tried out. As a general rule, there are two sources of inspiration when trying to develop a better model. First, there are theories which may suggest influences on choice behavior other than those already covered by the model; second, empirical observations may produce hunches or embryonic theories. There are few well-established theories in the field of travel behavior, but empirical observation in this and adjacent fields has prompted many embryonic theories of what influences spatial decision-making. These will be drawn on to justify the various modifications proposed below.

Generally, there are three ways to seek improvements to a trip distribution model such as equation (9). These are: (1) to redefine the measure of distance used; (2) to define a new variable, the values of which vary between O-D pairs; and (3) to redefine the composition of the model, i.e., how the terms in the model are combined mathematically. Only the first two options, which involve revised and additional measurements of the relationship between origins and destinations, are considered here.[3]

(i) *Redefining distance*   There are several ways to redefine distance. The most obvious is to define it as travel time rather than milage, since it is probable that journey time, rather than actual distance travelled, is the major deterrent in medium-distance travel. Of course, if distance and travel time were highly correlated, replacing one by the other would have no effect on the fit of the model. If more than one mode of travel is required to get from origin to destination, distance can be redefined in terms of the distance travelled by each mode. This enables separate parameters to be estimated which measure the different deterrence of each mode of transport.

Since car ferry, and road travel are involved in British Columbia, this extension of the model was tested. The results are shown in model 2 of Table 1, where R is road distance and F is ferry distance. Factoring out the lowest common value of their parameters reveals ferry distance to have three times the deterrent effect of road distance. Considering average ferry waiting times and crossing times involve about triple the time of an equivalent road distance, but nearly ten times the visible cost in 1976 prices, the parameter appears to indicate that on journeys of

---

[3]Note that no mention is made of redefining measures of destination characteristics. This is because no further precision is possible if, as in equation (9), a separate parameter measuring the drawing power of each destination has already been estimated.

this type it is travel time, rather than out-of-pocket cost, that has the major deterrent effect.[4] The very large improvement in fit indicates the necessity of retaining ferry distance in the model.

(ii) *The nearest opportunity effect* A common assumption in many classical location theories is that man is a distance-minimiser who, all other things being equal, chooses the nearest destination. Since we know that parks are not all equal in amenities, we do not expect people to frequent only their nearest park. However, it is possible that being an origin's nearest park, whether 10 or 50 miles away, may confer on the park a special absolute advantage reflected in higher patronage levels than relative distance alone would predict.

This belief is strengthened by evidence from a Scottish study of day trip behavior which indicated that models of trip distribution which use a conventional measure of distance significantly underpredicted the volume of trips to nearest destinations of a given type (Ewing 1982, Ewing and Baxter 1981). To formally test this nearest destination effect, model 3 in Table 1 was calibrated where the term Q_{ij} is a dummy variable indicating whether park j is origin i's nearest provincial park or is within 20 kilometers of being the nearest. Not only does Q_{ij} have the expected positive sign, but the improvement in fit is sizeable. Rewriting model 3 (see Table 1) reveals that being nearest is equivalent to being 48 kilometers closer than in actual fact, a sizeable bonus effect. The fact that the effect was revealed in an identical model calibrated on Alberta provincial park visitation data suggests, together with the Scottish evidence, that the nearest opportunity effect is possibly a general locational effect, at least in recreation travel data.

(iii) *A nearness threshold* In response to a suggestion by Stetzer and Phipps (1977), that travelers are indifferent to distance up to some threshold distance, models 4 and 5 were designed to discover whether recreational travelers are only moderately deterred by the distance of a destination up to some critical threshold, beyond which the burden of travel for a one-night stay becomes steadily heavier. Model 4 was used to test whether the distance deterrence function steps down abruptly at a given threshold distance. Using N_{ij} as a dummy variable with a value of 1 if the distance is less than the threshold and experimenting with a range of thresholds between 50 and 250 kilometers, there was only a small improvement in fit with any of the thresholds.

Another version of the same hypothesis is that there may be an inflexion point on the distance deterrence function at some threshold distance beyond which the function is steeper. While this may be true for individuals, it is questionable whether such a phenomenon would be detectable in aggregate trip distribution data. Inter-individual differences, for example, could mask the phenomenon in aggregate data. Model 5, shown in Table 1, tests for such an inflexion point. Algebraically, an inflexion point can be incorporated in the deterrence function by redefining $\exp \beta D_{ij}$ as $\exp(\beta_1 D_{ij} + \beta_2(D_{ij} - t)N_{ij})$ where t is the threshold distance and, as in model 4, N_{ij} equals one for $D_{ij} > t$ and zero otherwise.

---

[4]Due to linear dependence between ferry crossing time, waiting time, and fare it was impossible to estimate separate deterrence effects for each.

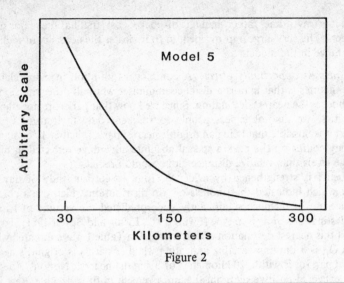

Figure 2

The Distance Deterrence Function for Model Five

To test for the inflexion point using a range of values for t, it was necessary to combine road and ferry distances in a single measure. Experiments showed that multiplying ferry distance by three or four gave best fits to the data. So in the remaining models total distance is defined as road distance plus four times ferry distance, R4F in Table 1.

The graph of the deterrence function (Figure 2) $\exp(-0.011R4F + 0.004(R4F - 150)N)$ in model 5 reveals no evidence of the hypothesized inflexion. Indeed, the slight inflexion is one that flattens the decay function beyond the 150 km threshold. However, given that for the same number of degrees of freedom model 5 has a modestly better fit than model 3, the inflexion point is retained in succeeding models.

(iv) *Pattern in residuals*   An approach commonly used to try to improve the fit between observed values and those predicted by a model, is to look for pattern in the differences between the observed (T_{ij}) and predicted ($\hat{T}_{ij}$) values, referred to as residuals. Just as we have a matrix of T_{ij} values, so we can draw up a matrix of residual values, $T_{ij} - \hat{T}_{ij}$, where each row of the matrix represents a different origin and each column a different destination. If adjacent origins and adjacent destinations are also set adjacent to one another in the matrix, it is sometimes possible to detect blocks of overpredictions (negative residuals) or underpredictions (positive residuals). This may suggest that a particular kind of relationship exists between a certain subset of origins and destinations, which a modified model should incorporate. Before doing that, however, it is necessary to verify whether the block of over- or under-predictions is as well defined statistically as it appears visually.

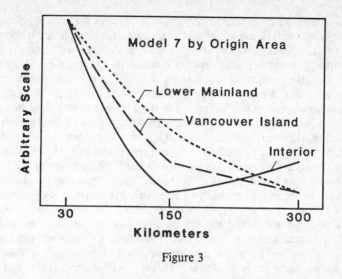

Figure 3

The Distance Deterrence Function for Model Seven

An inspection of the matrix of residuals from model 5 revealed one apparent block of underestimated flows and one of overestimated flows. The former were the flows from all origins in the Vancouver and adjacent lower Fraser valley area to the only three parks on a dead-end highway north of Vancouver. The latter were from the same origins, eight in all, to their three nearest provincial parks to the east of Vancouver which are close to the Trans-Canada highway, the province's main highway link with the rest of Canada. In model 6, these two sets of O-D pairs were distinguished from the rest by two dummy variables, SP1 and SP2, which were set equal to 1 for O-D pairs in the first and second block respectively. The large positive parameter on SP1 shows that the three parks on the 200 km dead-end highway north of Vancouver are much more attractive to this, its nearest cluster of origins, than to any others. This possibly reflects a perceptual effect, namely that places on dead-end highways, unless outstandingly attractive, are more likely to be known by residents living near the beginning of that highway than by those from further away. If this is so, it would tend to explain the observation in the Scottish day trip study (Ewing and Baxter 1981) that dead-end roads, such as follow certain mountain valleys, were rarely used on day trips to the countryside. In that case, none of the origins was close to any of the culs-de-sac.

The parameter for SP2 is not significant compared to its standard error. But since from model 9 onwards it has a large and significant negative value, it is retained in the sequence of models. The negative value indicates that the three nearest parks east of Vancouver are much less attractive to local origins than to others. This suggests that some "locals" avoid these parks because they are known to be congested or at least heavily used by campers from further afield who are travelling on the nearby Trans-Canada Highway.

(v) *Area-specific distance deterrence functions*   Besides the various refinements to the way distance is measured, as described in sections (ii) to (iii), it is also possible that the deterrent effect of distance is greater in some areas than others. While this is often thought possible between cultures, it is interesting to speculate whether it exists at a regional or sub-regional level. For example, people in areas with opportunities to recreate outdoors in many ways other than by camping at provincial parks, may be less willing to travel far afield to camp than those from areas with fewer alternatives. As a rough-and-ready test of this hypothesis, the study area was divided into three natural regions: Vancouver Island (SS1), the lower mainland (SS2), and the interior of southern B.C. (SS3). Model 7 in Table 1 shows the separate deterrence function estimated for each region of origins. There is a sizeable improvement in fit for the loss of four degrees of freedom. Figure 3 shows the shapes of the three deterrence functions. It is significant that the most central set of origins, the lower mainland, has the gentlest deterrence function and the most isolated, the interior, has the steepest. It would be comforting to conclude that the original hypothesis is supported and that the results show that people in the interior and, to a lesser extent on Vancouver Island, have a wider range of National Parks, private campgrounds, and other places for outdoor summer recreation than people in the metropolitan Vancouver and lower mainland area. However, without data on the level of these facilities in each region, the conclusion must remain speculative.

(vi) *A differential spatial competition effect*   As it stands, equation (8) implies that a destination's competition from other destinations for visitors from a given origin declines the further the competition is from the origin. However, an argument can be made that people first choose roughly what distance they want to go and then select a particular destination in that distance range. If that is so, one would expect parks in distance ranges containing many other parks to attract fewer visitors than if the competition at that distance was less. A version of this hypothesis is tested in model 8. In it the basic structure of the choice model in equation (4) is retained, implying that choice is a function of a destination's attractiveness and distance relative to other destinations, but there is another term added which measures the magnitude of the competition in the same distance band as j is from i. If the competition faced by j from these destinations is stronger than competition from destinations closer to or further from i, one would expect the estimated parameter, δ, to be negative. Specifically the added term is defined as the sum of the spatial utilities of destinations within 20 kilometers of D_{ij}, namely:

$$SAD_{ij} \, \delta \;\;=\;\; \sum_{k \in R_{ij}} A_k / f(D_{ik})^{\delta} \tag{11}$$

where R_{ij} =   the set of destinations within the same distance range of i as j

δ =   a parameter to be endogenously estimated in model 8

Since this term cannot be made linear in all its parameters, estimates of A_j and of the distance deterrence parameters from model 7 are used in place of the terms inside the curly brackets in (11) to produce the variable SAD_{ij}[5]. Using the notation of equation (9), for illustration, one can then linearize the modified equation such that its right-hand side becomes:

$$\log \hat{c} + \log \hat{0}_i + \log \hat{A}_j + \hat{\beta} D_{ij} + \hat{\delta} \log SAD_{ij} \tag{11}$$

In model 8, δ is estimated as -0.1, with a very small standard error, and there is an appreciable improvement in fit. The negative value of δ is consistent with the hypothesis that park j's patronage is reduced more by those parks in the same distance range as j than by others, and that this effect is directly related to the total spatial utility of these parks. This corroborates a slightly different conclusion by Fotheringham (1982) who found that airline passenger volumes to cities in the United States were negatively affected by the proximity of a destination to other population concentrations.

(vii) *An intervening opportunities effect*   Another category of destination which may compete more strongly than others with a destination are those actually on the route between origin i and destination j. A version of this hypothesis was supported in a study of eastern Pennslvanian state park trip distribution data (Baxter and Ewing 1979). The hypothesis was tested in a simple fashion in model 9 by incorporating a count of the number of intervening provincial parks between i and j, NIO_{ij}, into the distance deterrence expression. While the addition improves fit by over 100, the positive coefficient suggests that, holding other things constant, parks on routes with more intervening opportunities are more, rather than less, likely to be visited. The most likely interpretation of this surprising conclusion is that there may be an incidental correlation between the location of a few very attractive parks and the number of intervening parks on routes to them, compared to the number of intervening parks on routes to equally distant but less attractive parks.

(viii) *The effect of park features on local visitors*   It is well known from studies of environmental cognition that people have spatially biassed information fields, i.e., varying levels of information about places in different directions and at different distances. Applied to recreational travel, one might hypothesize that people within a given range of a park are more likely to know of its attractions or disadvantages than people from further away. In other words, certain positive or negative features of a park may have more of an influence on local attendance than on attendance by non-local visitors who are less acquainted with the park.

   To see whether any of several nominal park characteristics influence local attendance more than non-local, model 10 was calibrated. The park characteristics are listed in Table 2. To indicate to the model that we are interested in distinguishing between the possible effects of these features on local and non-local visitors, we use the nearness variable, N_{ij}, which has a value of one for local

---

[5]Since the estimates of A_j and of the distance deterrence parameters do not change significantly between models 7 and 8, the approximation used to define SAD_{ij} is appropriate.

Table 2

Park characteristics included in model 10

Model name	Characteristic
CH1	No identifying feature
CH2	On a river
CH3	On a waterfall(s)
CH4	On seaside; no beach
CH5	On seaside; with beach
CH6	On a lake; no boating allowed
CH7	On a lake; no power boating allowed
CH8	On a lake; all kinds of boating allowed

origins, i.e., those within 150 kms of park j, and zero for all other O-D pairs and define a set of eight so-called interaction terms, CH1.N to CH8.N, for each of which the model estimates a parameter. This parameter indicates what, if any, is the effect of a particular park characteristic on attendance from local origins compared to the effect on non-local origins. A positive value would indicate that this characteristic had a bigger positive effect on local than on non-local visitors; a negative value would indicate the reverse.

The addition of these eight additional parameters in model 10 improves the fit by a further 200 units of deviance. The estimated coefficients (see Table 1) reveal that in particular the presence of a lake, or beach, or waterfall have a greater effect on local than on non-local attendance. To a lesser extent, the same is true for parks by the sea without a beach and for parks on rivers. Contrariwise, the negative effect of having none of these characteristics is greater on local than on non-local attendance.

These results suggest that local residents are more aware of the presence or absence of desirable park characteristics than non-local residents. This would seem to corroborate the evidence for spatially biased information fields found in other areas of environmental cognition. However, to show how careful one must be in making inferences about cognition from aggregate data, consider the following alternative inference. Lakes, beaches, and waterfalls being the more desirable of the amenities listed, local residents are in a better position, spatially speaking, to take advantage of these amenities, in that it is easier for them than non-local residents to arrive at such parks before the "sorry, campsite full" sign appears.

One further distinction between local and non-local residents was tested, namely their differing reaction to park congestion levels. This was done in model 11 by

introducing an interaction term between nearness and the level of peak congestion at the park in the busiest month of the previous year, N.PK2 in Table 1. The
reduction in deviance by almost 60 and the small standard error on the negative
coefficient suggest the factor is significant. The negative coefficient indicates that
local residents avoid congested parks more than residents from further afield.
Again, this may in part reflect local residents' more accurate knowledge of park
congestion levels.

Conclusion

Clearly the sequence of models considered could be further extended, but the set
considered provides enough evidence to draw several conclusions.

1. The large reduction of the deviance measure from 3467 for the base model to
1456 for the final model at the expense of 19 extra parameters is noteworthy,
although about 1000 units of reduction are attributable to estimating separate
deterrence effects for road and ferry distance. This leaves about 1000 units of
reduction attributable to the other 18 parameters. The sequence demonstrates the
value of the linear estimation technique GLIM for experimenting easily with a
variety of alternative model specifications.

2. Besides quantitative distance measures, various qualitative measures of proximity, such as being a nearest destination, and interaction effects between proximity and certain park characteristics, as well as the cul-de-sac effect, also influence the aggregate pattern of spatial choice amongst parks.

3. One of the difficulties of aggregate analysis is that results can be suggestive
of alternative behavioral interpretations, but they provide no guide as to which is
more valid, if any.

4. The use of data with unknown levels of contamination increases the difficulty of interpreting results and of deciding what part of the lack of fit between
model and data is due to the presence of irrelevant data and what part is due to
model mis-specification. In this it highlights the problems of using data not collected with the analyst's modelling objectives in mind. As a corollary, it highlights
the weaknesses, common to many sectors of the recreation travel industry, both
public and private, of designing procedures to collect or record travel data
without giving much attention to what kinds of analysis will be possible with data
in a particular form.

References

Baker, R. J., and Nelder, J. A. *The GLIM System, Release 3: Generalised Linear Interactive Modelling.* Oxford: Numerical Algorithms Group, 1978.

Baxter, M. J., and Ewing, G. O. "Calibration of Production Constrained Trip Distribution Models and the Effect of Intervening Opportunities. *Journal of Reginal Science* 19(1979):319-330.

Baxter, M. J. "Similarities in Methods of Estimating Spatial Interaction Models." *Geographical Analysis,* 14(1982):267-272.

Baxter, M. J. "Esimation and Inference for Spatial Interaction Models." *Progress in Human Geography* forthcoming, 1983.

Bishop, Y. M. M.; Fienberg, S. E.; and Holland, P. W. *Discrete Multivariate Analysis.* Cambridge, Mass.: M.I.T. Press, 1975.

Box, G. E. P., and Cox, D. R. "An Analysis of Transformations." *Journal of the Royal Statistical Society,* Series E 26(1964):211-243.

Cesario, F. "Linear and Nonlinear Regression Models of Spatial Interaction." *Economic Geography* 51(1975):69-77.

Edwards, W., and Tversky, A. *Decision Making.* Harmondsworth, England: Penguin Books, 1967.

Ewing, G. O. "Modelling Recreation Trip Patterns: Evidence and Problems."*Ontario Geography* 19(1982):29-56.

Ewing, G. O., and Baxter, M. J. "Recreational Day Trips in East-Central Scotland." *Scottish Geographical Magazine* 97(1981): 147-157.

Flowerdew, R., and Aitkin, M. "A Method of Fitting the Gravity Model Based on the Poisson Distribution. *Journal of Regional Science* 22(1982):191-202.

Fotheringham, S. "A New Set of Spatial Interaction Models: the Theory of Competing Destinations. *Environment and Planning A* 15(1983):15-36.

Gaudry, M. J. I., and Wills, M. J. "Estimating the Functional Form of Travel Demand Models." *Transportation Research* B 12(1978): 257-289.

Ghoshal, A. "Price Elasticity of Demand for Air Passenger Service: Some Additional Evidence." *Transportation Journal* 20(1981): 93-96.

Huff, D. L. "A Probabilistic Analysis of Shopping Centre Trade Areas." *Land Economics* 31(1963): 81-89.

Huff, J. O., and Hanson, S. "Systematic Variability in Daily Travel Behavior." Paper presented at the Association of American Geographers Annual Meeting, San Antonio, Texas, 1982.

Lakshmanan, T. R., and Hansen, W. G. "A Retail Market Potential Model." *Journal, American Institute of Planners* 31(1965): 134-143.

Luce, R. D. *Individual Choice Behavior: A Theoretical Analysis.* New York: John Wiley, 1959.

Nakanishi, M., and Cooper, L. G. "Parameter Estimation for a Multiplicative Competitive Interaction Model - Least Squares Approach." *Journal of Marketing Research* 11(1974): 303-311.

Nelder, J. A., and Wedderburn, R. W. M. "Generalised Linear Models." *Journal of the Royal Statistical Society Series A* 135(1972): 370-384.

Richards, M. G., and Ben-Akiva, M. E. *A Disaggregate Travel Demand Model.* Lexington, Massachusetts: Lexington Books, 1975.

Rushton, G. "The Scaling of Locational Preferences." In *Behavioral Problems in Geography Revisited* edited by K. R. Cox, and R. G. Golledge. New York: Methuen, 1981.

Stetzer, F., and Phipps, A. G. "Spatial Choice and Spatial Indifference: A Comment." *Geographical Analysis* 9(1977): 400-403.

Straszheim, M. R. *The International Airline Industry.* Washington, D.C.: Brookings Institution, 1969.

Theil, H. "A Multinomial Extension of the Linear Logit Model." *International Economic Review* 10(1969): 251-259.

Wills, M. "On the Equivalence of Common Rearrangements for Sum Constrained Travel Estimation Problems." *Transportation Research* B 16(1982): 339-359.

Wilson, A. G., and Kirkby, M. J. *Mathematics for Geographers and Planners.* 2nd ed. Oxford: Clarendon Press, 1980.

Wilson, A. G. "A Family of Spatial Interaction Models and Associated Developments." *Environment and Planning A* 3(1971): 1-32.

5

Introduction to Dynamic Techniques for Forecasting Recreational Behavior

Ralph L. Levine
Weldon Lodwick

Recreation systems appear to be in flux. In the recent past, for example, recreational patterns have gradually adapted to changing conditions brought about by increased costs of gasoline and other factors, such as population increases, which affect recreation. Change is a key ingredient in developing recreational models and understanding adaptive processes associated with recreational systems.

This chapter stresses modeling changes in recreational systems over time. It is a general survey of dynamic approaches to recreation planning and forecasting techniques. Companion chapters will cover the use of simulation methodology in more detail, describing both the System Dynamic and control theory approaches to modeling changes in recreational patterns.

Figure 1 illustrates how the material will be organized and presented. One can follow the flow of concepts and issues from top to bottom, starting from the most abstract systems notions and ending with specific examples of models used for recreational planning and analysis. An important distinction will be made between energy processes and information. This distinction is very important in control theory and will resurface several times in the present chapter. Moreover, a knowledge of these processes will be absolutely fundamental in understanding the material on dynamic simulation techniques, which will be presented in our second chapter.

This figure also shows that we are going to cover the difference between dynamic and static perspectives involved in studying recreational behavior early in the chapter. The so-called "dynamic" approaches have been used in the past, and some of the reasons for attempting to supplement present statistical methodology with simulation and other dynamic techniques.

These general comments lead to the notions of models and of model building. After defining what we mean by a model, the chapter covers how models can be useful for the study of recreational systems. Models have several useful purposes. Among them are such functions as forecasting, allocating resources, explaining how recreational problems developed and can be solved, and finally analyzing the impact of new recreational policies. In order to see how these processes come into

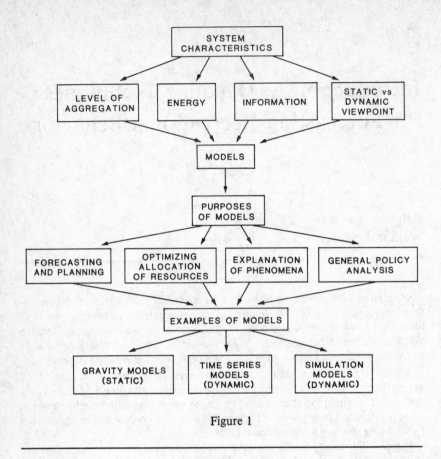

Figure 1

The Structure of the Chapter

play at a practical level, the chapter concludes with a description of specific models used by recreational planners and researchers. In addition, for those who have had a background and interest in problems of statistical estimation of model coefficients, we briefly bring up some of the issues involved in fitting models to actual data. These issues will be particularly important for the later chapter on simulation techniques, where there is much controversy over how to validate computer simulation models.

SYSTEMS: CHARACTERISTICS AND APPROACHES

Let us start off by giving a brief working definition of a system. A system is a collection of component processes and variables which, when coupled together, display an organizational structure and behavior (see Levine 1980). Recreation systems refer to those systems which are associated with recreational behavior patterns. As we shall see, the definition includes three major ideas, namely the notion of a set of components and variables, the idea of interactive couplings among components of the system, and finally, the set of behavioral patterns under study for any given period of time.

Components of A System

Systems can be categorized in several ways. For example, when dealing with recreational systems, it is important to note the level of aggregation at which one is working. Problems associated with recreational systems can be viewed from the national level, forecasting national demands for a specific recreation, down to the local level of a small lake, where one might want to study the causes of an increase in boating accidents as a function of spatial interaction patterns among boaters. Some examples of various levels of aggregation are: (1) National - The demand for national parks vs. other land uses for the area, (2) Regional - The effect of pollution in the great lakes region on water recreation, (3) State - The psychological or economic effects on a class of people due to closing state parks because of fiscal economic constraints, and (4) Local - The allocation of hours for two groups of recreationists using the same facilities.

In general, it is quite important to pick the level of aggregation at which one wants to work quite early in the game, for each level implies different kinds of statistical procedures and measurement principles. Moreover, from our point of view as modelers, it allows us to define the boundary and limitations of any planning model we might develop for forecasting future recreation behavior. The systems approach can be applied at any one of the mentioned above. However, the components of the system and their interactions would be vastly different.

A second dimension of systems deals with the distinction between energy and information processes. An energy process is associated with the flow and concentration of materials, people, cars, money, etc. in time and space. Energy is always involved in concentrating people at a beach, for example. Indeed, energy processes play a large role in understanding recreational behavior. Most of the models we shall be considering, such as gravity models, will largely depend on predicting the flow of people from points of origin to recreational facilities some distance away.

Information processes, a third general component of a system, deal with the control and management of energy processes. The notion of feedback is very important here. Control mechanisms have evolved to monitor the state of the systems, assess deviations from the system's goals, and to make corrections toward those goals. This description of what feedback mechanisms do is very general. In social systems, information is also used to manage and control the system towards one or more specific goal states. Our perceptions of how well the system is doing and how fast it is going can be used to make appropriate corrections. When these mechanisms are not working properly, energy systems may lack control. The study of feedback should be a primary task in the analysis of processes associated with recreation systems. Some examples of information processes associated with social and economic systems include: (1) expectations of inflation, (2) perceptions of crowdedness, (3) "testing the waters" before marketing a new product, and (4) becoming alarmed at the rise in fishing violations.

We hope the distinction between energy and information is clear at this point. Energy processes usually deal with physical flows and concentrations of materials. On the other hand, information processes usually deal with perceptions of those physical flows and concentrations. As one will see in the next chapter, where energy and information processes are examined in more depth, the two types of processes must be treated very differently when building dynamic models. The form of the equations are somewhat different, which could lead to inappropriate predictions if one fails to keep the two processes straight.

Systems Dynamics and Control Theory

There are two major ways in which information processes have been approached. The first deals with the analysis of problems involved with coordination of energy processes. This is primarily an analytic approach to the study of systems. It is typified by the use of System Dynamics, a problem oriented method used to understand the structural feedback mechanisms which frequently cause problems in industry and in public policy domains. System Dynamics can provide a set of analytic tools for the study of how information is used in decision making, and where community breaks down.

A somewhat different method for dealing with information processes has evolved from control theory engineering. This method places even less stress on energy processes than does the System Dynamic approach. Control theory applied to a system is an approach which classifies the system (recreational for example) into the states of the system and controls, those entities of the system which can be manipulated to direct the states in some manner. The states of the system are those variables which describe the conditions of systems. For dynamic (changing) systems, the states describe the system's condition in time. Often one of the states describes the position of the system in space. This is usually the case for recreational models in which spatial relationships are an integral part of a recreational system. For physical models, matter is often considered a state. Since control presupposes an expected direction or performance measurement criterion for the states of the system, it is normative.

Control theory is a synthetic approach to dynamics systems as opposed to an analytic approach, for it creates or constructs the controls from all possible controls in a given set which can be applied to the system over time. Controls that are constructed direct the system according to a specified performance measure. For example, a community may want to develop a set of policies (controls) such that within the next five years it has a park within no more than ten minutes walking distance from any home (states), and a minimum monetary outlay (performance criterion). If the community planners were politicians, the performance criterion might be to maximize political payoff. This problem could utilize control theory to synthesize or create policies "driven by" the performance measure. Note that the above approach is different from one which looks at forecasting of park usage over the next five years and then implementing policies to satisfy the demands.

To formulate policies utilizing control theory approaches, planners need infor-mation about the state of the system and not the energy/matter flows nor energy/matter interactions. Thus, in the above example, the performance criterion needs only information of costs (political payoff) to measure itself. The physical, biological, economic, sociological, etc. interactions are not what are being used. "Another aspect of control theory is that it avoids the concept of energy but, in-stead, deals with the phenomenon of information in physical systems.... Thus control theory rests on a new category of physical reality, namely information, which is distinct from energy or matter." (Markus 1976, p. 3)

An engineer constructing or improving a park must deal with energy/matter flows and interactions of the state. This is not the case for the policy maker above. The policy maker deals with information about the states. Looking at this concept from a different angle, suppose in driving, a car has to stop in the shortest amount of time possible utilizing the brake (control). The driver deals with information (feedback from the nerve sensors on the foot) about the system (car moving in time and space). This is distinct from the mechanic's problem of putting the car back together after the crash.

Energy and Information in Recreation Systems

Although System Dynamics and control theory appear to be quite different, they are really two sides of the same coin. Both focus upon information processes. System Dynamics is analytic and descriptive. It's strong point is that it is a useful method for explaining problem behavior. The method leads to understanding the system in terms of faulty feedback processing. Control theory, on the other hand, is useful for normative policy. It tells the decision-maker what the system should do in order to meet specified goals.

What is being stressed here is the very important role of information in systems and the various ways of studying these processes. It is important to remember, however, that most systems are characterized by both energy and information processes. Some social sciences, such as psychology, which specializes in the study of IQ, decision-making, perception, judgment, memory, and consciousness are almost totally devoted to the study of information processes. Economics, on the other hand, deals with the flow and concentration (e.g. inventories of materials, goods, and money) as well as information processes. At the macro level, the economist must be concerned with knowing the state of the economy, have a knowledge of the size of the money supply, the size of inventories, etc. This infor-mation is necessary for controlling the economic system through fiscal and monetary policies.

In many situations, then, both energy and information processes will be pre-

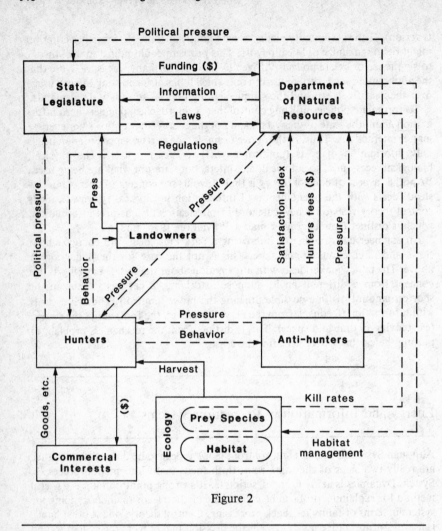

Figure 2

The Interaction Among Components of A Recreation System
at the State or Regional Level

sent. For recreation systems, Figure 2 represents the interactions among various components of a particular recreation system associated with hunting. The first question is at what level of aggregation does this system represent? The answer is clear just by looking at the boxes in the figure: this is a description of the interactions of components coupled together at the state or regional level. This representation may have been generated by the need of a state legislature to understand the origin and impact of "pressures" from various subgroups of the public, such as hunters and anti-hunters, who take very different positions concerning wildlife management and other issues.

Looking at the figure in more detail, one sees that some of the boxes represent components of the system and the arrows indicate the principal couplings or interactions among parts. The arrows also represent change in the system as well, through flow of materials and passing or transmission of information. To be more specific, most boxes represent the populations involved in this recreational system. Their numbers are cumulative over time. Social systems are represented by concentrations of people, while the biological systems in the figure are represented by the number of plants and animals in the biological populations involved.

As has been indicated, energy processes are characterized by just such concentrations. In addition, energy and materials flow from one place to another. The concept of flow is represented by the solid arrows. For example, consider the exchange of materials and money between hunters and commercial interests (e.g. sporting goods stores). Here goods and supplies are exchanged for money. Note also that in this type of systems representation, actual materials and services (in the form of human labor) flow in one direction and money flows in the opposite direction. This little portion of the system represents a nice illustration of the principles of energy processes. Information is also represented in the figure by broken arrows. Thus, for example, such concepts as "pressure" and information about so-called "kill" rates, generated by one portion of the system, will influence other parts as well. The impact of decisions, in the form of habitat management policies, laws, regulations, etc. work their way through the system in time. Again, all of these information concepts have evolved to keep the system from getting out of hand. The purpose of information processes is to make the system stable (see Weinberg and Weinberg, 1979). In the next chapter, which deals with simulation models, you will study cases where those control mechanisms have failed to do this.

DYNAMIC AND EQUILIBRIUM/STATIC PERSPECTIVES

Approaches to working with systems require two different perspectives in general. The first approach assumes that the majority of the variables do not change rapidly. The second approach assumes that time is an important factor to include within the description of the system, and that variable change relatively rapidly within the period of observation. The first perspective might be called the equilibrium or static view of systems, while the second perspective can be called the dynamic view. In the first case, one is mainly concerned with the state of the system at various points of equilibrium, under stable conditions, where the variables are not changing rapidly. In the dynamic case, on the other hand, the system is studied both in terms of equilibrium points, if they actually occur, and in terms of how the system moves from one point to another in time.

The two perspectives lead to different sets of methods, experimental designs, and analyses. An example of the static approach to the study of recreational systems might be predicting attitudes towards competitive sports as a function of personality characteristics. The emphasis here is on using the relationship between personality and attitudes to predict a given person's attitudes from one or more personality characteristics. There is no stress on change within a given person. Thus, to make the prediction by use of statistical techniques like multiple regression, changes in personality variables must correspond to differences between people, not changes within a person. Typically, data on attitudes and personaltiy characteristics were gathered simultaneously as dictated by a cross-sectional design (see Wood 1977). In the regression analysis itself there are no explicit functions of time, which might be gathered in a longitudinal study, nor are lagged (delayed) variables included in the regression equation.

A dynamic approach would predict how attitudes toward competitive sports would change over time as a function of specific experiences, programs, and opportunities to play competitive sports. For the static case, in the attitude personality model, change was not emphasized. On the other hand, in the second dynamic example, time and experience would be of prime interest.

To summarize, a dynamic approach to systems analysis stresses what happens in time, that is, it stresses the study of time series. Some dynamic approaches also attempt to understand the causal interactions among variables as they change in time. Moreover, many of the models we shall review in this chapter will attempt to account for change in the state of the system as a function of informational feedback processes. Coordination and management of all systems, including recreational systems, depend very much on viewing the interaction among variables in terms of feedback mechanisms, goals, etc.

Change in Static Models

At this point the reader should not assume that the static or equilibrium approach cannot address the problem of change. Although static descriptions of systems are most useful when system variables are at stable points, they can be used to predict the effects of changes in specific variables if one is willing to assume that very little else changes. Systems are usually represented abstractly by models. Static models, by the way, have been relatively successful in the social sciences. They can frequently predict how much change in the system to expect, given a change in a variable, but they cannot tell the decision-maker how fast those effects take place. Dynamic models, which stress lagged responses to a changing variable, are concerned not only with the magnitude of the effect, but also how long one will have to observe the system before those effects take place.

The difference between static and dynamic perspectives can be seen by taking an example from macroeconomics. Most working models of the interaction among economic variables, such as money supply, rate of inflation, unemployment, government spending, do not focus upon time delays, although lagged models, which view economic systems as dynamic in nature, are becoming more popular. In any event, the classical models are still taken seriously, for in theory they can predict change rather easily. They appear to be useful in predicting how the economy will react to changes in the economic variables.

How then is change predicted through the use of the static approach? This is accomplished through what the economists call "multiplier effects." The first step in the analysis is to assume that the economy is at a point of equilibrium. Next, sets of equations can be derived algebraically to outline the relationship among all of the major variables in the system. From those equations, one can derive an expression relating the change in any one variable in the system with any other variable of interest. Thus, the change in variable Y becomes a function of the change in variable X.

To see this more clearly a specific example is in order. Suppose an economist is asked to predict the effect of increased government spending on aggregate consumer income. The first step is to assume that the system is in equilibrium, and that the only change to occur is a change in government spending. According to the theory, the effect of this change will be to push the system to a new point of equilibrium. Under these assumptions, the macroeconomist can derive an explicit equation relating how much income will change with a change in government spending (Dornbush and Fisher 1981). Let ΔX be the change in government spending, ΔY be the change in aggregate income, and alpha be a constant equal to or greater than 1.0. Then, from macroeconomic theory, the relationship between the two changes can be expressed by the following equation:

$$(\Delta Y) = (\text{alpha})\,(\Delta X)$$

Alpha represents a constant that may take a value of 1.0 or greater. This means that it magnifies the effect of ΔX on ΔY, hence the term "multiplier effect."

In concrete terms what this means is that, for an increase in every dollar spent by the government over what they are currently spending, income will change by alpha dollars. Again, the theory assumes other factors are not changing during the period of observation. It is interesting to note that, although these equations deal with change, (ΔY) is not an explicit function of time. Indeed, the equations imply that change in government spending immediately affects income. Of course, in true economic systems, the impacts of policy, such as increased government spending, almost always take time. This may be one of the weakest points of the equilibrium or static approach. It cannot specify how rapidly the system travels toward its new equilibrium. Since in most complex economic systems other factors do not remain constant, the timing of their effects becomes crucial to accurately predict the outcome of any given economic policy.

Change in Dynamic Models

A dynamic representation of a system recognizes that many variables are functions of time. Secondly, the methods that shall be covered in this chapter will include ways of assessing the impact of delays in the system. It is known, for example, that attitudes take time to change, and so do recreational behavior patterns. Likewise, in a recreational marketing situation, advertising campaigns usually are not always effective immediately. Information concerning new facilities, for example, gets disseminated very slowly because it is a function of distance as well as time.

In this economic example, a policy of increased government spending will not have an immediate effect on income. A dynamic approach to this policy problem

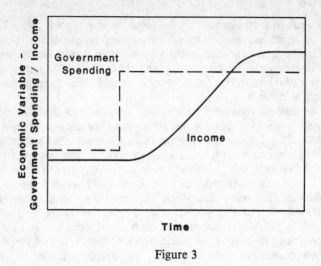

Figure 3

Delayed Response of Income To A Sudden Increase in Governmental Spending

would be to put systematic delays into the picture. For now, since only a simple point is being illustrated, assume other factors are held constant. We would make a very simple model of the effect of government spending on income. Figure 3 shows what such a model predicts if the government put more dollars into the economy. This has a delayed effect. At some point in time the government increased its spending from a lower level. This is represented by a dotted step function. The solid curve indicates how income might respond in time. Note that the shape of the income curve is not necessarily the same shape as the input function, which is, in this case, a sudden change in government spending.

This economic example assumes that all other factors remain constant. Indeed, in real life economic systems many other factors might change. Dynamic modeling techniques will handle multiple changes of the sort described above. Again it focusses upon changing patterns of interactions among variables. How this can actually be accomplished will be described in our chapter on simulation modeling, when we cover the System Dynamics approach to modeling societal problems.

The Use of Dynamic and Static Models in the Social Sciences

During the past twenty years there has been almost revolutionary progress in developing quantitative methods in the social sciences. Armed with a foundation of statistical tools, such as the analysis of variance and regression analysis, many social scientists now have a working knowledge of factor analysis, cluster analysis, discriminant function analysis, and other complex multivariate techniques (Morrison 1976, Bock 1975). The use and application of causal models and path analysis by psychologists, sociologists, and econometricians also expanded the level of sophistication of the social sciencist (Blalock, 1969). Finally, in applied areas of economics and operations research, there has been a rapid growth of the use of linear programming and similar optimization techniques (Intriligator 1971; Taha 1976; Hillier and Leiberman 1980).

Almost all of these methods have one thing in common: they usually assume equilibrium conditions. Most of these techniques view the system under investigation as being essentially static. The social sciences have a tremendous number of problems related to measurement compared to the physical sciences. Techniques, such as factor analysis and regression analysis, are very helpful in assessing static relationships among variables.

Currently, however, as more social scientists apply their theories to real world problems, there is a growing interest in time series analysis (e.g., see Cook and Campbell 1979) and other dynamic approaches to systems. This is especially true for those who are interested in forecasting and policy making and who must be aware of rapidly changing conditions. Currently, there are many econometric models which are based upon time series data and have accounted for lags and delays in economic systems (Johnson 1972).

Although as we have indicated, social scientists are beginning to analyze dynamic aspects of systems, nevertheless many still apply cross sectional designs (measuring all variables at the same time) and analyze data using static techniques, such as correlation analysis or linear programming, as a substitute for their dynamic counterparts. The reason for this is fairly simple. The social sciences are very young. Statistical analysis has proven to be useful in situations where measurement errors are large, variables lack validity, and little is known about the phenomena under study. Moreover, the art of teaching sophisticated statistical techniques has been developed to the point that now a student can learn to handle data well without spending time mastering calculus, a topic which would introduce the student to dynamics and time processes.

Where do these newer techniques come from? The techniques which will be introduced in this chapter come from a very different tradition. This is the legacy of Weiner and Ashby's cybernetics (Weinter 1966, Ashby 1963), the mathematical biology of Alfred Lotka (1956), the study of urban systems by Forrester (1969), MacArthur's work on geographic ecology (MacArthur 1972), Bellman's dynamic programming (Bellman and Angel 1970), and lastly, H. D. Odum's energy analysis of systems (Odum 1971, Odum and Odum 1976). All of the above works are modern versions of the study and management of dynamic systems.

What about the problems of recreational forecasting and planning? The literature indicates, with a few exceptions, that only a small number of articles stress the dynamic interaction of variables over time. This is understandable, because the study of recreation behavior as a scientific enterprise is just beginning. Because there are major problems in just finding the variables and measuring them reliably, static analyses are certainly appropriate and useful. For the most part, these newer techniques, which have not had a long history of application to the biological (Clerk 1976) and social sciences, may aid in supplementing other more familiar statistical tools.

These system techniques will also help to integrate many of the isolated contributions from various sciences (geography, psychology, economics, sociology, resource management, forestry, etc.). They should aid in the recreation planning process. The remainder of this chapter will be devoted to surveying various approaches to these dynamic systems. First, however, the concept of a model will be discussed.

MODELING BUILDING

Definition and Meaning of Models

The idea of a model is described next and distinguished from a system. The set of all variables or components and all interrelationships of the variables which describe the entity being studied is the system. A model is the abstracting or mental construct approximating the actual system. The mental construct is often mathematical. The abstraction is manipulated without affecting the system. This is both an advantage and a limitation. For mathematical models, the entities being manipulated are mathematical symbols and conclusions are drawn from the mathematical inferences. Thus the results of inferences are not the reality or what actually occurs to the system, but what occurs in the model. A model removes relationships into an abstract setting where it can be manipulated to arrive (hopefully) at solutions. These solutions have to be interpreted back to the system. Since there is a wealth of mathematical theorems that can be brought to bear in moving ideas to their conclusion, mathematical models are used.

It is preferable, of course, to draw conclusions directly from the system itself. However, when problems in the original setting (reality) cannot be solved because of their complexity or physical, biological, sociological, economic, etc. condition, a model may help to gain greater understanding of how the system operates. In this sense, a model is like laboratory experiments used in the physical or biological sciences.

Moreover, a model has at least two interfaces with the system. Firstly, the model, when initially constructed, interacts with the system. Secondly, the model solutions are compared and related back to the system. A model, when properly constructed, provides insight, understanding, and opens up opportunities for creativity and intuition. The modeler interprets results and compares her/his knowledge, intuition, and insight about the system with the model results. A model is after all a mere extension of human thought.

Purposes of Dynamic Models

Recreational systems are usually in a state of flux. Yet at the same time, decision-makers desire stability in funds, controlled expansion or contraction of facilities, etc. Recreational decision-makers must have a reasonably good idea of short-term and long-term trends in population size, economic conditions, and recreational habits and in their policy analysis use the tools of planning and forecasting. Thus, they have to have a good idea about what will happen in the future.

Over the years researchers have developed various kinds of models to aid in planning. Many of those models are static in form. In order to project the system into the future, planners often use the same technique as was used in our macroeconomic example when the basic model was applied to forecast the effect of a change in government spending on income (education). This was accomplished by literally making change as a function of change, i.e. having change variables on both the right and left side of the equation. Others are truly dynamic, where change is either a function of time, per se, or a function of the present state of the system.

How are models used then? This section will describe several different functions of models in the recreation area. There are at least four major interrelated functions of models: (1) to forecast future short-term trends, (2) to find optimal allocation of recreational resources, (3) to understand mechanisms which underlie recreational behavior, and (4) to provide the tools for policy analysis and recreational planning.

Forecasting Although models can be used for many purposes, certain models seem to be associated with specific types of problems. First there are what might be called predictive models used in making short-term forecasts. The problem might be to predict future recreational usage of a national park or a set of state parks. Frequently these models will focus upon following one variable, such as park attendance, over time. Forecasts are made from the analysis and extrapolation of past trends in the time series (see Stynes' chapter in this book on these forecasting techniques).

Another type of model, the so-called gravity model, which will be discussed early in the next section, can be used for short-term forecasts. Instead of extrapolating future values of attendance from past values, gravity models predict usage from other variables, such as the size of the populations inhabiting the points of origin, the distance to the recreational facility, and the attractability of the recreational sites.

Allocation Another application of models deals with the problem of allocating resources, personnel, and funds in recreational settings. This is a rational use of models, for they prescribe what would be the optimal allocation of recreational resources, given constraints on land availability, personnel, time, etc. These prescriptive or normative tools can be quite useful for minimizing costs or maximizing recreational satisfaction, when and where a manager has to plan a budget or design a schedule of activities under a set of constraints.

Explanation In contrast to the prescriptive applications, models give the manager or researcher insight into how the recreational system really works. This type of model, and many of the dynamic simulation model fall in this class, is more explanatory in nature. It focuses upon the causal relations among variables to explain why problems occur. In most cases these models are less concerned with short-term forecasting and concentrate more on long-term trends, over, let us say, a twenty to forty year time span.

Planning and Policy Analysis Finally, models are tools for general policy analysis and planning at various levels of aggregation. What would be the general impact of use fees for state forests? Would the opening of three new urban parks relieve some of the pressure upon the existing park system? What would be the effect of rising gasoline prices upon tourism in the southwestern portion of the United States? These are the types of policy issues some models can address.

Examples of Recreational Models

This section is a survey of many different types of models. Both static and dynamic models are presented here, but the emphasis in future sections will be on a class of dynamic models which can only become practical by using computer simulation techniques.

Just as was done at the beginning of the chapter, Figure 4 is intended to help you follow this last section on examples of models used in recreation planning and forecasting. The figure describes the overall organization of this very important concluding section on forecasting and planning models. Specific examples of each type of model will be given, starting from the left and progressing to the right of the figure. Note also that our discussion of simulation models will be organized along descriptive (non-optimizing) and normative (optimizing) lines. These categories are then broken down into models which focus upon discrete time periods or events and models which stress processes which change continuously over time.

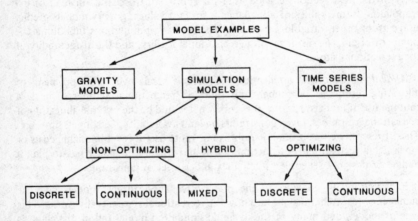

Figure 4

Examples of Models Used in Planning, Designing, and Forecasting
Recreational Systems

Gravity Models   Gravity and linear regression models (Cesario 1969) are the most popular models used to predict the intensity of recreational activities (see also, Malamud 1973, McAllister and Knott 1976, and Bell 1977). Since gravity models will be covered in great depth by Ewing in a separate chapter, they will not be discussed here in detail. Perhaps, however, from the point of view of systems analysis, the most interesting modification of the gravity model was made by Wolfe (1972), who noted an "inertial" effect of distance, an important variable. In the gravity model, if one were to plot the number of visitors as a function of distance, one would get a reflected J-shaped curve starting high and approaching zero visitors at very long distances away from the recreational site. This modification changed the form of the relationships between usage of a recreational facility and distance. He hypothesized that at short distances, facilities may not be as popular as one would expect from the predictions of the gravity model. This is because some people are reluctant or hesitant to travel any distance at all. There is an inhibitory process that has to be overcome. For those who do overcome this "inertia," there are some who, once they begin to travel, want to travel even a longer distance. Given these types of travelers, one would expect a higher number of visitors from far away cities than would be predicted by the reflected J-shaped curve generated by the gravity model. Once they start to move there is a tendency to keep on going for a while, hence the term "inertia."

From a systems perspective, perhaps Wolfe's concept of inertia can be understood from the standpoint of dynamic systems. In essence, the reluctance to travel can be represented by positing a set of inhibiting feedback loops delaying the action, while the tendency to travel long distances can be usefully described in terms of positive growth loops, so that the more one travels the more they want to travel.

What Wolfe's inertial theory does not explain is the fact that eventually people stop traveling, i.e. they reach an equilibrium point. By using some of the computer simulation methods which will be discussed later, one could supplement Wolfe's ideas by developing a model which would represent the inhibitory effects of constraints on traveling, such as time, boredom, illness, as well as Wolfe's inertial effects.

Time Series Forecasting Models   Unlike gravity models, which are most suited to be applied under slowly changing conditions, time series models are truly dynamic in nature. Since the use of this type of model has been treated extensively by D. Stynes in another chapter of this book, only a brief discussion of these forecasting techniques will be made.

A time series is, as its name implies, a description of the behavior of one or more variables over time. Economists have always been interested in time series, and indeed have developed methods to smooth out random fluxuations, seasonal trends, etc. in order to obtain valuable information concerning the state of the economy.

Many of the technical breakthroughs in time series analysis came from the work of Norbert Weiner (1966) and his colleagues at the Massachusetts Institute of Technology. There they developed the theory of statistical communication (Lee 1960), which is composed of a set of elegant techniques for handling time series. Their contributions eventually led to methodological breakthroughs in analyzing geophysical data, neurophysiological time series (Rosenblith 1962), and more recently in the analysis of psychophysiological data (Porges et. al. 1980).

During the past ten years or so, a second wave of interest in time series models came about with the development of a new set of techniques introduced by Box and Jenkens (1976) and Box and Tiao (1975). These techniques can be used for a number of related purposes. Psychologists and other social scientists, who are interested in program evaluation, use the Box-Jenkins times series approach to evaluate the statistical impact of a social intervention such as (for example) the effect of changing policy toward being leniant to speeders (see Campbell 1975). There is considerable literature on the use of the Box-Jenkins approach to time series analysis (see Cook and Campbell 1979, McDowall, McCleury, Meidinger, and Hay 1980). Also, Jenkins (1979) has written a book on the applications of these techniques for forecasting.

Models of time series analysis are very powerful techniques for preliminary examination of data and for short-term forecasting. Indeed, they have many strong points. They do have some problems, however. The interested reader can find a more complete discussion of their strong points and weaknesses in the chapter written by Stynes. Also, some of their limitations will be reviewed later in the authors' more advanced chapter dealing with computer modeling. In that chapter, time series analysis will be compared to models derived from System Dynamic techniques.

Simulation Models   In general, the forecasting models discussed previously were oriented towards fitting existing data. Gravity models utilize standard regression techniques to provide estimates of the parameters of the model. Likewise, in the use of time series analysis, emphasis is placed on fitting models to data.

There are some problems and limitations in placing so much stress on data fitting procedures. First, there is a tendency not to spend time on developing theoretical models of the process under study. Without a theory, researchers may lack insight and understanding of how the system works. When regression and time series models fail to predict future trends, they are at a loss to explain why and what to do about it.

An alternative approach to analyzing systems is to start first with a theoretical model, see its general implications for policy analysis and for planning, and then use past data for obtaining more exact parameter estimates used to predict the future. This approach puts more emphasis upon studying the dynamic implications of underlying processes and relationships among variables than on fitting data per se. Also, in most cases, gravity models, for example, only utilize a handful of variables to predict recreational usage. To really understand recreational systems, it might be better to develop a much richer model, composed of more variables, and representing more complex relationships among those variables.

Simulation does allow the modeling of a system in almost limitless detail. With the advent of the computer, more and more scientists are using simulation techniques to represent the system, generate potential behaviors, and to analyze potential problems. There is a large body of literature on simulation techniques and their application to systems analysis (e.g. see Ord-Smith and Stephenson 1975, Gordon 1978, Zeigler 1976). Although these methods have not been used widely in recreation research, today these methods are absolutely essential for business, land use, and most engineering applications. They are used in the design of autos, airplanes, ships, computers, and complex manufactured systems. They are used to train pilots and urban planners as well.

During the past twenty-five years or so, biologists and social scientists have begun to use simulation to model ecological and behavioral systems as well (Odum and Odum 1976, Loehlin 1968, Forrester, 1961). In the hands of the social scientists, the computer becomes a tool for developing a theoretical framework on which to base decisions on land use, recreational location, administrative policies, and planning. Before the advent of high speed computers, most systems could not be studied in any great detail. Mathematical models of systems were represented mathematically as simply as possible, because of the difficulty of finding general solutions to dynamic non-linear equations. The computer has made it possible to solve large systems of equations quickly and accurately. Simulation is becoming more common as a business tool through the availability of electronic spread sheets and simulation games for microcomputer. There is an active set of researchers who now use simulation techniques to model social systems. In the world of business and government, simulation models are becoming more utilized for decision-making and policy analysis.

One powerful aspect of simulation is that one can experiment with different policies and plans without large real world costs, since the computer is simulating the system. If the model represents the system well, not many resources, hours, and personnel have to go into finding a great deal of information concerning the social, financial, and physical impacts of proposed legislation or administrative policies.

Suppose, for example, administrators want to assess the effects of policies initiated to prevent conflict between cross country skiers and rabbit hunters, who frequently recreate on the same piece of public land during the same season. Several solutions might be proposed. They might hire more conservation officers to work in the field to keep order. Secondly, they could time zone the two groups, so that cross country skiers could only use the land in the morning and rabbit hunters could only hunt during the afternoon. Thirdly, the land could be zoned for rabbit hunters only. Fourthly, they could initiate a program of changing the cover or habitat so that cross country skiers would naturally use paths made for them and the hunters would find other parts of the area more attractive to hunt.

A model of this system could be developed to test the efficacy of each of the four policies proposed to reduce conflicts. The model, if suitably defined, could also handle any practical combinations of the four as well. It may be the case, for example, that the proposed solution which looked most reasonable at first might have lead in time to worse conditions than before. These models are very good at pointing out hidden consequences of any long-term action or policy.

Summary

This chapter has stressed the concept of change in recreational systems. The intention was to introduce a general dynamic perspective as an extension of the existing statistical techniques used in forecasting, planning, and recreation policy analysis.

The major distinction between energy and information processes was made early in the chapter to set the stage for understanding the role of feedback in recreation decision-making, marketing, and patterns of usage. Energy processes represent the flows and concentrations of people in time and space, and are represented in the gravity model, for example, by the size of the population at the origin and the costs of moving in time and space from the origin to the recreational facility. On the other hand, information processes are characterized by attractivity, recreational motivations, experiences at the recreational site, attachment to old recreational haunts, etc.

Many control processes are best understood by the study of feedback mechanisms. Although feedback mechanisms were described early in the chapter and reintroduced from time to time when relevant to the material, no attempt was made to go into detail at this point. However, it should be stressed that there is much to learn about how feedback works and the relationship between feedback and control theory. In the sequel, the authors will amplify these ideas by describing how to use feedback concepts to form a dynamic structure. Once formed, this structural "matrix" of interacting dynamic feedback loops can become an effective planning tool for predicting future recreational behavior patterns.

The difference between static and dynamic approaches to recreational systems was described. Both perspectives can handle changing conditions, although the limitations of the static approach, with its inability to predict how fast the system will change, have been brought out. The chapter continued by describing what models were and what was the purpose of modeling. The point was made that the lines between purposes of modeling are sometimes blurred, and indeed, any particular model might be used for several purposes.

The chapter also contained a description of a number of different models which could be used in forecasting, planning, and other aspects of recreational analysis. Although the gravity model, as presented here, represented a static approach to predicting usage, the authors indicated in a general way how the model might become more dynamic. Indeed, as an example of a simulation case study, in the next chapter the authors will present a dynamic version of the gravity model, which predicts the effects of energy supply problems and demographic changes on recreational facilities at the state level of aggregation.

The remainder of the chapter described the use of dynamic models for both descriptive and normative (e.g., optimization) purposes. With the exception of time series analysis, the application of dynamic models for forecasting and planning is relatively new. Recreational systems are by no means simple. Discrete and continuous computer simulation models have been developed to handle the complex relationships among variables, which is certainly characteristic of recreational systems. Potentially, the dynamic approach offers insight into the causes of recreational patterns, and can be used for the design of recreational systems built for multiple goals. Control theory and System Dynamics, which comprise major forces wihin the simulation community of researchers, are really two sides of the same coin. When applied as a supplement to traditional static techniques, it is felt that simulation methods can become a powerful set of tools for the recreational planner and researcher.

Many control processes are best understood by the study of feedback mechanisms. Although feedback mechanisms were described early in the chapter and reintroduced from time to time when relevant to the material, no attempt was made to go into detail at this point. However, it should be stressed that there is much to learn about how feedback works and the relationship between feedback and control theory. In the sequel, the authors will amplify these ideas by describing how to use feedback concepts to form a dynamic structure. Once formed, this structural "matrix" of interacting dynamic feedback loops can become an effective planning tool for predicting future recreational behavior patterns.

The difference between static and dynamic approaches to recreational systems was described. Both perspectives can handle changing conditions, although the limitations of the static approach, with its inability to predict how fast the system will change, have been brought out. The chapter continued by describing what models were and what was the purpose of modeling. The point was made that the lines between purposes of modeling are sometimes blurred, and indeed, any particular model might be used for several purposes.

The chapter also contained a description of a number of different models which could be used in forecasting, planning, and other aspects of recreational analysis. Although the gravity model, as presented here, represented a static approach to predicting usage, the authors indicated in a general way how the model might become more dynamic. Indeed, as an example of a simulation case study, in the next chapter the authors will present a dynamic version of the gravity model, which predicts the effects of energy supply problems and demographic changes on recreational facilities at the state level of aggregation.

The remainder of the chapter described the use of dynamic models for both descriptive and normative (e.g., optimization) purposes. With the exception of time series analysis, the application of dynamic models for forecasting and planning is relatively new. Recreational systems are by no means simple. Discrete and continuous computer simulation models have been developed to handle the complex relationships among variables, which is certainly characteristic of recreational systems. Potentially, the dynamic approach offers insight into the causes of recreational patterns, and can be used for the design of recreational systems built for multiple goals. Control theory and System Dynamics, which comprise major forces within the simulation community of researchers, are really two sides of the same coin. When applied as a supplement to traditional static techniques, it is felt that simulation methods can become a powerful set of tools for the recreational planner and researcher.

References

Ashby, W. R. 1963. *An Introduction to Cybernetics.* New York: John Wiley & Sons, Inc.

Bell, M. 1977. "The Spatial Distribution of Second Homes: A Modified Gravity Model." *Journal of Leisure Research,* 9:225-233.

Bellman, Richard E. and Edward Angel. 1970. *Dynamic Programming and Partial Differential Equations.* New York: Academic Press.

Blalock, Hubert, M. 1969 *Theory Construction.* Englewood Cliffs, New Jersey: Prentice-Hall.

Block, R. D. 1975. *Multivariate Statistical Methods in Behavioral Research.* New York: McGraw-Hill Co.

Box, G. E. P. and G. M. Jenkens. 1976. *Time Series Analysis*. San Francisco: Holden-Day.

Box, G. E. P. and G. C. Tiao. 1975. Intervention analyses with applications to economic and environmental problems. *Journal of the American Statistical Association*, 70:70-92.

Campbell, Donald T. 1975. Reforms as experiments. In E. L. Struening and M. Guttentag (ed.), *Handbook of Evaluation Research*, Vol. 1. Beverly Hills, California: Sage Publications.

Cesario, Frank J. 1969. Operations research in outdoor recreation. *Journal of Leisure Research*. 1(1):33-51.

Clarke, Colin W. 1976. *Mathematical Bioeconomics, The Optimal Management of Renewable Resources*. New York: John Wiley & Sons, Inc.

Cook, T. D. and D. T. Campbell, 1979. *Quasi-Experimentation: Design and Analysis Issues for Field Settings*. Chicago: Rand McNally Co.

Forrester, J. W. 1961. *Industrial Dynamics*. Cambridge, Massachusetts: M.I.T. Press.

Forrester, J. W. 1968. *Principles of Systems*. Cambride, Massachusetts: M. I. T. Press.

Forrester, J. W. 1969. *Urban Dynamics*. Cambridge, Massachusetts: M. I. T. Press.

Gordon, Geoffrey, 1978. *System Simulation*. Englewood Cliffs, New Jersey: Prentice-Hall.

Hillier, F. S. and Leiberman, G. J. 1980. *Introduction to Operations Research*. San Francisco: Holden-Day, Inc.

Intiligator, Michael D. 1971. *Mathematical Optimization and Economic Theory*. Englewood Cliffs, New Jersey: Prentice-Hall, Inc.

Jenkins, G. M. 1979. *Practical Experiences with Modeling and Forecasting Time Series*. St. Helier: Jenkins and Partners.

Johnson, John. 1972. *Econometric Methods*. New York: McGraw-Hill.

Lee, Y. W. 1960. *Statistical Theory of Communication*. New York: John Wiley & Sons, Inc.

Levine, Ralph L. 1980. Human behavioral ecology. In M. R. Denny (ed.), *Comparative Psychology: An Evolutionary Analysis of Animal BEhavior*. New York: John Wiley & Sons, Inc.

Loehlin, John C. 1968. *Computer Models of Personality*. New York: Random House.

Lotka, Alfred J. 1956. *Elements of Mathematical Biology*.

MacArthur, R. H. 1972. *Geographical Ecology*. New York: Harpter & Row.

Malamud, B. 1973. Gravity model calibration of tourist travel to Las Vegas. *Journal of Leisure Research*. 5:22-33.

Markus, L. 1976 *Control Theory and Topics in Functional Analysis*, International Atomic Energy Agency, Seminar Series, Volume 1, Washington, D.C.

McAllister, D. M. and F. R. Klett, 1976. A modified gravity model of regional recreation activity with an application to ski trips. *Journal of Leisure Research*, 8:21-34.

McDowall, David, McClearn, Richard, Meidinger, Errol E., and Richard A. Hay. 1980. *Interrupted Time Series Analysis*. Beverly Hills, California: Sage Publications.

Morrison, D. F. 1976. *Multivariate Statistical Methods*. New York: McGraw-Hill Co.

Odum, H. T. 1971. *Environment, Power, and Society*. New York: Wiley-Interscience.

Odum, H. T. and E. C. Odum. 1976. New York: McGraw-Hill Co.

Ord-Smith, R. J. and Stephenson, J. 1975. *Computer Simulation of Continuous Systems*. London: Cambridge University Press.

Porges, Steven, Bohrer, Robert, Cheung, Michael, Drasgow, Fritz, McCabe,Philip, and Gideon Keren. 1980. New time series statistic for detecting rhythmic co-occurrence in the frequenty domain. *Psychological Bulletin* 88:580-588.

Pritsker, A. A. and Pegden, C. D. 1979. *Introduction to Simulation and SLAM*. New York: John Wiley & Sons, Inc.

Rosenblith, W. A. 1962. *Processing Neuroelectric Data*. Cambridge, Massachusetts: M. I. T. Press.

Smith, U. K. and Krutilla, J. V., 1976. *Structure and Properties of a Wilderness Travel Simulator*. Baltimore: The John Hopkins University Press.

Taha, H. A. 1976. *Operations Research: An Introduction*. New York: Macmillan Publishing Company.

VanDoorn, J. 1975. *Disequilibrium Economics*. New York: John Wiley & Sons, Inc.

Weinberg, G. M. and D. Weinberg. 1979. *On The Design of Stable Systems.* New York: John Wiley.

Weiner, N. 1966. *Time Series.* Cambridge, Massachusetts: M. I. T. Press. New York: Dover Press.

Wolfe, R. I. 1972. The inertia model. *Journal of Leisure Research,* 4:73-77.

Wood, Gordon. 1977. *Fundamentals of Psychological Research.* Boston: Little, Brown and Co.

Zeigler, Bernard P. 1976. *Theory of Modeling and Simulation.* New York: John Wiley & Sons, Inc.

6

Continuous Simulation Methodology: A System Dynamics Approach to Planning, Forecasting, and Analysis of Recreational Usage[1]

Ralph L. Levine
Weldon Lodwick

There are a number of different approaches to modeling change in recreation systems. The previous chapter included a general overview of how change can be handled through traditional statistical techniques, such as regression analysis, or through alternative dynamic methods, such as time series analysis or computer simulation. There are some technical details, however, which are quite useful in the scientific study and management of recreational systems. These concern how to actually model recreational change in a given situation.

Of all the examples of models mentioned in the previous chapter, computer simulation techniques present the practical opportunity to model reality as closely as possible. Since gravity models and the analysis of time series have been discussed elsewhere, this chapter will cover only simulation techniques, and even here, mostly continuous simulation methods. Much of the social science literature is often quite terse, mathematical, and difficult to read. Yet these methods may have profound implications for control and management of recreational problem areas. This chapter is an attempt to bridge the gap between the systems literature, which is relatively inaccessable to many who might find these modeling methods useful, and traditional statistical analysis, in which the student has already attained at least an elementary background.

---

[1]Due to severe constraints on the length of the chapter, the present version only briefly mentions some of the work done by recreational modelers who use discrete simulation techniques. In the original version, twelve typewritten pages were devoted to reviewing this vital area of simulation research. We invite the interested reader to write for a copy of the more detailed original manuscript, which not only reviews this area of the literature, but also deals with many statistical questions concerning the estimation of parameters and the empirical verification of dynamic models in general.

CONTINUOUS EXPLANATORY MODELS: AN INTRODUCTION TO SYSTEM DYNAMICS

It is quite common to find physical systems described in terms of continuous dynamic models. This is not always the case in applications to the social sciences. Indeed, as was indicated in the previous chapter, discrete simulation has been utilized fairly widely in management sciences, as well as in he analysis of recreational systems (e.g. see Stynes 1980, Greenberg 1972, Cesario 1975, Smith and Krutilla 1976, Schechter and Lucas 1978). However, continuous dynamic modeling is a methodology which is also available to social scientists for exploring the dynamics of social systems, and can be used for modeling physical components within a social system. Although we shall review other approaches to the simulation of continuous social processes, almost the entire chapter will be devoted to System Dynamics methodology.

The methodology of System Dynamics has a history and literature that spans a period of about twenty-five years. It is perhaps the most sophisticated approach to simulating social systems available at the present moment. Those who learn the Systen Dynamic method have the opportunity to express very complex substantive theoretical relationships with less effort than most other modeling methodologies. Finally, we like it because it has a long history of shaking up established thought in such areas as economics and urban studies. It leads to new substantive insights and a rethinking of one's methodology. The application of System Dynamics to social systems is sometimes controversial! We like controversy.

Historical Background of System Dynamics

System Dynamics was developed at the Massachusetts Institute of Technology almost twenty-five years ago by a small group of modelers led by Professor Jay Forrester, who set up the first System Dynamics program at M.I.T.'s Sloan School of Management. During the past ten years other large research programs have been established at places like Dartmouth College in New Hampshire, University of Bradford in the United Kingdom, and in varying locations elsewhere in Europe and South America. Originally, Professor Forrester's work was primarily concerned with physical systems. Indeed, Dr. Forrester was a pioneer in the area of computer memory, and made major contributions to this field when the modern digital computer was in its infancy. With this background in physical science and computers, he and a group of students began to apply techniques of systems analysis to problems of society. The first applications of System Dynamics focussed on problems of industry (Forrester 1961). Indeed, even today much of the simulation modeling performed by Dr. Forrester and his colleagues deal with both industrial and general economic problems. For applications to planning and policy design the reader can obtain a very clear picture of how to apply these methods to corporate management problems by reading a recently published book by James Lyneis (1980), which appears to be the state of the art in this area. Lyneis develops a comprehensive System Dynamic model which addresses such problems and delays in supplier responses, inventories which are over or under target levels, labor instability, etc.

Forrester and his colleagues also devoted much of their time modeling the dynamics of urban systems, focussing upon problems of overcrowding, lack of economic development, etc. (see Forrester 1969; Mass 1974; Schroeder, Sweeney, and Alfield 1975; and Alfield and Graham 1976). These models should be of much interest to regional and urban researcher, for they lead to insights concerning how urban problems are generated and perhaps solved.

Perhaps the most influential applications of System Dynamics models to societal problems came from their dedication to understanding causes of world hunger, pollution, and limits of economic growth. The original World Dynamics model was developed by Forrester (1973) as a means of providing a framework to deal with future problems of society. Professor Forrester's original model generated a great deal of interest, and from this initial work, a second, larger modeling project came into being, under the leadership of Professor Dennis Meadows, a former student and colleague of Forrester. The new model was more detailed and comprehensive, although it still was aggregated at an extremely high level. A series of three books were published consecutively: *The Limits to Growth* (D. H. Meadows et. al. 1972); *Toward Global Equilibrium* (Meadows, and Meadows 1973); and *Dynamics of Growth in a Finite World* (D. L. Meadows et. al. 1974).

The emotional impact of these books was explosive! Indeed, during the twentieth century, few scientific writings have been so carefully studied and have been brought under such scrutiny by readers which included researchers and business people, as well as politicians. Many with engineering backgrounds found the methodology relatively familiar. Others, especially economists who were unfamiliar with the System Dynamics methodology and simulation techniques, made a concerted effort to attack the assumptions and conclusions of the study by pointing out what they thought were glaring methodological and statistical errors (e.g. see Cole, Freeman, Jahoda, and Pavitt 1973). Most of the criticisms reflected the differences in backgrounds between systems scientists and those who were heavily trained in statistical analysis. The critics also misunderstood many of the techniques used in computer simulation methodology. Perhaps this indicates to us that there certainly is a need for these methods to be made better understood, so that they can be examined for their potential application to social problems.

System Dynamic Philosophy

Since the term "System Dynamics" will be used so frequently, just for the sake of variety, sometimes we shall call System Dynamics, "S/D", and those who use this methodology will be called "System Dynamicists." We hope that our resorting to jargon will aid in communication and not confuse matters. System Dynamic methodoogy is composed of a set of techniques for constructing non-optimizing models of social systems. However, it is more than a methodology. There is an attitude and a set of philosophical assumptions that makes it relatively different from other approaches to modeling and interpreting the dynamics of systems.

Briefly, S/D has the following characteristics:

— S/D is problem oriented. One models a problem, not a system.
— S/D is oriented towards deterministic, non-linear causes of behavior.
— S/D is oriented toward how people use information.
— S/D translates information use into the concept of feedback.
— S/D explains the origin of the problem in terms of feedback structures.
— S/D stresses the dynamic impacts of internal problems and attempts to minimize the effects of external or exogenous variables as much as possible.
— S/D is wholistic in the sense that it is oriented towards long-term qualitative forecasting and analysis rather than toward making short-term quantitative forecasts.

1. *Problem Orientation*   The System Dynamics approach is particularly useful to either solve existing problems, or better yet, problems which are small now, but may become quite serious in a few years without an appropriate shift in policy or management. Its focus is upon problems, not on modeling systems in general.

2. *Deterministic and Non-linear Models*   The S/D method attempts to put much details concerning causal relationships as seems to be practical in the situation. Deterministic equations are used, because it is felt that one has greater insight into the dynamic behavior of the system if structural relationships among the variables of the system are studied rather than studying relations among probabilities, which by definition are rather fuzzy.

Social systems display rich and complex relationships among variables. S/D models reflect much of the complexity of social systems by use of non-linear functions such as U-shaped functions, for example. The stress here is on reflecting reality. If the system acts in a non-linear manner, then it would be modeled to reflect those non-linearities. If not, it would be modeled as a linear system.

This is a place where System Dynamics departs from much of what one might call classical system theory, which had its origin in modeling energy systems of various types, such as hydraulic, electrical, and mechanical systems. Engineers who work with these systems found out quite early that, for the most part, their systems were approximately linear. On the other hand, some physical systems, such as those associated with chemical reactions, are notoriously non-linear. Here, for example, all types of interactions are known to occur. Frequently, when two chemicals are mixed to obtain a completely different substance, the rate of formation of the new substance is proportional to a weighted product of the concentrations of the original interacting chemicals. The equation for the rate of recreation looks very much like the gravity model (equation 3, survey chapter), as indeed it should. In complex enzyme systems, the equations for the rate of reaction looks very much like the gravity model covered in other chapters of this book. In complex enzyme systems, the equations for the rate of chemical reactions also appear to have the same form as the gravity model (see Savageau 1976).

Likewise, social systems display non-linear interactions. Without a quorum, one does not have a meeting. It is a well known fact that in a swim meet, most people swim faster if other swimmers are in the race than if they swim the heat alone. They even have a name for it. It is called "social facilitation." The use of the computer allows the S/D modeler to put those non-linear processes into the model at the initial stages of modeling. Also, it might be added that linear models usually predict the dynamic behavior of the system under normal conditions just as well as a non-linear model. However, linear models fail to predict how the system will behave under extreme conditions (e.g., see Senge 1975). Since the model is being constructed to understand how the system functions under abnormal conditions, there is an advantage to using non-linear modeling techniques.

3. *Information and Energy*   Throughout this and our previous survey chapters the terms "energy" and "information" processes were used rather loosely. Here we provide more details about them, because they are absolutely essential to the System Dynamics method. Pure <u>energy</u> processes characterize conservative processes. This means that one has to account for material flows and storages within the system. For example, picture water flowing from a tap into a sink with a drain. In this situation, water can either flow in, be stored in the sink, evaporate into the air, or flow out the drain. It must do one of these four things. Likewise, all energy processes have this conservative characteristic, so that one can track any unit or entity throughout the whole system.

Here is another example. Consider a parking ramp which is used for storing parked cars and trucks. Suppose there is only one entrance and one exit. Further suppose an observer counted every truck that entered and left the parking ramp during a specific period of time. If during the first hour, four trucks entered and none came out, the observer would most likely assume that, if there are no other exits, the trucks were in the parking ramp, and not a thousand miles away. Likewise, if one happens to have a bunch of keys in his or her hand and drops them, then one looks on the floor for the keys.

People act this way because they must deal with energy processes and have adjusted to a world that has a lot of them around. Likewise, money is conserved, as any person who works in a bank will know. At the end of the working day, all money flows and storages have to be accounted for.

<u>Information</u> processes are not generally conserved. For example, child psychologists frequently study sibling rivalry. Suppose, Joe, who is four years older than Jim, makes fun of Jim for wearing diapers. The observer, the child psychologist, notes that the younger brother is in tears and from his remarks about himself, he appears to have a lower sense of self-esteem. Psychological processes dealing with self-esteem are information processes. Most likely, there is no conservation of self-esteem. Thus, if Jim lost his self-esteem, one does not look for it on the floor as if self-esteem were the same as keys. Likewise, if Jim lost two psychological units of self-esteem after his older brother said nasty things about wearing diapers, one does not expect Joe to gain those two units of self-esteem.

Signal or information processes, then, are not conserved. These processes provide feedback about how the system is progressing over time and space. They aid in the coordination and control of conserved systems. Recreation activities manifest many of the characteristics of both energy and information systems. The movement in time and space of recreationists, such as boaters, represents energy processes, and indeed, the use of the wind for sailing, and the fueling of motor boats places boating within an energy framework. On the other hand, advertising exotic trips to distant vacation islands represents the passage of information in recreational settings.

4. *The Use of Feedback Loops:*   The fundamental building block on which S/D methodology rests is the feedback loop. This is the idea that the effect of a change in a given state variable X will move through the system and eventually feed back to X again at a later time. Feedback mechanisms come in two varieties: positive and negative feedback loops. A positive loop accounts for the growth or collapse of a system. If variable X is part of a positive loop, then changes in any of the variables around that loop would either lead to a rise in X or a decrease in X. Negative loops, on the other hand, lead to stability. If the system is increasing rapidly, negative loops inhibit growth. On the other hand, if the system is decreasing, a negative loop reverses the decreasing trend. Thus, for example, if our variable were to be a part of a negative feedback loop, an initial increase in X would eventually lead to a decrease in X and vice versa.

It should be noted that any given variable can be part of more than one loop. The fact that variables are embedded in a network of positive and negative loops leads to another important concept in S/D, namely, the idea of a dynamic loop structure. Figure 1 illustrates a simple dynamic structure representing a positive loop functioning as a growth process, opposed by a negative loop which has an effect of inhibiting growth. In the positive loop, an increase in C will eventually lead to an increase in the same variable at a later time. On the other hand, following the same increase in C around the right hand negative loop leads to an eventual decrease in C in time. Now what happens when both loops are operating simultaneously? This is the fundamental dynamic question to ask when analyzing this structure. The answer can be obtained by deriving an explicit model to cap-

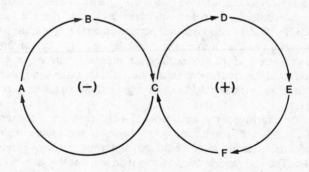

Figure 1

Dynamic Structure of Opposing Loops

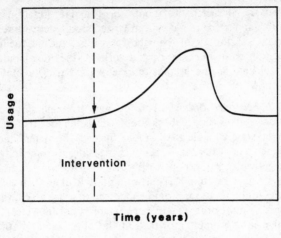

Time (years)

Figure 2

Potential Impact of an Intervention, Such as Dredging of A Lake,
on Recreation Usage

ture the dynamic structure and simulating it on a computer. In general, the behavior of the system will depend upon how fast the variables change in each of the loops. In many cases, the growth process will dominate at first, followed by the increasing influence of the negative loop acting as a delayed brake on the system.

5. *Relationship Between Behavior and Structure:*   The idea of dynamic structure underlying the behavior of the system is used by the system dynamicist to gain insight into why problems are not solved by simple changes in policy. Figure 2 shows a fictitious set of data on public use of a small lake for swimming after the lake was dredged, the beach was cleaned up, and parking facilities were renovated. If a time series analysis was performed on these data, the decision concerning the effect of the intervention would depend very much on how long one observed the system. If the time horizon was only two years, one might conclude that the effect of the dredging was significant. On the other hand, using all of the data, a test of significance might show marginal if any significance of the dredging project.

System dynamicists look at time series in a different way. For example, in the case represented in Figure 2, one would begin to hypothesize reasons for the growth of attendance just after the change, and why attendance eventually fell to a new level. The S/D modeler might try to represent positive growth and negative processes, such as curiosity, boredom, etc. as a set of interconnected dynamic loops. The method for doing this will be described briefly later. The point here is that there is a difference between the methods of time series analysis described in the previous chapter and the S/D approach. In the former case, one takes the time series pretty much as given, and then decides whether or not the policy took hold, based upon an empirical analysis of the data. The System Dynamicist, on the other hand, first hypothesizes what forces should come into play in this situation. He or she then derives a dynamic structure of the interaction among those forces, followed by building and testing a dynamic model of the situation on the computer. The purpose of these steps is to see whether or not the structure will indicate why the dredging, in the long run, could not produce a large stable increase in attendance at the beach.

Richardson and Pugh (1981), in their introductory text on System Dynamics, illustrate the point about thinking in terms of loop structures by giving an example of managing a public recreation area. In this example, the managers want to initiate a program to increase the quality of outdoor experience and, at the same time, they want to preserve the natural environment as much as possible. Richardson and Pugh show very graphically that one must remember that any program which is instituted to make the quality of wilderness experience better, will, through feedback mechanisms (e.g., such as word of mouth), draw more visitors. Thus, unless other forces intervene, usage goes up and crowding effects increase, causing a drop in the quality of wilderness experience.

The purpose of the program was to increase wilderness experience and to protect the environment. However, because of negative feedback linking the number of visitors, crowding, and the quality of wilderness experience, their management policies brought about opposite effects. An increase in the quality of the outdoor experience, brought about by the programs, increased the number of visitors. More visitors generated crowding and high population density, which affected the environment and led to a decrease in the quality of the outdoor experience, which originally had increased.

6. *Internal Structures:* An interesting aspect of S/D methodology is the emphasis placed upon the role played by internal structure in determining the origin and solution of social problems. It is thought that the causes of most problems are due to internal inadequacies rather than external factors. Frequently, the solution to a problem comes from a change in internal loop structure rather than from a change in the external environment.

System Dynamicists look for ways to buffer the system from exogenous sources, if at all possible. In an application of the method to urban systems, for example, Forrester's model indicated why most federally funded housing projects failed to relieve conditions of overcrowdedness, underemployment, etc. (Forrester 1969). Although at first conditions improve, inhibitory mechanisms embedded within urban system structure come into play and within twenty or thirty years, conditions may become even worse. When systems do not grow towards social goals, frequently the cause is strong dominant negative feedback loops which interfere with change.

There are some systems, of course, where exogenous factors, like weather, do affect the behavior of the system in a major way. Usually, system dynamicists attempt to close the loop structure by broadening the boundary of the system and by deriving at least a small model of the source of input. In many cases, there are important mutual influences between the original smaller system under study and the subsystem inputting into that system. This would provide the basis for extending the model.

7. *Qualitative vs. Quantitative Predictions:*   In most of the applications of statistical modeling techniques, such as regression analysis, to the social sciences, there is a great emphasis upon fitting curves to data points as a major criterion of success. This is particularly true of economists who are called upon to make short-term forecasts. For example, an economist might predict how much interest rates will go up or down in the next three months, or when the stock market will reach its low. Usually system dynamicists are called upon to help analyze problems which are not well defined in many cases, and appear not to disappear over night. S/D methodology is particularly strong on testing long-term impacts of policies. Many of the models will look at the effects of alternative policies over a time horizon of fifty or sixty years, for example.

Since the models address general trends of what would happen given the application of certain policies over very long periods of time, there is less concern about the fitting the model exactly to past or present data than there would be for someone who only wants to forecast what is going to happen two months ahead of time. Also, System Dynamic models are particularly useful in understanding the nature and causes of behavioral and economic cycles (Mass 1975, Forrester 1980, Graham and Senge 1981). Many of those cycles have a length of fifty years or more years and might have profound impacts upon the economy, perhaps even more than short-term cycles.

THE ART OF SYSTEM DYNAMICS MODELING

The preceeding section outlined the general characteristics of the S/D approach to modeling continuous explanatory models. Before describing the modeling process, it might be beneficial to indicate additional sources of information concerning S/D methodology. One of the first texts on S/D methods was written by Forrester himself (Forrester 1961). This is the classical text for industrial dynamics. The appendices are particularly useful in understanding the modeling process. Forrester (1968), Jarmain (1963), and Goodman (1974) have been among those who have contributed to explicating the methodology by publishing extended sets of notes, examples of models, and problems to aid the aspiring modeler in acquiring some degree of facility in building and analyzing models. Coyle (1977) has written a very interesting and useful book on management system dynamics. He has integrated much of what modern engineering has to contribute to the analysis of the dominance of non-linear feedback loops within a System Dynamics framework. In general, it is not an easy book to understand, but for those who have some knowledge of S/D, it is full of rich insights and is quite rewarding.

Table 1

Steps in the Modeling Process

Step	Comments
1. Problem recognition and formulation of dynamic hypothesis	Specifying reference mode and time horizon
2. Formulation	Construction of causal loop diagram
3. Dynamic equation writing	Flow diagrams and computer equations
4. Testing the model	Comparison with reference mode. Other explicit test
5. Evaluating, communication, diffusion of study insights	Sensitivity testing, policy analysis

Stages of Modeling

Recently system dynamicists have become more concerned with methodological issues, such as using more powerful parameter estimation procedures. A book edited by Randers (1980) addresses many of these issues and gives a reader an excellent idea of the modeling process, estimation of parameters, etc. The book also gives procedures for implementing the model as a useful policy book. Several case studies, including efforts to model problems within the public domain, such as those encountered at Scandinavian forest sector development, give helpful hints about achieving implemented results from System Dynamics projects.

The most general text on the System Dynamics approach to modeling has recently been written by Richardson and Pugh (1981). This is an outstanding text in the area, covering more aspects of modeling social and economic problem areas using the S/D approach. The book has clear examples and illustrations of the art of modeling social processes. In addition, it describes the use of the DYNAMO, a computer simulation language frequently used by System Dynamicists for specifying and running models on the computer.

There is also a second general text, written by Roberts et. al., entitled *Introduction to Computer Simulation, the System Dynamics Approach,* which should prove to be extremely helpful for learning the modeling process. It was written by an interdisciplinary group of modelers whose backgrounds range from public administration to chemistry. They show applications to a variety of fields, and demonstrate, through numerous exercises, the general principles of model building and policy analysis.

Randers (1980) was one of the first to describe this process of modeling in detail. The general stages of the System Dynamics approach are outlined in Table 1. One should realize that the real life process of model building involves continual movement back and forth through these stages, and that there are considerable individual differences among System Dynamic modelers with respect to spending time in each stage.

1. *Problem Recognition:*   The first step in the modeling process is to formulate the problem in exact detail. Usually problem formulation should be accomplished by working with an advisory group, such as a group of decision-makers who are familiar with the system and can develop a set of statements concerning where the system is displaying unsatisfactory behavior. Once a small set of problems have been described, the usual method for representing the problem is to draw it as a graph of how variables perceived to be important change over time. This graph does not have to be completely accurate nor be based upon totally "hard" data. The purpose is to represent the qualitative aspects of the problem, per se. The quantitative aspects might come later. In any event, this time graph is called a reference mode.

The reference mode provides the modeler with a blue-print of the level of aggregation and the relative degree of details needed to look at a problem, as well as the time horizon to be modeled. Also, once the modelers obtain the reference mode, it gives them an initial idea of what is perceived as the key concepts and variables of the system which are used by people facing the problem. Every effort is made in system dynamics to tie each variable to usable concepts. Rarely does one find arbitrary parameters in these models which have no realistic meaning for those who would be using the model. Indeed, if the modeling procedure is correctly followed, all variables will be closely examined to screen out ambiguity and more realistic concepts substituted for them.

2. *Specification of a Dynamic Hypothesis:*   The next stage is to develop the major organizing concepts to characterize the causes of the problem, specified in stage 1. The organization takes the form of two or three central feedback loops composed of half a dozen variables. When one has a good organizing concept, suddenly everything becomes much clearer and the structure begins to emerge. Moreover, even though systems appear to be radically different in form, frequently upon analyses there are communalities of structure which aid in understanding the problems in greater depth as well as their solutions.

Once the organizing concepts have been specified, one next develops clear causal loop diagrams, so that the modeler can communicate his or her understanding to others. This procedure clarifies hidden assumptions and aids in gaining better insight concerning the relative effects of each positive and negative loop at this early stage of the modeling process.

Briefly, the causal loop diagram displays the dynamic hypothesized relationships among variables. Methods for the construction of these diagrams have been developed by system dynamicists and other system scientists, such as Warfield (1976), who has become interested in generation of causal structure. The major way to discover the pathways among variables is to only consider the relationship of two variables at a time, considering all other variables constant, for that moment. Given variables X and Y, for example, one asks if an increase in X increases Y, decreases Y, or has no effect on Y. Again all other factors which normally may enter in must be eliminated from consideration for the moment.

Most experts in any given problem area at first find this task extremely difficult, for they know too much about possible interaction effects among variables. The idea here is to put all the effects of other variables out of one's mind for the moment, somewhat analogous to finding a partial correlation between the two variables, with all other variables partialled out. Additional effects of those other variables can be looked at later, using the same method. Once this procedure is learned, there is usually an amazing consistance among people making judgments about relationships. Feedback loop structure soon begins to emerge giving some idea about how various state variables grow or decline over time.

The recreational example suggested by Richardson and Pugh (1981) might serve to illustrate some of these points. Suppose a manager of a national forest area was having an increased problem with environmental damage, crowding of hikers on trails, and a decrease in reported quality of wilderness experience by those using the area. He or she might work with a System Dynamicist to analyze the nature of the problem and to evaluate the one or more policies, such as building more trails, encouraging the use of less-traveled trails, and in general, providing more services to increase the quality of outdoor experience.

Once the problem has been defined in terms of the reference mode, the system dynamicist might present the manager with a set of structural loops to represent major dynamic hypotheses concerning the mechanisms underlying the development of the problem. This situation has been simplified a bit by only showing in Figure 3 part of what might be presented to the manager. Usually at this stage,

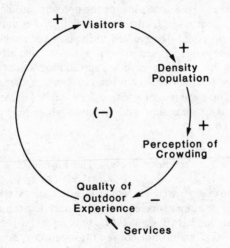

Figure 3

Negative Loop Representing the Dynamic Interaction of the Quality of Outdoor Experience and the Number of Visitors to A Recreation Facility

one might focus upon three or four major explanatory loops, but an attempt here is to keep it simple.

The causal diagram, Figure 2, was formulated in the following way. Assuming that all factors (such as contact area) remain constant, then an increase in visitors per year should increase population density. Again under the same constancy assumption, an increase in population density increases the perception of crowding. On the other hand, increases in the perception of crowding decreases the quality of outdoor experience. And finally, to close the loop, an increase in the quality of outdoor experience will increase the number of visitors per year.

Examining the loop in the figure, one finds that it represents a negative feedback process. Why is this the case? First, begin increasing visitors per year. An increase in this variable increases population density, which in turn, is perceived by the recreationist as an increase in crowding. The more crowded the area is perceived, the less the quality of the outdoor experience. A decrease in this variable will decrease the number of visitors per year which initially had been increasing.

Now consider the effect of services on the quality of outdoor experience. In looking at the relationship between services and the quality of experience variable, it is important to mentally screen out the potential effect of the perception of crowdedness which a moment ago we had considered. Services, such as better maintained trails, will increase the attractability of the forest area and hence increase the quality of outdoor experience. Quality has multiple (only two in this simple case) causes. The quality of outdoor experience increases with an increase in services and decreases when the perception of crowding goes up.

Although only one explanatory loop has been considered, the System Dynamicist can already point out some of the potential problems of initiating a new policy of putting more funds into service activities. The purpose of the policy is to prevent environmental damage and to increase the quality of outdoor experience. At first increasing services will appear to have that effect, but as part of a negative feedback loop, in time word will spread around that the area is a good place to go. Visitors will then increase instead of decrease, damaging the environment even more. These are the long-term effects implied in this one loop structure, which have to be taken into consideration when designing policy which might solve the problem.

3. *Formulation of the Computer Model:*   This stage involves the identification of the major state variables, rates, delays of various types, and what system dynamicists call auxiliary variables, which in effect break down complex rate equations into shorter more manageable expressions. The causal loop diagrams, unlike path analytic models (Blalock 1969), only represent general relationships among the variables. They do not convey information concerning the specific non-linearities of the system. The next step is to draw a "flow diagram" showing precise interrelationships of the state variables, which accumulate over time, and their rates of change. One can go from this flow diagram representation of the dynamic system to a set of computer equations with very little difficulty. The non-linear relationships are placed right within the framework of the simulation model by either writing out explicit equations or formulating tables to represent the hypothesized non-linear functional relationship between variables.

At this point, the first version of the model has been formulated and represented as a computer simulation model. Next, the parameter values (time constants) will be selected. During the early stages, system dynamicists frequently will use rough estimates of the time constants. There is no need at that moment to initiate a costly research program to obtain more precise data. In many cases, "ball park figures" will serve to get the model off the ground and running for further examination and refinement.

Various estimation procedures have been used to fit dynamic models to empirical time series data (e.g., see Senga 1977, Graham 1980, Hamilton 1980, Peterson 1980). The topic of estimating the parameters of non-linear models goes far beyond the scope of this chapter.[2] It is, however important to note that most of the standard statistical methods for estimating the size of the parameters break down in the case of non-linear systems. In recent years, Peterson and Schweppe (1974) have developed a program called GPSIE, which handles many of the problems encountered by traditional statistical estimation procedures.

Consider now how one goes about putting the model onto the computer. Although it has been implied that the model can be represented as a computer program, little has been said about what that program might look like. This section will be concluded by briefly describing some of the computer languages used by S/D modelers. The interested reader is also referred to the journal *Simulation,* published by the Society for Computer Simulation, which has a number of articles introducing other approaches to continuous simulation modeling languages.

Historically, however, System Dynamics has used DYNAMO as a vehicle for representing the dynamic model on the computer. DYNAMO is a very useful tool for making the approach practical. It was developed and is maintained by Pugh-Roberts Associates of Cambridge, Massachusetts. The language has been adapted to be run on most large mainframe computers. They also have a MINI-DYNAMO version which runs on a number of mini-computers. Finally, a MICRO-DYNAMO has been released for the Apple computer, and is distributed by Addison-Wesley Publishing Company. This version requires PASCAL and the Apple language card.

Another language similar to DYNAMO was developed at the University of Bradford, United Kingdom. The language is called DYSMAP, and it has very extensive facilities for model checking and analysis. DYSMAP can run on a number of mainframe computers.

There are a few other simulation langauges patterned after DYNAMO, which can be used on some smaller computers. ND-TRAN, developed at the University of Notre Dame, can run on some of the more powerful mini-computers made by Digital Equipment Corporation.

There is another similar computer simulation language called MYNAMO, which is written in BASIC. MYNAMO runs on a number of mini-computers, including Hewlett-Packard computer models (HP1000, HP2000, and HP3000), and the PDP 1140. Information concerning this language can be obtained from

---

[2]A discussion of the details concerning estimation procedures goes beyond the cope of this book. The interested reader can write us for a copy of the original manuscript which described in detail a number of sophisticated filtering methods for optimal estimation of model parameters.

Stochos, Inc., Schenectady, New York. Stochos also offers a micro version of the language, called MICRODYN, for CP/M based computers. The models are written in either CBASIC or CB-80, a compiled version of CBASIC. Programming a model on a micro using this simulation language is quite easy. All the hard parts are taken over by the MICRODYN program, and it is menu driven so that the user is guided through the process of transferring the model to the computer in easy steps.

Finally, there are those who like to use more general purpose languages, such as FORTRAN or PASCAL for simulation. Most of the basic subroutines, functions, and processes needed to generate delays, table functions, formatted output, and graphs are not too very difficult to program, once you understand the logical principles underlying them. At Michigan State University, through the auspices of the Department of Agricultural Economics and the Department of System Science, a library of FORTRAN subprograms for use in simulation studies are available. These were developed originally for an extremely large simulation study of the Nigerian agricultural sector performed at Michigan State University about a decade ago (Johnson 1971, Manetsch 1974).

4. *Testing the Model:*   Once the model has been formulated and the time constants have been chosen, the next step is to specify initial values of all of the state variables in the system. This is what the state of the system is defined to be at the start of the simulation run. Many times the system dynamicist will pick a point of equilibrium, where the system is stable at least momentarily, as the initial state. The simulation run might start off that way, and then, after a certain number of time periods, part of the system will be changed to represent the initiation of a new condition, such as a new law, the influx of a new group, or perhaps the introduction of a new policy.

The testing phase is one of the most exciting parts of the simulation process. There are many tests that must be made before one can be confident enough to use it in policy purposes. Since the dynamic hypothesis was formulated to gain insight into the nature of the problem being modeled, the first test is to check whether or not those loop mechanisms can lead to the reproduction of the reference mode, recalling that the reference mode represents the original problem. There is no guarantee that the model's theoretical curves will look anything like the reference mode. For example, if the reference mode addressed the problem associated with housing cycles, one would ask whether the proposed loop structure generates cyclic behavior similar to the reference mode. If the reference mode goes up, overshoots, and then goes down again such as in Figure 2, which shows the response of recreationists to the dredging of a lake, can the model predict overshoot? It is the qualitative characteristics of the behavior that are important, at least at that point.

Once the model can reproduce the reference mode, then it can be examined more closely both by the modeler and by the decision-maker, who will eventually use the model as a policy tool. Several questions concerning the nature and number of variables come to mind. Does the model exclude any important variables, even though it can reproduce the reference mode? In many cases, the decision-maker will broaden the problem a bit and want the model to include more detail to make it seem more realistic. In addition, some values of the time constants may not seem correct. For example, if the time horizon is broadened slightly, some of the time constants may not remain constant during longer periods of time, and they will have to be modeled as variables influencing the system.

Forrester and Senge (1978) discuss a number of tests for building confidence in System Dynamics models. Space does not allow us to enumerate the details of these tests. There is one test, however, which is particularly interesting and useful in evaluating the validity of one's model. This is called the "surprise behavior test." This test is performed when unexpected results are shown in the output of the model. The model is then used to understand the dynamic mechanisms underlying the emergence of this surprise behavior. If the model explains the plausibility of the emerging behavior, then the next step is to compare the behavior and its causes to those in the actual system being modeled.

An example of the model's ability to discover and understand the emergence of new behavior, comes from a corporate sector model derived by Richmond (1981), who considered why some companies appear to suddenly fail for very little known reason, except for bad management. Richmond explored those conditions where a company had all the normal signs of health for long periods of time, and yet suddenly, in some simulation runs, the corporation changed from a healthy to an unhealthy status overnight and soon went bankrupt. He was able to show under what conditions the cumulative negative effects of so-called "minor" variables contributed to the company's demise.

If the model does show surprise behavior, which can be understood by tracing through the dynamics of the model, then one can look for those same mechanisms and behaviors in the real system. If those phenomena have been identified correctly, then the surprise-behavior test gives additional validity to the model.

5. *Implementation:* The last stage really might be divided into three major divisions. First there is a period of further testing and analysis of the model to see its reactions to small changes in conditions. This is called sensitivity analysis. Secondly, the model is explored to ascertain the impacts of policies suggested by decision-makers to solve the problem. The last phase deals with the actual implementation of the model as a useful planning tool, applied on an on-going basis.

Once the previous testing stage has been completed, both the modeler and the people who will be using the model for future applications will have gained some degree of knowledge about the validity of the models. The sensitivity analysis which follows is actually an extension of the previous period of probing the model for its strong points as well as its inadequacies. This time one attempts to find the model's robustness with respect to small perturbations of the model's variables, parameters, non-linear relationships, and lastly, feedback structure itself.

In statistical approaches to modeling social behavior, such as regression analysis or analysis of variance, one not only finds whether or not a given variable is statistically significant, but also the importance of each significant variable in the equation. Although this can be somewhat tricky in the case of regression analysis (Hunter and Levine, in press), in general one finds that indeed some variables have a great effect on the system, while others play only a minor role. If the important variables are variables one can control and manipulate, then future policies should be geared toward those variables that have the most effect on the system.

In system dynamic models, there is an additional element, namely a structure of positive and negative feedback loops to represent growth and inhibitory processes. This difference, coupled with the fact that most S/D models have a very large number of variables, usually leads to a very different result. Most variables have little effect on the quantitative predictions of the model. Moreover, seldom do most variables have even qualitative effects on the behavior of the system over time. This is because the feedback structures compensate for any changes in variables. Thus, for example, if under normal conditions, the system grows rapidly for a period of time and then eventually levels off, it will display a very similar s-shaped curve to that which would be generated when the value of most variables are doubled. The only difference between the two cases is that in the new case, the leveling off stage occurs a bit faster. The shape of the curve remains basically the same.

This principle appears to be true when quantitative modifications of non-linear relations are introduced. It should be recalled that DYNAMO and other simulation languages have facilities for generating table functions of relationships between variables. Usually the modeler has a general idea about the shape of the non-linear function, but cannot specify the exact shape on a point by point basis. The question is whether or not it really matters. During the sensitivity analysis phase, the modeler can make one simulation run using the original table function and then make a series of runs in which the table function is modified. This provides a test of how radical a change has to be made to obtain a reversal of the behavioral trends. The original table function is usually constructed as rationally

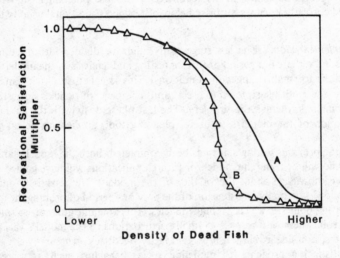

Figure 4

Two Qualitatively Similar Curves

as possible, given the literature, common sense, and/or the judgments of experts. In general, it is found that most reasonable modifications of the shape of the function have little ultimate qualitative impact on the system.

Suppose one has hypothesized a relationship between the density of dead fish on a beach and recreational user satisfaction. Figure 4 shows a set of theoretical curves which are qualitatively similar to each other. The idea here is that at first, low densities have very little impact on satisfaction for the multiplier effect is approximately 1.0. However, at intermediate density levels, satisfaction drops off. In curve A, the drop is less sharp than curve B, which may perhaps be closer to reality, let us say. In the context of a simulation run, the difference in effects between the two functions may be very minor, for both may lead to the same general conclusions.

Sometimes a particular variable or table function can change the system quite radically with only a small perturbation. This has at least two consequences. First, empirically, since most of the other variables had little effect on the system, finding a sensitive variable or relationship should indicate the area in which further empirical research and modeling should be performed to better understand why the variables were so powerful. This is much more efficient and economical than attempting to gather data on the system as a whole. Secondly, if and when a crucial variable or relationship has been discovered, then undoubtedly it should be stressed as a policy variable, if it can be observed and controlled by the manager or decision-maker.

Within these models, by far the most powerful effects are generated by changes in loop structure. If you want to assess the impact of a specific loop on the model's behavior, the first way is to put the loop out of commission by setting the value of one of the variables of the loop equal to a constant. This value should be within the normal operating range of the chosen variable, so that the prior runs with the loop intact will be comparable. By making one of the variables in a loop constant, you are in effect making the loop insensitive to changes in any of the other variables in that loop. There is no differential response to changes any more, for the response of a constant (which was previously a variable) will always be the same, no matter whether there was an initial increase or decrease around the loop.

The behavior of the model can be systematically studied in additional simulation runs by selectively turning on and off the positive and negative loop structure underlying the dynamics. Not all loops are as important as others. The study of the relative dominance of one feedback loop over the other is an extremely important subject. Coyle (1977) has an excellent discussion of this topic for those interested readers.

In the realm of policy analysis, again it is important to specify information flows in the system in the form of loop structure. For those loops already in the model, the effects of eliminating the selective loops can be ascertained by the method described previously. On the other hand, sometimes policies will be suggested at a later stage after the initial model has been analyzed and the mechanisms underlying the problem are better understood. It may be necessary at that point to elaborate the model a bit so that the impacts of the new policies can be studied in more detail. This would enlarge the boundary of the model somewhat, but the cost might still be worth it.

Here is an example of this process. Manetsch (1977) used simulation modeling to study the factors leading to world food shortages and starvation. He developed a general simulation model of how a country might survive during a sudden acute food shortage. His methods were quite similar to those used by the System Dynamicists. During the policy analysis phase, Manetsch attempted to apply most of the government policies suggested in the literature, such as supplementing the supply of food by emptying the government's food reserves, or initiating price controls to keep the price of food from rising. All those simulated policies eventually failed and were not adequate to prevent wide spread starvation in the simulated population. The policy that did work, and only under very delicate conditions, was one of initiating a food rationing system. The government had to be very sensitive to subtle indicators of the coming calamity and must have had enough lead time to get the rationing into motion for this policy to be successful.

Not all of the ramifications of the rationing policy were known at the sensitivity stage of the model building process. It did show an area that needed expansion. Manetsch and his associates knew then what part of the model needed more elaboration, namely the design of an information system that would be capable of sensing early warning signals of food shortages.

Another facit of the implementation stages is translating the insights gained from the model into an accessible form for others to use. System Dynamicists attempt as much as possible to work with the decision-maker at all of the previous stages. It is very helpful having staff members from the company or organization as part of the research team. An even better practice is to get the top administrators involved in checking the assumptions, suggesting additional factors, and getting the benefit of using the model as a policy tool.

Quite frankly, administrators are usually quite critical of simulation modeling at first. If you can get them to become involved in keeping the model addressed to the organization's problem, the model will most likely be accepted, and eventually used. This is because the person who is going to apply the tool understands where the model came from, and has contributed to most phases of model development. In addition, he or she has had the opportunity to test its validity at many stages along the way. Thus the administrator has both developed confidence in the model and has a realistic idea of the model's boundaries and limitations. For the interested reader, Roberts (1978) does an excellent job describing how to make a good model into a practical tool, and Lyneis (1981) discusses methods for making the model more effective in preventing the problem from reoccuring after it has been solved once.

AN EXAMPLE OF POLICY ANALYSIS IN RECREATION

In the previous survey chapter and in other places in this book, characteristics of gravity models were described in detail. In his research on recreational usage, the first author of this chapter has used the S/D approach to extend the power of the gravity model to predict long-term trends in recreational choice and behavior (Levine 1981). The motivation for developing this model came from an interest in the dynamics of recreational behavior, as well as in response to pressing applied problems faced by the tourism industry in Michigan and by state recreational officials. The economic climate in the midwest has steadily declined over the past three years. Even though currently there appears to be an oil glut, the combination of high gasoline prices and unemployment can have a powerful negative effect on the tourist industry, as well as on the use of our recreation resources far from urban centers. The problem was expressed well through conversations with officials of the Michigan Department of Natural Resources, who were very aware of the implications of the changing energy picture. Their scenario for the future, which was used as the reference mode for the model, was that if economic conditions worsen, outdoor recreational patterns will change profoundly over the years. There will be a switch to activities which do not depend as much on extensive traveling, and the demand for local outdoor recreation facilities will eventually outstrip the supply. They forecasted an initial increase in the number of recreators going to nearby parks, followed by a steady decline of visitors as transportation costs went up, and people changed to neighborhood recreational activities.

These were long-term forecasts, spanning a time horizon of perhaps sixty years or more. Levine hypothesized that the inertia model, mentioned in the previous chapter would break down under rising costs of gasoline and the original gravity model would better describe user behavior. However, there is no way to utilize the gravity model in its static form to make projections over such a long time span. The modal can be made dynamic though. Cesario (1975) simulated the usage of a system of parks in northeastern Pennsylvania on an hourly basis during a single day. Since the current problem dealt mostly with changes in trip costs which take much longer periods of time to change and have an effect on recreators, many of the factors, which would be constant in a single day, were allowed to vary in this model. It was also known that there were significant time delays for recreators to perceive changes in population density, attractivity, and other conditions at each recreational site. The author wanted to find the impact of these time delays as the system changed characterstics.

It was realized early that the interaction among recreational sites had to be captured directly within the structure of the model. Some gravity models incorporate this interaction by including a competing opportunity factor as part of the model.In the S/D model, it was hypothesized that an increase in the use of one park would mean a decrease in the use of a second park and vice versa. Also, the dynamics of the recreational populations involved had to be specified, allowing them to leave the region when the economic conditions were too unfavorable. Finally, a set of hypotheses concerning the mechanisms for switching from the outdoor recreation under study to another set of activities which required little or no travel was developed. This was based upon the total attractive strength of the recreation facility nearest the person's origin.

Currently the model is at the early stages of testing and policy analysis. The recreation patterns for the use of beaches in a large region were simulated over a period starting from conditions approximated in 1970 (about four years before the original energy crisis), to the year 2020. The qualitative characteristics of the output of the simulation model matched the original reference mode. Indeed, as economic tensions built up, the overall population of the region decreased by emigration from the area and the distribution of usage of parks shifted from more distant, more attractive parks, to beaches nearer to home. As time went on, however, even here usage declined.

As far as is known, this is one of the first System Dynamics models to simulate dynamic interactions at the regional level of aggregation. The nearest to that, of course, are the urban dynamics models mentioned previously. The difference between the urban models and the present regional model is that the present model is concerned with what happened to recreational behavior in both time and space. Indeed, one of the first ideas generated from the examination of the model's output dealt with a suggestion that the problem of the demand for local recreation facilities could be met by the development of urban parks. The model can address itself to the impacts of locating any new facility at any spot in the region. By including the spatial dimension within the framework of the model, it opens up the possibility of using this dynamic simulation approach for locational purposes when conditions, such as concentrations of recreationists, shift in time.

The basic mechanism for predicting usage stemmed from the application of any relatively well established model of decision-making developed by Luce (1959). In some areas of learning and decision-making, this model still enjoys a certain degree of popularity today (e.g., see Prelec 1982). Also, within the recreation area, Goodchild and Booth (1980) have applied the static version of the Luce model to solve locational and allocation problems. Although Goodchild and Booth were more concerned with optimal solutions to these problems, their approach to recreation choice is very closely allied to the approach taken by this System Dynamics model.

The fundamental assumption of the Luce model of choice is that relative preference between two alternatives are added or deleted from a set of choices. For example, suppose there are only two recreational choices in the region. If 60 percent of the recreational population goes to site A and 40 percent to B, then the relative preference is the ratio of A to B or 1.5. Next, consider building one additional facility, C. Now there are three facilities to choose from, but according to the Luce model, the new ratio of A to B under these new conditions will again be equal to 1.5, even though the percentages that went into the ratio of A to B might be different. Thus, for example, one might find that now, with three alternatives, 21 percent went to A, 14 percent went to B, and 65 percent went to the third alternative. The percentages going to the first two sites may have changed but the ratio of the two remains equal to 1.5.

A set of simulation runs were initiated to test the logic of the model more extensively and to evaluate the impacts of building and introducing two new urban parks near one of the large cities in the hypothetical region. The simulation "experiment" started with a total of three large parks in the region (parks #1, #2, #3), and then two other facilities, located near the urban center were systematically introduced in either 1985, 1995, 2005, or the year 2015, depending on the computer run.

For some of the runs, the average price of gasoline was only increased three to five percent per year, which is conservative to say the least. An example of the impacts on annual population density at each of the five sites is given in Figure 5. This particular figure indicates the response of the system when the urban parks were introduced relatively early in the time horizon. Originally, park #2, which in the experimental region was somewhere between two large urban centers, was very popular, simply because of its physical features and its general attractability. However, when in 1985 two new parks, #4 and #5, were introduced, economic conditions were poor enough to draw most of the people to the new urban parks.

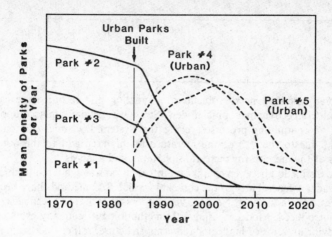

Figure 5

Projected Mean Visitor Density As A Function of the Introduction of
Two New Urban Parks

The population density of site #2, the previously most popular recreational spot, came down very fast. In most cases, the lack of density would enhance its attractive strength. However, in this situation, distance representing trip costs seem to prevail.

When the two new parks were introduced at a later date, such as 2010, for example, the system did not respond as strongly to the establishment of two new sites. It was too late. By then many of the recreationists had shifted activities, and since prices were so high, there was no incentive to shift back to the original outdoor activity.

This gives the reader the flavor of how the dynamic models of recreational behavior can be formulated to predict the impacts of new policies. It might be added that in going through the testing stage, some problems in applying the Luce model came to light. When any new facility was either added (as we just described) or closed, the Luce model predicts that the system will normalize itself, with an appropriate lag, and carry on from there. In general it is known that this is not entirely realistic, for there are what systems analysts call a "hysteresis" effects. What does this mean? Some people become attached to old places and others go to new recreation sites out of curiosity.

Currently the model is being enriched to take into account reasonable positive and negative feedback mechanisms, such as curiosity on the one hand, balanced by the negative loop representing attachment and boredom. If there is a hysteresis effect, then, for the same people, introducing urban parks early would produce more shifting to those new parks than under conditions where the urban parks were developed later in their lives. This is because the recreators would have less time to become attached to the old parks before the urban facilities came on line.

Summary

This chapter described how problems of recreation and resource use can be understood from a dynamic point of view. Stress was primarily placed upon explanation of continuous processes, using the System Dynamics approach to simulation, due to the size of the literature in this area and to the potential usefulness of the method for recreation planning and analysis.

First the distinction between energy and information was again reintroduced to give the reader a general idea of the context in which S/D methods have been applied successfully in the past. Next the very important concept of feedback structure was introduced. Modelers using S/D methodology frequently explain problem behavior in terms of inadequate internal structure, rather than from external causes. The S/D philosophy is translated to a set of operational stages outlined in this chapter. Every effort is made to incorporate the ideas and goals of decision-makers in each stage of the modeling process. This insures that the validity of the model will be tested constantly from early problem formulation to the actual implementation stage.

System Dynamics is an ideal method for getting to understand how problems of recreational behavior developed over time. Another traditional field of systems science comes from optimal control theory, which is devoted solely to addressing normative issues. The two methods can be highly compatible, if used appropriately. The next chapter will describe how to manage continuously changing recreational systems by use of optimal control modeling procedures. When used in conjunction with the System Dynamics approach, optimal control technique should provide decision-makers and planners with an additional and valuable set of tools for analyzing recreational systems.

References

Alfield, L. E., and Graham, A. K. *Introduction to Urban Dynamics.* Cambridge, Massachusetts: Wright-Allen Press, 1976.

Blalock, H. M. *Theory Construction.* Englewood Cliffs, New Jersey: Prentice-Hall, 1969.

Cesario, F. J. "A Simulation Approach to Outdoor Recreation Planning." *Journal of Leisure Research* 7(1975):38-52.

Cole, H. S. D.; Freeman, C.; Johoda, M.; and Pavitt, K. L. R. *Models of Doom: A Critique of the Limits to Growth.* New York: Universe Books, 1973.

Coyle, R. G. *Management System Dynamics.* New York: John Wiley & Sons, 1977.

Forrester, J. W. *Industrial Dynamics.* Cambridge, Massachusetts: M.I.T. Press, 1961.

Forrester, J. W. *Principles of Systems.* Cambridge, Massachusetts: M.I.T. Press, 1968.

Forrester, J. W. *Urban Dynamics.* Cambridge, Massachusetts: M.I.T. Press, 1969.

Forrester, J. W. *World Dynamics.* Cambridge, Massachusetts: Wright-Allen Press, 1973.

Forrester, J. W. "Understanding Economic Change." System Dynamics Group, Alfred P. Sloan School of Management, *M.I.T. Bulletin* #D3210, 1980.

Forrester, J. W., and Senge, P. M. "Tests for Building Confidence in System Dynamics Models." System Dynamics Group, Alfred P. Sloan School of Management, *M.I.T. Bulletin* #D29264, 1978.

Goodchild, M. F., and Booth, P. J. "Location and Allocation of Recreation Facilities: Public Swimming Pools in London, Ontario." *Ontario Geography,* 15(1980): 35-49.

Goodman, M. P. *Study Notes in System Dynamics.* Cambridge, Massachusetts: M.I.T. Press, 1974.

Gordon, G. *System Simulation.* Englewood Cliffs, New Jersey: Prentice-Hall, 1970.

Graham, A. K., and Senge, P. M. "A Long-Waive Hypothesis Innovation." System Dynamics Group, Alfred P. Sloan School of Management, *M.I.T. Bulletin* #D31641, 1981.

Greenberg, S. *GPSS Primer.* New York: John Wiley & Sons, 1972.

Hunter, J. E., and Levine, R. L. "Regression Methodology: Correlation Meta-Analysis, Confidence Intervals, Reliability." *Journal of Leisure Research,* (in press).

Jarmain, E. W. *Problems in Industrial Dynamics.* Cambridge, Massachusetts: M.I.T. Press, 1963.

Johns, G. L. *A Generalized Simulation Approach to A Sector Analysis.* East Lansing, Michigan: Michigan State University, 1971.

Levine, R. L. "A Dynamic Model of Recreational Usage." 1981 Systems Dynamics Research Conference. Rensselaerville, New York, 1981.

Luce, R. D. *Individual Choice Behavior.* New York: John Wiley & Sons, 1959.

Lyneis, J. M. *Corporate Planning and Policy Design: A Dynamics Approach.* Cambridge, Massachusetts: M.I.T. Press, 1980.

Lyneis, J. M. "Increasing the effectiveness of corporate models." 1981 System Dynamics Research Conference. Rensseaerville, New York, 1981.

Manetsch, T. J. "Basic Systems Theory and Concepts Underlying Construction of the Korean Sector Model with Implications for Further Work." United States AID Conference for Evaluation of the Korean Sector Symposium Model. Virginia: Airlie House, 1974.

Manetsch, T. J. "On the Role of System Analysis in Aiding Corporate Facing Acute Food Shortages. *IEEE Transactions on Systems, Man, and Cybenetics,* 7(1977): 264-273.

Mass, N. J. *Readings in Urban Dynamics,* vol. 1. Cambridge, Massachusetts: Wright-Allen Press, 1974.

Mass, N. J. *Economic Cycles: An Analysis of Under.* Cambridge, Massachusetts: Wright-Allen Press, 1975.

Meadows, D. L.; Behrens III, W. W.; Meadows, D. H.; Halle, R. F.; Randers, J.; and Zahn, E. K. O. *Dynamics of a Finite World.* Cambridge, Massachusetts: Wright-Allen Press, 1974.

Meadows, D. L., and Meadows, D. H. *Toward Global Equilibrium.* Cambridge, Massachusetts: Wright-Allen Press, 1973.

Meadows, D. H.; Meadows, D. L.; Randers, J.; and Behrens III, W. W. *The Limits to Growth.* New York: Universe Books, 1972.

Peterson, D. W., and Schweppe, F. C. "Code for a General Purpose System Identifier and Evaluator: GPSIE" *IEEE Transactions on Automatic Control.* AC-19(1974):852-854.

Prelec, D. "Matching, Maximizing, and the Hyperbolic Reinforcement Feedback Function." *Psychological Review,* 89(1982):189-230.

Randers, J. *Elements of the System Dynamics Method.* Cambridge, Massachusetts: M.I.T. Press, 1980.

Rausser, G. C. "Active Learning, Control Theory, and Agricultural Policy." *American Journal of Agricultural Economics,* August 1978, pp. 476-490.

Richardson, G. P., and Pugh, A. L. *Introduction to System Dynamics Modeling with DYNAMO.* Cambridge, Massachusetts: M.I.T. Press, 1981.

Richmund, B. M. "Endogenous Generation of Structural Change in System Dynamics Modelers: An Illustration from a Corporate Context." 1981 System Dynamics Research Conference. Rensselaerville, New York, 1981.

Roberts, E. B. "Strategies for Effective Implementation of Complex Corporate Models." In *Management Applications of System Dynamics,* edited by E. B. Roberts. Cambridge, Massachusetts: M.I.T. Press, 1978.

Roberts, N.; Anderson, D. F.; Deal, R. M.; Garet, M. S.; and Shaffer, W. A. *Introduction to Computer Simulation: the System Dynamics Approach.* Reading, Massachusetts: Addison-Wesley, forthcoming.

Rosenblith, W. A. *Processing Neuroelectric Data.* Cambridge, Massachusetts: M.I.T. Press, 1962.

Savageau, M. A. *Biochemical Systems Analysis*. Reading, Massachusetts: Addison-Wesley, 1976.

Schechter, M., and Lucas, R. C. *Simulation of Recreational Use for Park and Wilderness Management*. Baltimore: The John Hopkins University Press, 1978.

Schroeder, W. W.; Sweeny, R. E.; and Alfield, L. E. *Readings in Urban Dynamics*. vol. 2. Cambridge, Massachusetts: Wright-Allen Press, 1975.

Senge, P. M. Multiplicative formulations in urban dynamics. In *Readings in Urban Dynamics*. vol. 1, edited by W. Schroeder; R. Sweeney; and L. Alfield. Cambridge, Massachusetts: Wright-Allen Press, 1975.

Smith, V. K., and Krutilla, J. V. *Structure and Properties of a Wilderness Travel Simulator*. Baltimore: The Johns Hopkins University Press, 1976.

Stynes, D. J. "An Economic Model of Deer Hunting." *Leisure Sciences*. 3(1980): 99-119.

Warfield, J. N. *Planning, Policy, and Complexity*. New York: John Wiley & Sons, 1976.

Section Three:
Information for
Planning and Management

1

Measuring Visual Features of Recreational Landscapes

Herbert W. Schroeder

Scenic landscapes are an essential part of the experiences of visitors to natural resource recreation areas such as national parks and national forests. Whether sightseeing, hiking, camping, taking photographs, or hunting, recreationists find that attractive natural scenery contributes immensely to their enjoyment of outdoor activities. The importance of the scenic landscape expresses itself through people's decisions about what recreation sites to visit. For example, large numbers of people visit the Grand Canyon every year, primarily to enjoy its spectacular scenic vistas. To provide high quality recreation opportunities and to forecast the amount of use that existing and planned sites will receive, managers and planners need to understand how people perceive landscapes and which landscape features are the most important for creating attractive scenic views.

Attractive landscapes are an important part of users' experiences in natural resource recreation areas. Careful measurement of landscape features can lead to better planning and improve recreation opportunities. Landscape features fall into two broad categories: physical features, which are tangible components of the landscape (e.g., trees and mountains); and perceptual features, which are subjective landscape characteristics (e.g., scenic beauty and mystery). Methods for measuring both kinds of features must satisfy the criteria of reliability, sensitivity, validity, and utility. To illustrate measurement procedures, an example study is described in which physical landscape features were measured in the field. Perceived scenic beauty was evaluated by observers viewing color slides of the landscapes. The study produced a model that predicts how scenic beauty will be affected by managers' decisions to alter the landscape, for example by harvesting timber. Scenic beauty models provide information for designing and locating recreation sites, trails, and roads, and for evaluating the tradeoffs and costs involved in maintaining visually attractive landscapes.

QUANTIFYING LANDSCAPE FEATURES

In the past twenty years, numerous research studies have been done on landscape perception. The general goal of this research has been to quantify landscape features; that is, to use numerical measurements to describe visual characteristics of the landscape. Quantitative measurements of landscape features are important for outdoor recreation management and planning because they allow us to precisely predict how site management will effect landscape quality.

For example, suppose that a forest management plan calls for cutting some mature timber in an area used by hikers and hunters. When the plan is carried out there will be fewer large trees, but the additional sunlight reaching the ground will allow more vegetative ground cover (grass and other herbaceous plants) to grow. Common sense might tell us that removing large old trees will tend to decrease scenic beauty and that increasing vegetative ground cover will tend to enhance it. But what will be the combined effect of both changes occuring at once? Will the positive effect of the increase in ground cover offset the negative effect of the timber harvest? To answer these questions we need precise measurements of specific features of the forest landscape and also of the landscape's overall scenic quality as perceived by users of the forest.

Forest managers must balance many different resource uses, such as timber production, cattle grazing, watershed, wildlife, recreation, and landscape esthetics. Quantitative measurements are necessary for evaluating tradeoffs between these multiple uses. Measuring landscape quality on a numerical scale helps to ensure that scenic enjoyment is given equal footing with other resource uses in planning, rather than being added only as an afterthought.

Planning for recreation sites is easier when landscape features can be measured and when their effects on landscape quality are understood. Models for predicting the amount of use that recreation sites receive require quantitative data about populations and recreation sites. Quantitative measurements of the socioeconomic characteristics of users are routinely recorded in recreation surveys. Measurements of the attractiveness of recreation sites and facilities are also used to increase the accuracy of models for predicting use (Ravenscraft and Dwyer 1978). Landscape scenic beauty is an important aspect of site attractiveness. Therefore, quantitative measurements of landscape features may be an important component of the site attractiveness indices that are frequently used in site demand models.

This chapter will present an overview of basic approaches to visual landscape assessment, followed by an example of a study that measured specific landscape features and derived models for predicting landscape scenic quality. The chapter concludes with a discussion of how landscape measurements may be used in planning and managing outdoor recreation areas and in assessing the costs of providing attractive scenic landscapes. For extensive reviews of the landscape assessment literature, see Arthur and Boster (1976), Arthur et. al. (1977), as well as the forthcoming reviews by Zube et. al. (in press) and Daniel and Vining (in press).

DEFINING LANDSCAPE FEATURES

Before we can measure features of the landscape, we must decide which features to measure and what methods to use for measuring them. Features must be defined so that they are relevent to management and planning concerns, and so that they can be readily measured using the resources available to the planner or manager. Features studied in landscape perception research may be placed into two broad categories: physical features and perceptual features.

Physical features are tangible components of the landscape, such as trees and landforms, that influence the overall quality of the landscape. That is, physical feature measurements reflect objective elements of the landscape that combine to determine the scenic quality of the landscape as perceived by users. A wide variety of physical landscape features and characteristics can be measured for example: numbers of trees, area of water, thickness of ground cover, and prominence of distant mountains. Physical feature measurements are useful because they allow us to anticipate how people will respond to the landscape, based on our knowledge of objectively measured landscape features.

Perceptual features represent subjective characteristics of recreational landscapes as experienced by users. Perceptual measures such as "scenic beauty" often are defined to reflect people's overall preference for or enjoyment of the landscape (Daniel and Boster 1976). The goal in measuring features such as scenic beauty is to assign numbers to particular landscapes so that preferred or beautiful landscapes receive the highest numbers. Such measurements are of concern to the recreation planner because ultimately the recreator's decision of what sites to visit depends on his or her subjective impression of the attractiveness of the site.

Perceptual features may also be defined to reflect more specific psychological attributes or components of the landscape. For example, the overall quality of a landscape may depend on how people perceive its coherence, complexity, and mystery (Kaplan 1975). Psychological attributes such as these may help us to understand the basic processes by which people perceive and evaluate landscapes. Because perceptual features involve individuals' subjective reactions to landscapes, they cannot be measured in as direct and objective a way as physical features. But this does not mean that they cannot be measured. As will be seen below, well-established methods exist for measuring perceptual features of landscapes.

CRITERIA FOR DESIGNING LANDSCAPE MEASUREMENT SYSTEMS

Before methods for measuring landscape features can be designed for use in recreation planning, we need to know the characteristics of a good measurement system. "Goodness" of a measurement system can be judged according to a number of criteria. Several important standards for measurement are summarized below (Daniel 1976).

Reliability A measurement method is reliable if it yields the same results when it is applied repeatedly to the same set of landscapes. For example, a procedure for measuring the sizes of trees is reliable if it gives the same results when applied to the same landscape on different days and by different people (assuming, of course, that the trees have not grown appreciably between the measurements).

No measurement system is completely reliable; there are always some random variations when measurements are made. If these random errors are large, the measurements will be of little use. One way to improve the reliability of a measurement system is to make many measurements of the same features. When the repeated measurements are averaged together, the random errors tend to cancel out and a higher degree of reliability can be achieved.

Sensitivity A good landscape measurement system must be sensitive to differences in relevant features among landscapes. A measurement scheme that gives the same result with all landscapes is reliable because it can be repeated with consistent results, but it is of no use to a planner or manager. Management decisions must be based on the differences that result from alternative landscape management plans, so a landscape measurement system must be able to reflect those differences.

Validity A measurement scale is valid if it actually measures the landscape feature that it was designed to measure. For example, schemes for measuring landscape scenic quality often require individuals to rate their preference for landscapes shown in photographs. The measurement system would be invalid if ratings were determined more by the skill of the photographer than by the appearance of the landscape itself. Careful design and testing of measurement procedures are important to ensure that measurements of landscape features are valid, especially when subjective judgments are involved.

Utility A final standard for evaluating landscape measurements is utility; that is, can the measurements be easily and economically applied to actual landscape management decisions. A measuring scheme that is reliable, sensitive, and valid will still be useless if it costs so much to apply that no one can afford to use it, or if it takes so long to carry out that the information is not available in time to make decisions. Important tradeoffs must be made in developing landscape measurement systems, because greater reliability and validity can usually only be obtained at greater cost.

METHODS FOR MEASURING LANDSCAPE FEATURES

There are as many ways of measuring landscape features as there are features to measure. The choice of a measurement method depends on the particular needs and uses for which the measurements are being made as well as on the funds and resources available for data collection.

Measuring Physical Features

Measurements of physical landscape features can be made in the field using standard forest mensuration (measurement) methods (Husch et. al. 1972). For example, Schroeder and Daniel (1981) measured forest landscape features such as number of trees per acre, tree diameters, amount of vegetative ground cover, and amount of downed wood. Forest management plans are usually developed using field inventory data about these kinds of physical resources. Therefore a landscape assessment system that uses field inventory data can be readily applied to forest planning decisions.

Measurements of physical landscape features can also be made from photographs of the landscape. One approach is to measure the area of the photograph covered by particular landscape features such as vegetation, water, and mountains (Shafer et. al. 1969, Buhyoff and Leuschner 1978, Buhyoff and Riesenman 1979). The measurements can be made by placing a square grid over the photograph and counting the number of grid cells covered by each landscape feature.

Another approach to estimating physical landscape features was used by Arthur (1977). She had observers view photographs of forest landscapes and make rating-scale judgments of the amount of several forest features present in each photograph (e. g., downed wood, vegetative ground cover, tree density, and tree size).

Obtaining physical feature data from photographs of landscapes is often less expensive and less time-consuming than field inventories. However, the information may be less easy to apply to management decisions because it is not as directly related to the landscape features with which managers must deal. For example, it is difficult to say exactly how the area of a photograph covered by foreground vegetation will change as a result of the decision to harvest 60 percent of the mature timber in a forest stand.

Measuring Perceptual Features

Perceptual features of landscapes cannot be measured as directly as physical features, but there are well established procedures that can be used to quantify people's perceptions of landscapes. Most commonly, individuals are instructed to use a rating scale (e. g., from 1 to 10) to express their perception of a subjective attribute of a landscape. Alternatively, individuals may be shown pairs of landscapes and instructed to choose the member of each pair possessing more of a specific attribute (Buhyoff and Wellman 1980). The landscapes are usually presented to the observers as photographs or in other pictorial forms. Of course observers could be brought to the actual landscapes to make their judgments, but this is much more expensive and time-consuming. For many applications photographs are the most practical method for representing landscapes, provided, of course, that they adequately represent the appearance of the real landscape.

Individuals' subjective judgments of landscape features may be analyzed in a number of ways. Frequently, ratings from a group of observers are simply averaged together to form a single mean rating for each landscape. Theories of psychological perception and measurement also provide procedures for standardizing ratings of subjective features and constructing numerical scales of perceived attributes (Thurstone 1927, Torgerson 1958, Guilford 1954). Daniel and Boster (1976) developed a procedure based on the theory of signal detectibility (Green and Swets 1966) for analyzing observers' ratings of landscape photographs and obtaining measurements of perceived scenic beauty. A series of tests showed that these procedures are reliable and sensitive and that they produce

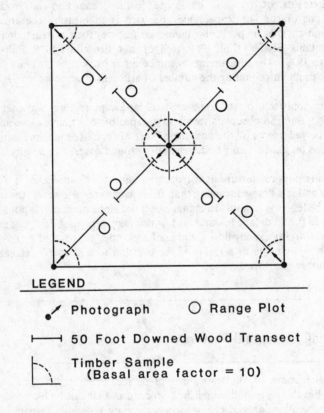

LEGEND

✓• Photograph   ◯ Range Plot

⊢—⊣ 50 Foot Downed Wood Transect

⌐◡ Timber Sample
     (Basal area factor = 10)

Figure 1

Sampling Locations For Photographs

valid indices of landscape scenic quality. Comparisons between ratings of photographs and ratings made on-site by observers viewing the actual landscapes, showed that photographs adequately represented the appearance of the land-scapes. The next section will describe how this approach was used along with measurements of physical landscape features to develop models for predicting landscape scenic quality.

Example Study

To illustrate the uses of landscape measurement procedures, I will describe a study by Schroeder and Daniel (1981) in which physical and perceptual features of forest landscapes were measured. The purpose of the study was to provide forest managers with information about how alternative timber management plans would affect the scenic beauty perceived by recreators using the forest. To ensure that the results of the study would conform as closely as possible to the in-formation that forest managers commonly deal with, physical features of the forest that would be affected by timber management actions were measured using standard forest inventory procedures. The perceptual landscape feature in this study was the scenic quality of the forest.

Measurement of Physical Features

Ninety 1-acre square plots were selected in Ponderosa pine forests in northern Arizona, representing a wide range of forest conditions and landscapes. Feature measurements were made on each of the plots (Figure 1). To increase reliability, each physical feature on each plot was measured eight times and then these measurements were averaged to give one mean value for each feature per plot. Three general types of physical features were measured: timber, vegetative ground cover (range), and downed wood.

Timber   Trees were inventoried according to species and size using an angle-count cruise (Husch et. al. 1972). Trees were counted from points at the center and corners of the 1-acre plot. Tree counts were later converted into estimates of trees per acre of each species in each of several size classes.

Ground cover   Shrubs and nonwoody vegetative ground cover were measured on small sample plots close to the diagonals of the 1-acre plot. The weight of each species of plants growing within each small sample plot was estimated by eye. One randomly selected sample plot was clipped at each inventory site and the plants were weighed. The actual weights were compared to the estimated weights and the other field estimates were adjusted accordingly. Field estimates were finally con-verted to estimates of pounds per acre of vegetative ground cover.

Downed wood   Downed wood on each 1-acre plot was measured by placing a 50 foot transect on the diagonals of each plot and then recording the number and size of pieces of downed wood crossing the transect (Brown 1974). Downed wood was recorded as either natural or man-caused (slash). This information was con-verted to estimates of the volume of downed wood on the 1-acre plots.

Measurement of Scenic Quality

To represent the appearance of the forest landscape, eight photographs were taken of each plot: four at the center of the plot and one from each corner. The photographs were later shown to groups of observers who rated them on a 1 to 10 scale of scenic quality. These ratings were converted into standardized scenic beauty estimates (SBE's) (Daniel and Boster 1976). The SBE's for the eight photographs of each plot were averaged into a single estimate of the scenic quality of the forest landscape.

Scenic Beauty Model

The next step, after measuring the physical and perceptual features of the ninety forest plots, was to study the relation between the physical landscape features and perceived scenic quality using multiple regression analysis. The analysis tells how information about forest physical features can be combined to predict the perceived scenic quality of the forest. Using the data collected on the field plots, we found that the following equation predicted scenic quality for Ponderosa pine landscapes:

$$SBE = .0808\ HB + .3503\ LP - .0160\ SL \qquad\qquad (1)$$
$$+ .6180\ SH - .0795\ MP + 3.43$$

where

SBE = scenic beauty estimate,
HG = herbaceous ground cover (lbs/acre),
LP = large (> 16" diameter) pine (trees/acre),
SL = slash (cubic ft./acre),
SH = shrubs (lbs/acre), and
MP = medium (5-16" diameter) pine (trees/acre).

This equation provides managers with a "model" of the forest landscape. That is, if they know how a proposed site management plan will affect the physical features of the landscape, they can use the equation to predict how scenic quality will change if the plan is carried out.

USING LANDSCAPE MEASUREMENTS IN RECREATION PLANNING

Landscape measurement can provide valuable information for recreation planners to use when planning for the location and design of new recreation sites and for managing existing sites. A survey of scenic quality over an area can show which locations have the most attractive landscapes and would be the most esthetically pleasing for campsites and other facilities.

Scenic beauty maps can be particularly useful for this purpose (Daniel et. al. 1977). A scenic beauty map was created for a forested area by taking photographs at locations across the study area, having observers rate the photos, and obtaining SBE's from these ratings. A computer program than interpolated the scenic values between photo locations and printed a map showing how scenic beauty

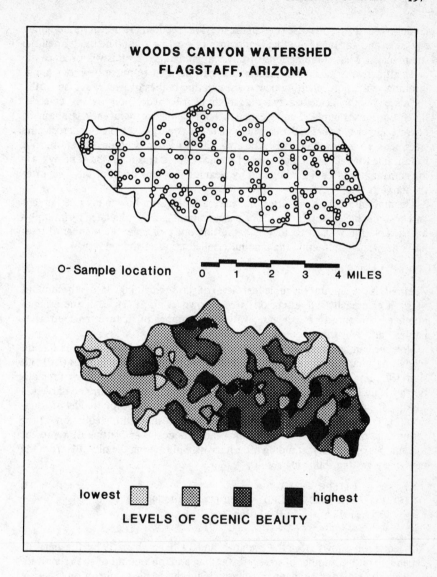

WOODS CANYON WATERSHED
FLAGSTAFF, ARIZONA

O- Sample location

0   1   2   3   4 MILES

lowest   highest
LEVELS OF SCENIC BEAUTY

Figure 2

The Study Area

varies from point to point within the area (Figure 2). Maps of this type can serve as guides for placing recreation sites, trails, and roads to take full advantage of the scenic resources in an area (Schroeder and Daniel 1980). Scenic beauty models, such as the one discussed in the previous section, are useful for designing new sites and for managing the landscapes of existing sites. The models tell the site manager what combinations of physical landscape features will produce the most attractive results. This information can be used to make decisions about thinning vegetation, planting new trees, creating bodies of water, and so forth.

To see how the scenic beauty model might be used in decision-making, consider the following example. Suppose that a land management agency is about to harvest timber in a forested area where there are twenty-two large Ponderosa pine trees per acre. After the harvest, the area will be used mostly for recreation, so it is desirable to maintain a high level of scenic beauty. This might be done by leaving some mature trees standing and by cleaning up some or all of the slash after the harvest.

The amount of slash left after the harvest depends on how many trees are cut and how much clean-up is done. The exact amount can be calculated by multiplying the amount of slash created by harvesting one tree times the number of trees harvested, and subtracting the amount cleaned up after the harvest:

$$SL = 35.8 (22 - LP) - R \tag{2}$$

where SL is the amount (in cubic feet/acre) of slash remaining, 35.8 is the amount of slash created by harvesting one tree (Brown et al. 1977), 22 is the original number of mature trees per acre, LP is the number of mature trees left after harvest, and R is the amount of slash cleaned up.

Now we can combine the formula for slash with the scenic beauty prediction model. Assume that there is no slash before harvest and that large trees (LP) and slash (SL) are the only landscape features that change during the harvest (in reality, this is unlikely to be absolutely true). The scenic beauty before the harvest is found by letting LP equal 22 and SL equal 0 in the scenic beauty model of equation (1). The scenic beauty after harvest is found by substituting equation (2) for the amount of slash (SL) into the scenic beauty model (1) and letting LP represent the number of trees left standing after harvest. Subtracting the old SBE from the new one gives the following result:

$$\begin{aligned}
\text{New SBE} - \text{Old SBE} &= \tag{3} \\
(.3503\, LP &- .016\, [35.8(22 - LP)]) - (.3503(22) - .016\, [0]) \\
&= .3503\, LP - 12.6 + .57\, LP + .016R - 7.71 \\
&= .92\, LP + .016\, R - 20.31.
\end{aligned}$$

This equation shows how the scenic beauty will be changed by the harvest, depending on the number of trees left standing and the amount of slash removed.

Using the equation, a planner can anticipate the scenic results of any specific decision about how many trees to harvest and how much slash to remove (Figure 3). This information can be used to help tradeoff esthetic benefits with other uses of forest resources. Although the model presented here was based on the natural features of back-country forest landscapes, such models can also be developed for urban recreation sites and can include measures of built features and recreation facilities. For example, Wohlwill (1979) and Wohlwill and Harris (1980) showed that the effect of structures on landscape quality depends on whether the structures are perceived as fitting into their natural surroundings. With this knowledge, a recreation site can be designed so that the facilities do not interfere with the quality of the natural landscape.

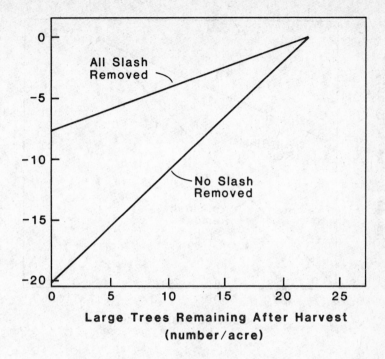

Figure 3

The Cost of Scenic Beauty

EVALUATING COSTS

Managing landscapes in recreation areas involves costs, and these costs are an important factor in the planning process. Costs may be direct, such as those for labor and equipment to manipulate landscape features and build attractive facilities, or they may be indirect, such as the "opportunity costs" in preserving scenic beauty when other uses of the land compete with recreation. For example, the scenic beauty model shows that large trees have a positive influence on perceived scenic beauty, so at least some of the large mature trees should be left standing to preserve a high level of scenic quality in a forest used for recreation. But the trees also have market value if they are harvested and sold for lumber and wood products. Opportunity cost means simply that to maintain a high level of scenic beauty the manager must forego some of the revenue that could be obtained by selling the trees.

Landscape feature measurements and scenic beauty models can be used to

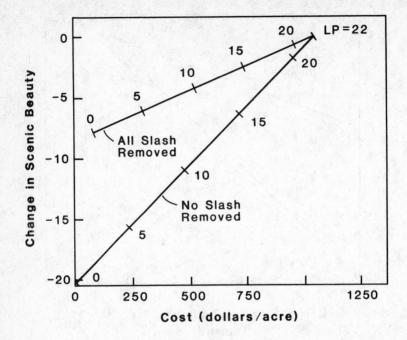

Figure 4

The Cost of Scenic Beauty

evaluate the costs of creating and maintaining recreation landscapes with high perceived scenic beauty. To see how this can be done, consider the example of the timber harvest. The cost of maintaining a given level of scenic beauty in the forest area harvested is the additional amount of revenue that the agency would have received by selling all of the timber, plus the amount the agency must pay for labor and equipment to close up the slash. If these costs are known, we may construct opportunity cost curves showing how much revenue the agency must forego in order to maintain a given level of scenic beauty (or how high a level of scenic beauty can be achieved at a given cost).

The maximum loss of scenic beauty occurs with harvest of all mature trees (LP = 0) and no cleanup of slash (Figure 4). This corresponds to a cost of zero because no money is being spent for cleanup and no timber-sale revenue is being sacrificed for scenic enhancement. The cost for maintaining the initial level of scenic beauty is more than $1,000 per acre (Figure 4). That is, to maintain this level, the agency would have to give up more than $1,000 per acre in timber-sale revenues that could have been used to finance recreation facilities. If the agency can only afford a cost of about $500 per acre to carry out recreation development plans, it should leave about 10 trees per acre standing (Figure 4). Also, because the expense of cleanup is small compared to the market value of trees, a much higher level of scenic beauty can be maintained at a little extra cost by cleaning up the slash.

Cost curves for actual forest sites will probably differ from those in the simple example presented here because market prices vary among regions and over time. Also, this example does not take into account that changes in the forest overstory will cause changes in other vegetation as well, and that the appearance of the forest will change as trees grow and the evidence of cutting disappears after the harvest. When scenic beauty cost curves can be developed that reflect all of these factors, they will provide a good basis for balancing the costs and benefits of providing scenic recreational landscapes.

References

Arthur, L. M. "Predicting Scenic Beauty of Forest Environment: Some Empirical Tests." *Forest Science* 23(1977):151-160.

Arthur, L. M., and Boster, R. S. "Measuring Scenic Beauty: A Selected Annotated Bibliography." USDA Forest Service General Technical Report RM-25, Fort Collins, Colorado: Rocky Mountain Forest and Range Experiment Station, 1976.

Arthur, L. M.; Daniel, T. C.; and Boster, R. S. "Scenic Assessment: An Overview." *Landscape Planning* 4(1977):109-129.

Brown, J. K. "Handbook for Inventorying Downed Woody Material." USDA Forest Service General Technical Report INT-16. Ogden, Utah: Intermountain Forest and Range Experiment Station, 1974.

Brown, J. K.; Snell, J. A. K.; and Bunnel, D. L. "Handbook for Predicting Slash Weight of Western Connifers." USDA Forest Service General Technical Report INT-37, Ogden, Utah: Intermountain Forest and Range Experiment Station, 1977.

Buhyoff, G. J., and Leuschner, W. A. "Estimating Psychological Disutility From Damaged Forest Stands." *Forest Science* 2(1978):424-432.

Buhyoff, G. J., and Riesenman, M. F. "Experimental Manipulation of Dimensionality in Landscape Preference Judgments: A Quantitative Validation." *Leisure Sciences* 2(1979):221-238.

Buhyoff, G., and Wellman, J. D. "The Specification of a Non-Linear Psychophysical Function for Visual Landscape Dimensions." *Journal of Leisure Research* 12(1980): 257-272.

Daniel, T. C. "Criteria for Development and Application of Perceived Environmental Quality Indices." *Perceived Environmental Quality Indices,* edited by E. Zube and K. Craik. New York: Phenum, 1976.

Daniel, T. C., and Boster, R. S. "Measuring Landscape Aesthetics: The Scenic Beauty Estimation Methods." USDA Forest Service Research Paper RM-167, Fort Collins, Colorado: Rocky Mountain Forest and Range Experiment Station, 1976.

Daniel, T. C., and Vining, J. "Methodological Issues in the Assessment of Landscape Quality." *Human Behavior and Environment.* vol. 6, edited by I. Altman and J. F. Wohlwill. New York: Phenum, in press.

Daniel, J. C.; Anderson, L. M.; Schroeder, H. W.; and Wheeler, L. W. III. "Mapping the Scenic Beauty of Forest Landscapes." *Leisure Sciences* 1(1977):35-53.

Green, D. M., and Swetts, V. A. *Signal Detection Theory and Psychophysics.* New York: John Wiley & Sons, 1966.

Guilford, J. P. *Psychometric Methods.* New York: McGraw-Hill, 1954.

Husch, B.; Miller, C. I.; and Beers, T. W. *Forest Mensuration.* New York: Ronald Press, 1972.

Kaplan, S. "An Informal Model for the Prediction of Preference." In *Landscape Assessment: Values, Perceptions, and Resources,* edited by E. H. Zuke, R. O. Brush, and J. A. Fabors. Stroudsburg, PA: Dowden, Hutchinson, & Ross, 1975.

Ravenscraft, D. J., and Dwyer, J. F. "Reflecting Site Attractiveness in Travel Cost-Based Models for Recreation Benefit Estimation." Forestry Research Report no. 78-6. Agricultural Experiment Station University Illinois at Champaign-Urbana, 1978.

Schroeder, H. W., and Daniel, T. C. "Predicting the Scenic Quality of Forest Road Corridors." *Environment and Behavior* 12(1980):349-366.

Schroeder, H. W., and Daniel, T. C. "Progress in Predicting the Perceived Scenic Beauty of Forest Landscapes." *Forest Science* 27(1981):71-80.

Shafer, E. L.; Hamilton, J. F.; and Schmidt, E. A. "Natural Landscape Preferences: A Predictive Model." *Journal of Leisure Research* 1(1969):1-19.

Thurstone, L. L. "A Law of Comparative Judgment." *Psychological Review* 34(1927):278-286.

Torgerson, W. S. *Theory and Methods of Scaling.* New York: John Wiley & Sons, 1958.

Wohlwill, J. F. "What Belongs Where: Research of Fittingness of Man-Made Structures in Natural Settings." In *Assessing Amenity Resource Values,* edited by T. C. Daniel, E. H. Zube, and B. L. Driver. USDA Forest Service Technical Report RM-68. Fort Collins, Colorado: Rocky Mountain Forest and Range Experiment Station, 1979.

Wohlwill, J. F., and Harris, G. "Response to Congruity or Contrast for Man-Made Features in Natural Recreation Settings." *Leisure Sciences* 3(1980):349-365.

Zube, E. H.; Sell, J. L.; and Taylor, J. G. "Landscape Perception: Research, Application, and Theory." *Landscape Planning,* in press.

2

Developing An Information Gathering System for Large Land Areas

Kenneth C. Chilman*

The concept of an outdoor recreation opportunity spectrum to provide for diverse recreation visitors has been discussed for many years (Wagar 1951, Carhart 1961, Lucas 1964). Only recently has the concept been made operational as a recreation opportunity spectrum (ROS) system for land management planning (Driver and Brown 1978; Brown, Driver, and McConnell 1978; USDA Forest Service 1980); the rationale for the ROS system is discussed by Becker and Jubenville (1983) in another chapter of this book.

The Recreation Opportunity Spectrum system utilizes six land classifications from primitive to urban to describe recreation opportunity characteristics of large wildland areas. However, some of the ROS land classes are too large (e.g., primitive class minimum size 5,000 acres) to provide the very specific information needed by land managers who are often required to make decisions about individual recreation settings (usually where visitors tend to congregate). In the past, managers have made these decisions with general knowledge of the recreational uses and region, but are now being increasingly pressed to state the basis of their decisions in a systematic way. Managers need a system to (1) identify settings requiring management attention in a comparative way within large (thousands of acres) wildland areas, and (2) methods to gather specific information about these settings, including visitors' perceptions of quality of recreation experiences. Therefore, the purpose of this chapter is to illustrate how a new Recreation Area Division and Subdivision (RADS) system can be used to identify these management settings for data collection so that the ROS system concept can be more fully operationalized.

The information gathering system was developed and tested on 300 square miles of national forest lands in the Lake Tahoe Basin of California and Nevada (Chilman and Hampton 1981), and was also tested on an equivalent area of na-

*Acknowledgement is made to Yen-Pin Jem Kao, former graduate student at Southern Illinois University, who gathered the field data for the study reported here and wrote about the procedures (Kao 1982).

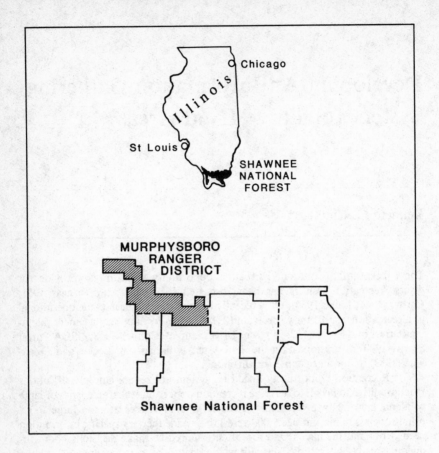

Figure 1

The Southern Illinois Study Area

tional forest in the eastern United States (Kao 1982). It was additionally tested on Tennessee Valley Authority lands during summer 1982.

Five sections comprise this chapter: the first is a description of the ROS mapping of the study area, the second part of this chapter involves RADS identification for the study area, the third section of the chapter describes the criteria for the development of subunit priorities, the fourth section describes simple procedures for the assessment of site impacts and the evaluation of visitor survey data, and the last section describes the major conclusions drawn from use of the information gathering system, especially in light of the availability of local management resources.

The Recreation Inventory Study Area

Murphysboro Ranger District is one of the four districts of the Shawnee National Forest. It is located in the northwest portion of Shawnee National Forest in southern Illinois (Figure 1) and encompasses 274 square miles. This includes private, state, and federal lands (approximately 30 percent is National Forest).

The area is thought to be representative of many forest areas in the eastern U.S., with primarily deciduous forest cover, hilly but not mountainous terrain, and scattered U. S. Forest Service ownership. It provides a variety of dispersed recreation activities (hunting, hiking, camping, scenic viewing) and some developed sites. Recreation use is heaviest in late spring and early fall because July and August are hot and humid. Estimated recreation use for Murphysboro Ranger District during 1980 was 196,300 visitor days (Barker 1981).

ROS Classification and Mapping

The purpose of Recreation Opportunity Spectrum land classification is to classify the recreation use attributes of large scale wildland areas so that wildland managers can obtain information needed to maintain the quality of recreation experiences and protect the natural resources of an area (USDA Forest Service 1980).

There are six classes in the U. S. Forest Service's ROS land classification and each involves a physical, social, and managerial component (Tables 1 and 2).

Table 1

Land Classes in the Recreation Opportunity Spectrum

Class	Abbrevation
Primitive	P
Semi-Primitive Nonmotorized	SPN
Semi-Primitive Motorized	SPM
Roaded Natural	RN
Rural	R
Urban	U

Table 2

Criteria Used for ROS Class Delineation

Setting Component	Mapping Criteria
Physical	Remoteness Size Human Evidence
Social	User Density
Managerial	Managerial Regimentation and Noticeability

Among the three setting components, the physical setting usually represents the more permanent (or less easily changed) component; social and managerial components can often be altered in shorter time frames. The criteria for defining the type of physical setting that exists in an area is a function of the absence or presence of human sights and sounds, area size, and the amount of environmental modification caused by human activity. Essentially, determination of the type of physical setting is done by mapping remoteness, size, and human evidence.

Remoteness from human sights and sounds is used as the indicator of the opportunity to experience lesser or greater amounts of social interaction, as one

Table 3

Remoteness Criteria

Class	Distance from the Class to Road
	PRIMITIVE ROAD
P	More than 3 Miles
SPN	Between 3 Miles and ½ Mile
SPM	Within ½ Mile
	ROAD BETTER THAN PRIMITIVE ROAD
SPM	Outside ½ Mile
RN	Within ½ Mile
R	Within ½ Mile
U	Within ½ Mile

Table 4

Road Level

Levels	Description
Primitive Road	Not Graded and Drained For example: Cross-Country Trail, Trail, Trail with Motorized use, Way, Rut, Track.
Road Better than Primitive Road	Graded and Drained Suitable for Highway use For example: Gravel, Aggregate Surface, Well Developed, Paved Road.

---

moves across the spectrum from primitive to urban, and is measured by the distance from a road to the area classified (Table 3). Table 4 shows the definition of road levels.

Using these criteria for remoteness and the intensity of road development, one may subdivide the six classes into two categories. The first category includes Urban, Rural, and Roaded Natural classes. The other category includes Semi-Primitive and Primitive classes of recreational environments. The size criteria (Table 5) is then used to further subdivide these classes—Primitive, Semi-Primitive Nonmotorized, and Semi-Primitive Motorized classes. If a map area does not meet a particular size criteria, it is merged into the next smaller sized class.

Table 5

Size Criteria

P	SPN	SPM	RN	R	U
5,000 Acres	2,500 Acres	2,500 Acres	NO	NO	NO

To divide the Roaded Natural, Rural, and Urban classes, measures of human evidence such as structures or farmlands made are used. Finally, after considering social and managerial setting criteria (same USDA reference) the ROS land classification is completed. Once the areas are classified, one can evaluate the kind of recreation activity opportunities that could be provided by each of the classified areas. However, when the physical, social, and/or managerial settings are not the same on the same piece of ground, a setting inconsistency is occurring. The Forest Service ROS handbook indicates that mapping the existing recreation opportunity spectrum class as the one which best reflects current management direction is the way to lessen potential setting inconsistencies.

Base maps were obtained from the Ranger District office in Murphysboro, along with additional information about area conditions. Mapping initial ROS land classes on the District was done during several days of field checking and in discussions of criteria with Southern Illinois University personnel and District recreation specialists. The result was a slight modification of ROS mapping procedure originally undertaken by Shawnee National Forest personnel (Zdzieblowski 1981) because the delineation of more specific land class boundaries was possible with aerial photography.

RADS Identification Procedures

The purpose of Recreation Area Division and Subdivision (RADS) is to organize management activities related to conditions occurring on specific land areas. Although subdivision of large land areas for management purposes is commonly done, procedures for subdivision are rather briefly elaborated in management texts (Chapman 1931, Davis 1966). Generally, the boundaries of land ownership by a private or public organization are first considered (Avery 1975). Aggregates of land ownership units to constitute an entire national forest depend on protection and management workloads and travel times involved, and may change as technologies and workloads change over time. Patterns of ownership within the total aggregate may directly influence management.

Within the forest district, obvious differences exist because of inherent variability. Topographical differences, e.g., contrasts between Oakwood Bottoms flatlands and Little Grand Canyon uplands, are often distinctive. Vegetational differences between timber types and/or other vegetation types may be readily apparent. These physical/biological differences often relate to previous and present land uses, and to road systems. The point is that these obvious differences can be used to divide district size areas of 200,000 or 300,000 acres into zones with different management needs. These zones may still be quite large, areas of 50,000 acres or more, and need to be further subdivided into smaller compartments where particular conditions exist and where specific management actions take place.

Previous research has established the concept of "workable units" in a recreation resource management system and Table 6 shows the equivalent relationship between timber management and recreation management work units.

Zones are similar to timber management units called blocks, which are generally distinctive in the characteristics of topography, location, access, and use. A subunit which is called a "Travel Pattern Concentration" (TPC) for recreation purposes is similar to a timber management compartment. The designation of

Table 6

Equivalent Relationship Between Timber and Recreation Work Units

Management	Division	Subdivision	
Timber	Working Circle	Block	Compartment
Recreation	Unit	Zone	Subunit*

*Subunit - Travel pattern concentration.

TPC is assigned to these places where highest intensity of use is now occurring, and/or where environmental disturbance from recreation is greatest. These areas are usually known to district personnel, but additional TPC's may be located during ROS field checking. Each TPC indicates land areas containing a travel pattern for particular recreation activity concentrations, usually from parking area, activity area and return. For some activities which take place over large areas (i.e., wilderness hiking), a TPC may consist of one segment of the total trip pattern.

Establishing Subunit Priorities for Management Attention

Many different circumstances cause recreation land managers to give attention to specific recreation settings. Probably most frequent is some increase in the amount or type of recreation use. But other items, such as unique features, fragile ecosystems, or proposed chances in use, may be criteria for an area that needs management attention. The important aspect here is that the managers need to specify the criteria they believe most important at a particular point in time, and their reasons for ranking various criteria as important. The criteria used for assessing priorities may change over time, but the basis for change must be made explicit.

Based on the criterion of high density recreation use (causing related and potential impacts on recreators and recreation areas), priorities of subunits (TPC's) for management attention were established and recommended at Lake Tahoe (Chilman 1980). The same criterion was also utilized for selecting the top priority TPC in the Murphysboro District.

Following designation of zones and TPC's within each zone, the TPC's were ranked for priority within each zone using the criterion above. This ranking was done through discussions with district personnel who usually have an extensive working knowledge of TPC's and what generally occurs in each Travel Pattern Concentration. Of course, these rankings may be subject to later modifications as more information is acquired or as conditions change.

The top priority TPC's for each zone within a district can then be compared. A judgment about which district TPC's should receive top district priority for management attention can be made from this comparative basis, and reasons for the judgment can be specified. The basis of this comparative assessment is readily indicated with maps and assessments of use, and additional information may be acquired as needed for quantitative verification.

Assessing Site Impacts on Priority Subunit

After selection of the top priority Travel Pattern Concentration, a reconnaissance is made of the TPC area. Reconnaissance is a very important step in site impact assessment to evaluate amounts and locations of impacts, and priorities for management attention. Typical site impacts include loss of ground cover vegetation, and soil compaction and erosion, from repeated foot trampling or wheeled vehicle contacts. Mapping of the TPC to indicate patterns of recreation use and site impact problem areas was done using site analysis techniques (Rutledge 1977). Then measurements of specific kinds of site impacts (on vegetation, soil, wildlife, etc.) can be made to indicate amounts and types (McEwen 1978, Hendee et. al. 1976).

After reconnaissance visits to the top priority TPC of the Murphysboro Ranger District, preliminary evaluation indicated that it was unnecessary to establish any site impact measurement for the time being because the top priority subunit had recently received intensive site maintenance treatments, i.e., paving of steep trail sections to alleviate soil erosion.

Visitor Survey Procedures for the Priority TPC

Two principal methods of gathering quantitative and qualitative information in terms of recreation visits and recreation experiences were applied during the top priority TPC visitor survey. They were (1) observations recorded in a diary and (2) on-site interviews. The on-site research started with reading existing Forest Service reports about the top priority subunit in order to gain an overview of conditions on the study site, this was followed by reconnaissance trips so that the researcher gained familiarity with the study area. These reconnaissance trips also were useful in establishing survey interview times and locations.

The top priority TPC in the Murphysboro Ranger District is a day-use hiking area with most of the visitation occurring from sunrise to sunset. District management personnel normally work from 8:00 A.M. to 5:00 P.M. on weekdays and the ranger district office is nine miles away from this area. Because there are many demands on managers and because rangers may get to any particular site infrequently, initial observation periods were scheduled from 6:00 A.M. through 6:00 P.M. to learn about various activities occurring that Murphysboro Ranger District staff might not normally notice (Burch 1964; Selltiz, Wrightsman, and Cook 1976). During those observation periods, visitors arrived and departed in automobiles, therefore the one parking area at the top priority subunit was determined to be the best place to conduct interviews for the survey. Initial observations indicated that in the early morning before 10:00 A.M., the only visitors observed were squirrel hunters with total numbers of less than 10 persons. In the morning from 9:00 A.M. to noon, only a few groups were observed in the area and almost everyone left by 5:00 P.M. Therefore, the most appropriate interview periods were chosen as being from 1:00 P.M. to 5:00 P.M.

Interviews with visitors to the priority subunit were conducted during the months of September, October, and November 1981. These months were chosen for the survey because, according to past records, fall is the most heavily used park visitation period; temperatures are mild, precipitation is low, insects are fewer, and fall vegetation is colorful. Furthermore, highest visitation periods are of primary concern to managers because that is when site impacts and visitor conflicts are most likely to occur.

The mid-fall period selected for this research included thirty-five days, including ten weekend days and twenty-five weekdays. Interviews were divided into two strata because populations of recreation visitors are usually different between weekends and holidays. Additionally, because the precision of sample estimates of the population mean depend on two factors (the size of the sample, and the variability or heterogenity of the population), stratified sampling was used to, as efficiently as possible, reduce the heterogenity of the population and to increase the precision of estimates (Sukhaltmel 1954).

Beyond these concerns, stratified random sampling often results in increasing information for a given cost: (1) The data should be more homogeneous within each stratum than in the population as a whole, (2) the cost of conducting the actual sampling tends to be less for stratified random sampling. When stratified sampling is used, separate estimates of population parameters can be obtained for each stratum without additional sampling (Mendenhall, Ott, and Schaeffer 1971).

Given these considerations, equal numbers of weekdays and weekend days were selected as the two strata and each stratum included ten days. In this research, all ten weekend days (among the 35 days in the research periods) were utilized as the weekend stratum and a simple random sample for ten weekdays was taken from the twenty-five weekdays of survey research. Besides the weekday-weekend category, there were two more research conditions that were taken into consideration. They were: (1) no more than two weekdays can be selected from the same week among the five different weeks, and (2) no more than two days can be selected from the same day category, such as Monday, Thursday, etc. The reason for these special conditions was to spread the sample days more evenly in the research periods. Obviously, one could call the technique of sampling used in this research, "stratified random sampling with two special conditions." For the survey, no visitors came on foot and at least one adult was included in each visitor group. Therefore, an adult (over 15 years of age) representative of each visitor group was interviewed after coming back from the hike and preparing to leave.

Questionnaire Design   The design of the initial questionnaire utilized in this study involved two important aspects: (1) measurement of "quality of recreation experience" indicators, and (2) limitation of the number of questions asked to less than ten.

Management for improved recreation quality has been advocated for some time (Wagar 1966). Avery (1975) in a widely used natural resources measurement text, reminds us that the "quality of the (recreation) experience may be as important as (or more so than) the total numbers of persons utilizing a recreational site. Unfortunately, we have not devised operational inventory systems that will provide reliable definitions and measurements of such products." Recent advances have, however, been made in definitions and measurements and Driver and Brown (1978) have indicated that the combination of recreation activity and setting are basic components of a recreation experience.

Following Driver and Brown (1978), the survey questions were organized into four categories: (1) visitor characteristics (including purpose of visit as activity), (2) importance of the setting for desired recreation experiences, (3) changes that visitors have noticed in the setting since they first started visiting the setting (these changes influence expectations for desired experiences), and (4) comments the visitors may have about the area and its management. Questions about visitors' perceptions of the recreation setting's importance and changes occurring are particularly useful for management purposes because the managers have more direct control over setting factors than visitors' choice of activities.

Questions were kept to less than ten to minimize interference with recreation visits, but more importantly to keep management costs of data collection and analysis low. Such a short set of questions can be administered by field personnel on a repetitive basis as part of a continuing series of studies (Chillman 1976). In addition, this short set of questions can be administered more informally, in a conversational mode, without a formal survey instrument, and the responses can be recorded after the interview. Notwithstanding these advantages, the responses were self-recorded by visitors on a questionnaire to obtain more samples at busy times in the park lot.

To reduce response error, open-ended questions were used (Moser 1961). Open-ended questions give respondents the opportunity to answer in their own terms and with their own frames of reference (Kidder 1981). To eliminate confusion and response problems, a pretest was administered from September 18 to 20, 1981. One hundred and eighty-four interviews were conducted between September 28 and November 1, 1981.

Analysis of the interviews identified the user profile of the visitor population (mostly local, 40 percent university students), the purposes of visits (types of hiking interests), the recreation spectrum position and importance of the TPC to the visitors (wooded hiking area with special trail and area features), and their particular likes and dislikes (especially in regard to recent paving of portions of the trail). The visitors also perceived use of the area as increasing, and suggested some management options relating to managing the increasing use.

Summary

Wildland recreation managers deal with maintaining and improving a variety of recreation setting opportunities. Wagar (1974, p. 276) has observed that "examining one area at a time may be the trap that has caused so much confusion about use limits for specific areas." What wildland recreation managers need are methods to systematically compare recreation areas located within or near their management units so that they can better explain their priorities for budget requests or other concerns.

This chapter has described one part of a series of studies aimed at developing a practical, cost-effective recreation resource inventory system for large wildland areas. Specifically, this research replicates inventory methods that were initiated for the Lake Tahoe Basin Management Unit in California and Nevada and for Rockwoods Reservation (a small urban forest) in Missouri.

The Recreation Opportunity Spectrum land classification system developed by researchers at the Rocky Mountain Forest and Range Experiment Station provides a useful assessment of recreation activities settings for large scale areas but does not provide detailed or comparative assessments of specific sites necessary for establishing priorities for area management actions. In this research, the ROS system was combined with a recreation area division and subdivision (RADS) system so that detailed management priorities could be defined in a graphic and cost-effective manner. The visitor survey provided valuable information about visitors' perceptions of quality of recreation opportunities for a priority recreation site.

Several observations can be made about the utility of the information gathering system from this study. First, the inventory methods initiated under western wildland conditions were readily applied to eastern forest conditions. One might have suspected that different conditions of topography, vegetation, land ownership patterns, etc. would require different inventory strategies thereby making the transferability of the system difficult and thereby limiting the development of generalizations from the system. Similarities of large size management units (300 square miles of Tahoe Basin and 274 square miles of Murphysboro Ranger District) and diversity of conditions existing within these large units appear to be important for operation of the combined ROS-RADS approach. One modification of ROS did include the mapping of smaller size Semi-Primitive Motorized areas (2,000 acres in MRD area) than those called for in the ROS handbook (2,500 acres). Such a change called attention to the scarcity of areas at the primitive end of the spectrum in Shawnee National Forest.

Second, the application of ROS served to provide a systematic orientation to field conditions that were useful when making RADS designations. Two aspects of the method that were emphasized in both the Tahoe and Shawnee studies were (1) careful field examination (access road types in conjunction with ecological and land use conditions) and (2) considerable discussion of area conditions with district field personnel. The ROS classification instructions are a useful conceptual framework for these field examinations and discussions, and field personnel usually have a detailed observational knowledge of area conditions that would be costly to obtain by other means.

Third, field managers appear to readily understand the logic of both ROS and RADS. The systems are based on readily observable differences in area conditions. Managers recognize and use these differences as a general factor in determining management actions and workloads. The systems also are conceptually similar to other resource management systems, e.g., timber, range, or wildlife management, that usually are part of the training of field management personnel. For example, ROS parallels timber type mapping or wildlife habitat type mapping to provide an overview of conditions on the entire area. RADS parallels forest organization and subdivision procedures and range management "key area" concepts to indicate why management attention is focused on particular areas. Visitor surveys parallel timber sale studies to provide quantitative and qualitative resource evaluations for specific areas.

Finally, applications of ROS and RADS appear to be economical and flexible in adapting to changes in area conditions. Only a few days are needed to initially institute the systems and the method of establishing priorities for management of Travel Pattern Concentration areas is (1) definitive in establishing initial priorities, (2) economical in enabling the ready definition of only the number of areas that will be dealt with at one point in time (i.e., establishing the top one or two priorities rather than examining all thirty-five), and (3) flexible in allowing changes in priorities related to changes in area conditions when selecting the next one or two TPC's to work with at a particular time. The execution of the entire inventory system (including ROS, RADS, and visitor survey) can be performed by one or two researchers, management personnel, or rangers and could be considered as relatively low cost. With appropriate instructions, maybe only one field level employee could be used to perform this task, if he or she has experience and knowledge about the area.

As Wagar (1974, p. 278) suggested, "the crucial question becomes: what management pattern, including kinds and amounts of use, will permit this recreation area to make its maximum contribution to the sustained benefit provided by the whole system of recreation areas?" This chapter has illustrated how a land classification information system can be developed into a commonly used, generalizable recreation resource management tool to identify areas that require management attention to maintain or improve high quality recreation opportunities.

References

Avery, T. E. *Natural Resources Measurements*. 2d ed. New York: McGraw-Hill, 1975, pp. 284-300.

Barker, P. "Personal Communication." Murphysboro Ranger Station, Shawnee National Forest, Illinois, 1981.

Brown, P. J.; Driver, B. L.; and McConnell, C. "The Opportunity Spectrum Concept in Outdoor Recreation Supply Inventories: Background and Application." In *Proceedings of Integrated Renewable Resources Inventories Workshop*, pp. 73-84. Fort Collins, Colorado: USDA Forest Service General Technical Report RM-55, Rocky Mountain Forest and Range Experiment Station, 1978.

Burch, W. R. "Observation as a Technical for Recreation Research." In *Land and Leisure: Concepts and Methods in Outdoor Recreation,* pp. 130-145. Chicago: Maroufa Press, 1964.

Carhart, A. H. *Planning for America's Wildlands.* Harrisburg, Pa.: Telegraph Press, 1961.

Chapman, H. H. *Forest Management.* New York: J. B. Lyon Co., 1931, pp. 196-212.

Chilman, K. C. "Reading the Visitor Mind." In *Managing Recreation Resources for Century III: Proceedings of John Wright Forestry Conference,* pp. 50-59. West Layfayette, Indiana: Department of Forestry, Purdue University, 1976.

Chilman, K. C. "Recommendations for a Dispersed Recreation Management Plan for the Lake Tahoe Basin Management Unit, California and Nevada." Report on file at Lake Tahoe Basin Management Unit, USDA Forest Service, South Lake Tahoe, California, 1980.

Chilman, K. C., and Hampton, G. "A new Recreation Inventory System to Aid Land Management Decision-Making: An Application at Lake Tahoe." Paper presented at National Recreation and Parks Association research symposium, Minneapolis, October 1981.

Chilman, K. C., and Kao, Y. J. "Quality of Outdoor Recreation: A Short Set of Questions Used for Field Level Resource Management." Paper presented at National Recreation and Parks Association research symposium, Louisville, October 1982.

Davis, K. P. *American Forest Management.* New York: McGraw-Hill, 1966.

Driver, B. L., and Brown, P. J. "The Opportunity Spectrum Concept and Behavioral Information in Outdoor Recreation Resource Supply Inventories: A Rationale." In *Proceedings of Integrated Renewable Resources Inventories Workshop,* pp. 24-31. Fort Collins, Colorado: USDA Forest Service General Technical Report RM-55, Rocky Mountain Forest and Range Experiment Station, 1978.

Hendee, J. C.; Clark, R.; Hogan, M.; Wood, D.; and Koch, R. "Code-a-site: A System for Inventory of Dispersed Recreational Sites in Roaded Areas, Back Country, and Wilderness." Portland, Oregon: USDA Forest Service Reearch Paper RNW-209, Pacific Northwest Forset and Range Experiment Station, 1976.

Kao, Y. J. "Application of Recreation Resource Inventory Techniques on Shawnee National Forest, Illinois." M.S. thesis Southern Illinois University, Carbondale, Illinois, 1982.

Kidder, L. H. *Research Methods for Social Relations.* 4th ed. New York: Holt, Rhinehart and Winston, 1981.

Lucas, R. C. "The Recreational Capacity of the Quetico-Superior Are." St. Paul, Minnesota: USDA Forest Service Research Paper LS-15, Lake States Forest Experiment Station, 1964.

McEwen, D. N. *"Turkey Bay* Off-Road Vehicle Areas at *Land Between the Lakes:* An Example of New Opportunities for Managers and Riders." Carbondale, Illinois: Report no. 1, Recreation Department, Southern Illinois University, 1978.

Mendenhall, W.; Ott, L.; and Scheaffer, R. L. *Elementary Survey Sampling.* Belmont, California: Wadsworth, 1971.

Moser, C. A. 1961. *Survey Methods in Social Investigation.* London: Heinmann Educational Books Ltd, 1961.

Rutledge, A. J. *Anatomy of a Park.* New York: McGraw-Hill, 1971.

Selltiz, C.; Winston, L. S.; and Cook, S. W. *Research Methods in Social Relations.* 3d ed. New York: Holt, Rhinehart and Winston, 1976.

Sukhaltme, P. V. *Sampling Theory of Surveys with Applications.* Ames, Iowa: The Iowa State College Press, 1954, pp. 83-137.

USDA Forest Service. "Recreation Input to Land and Resource Management." Washington, D.C.: Forest Service Handbook 1909.12. 1980.

Wagar, J. V. K. "Some Major Principles in Recreation Land Use Planning." *Journal Forestry* 49(1951): 431-435.

Wagar, J. A. "Quality in Outdoor Recreation.' *Trends in Parks and Recreation* 3(1966): 9-12.

Wagar, J. A. "Recreation Carrying Capacity Revisited." *Journal Forestry* 72(1974):274-278.

Zdzieblowski, A. "Recreation Opportunity Spectrum." Report on file at Supervisor's Office, Shawnee National Forest, Harrisburg, Illinois, 1981.

3

Survey Research and Data Collection Procedures

Neil J. Dikeman, Jr.

The scarcity of timely secondary data relating directly to the recreation/leisure industry and its customers often necessitates the use of survey research in the acquisition of suitable data. The researcher interested in leisure research should recognize that, while generally accepted sampling procedures are applicable to this subject, there are certain specific methods of sampling which are more suited. In addition, there are two broad locations at which samples of recreators can be drawn and interviewed (i.e. at home or at the recreation facility). The choice of the method used and the place at which the interview takes place depend in large measure on the composition of the population to be interviewed and the data requirements of the study. (See *Handbook on Sampling Methods Applicable to Tourist Research,* World Tourist Organization, Avda. Del Generalisimo, 59-Madrid-16, for further discussion.) The recreation researcher should also recognize the vast complexity of the leisure industry and the approaches taken by others to examine its micro-elements. At least two associations, The Travel Research Association and the National Recreation and Park Association, publish annual bibliographies of studies, reports, and articles which focus on recreation research activities by subject matter. The Travel Research Association bibliographies can be obtained through the Business Research Division, University of Colorado, Boulder, Colorado and the National Recreation and Park Association bibliographies are published by the *Journal of Leisure Research,* Alexandria, Virginia.

The remainder of this chapter deals principally with those standard, basic sampling procedures which can be applied to the data gathering process necessary to conducting most types of survey research projects. These procedures can be altered to fit the various leisure research problems.

SURVEY METHODS

Timely and valid primary data can be obtained by either of two general methods: (1) a complete canvass of a target population or, (2) a sample of the units which make up that same population. Each of these methods have their unique advantages and disadvantages. In the case of a complete canvass (or census), the apparent advantage is obvious — that of a complete (or assumedly so) concensus or count of the target population. The disadvantages of a data gathering effort of this magnitude are equally obvious — the high cost of the project in terms of time and money and the difficulty of controlling the quality of the results. The alternative to the complete count is a sample of the members of the target population. This method too has its advantages and disadvantages. The advantages of the sample survey include lower costs, less time required (therefore, more timely data), and improved quality control. It's principal disadvantage is that it provides less precise results than those obtained by canvass, although the degree of precision attained in a sample survey can be defined.

Because of the extreme costliness of the canvass, only the methods and procedures applicable to sampling and sample surveys will be addressed in the discussions which follow.

Target Population   The population (or group) to be studied. For example, if a survey of residential consumers is to be conducted by telephone, the target population might be defined as "all residences (in an area) with telephones."

Sampling Frame   There are basically two types of sampling frames. The first consists of lists of actual elements to be sampled. Thus, the sample frame of a sample survey conducted by telephone from a population having listed numbers would be those telephone directories covering the study area.

The second type of sampling frame does not involve a list of elements to be sampled but provides a systematic description of those elements within which the target population is contained (Dommermuth 1975). For example, the sampling frame of this second type may be a map of an area within which the target population resides.

Sampling Unit   A sampling unit is a single element of the target population from which the sample is to be selected. The sampling unit may be the head of a household, a member of the household, etc. (Crisp 1957).

Random   In the sampling context, a sample can be said to have been randomly selected only if the method used in the selection process insures that every sampling unit had an equal chance of being selected.

Types of Samples

Samples are generally classified as either random probability samples or nonrandom samples. Random probability samples are chosen so as to insure that all members of a target population have an equal chance of being selected and that none of the respondents (or sample units) are chosen judgmentally. The advantage of this type of sample is that, since it was chosen randomly, it can provide the basis for statistical inference. That is, its results can be inferred to the target population as a whole. In effect, a probability sample is one whose error can be measured. This condition exists only when random selection techniques are employed (Ferber, Blankertz, and Hollander 1964).

There are several types of randomly selected, probability samples which are generally recognized as acceptable sampling procedures. These include the stratified random sample, the simple random sample, the area sample, the cluster sample, the systematic sample, and the sequential sample (Worcester 1972).

Nonrandom or judgmental samples are not chosen randomly but consist of respondents selected arbitrarily for some specific purpose and thus the errors and variations contained in the results of this form of sampling cannot be measured. This means that inferences to the target population cannot be based on the results of a judgment or nonrandomly-selected sample.

Simple Random Sample   The simple random sample is relatively unsophisticated. It is simply a randomly selected series of sampling units drawn from the sampling frame without regard for the social or demographic characteristics of the target population. Because of its design, the simple random sample can be expected to have a relatively high sampling error when compared with those of samples whose design provide more error control such as the stratified random sample.

Stratified Random Sample   The sample stratification process represents one acceptable method for reducing the sampling error without increasing the sample size (Schreier 1963). The procedure for selecting a stratified random sample is first to divide the population into groups which in themselves are relatively homogeneous but which are differentiated one from another by selected characteristics. The key to defining the strata is the selection of a key variable which may influence the tendency or ability of the target population to use some good or service. One such characteristic which would be useful in the development of sample strata for a survey of the recreation market is average annual household income. The assumption here is that different income groups are markets for differing types of recreational facilities. In a sample in which income groups are used to delineate strata, each income group is represented in the sample in proportion to its representation in the population. Thus, if the income category of $10,000 - $19,999 represented 10 percent of the population, a total of 100 respondents in a sample of 1,000 would be selected randomly from those members of the target population receiving annual incomes in this range.

Stratified random sampling can be further refined by using multiple stages of stratification (i.e., sampling by substrata). For example, if the research team desired to further reduce the sampling error from that attained by merely stratifying by income groups, it could further subdivide each income group into urban and rural strata thus developing a two-stage stratified random sample. Then if further refinements were desired, it might add still another substratification step and divide the urban rural distribution into age groupings thereby creating a three-stage stratified random sample. It is important to insure that not only the first stage strata be proportionate to the sector of the target population they represent, but each successive stage be in proportion to its share of the target population (Green and Tull 1966).

Sequential Sample   When conventional sampling methods are employed, the sample size is fixed before interviewing begins and the results of the survey are analyzed after the data gathering efforts are completed. Sequential sampling, however, differs significantly in its approach in that the sample size is not fixed and its results are analyzed as the survey proceeds. The purpose of the ongoing analysis is to detect any significant and pronounced trends relating to the hypotheses tested. At such time as these trends become so clearly prevalent that the desired level of precision has been reached, as determined by appropriate tests of validity, sampling is halted (Ferber, Blankertz, and Hollander 1964). Studies have indicated that the results of this form of sampling are as reliable as those obtained from the more conventional methods despite the fact that the sample size may be greatly reduced.

Sample units drawn for use by sequential samples are always selected randomly. In addition, sequential samples may be of any of the random sample structures (i.e. simple, stratified, clustered, area, etc.).

Systematic Sample   Systematic sampling offers a relatively simple method of randomly choosing sampling units without extensive use of tables of random numbers or computerized random number generators. The use of this method entails first, the determination of the size of the sample desired and second, the division of the size of the sample into the size of the target population. These steps then provide the periodicity of the sample unit selection process. The next step in the process is to enter the sample frame at some random point, usually determined by a table of random numbers, and then to select each Nth item from the sample frame listing (i.e., the sample selection period) after that point of entry. This process continues until enough sample units have been selected to equal the size of the sample (Dommermuth 1975). For example, assume that the purpose of a research project was to measure the expenditures of students at a university. Also, assume that a sample of 400 students from a student body of 9,000 students was sufficiently large to provide the precision required. The sample selection process would be to first select a number from 1 to 9,000 from a table of random 4 digit numbers. Assume that the number so selected was 1,662. Next, to determine the periodicity of the sample selection process, the total number of students (9,000) is divided by the size of the sample (400) resulting in a sampling period of 22. The roster of all students (the sampling frame) would then be entered at the 1,662nd student (the first sampling unit chosen). The second sampling unit chosen would be the 1,684th student, (i.e., 1,662 + 22 = 1,684) and so on until a sample of 400 students was chosen. It should be noted that only 333 sampling units will have been chosen at the time the end of the student roster has been reached. In this event, the counting reverts back to the beginning of the roster (i.e., the first name on the roster) and continues until 400 items have been selected.

If a systematic sample is to be stratified, it becomes necessary to stratify the sampling frame and select subsamples from each strata in proportion to the number of items in that frame. In the example of student expenditures, assume that the expenditures were to be stratified by the classification of the student (i.e., freshmen, sophomores, etc.). Assume also that the freshman class represented 22 percent of the total student body. Then, the subsample to be drawn from the roster of freshmen would be 88 sample units. The listing of the 2,200 freshmen would be entered at some random point and every 22nd student from that point would become a sampling unit. This same procedure would be followed for the other classes.

Cluster Sample   Cluster sampling represents yet another method of random sampling which offers savings in both time and money when personal interviewing is involved. It is not, however, readily adaptable to telephone interviewing procedures. By sampling in clusters, considerable travel time and costs are saved and thus the time and money required in the sample selection and interviewing process are greatly reduced.

The selection of sample units for the cluster sampling process involves first dividing the sampling frame into clusters equal to the size of the total sample and then selecting one such cluster at random. This selected cluster then would become the sample.

Cluster sampling works effectively if the characteristics of the target population being studied are distributed throughout the sampling frame. If, however, the listing which represents the sampling frame is composed of particular groupings (such as a listing of households arrayed by income size) then cluster sampling loses statistical efficiency (Schreier 1963). This loss is due to intraclass correlation.

Area Sample   Area sampling is a special form of cluster sampling which utilizes broad areas such as city blocks, census tracts, etc., as sampling frames. The sample selection procedure begins with a listing of the subareas within the area containing the target population. Next, those subareas to be included in the sample will be chosen by one of the random methods. All households (or other specified sampling unit) within the selected subareas would then be treated as the sample (Dommermuth 1975).

Other Random Sample Designs   There are a number of other types of random sample designs available for use in specific situations. These, however, are for the most part special adaptations of those discussed herein. All such sample designs have at least one item in common, which is that the random sample unit selection procedures must be followed if the results of the sample survey are to be statistically inferred to the target population.

Non Random Sample   Generally, non-random-sampling methods are not appropriate for use as data gathering mechanisms for formal research projects. Since such samples cannot be evaluated with regard to their precision, they lack the vital quality of statistical inference. This renders any results of such samples relatively useless as indicators of a target population and thus of little practical value to a research project.

DATA GATHERING MEDIA

Three general media are available for use as data gathering mechanisms for survey research: personal interview, telephone, and mail. The selection of the method to be used to compile survey data depends in large measure on the resources and needs of the project. The advantages and disadvantages of each method should be considered carefully before one is selected so as to insure that the data needs of the project will be met.

Personal Interview Surveys conducted by personal interview involve a personal interface between an interviewer and a respondent (or sample unit). This form of surveying can accommodate more extensive interview schedules and thus can provide greater depth and more detail in the information being gathered. In addition, the personal interview survey provides the analysts with the comments of the interviewer vis a vis the respondent, including the setting of the interview and conditions surrounding the interview. Add to this the greater willingness of respondents to provide such information as annual income to an interviewer in person rather than to a telephone interviewer for example, and the enhanced value of data obtained through personal interviewing methods becomes obvious.

Three major disadvantages are inherent in the personal interview method for obtaining data. The first of these is cost. In the conduct of personal interviews, several cost factors are present which do not exist in the same magnitude with the other methods. Travel costs for instance, must be included in the budget of a personal interview based survey since the interviewers must travel from interview to interview. Because of the time required to travel, the personal interviewer must be paid more per hour to compensate for this relatively unproductive time. Travel time also impacts on the speed with which data are compiled. This in itself is costly both in terms of time and interviewing costs. The second disadvantage is the difficulty in locating persons who are interested in and adept at "face to face" interviewing. Only a certain personality is comfortable in the role of a personal interviewer. The final disadvantage in the use of the personal interview approach is the growing resistance on the part of the population to participate in personal interviews. A portion of this resistance is due to a suspicion that such interviews are a subterfuge on the part of government agencies to recheck answers provided these agencies by other modes. Another part of this resistance is attributable to a increasing desire for privacy and a concurrent resentment of intrusions into this privacy. A final portion of this resistance to participating in personal interviews is traceable to door-to-door salespersons who gain entry by representing themselves as agents of a survey research operation.

Despite the disadvantages noted in the use of personal interviews as a data gathering mechanism, the high quality and potential quantity of data obtained through personal interviews usually more than offsets the costs in terms of money, time, and extra efforts required to obtain respondent participation inherent in surveying by personal interview.

Telephone Interview   The telephone as an instrument for conducting surveys is becoming increasingly popular and important. This new interest in telephone surveys is due both to the fact that a growing proportion of the population has telephone service, as well as to the development of new sample selection techniques which tend to broaden the target population. These improved techniques include random digit dialing and the number plus one methods of sample selection (Glasser and Metzger 1972; Hauk and Cox 1974).

1. Sample Selection: The most common procedure for selecting telephone sample units when using the random digit dialing technique is first to obtain the three digit numbers for each exchange included in the geographic area to be sampled. Then, using one of several available computer software packages, generate the appropriate number of four digit numbers for each exchange. If the sample is to be of the simple random sample variety, an equal amount of four digit numbers might be generated for each exchange. If, however, the sample is to be stratified, the number of sample units drawn for each exchange could be proportionate to the total number of residential telephones served by each exchange.

The use of the number plus one method involves the random selection of the appropriate number of sample units from a telephone directory (or directories) of the area to be sampled. Each number so chosen is then increased by one in the last digit to arrive at the telephone number of the sample unit. The choice of the original number can be accomplished by use of a table of random numbers, or one can utilize the systematic sampling methods described elsewhere in this chapter (Landon and Banks 1977).

2. Advantages and Disadvantages: Telephone interviewing has a number of advantages over both the personal interview and the mailed questionnaire. Among those advantages afforded by this media relative to personal interviews is the reduction both in survey costs and in the time required to gather data. A second major advantage of using telephones to gather data is the greater control over the quality of the data being gathered afforded the principal investigator. This is particularly true when the telephone interviewing process is centralized and has the capability of being monitored during interviews. Its disadvantages relative to personal interviews are the general lack of depth and detail in the information it secures, and its inherent tendency to reach telephone numbers of entities which are not a part of the target population (i.e. commercial establishments when conducting a residential survey). Another important disadvantage is that telephone interviews encounter more resistance from respondents in obtaining data on income and family finances than is the case with personal interviews (Tyebjee 1979). Also, like personal interviews, it is possible that the interviewer can inject bias into the survey's results by the way in which questions are asked.

3. Problem Areas: The problems associated with the use of telephones as a data gathering device are largely similar in nature to those associated with other methods. First, the question of the validity of the data gathered by telephone often arises. Several studies conducted on this topic (Schmiedeskamp 1962; Sudman and Ferber 1974; and Wheatley 1973) found that data collected by different interview methods were generally equivalent but that some important differences were also found (Tyebjee 1979):

a. Different interview methods can result in differences in sample characteristics (Linsky 1975).

b. Telephone interviews generally have a higher refusal rate on questions dealing with income.

c. Telephone interviews generally tend to minimize the probability of receiving "socially acceptable" answers relative to those received from personal interviews but may tend to receive more such answers than would result from mail surveys (Hochstim 1967).

d. Telephone interviews provide less opportunity for in-depth probing than personal interviews but are superior to mail surveys in this respect (Telser 1976).

Mail Surveys   The use of mail surveys remains the least desirable of the three methods for obtaining primary data. The principal problems associated with the use of the mails as a means of gathering data are first, that a considerable amount of time is required to obtain completed interview schedules and next, the lack of assurance that the sample returns are actually representative of the population. In addition, the questionnaire must be short, which precludes any appreciable in-depth exploration into the answers. Finally, certain segments of the population are, by the very nature of this method, excluded (i.e. blind, illiterate, etc.).

The advantages offered by mail surveys are generally associated with cost since they are potentially the least expensive of the methods discussed for large area surveys. This characteristic would render the mail survey an extremely desirable choice when survey budgets are very limited but time is of little importance.

Selection of the Data Gathering Method

The selection of the method for obtaining survey data depends on a number of factors including the availability of funds, time restrictions, and the need for in-depth information, to mention a few. Table 1 provides a tabular summary of the advantages and disadvantages of each of the three survey methods.

SURVEY PROCEDURES

The conduct of a survey should proceed in an orderly and logical fashion, utilizing the step by step procedures common to most scientifically oriented research projects. The first step in this procedure is the definition of the problem. This definition should include the goals of the project (i.e., the questions to be answered), the hypotheses to be tested, and the population to be described. Each

Table 1

Ratings of the Important Characteristics of Three Survey Media

Characteristics of the Media	Personal Interview	Telephone Survey	Mail Survey
Cost	1	2	3
Time required for results	2	3	1
In-depth data available	1	2	3
Management control	2	1	3
Visual evaluation	1	0	0
Precision	1	2	3
Nonresponse rate	2	3	1
Ability to obtain sensitive data	1	2	3
Interview time required	1	3	2
High personnel skills required	1	2	3

Ratings

1 = High
2 = Medium
3 = Low
0 = None

of these should be determined in the context of the funds, time, personnel, and physical resources available for the project.

The next step is the assembly of the research team and the assignment of responsibilities for completion of the various aspects of the project. The research design, scheduling, and establishment of target dates for each portion of the study should then be developed by the research team.

The next phases of the study can be conducted concurrently since neither is dependent upon the other. The first of these phases is the development of the interview schedule or questionnaire based on the goals of the project and the hypotheses to be tested. Great care must be exercised in the construction of the questions to minimize any respondent bias which can result from leading questions, the sequence of questions, and the methods provided for answering the questions. Attention must also be given to the inclusion of questions which will be used to check the answers given for internal consistency and to validate the sample (i.e., to determine the precision of the sample). Following the initial structuring of the interview schedule, it should be pretested on a sampling of the population to determine the extent to which the questions are understandable and the document will elicit the information needed. Wherever possible, the questions should be phrased so that short answers will be forthcoming. Also, to the extent possible, open ended questions should be avoided. It is often desirable to review the structure of the questionnaire with the editing and computer staff to insure that a minimal amount of work will be required to transcribe the data to machine processable form.

During the period in which the interview schedule is being developed, the sample itself can be designed and drawn. During this phase, the research team should determine first the degree of precision desired in the results. This desired degree of precision then will be used to determine the sample size (Schreier 1963). Next, the decision should be made as to what media should be used to gather the data — personal interview, telephone, or mail. Usually, this decision rests on the amount of money and time available to the project and on the degree to which key questions should be examined in some depth.

The actual selection of the sampling units is the next step in this phase of the activity. The method by which the sample is selected depends somewhat on the media to be used in gathering the data. For example, if a stratified random sample is to be drawn, the stratification process for each method differs significantly as do the bases for stratification. Regardless of which data gathering method is used, the selection of sampling units must be one of the accepted random processes thus insuring that the precision of the sample can be measured and that the results of the survey can be inferred to the target population.

During the time the sample is being selected, the interviewers should be trained in the administration of the interview schedule. This training should include a discussion of the meaning and intent of each question, interrelationships which exist among and between the various questions, methods of approaching the respondents, and the necessity of probing for the real meaning of some of the answers. Actual application of the schedule to a group of respondents prior to beginning of the interviewing process is usually desirable, not only from the point of view of training the interviewer, but also from the point of view of the survey supervisor who can then point out where improvements or changes in approach are needed.

After the inventory phase of the study is terminated, the consumated schedules are edited for completeness and consistency and samples of these schedules are selected for use in verifying each interviewer's work. The supervisor selects the schedules to be verified, makes the callbacks, and checks the answers with the original respondent for accuracy of recording the replies and for the interpretation of the replies where needed.

During the verifying and editing process, the answers may either be coded on the left margin of the schedule or transferred to a special coding sheet. The purpose of this step is to simplify the transcription of the results from the interview schedule to machine processable documents or media (i.e., punch cards or magnetic tape).

Next, the results are tabulated (usually by computer) for use both in validating the sample and in preparing the outline of the final report. Prior to beginning the report preparation phase, the sample should be tested to insure that it replicates the target population and that its error does not exceed that originally desired. Several statistical procedures are available for use in this testing process including the Chi Square, students' t and the z tests. A number of software packages are available for use in tabulating and testing survey results. These include the OSIRIS series, SAS, and SPSS. Each of these contain subroutines which create cross-tabulations, and test various aspects of the survey results.

The final step in the survey procedure is the preparation of the report of findings. This report should contain, in addition to the findings, a complete description and documentation of the methods used to complete all phases of the data compilation and analyses. This methodological description should be augmented by a bibliography of all references used during the course of the study.

Records and Controls

In case either the personal interview or the telephone survey approach has been chosen, after the sample has been selected, the interview schedule finalized, and the interviewing staff trained, the survey supervisor should assign lists of respondents to each of the interviewers. In doing this, the supervisor should maintain a master list of all respondents grouped by interviewers to which each was assigned. This will allow the supervisor to maintain an up-to-date record on the status of each respondent and on the progress of each interviewer. These control sheets should reflect such interviewing phases as:

   Date of first contact
   Action taken (or result of first contact)
   Date of appointment (or call back)
   Date the interview was completed
   Date the schedule was edited
   Date the schedule was keypunched
   Remarks

The maintenance of records of this type enable the research team to note areas in which progress is not satisfactory, thereby providing a forewarning of problem areas in which added effort is needed before schedule target dates are endangered. These records also allow the supervisor to evaluate the effectiveness of the members of the interviewing staff.

Problem Areas and Solutions

During the interviewing process, there will inevitably be those respondents who are not at home or are not available for an interview at the time of the first contact. This problem can usually be handled by use of callbacks and/or appointments. Callbacks to not-at-homes should be made at various times of day and on differing days of the week until the proper respondent is contacted or until it is deemed unlikely that the respondent is available (Dunkleberg and Day 1973). Usually, four callbacks are made before abandoning a respondent (Falthzik 1972). A second problem faced during the interviewing are nonresponses which are due to refusals to participate in the survey.

This latter problem is somewhat more difficult to solve, especially when the survey is conducted by telephone since little is known about the respondents except their telephone numbers, thus adjustments for their absence from the findings of the survey are not possible. However, when personal interviews are conducted, the interviewer can acquire considerable knowledge about the respondent (i.e. approximate income, standard of living, etc.) and, by comparing these observed indicators with those of others with the same or similar characteristics who have completed the questionnaire, some adjustments for these nonresponses can be made to the total results (Tyebjee 1979).

One school of thought continues to support the use of substitutions of sample units in the sample for nonresponses. If substitutions are used, methods are available to insure that the substitute sampling units are randomly drawn from the same strata as those from which the nonresponse units were drawn, thus minimizing the possibilities of injecting bias into the sample. It should be noted, however, that the use of substitutions is not universally accepted and should be used with extreme care and only in the event that a large proportion of the sample units fail to respond for whatever reason.

Surveys conducted by mail also present nonresponse problems, some of which can be solved by followup letters or telephone calls. However, the mail method of conducting surveys consistently has more nonresponses than do surveys using either telephone contacts or personal interviews. Adjustments to mail survey results for nonresponses are seldom possible since practically no information is available on those respondents who fail to complete the interview schedule.

References

Crisp, D. Marketing Research. New York: McGraw-Hill, 1957.

Dommermuth, W. P. The Use of Sampling in Marketing Research: Marketing Research Techniques. no. 3. Chicago, Illinois: The American Marketing Association, 1975.

Dunkelberg, W. C., and Day, G. S. "Non Response Bias and Call Backs in Sample Surveys." Journal of Marketing Research 10 (May 1973): 160-168.

Falthzek, A., "When to Make Telephone Interviews." Journal of Marketing Research 9 (November 1972): 451-452.

Ferber, R.; Blankertz, D. F.; and Hollander, S., Jr. Marketing Research. New York: The Ronald Press, 1964.

Glasser, G., and Metzger, G. D. "Random Digit Dialing as a Method of Telephone Sampling." Journal of Marketing Research 9 (February 1972): 59-64.

Green, P. E., and Tull, D. S. Research for Marketing Decisions. Englewood Cliffs, New Jersey: 1966.

Hauck, M., and Cox, M. "Locating a Sample by Random Digit Dialing." Public Opinion Quarterly 3 (Summer 1974): 253-260.

Hochstim, J. R. "A Critical Comparison of Three Strategies of Collecting Data from Households." Journal of the American Statistical Association 62 (September 1967): 976-989.

Landon, E. L., Jr., and Banks, S. K. "Relative Efficiency and Bias of Plus One Telephone Sampling." Journal of Marketing Research 14 (August 1977), 294-299.

Linsky, A. S. "Stimulating Responses to Mailed Questionnaires: A Review." Public Opinion Quarterly 39 (Spring 1975): 82-101.

Schmiedes Kamp, J. W., "Reinterviews by Telephone." Journal of Marketing 26 (January 1962): 28-34.

Schreier, F. T. *Modern Marketing Research: A Behavioral Science Approach*. Belmont, California: Wadsworth Publishing Co., 1963.

Seidman, S., and Ferber, R. "Comparison of Alternative Procedures for Collecting Consumer Expenditures Data for Frequently Purchased Products." *Journal of Marketing Research* 11 (May 1974): 128-135.

Telser, E. "Data Exorcises Bias in Phone versus Personal Interview Debate." *Marketing News* 10 (September 10, 1976) 6-7.

Tyebjee, T. T. "Telephone Survey Methods: The State of the Art." *Journal of Marketing* 43 (Summer 1979): 68-79.

Wheatley, J. "Self Administered Written Questionnaires or Telephone Interviews?" *Journal of Marketing Research* 10 (February 1973): 94-95.

Worchester, R. M., editor. *Consumer Market Research Handbook*. London: McGraw-Hill, 1971.

World Tourist Organization. *Handbook on Sampling Methods Applicable to Tourist Research*. Madrid, n.d.

4

Surveys and Forecasts

Thomas L. Burton

It is useful to consider the problems associated with outdoor recreation surveys under two broad categories: technical problems, having to do with the collection and statistical manipulation of data; and substantive problems, having to do with the reasons why survey data are sought and what kinds of data are required. Schroeder, Dikeman, and Chilman in the three previous chapters of this book have dealt extensively with issues concerning the technical aspects of surveys, measurement problems, and data collection. Through his careful outline of procedures, Dikeman has illustrated how many of the pitfalls of survey research can be avoided: for example, the biased sample and the leading question. By emphasizing the importance of proper procedure, he has shown how the likelihood of error or bias can be reduced. Schroeder has illustrated the variety of measurement problems associated with the evaluation of aesthetics. Chilman has focussed upon the technical problems associated with the development of a particular information gathering system for a specific type of recreational land area. He, too, emphasizes appropriate procedures for the collection of data—in this case through visitor surveys. Chilman, however, also addresses a broader question, at least implicitly. This has to do with the appropriateness of the data that are collected through surveys. By placing his discussion of visitor survey procedures into the context of a land and resource management system for large wildland areas, he implicitly acknowledges the substantive problems noted earlier; namely, why are survey data sought and what kinds of data are needed?

Determining Collective Goods

The primary reason why outdoor recreation surveys are carried out is to provide a basis for the development of forecasts or predictions which can then be employed in planning and management activities. In Canada and the United States, many outdoor recreation facilities, programs, and services are provided as free goods or at nominal prices only: that is, the consumer is not asked to pay for them as he uses them, or else he is asked to pay only a nominal fee which in no way covers the cost of supply. These collective or public goods as they are called have a well established history and consist of two basic kinds. First, there are pure public goods which can only be provided on a collective basis: it is impossible to separate out the value of such goods to any particular individual. An example of such a pure public good is national defense; another example is public health protection against typhoid epidemics in urban centers. Everybody in society benefits from national defense to the same extent (allowing for variations caused by the specific location of defense units). One individual does not benefit more than another. Similarly, all members of the community benefit from the provision of public health services aimed at the prevention of a typhoid epidemic in an urban centre. One individual does not benefit more than another.

The second type of public good may be described as an optional collective good. It is the kind of good which society has chosen to provide collectively, even though it is possible to separate out the value of such a good to the individual consumer and to charge him directly for his consumption of it. There are two primary types of optional public goods. The first is the type of good that would be wholly uneconomic to provide to individual consumers through normal market mechanisms. An example might be a scenic highway in a remote area of the country. Theoretically, it is possible to charge a price for the use of the highway. But the elasticity of demand for its use is such that there is no price at which the costs of providing the highway, including the costs of collecting the fees from users, will be covered by the revenues obtained. The only way that the highway can be provided, therefore, is through a societal decision to provide it as a public good. Some individuals (the users) will benefit more than others (the nonusers) from the provision of this as a public good.

The second type of optional public good is one that could be provided to individual consumers on a profitable basis through normal market mechanisms. Notwithstanding this, society opts to provide it as a public good. An example of such a good might be public tennis courts in a city park. It is possible to charge a price for the use of such courts. Moreover, a price could be set which would enable the operator to make what the economist calls a normal profit. In spite of this, many communities in North America have chosen to provide tennis courts as public goods, and to charge only nominal fees for their use. Some individuals (the users) will benefit more than others (the nonusers) from the provision of this public good. Moreover, there will be different degrees of benefit to users—for example, between those who would have used a market facility anyway and those who would have been unable to do so.

Many outdoor recreation facilities, programs, and services in North America consist of one or other of the two types of optional public goods: for example, national, state or provincial, and local parks; campgrounds; interpretation programs; hiking and cross country ski trails; and many urban recreation facilities, such as baseball diamonds and playgrounds. But whatever form they may take, such goods present a major problem for decision-makers in that there is no readily available basis for measuring the demand for them and, hence, no simple formula for determining how much of each to provide. In the normal market, demand and supply combine to determine price. Suppliers regulate the amount of a good that they supply by reference to price and their costs of production.

But how does the supplier of public goods determine how much to provide, given that there is no demand schedule relating quantities demanded to a range of prices: that is, when there is no price, or else it is set arbitrarily? Generally, the supplier, which is usually a government agency, attempts to ascertain what is the current quantity demanded for the particular good—say, visits to National Parks. A survey is carried out which seeks to discover not only the current number of visits to National Parks but also how these relate to presumed determining characteristics, such as age, income, level of education, and possession of various items of recreational equipment. The results are then employed to forecast changes in the numbers of visits that can be expected with anticipated changes in these determining, or predictor, variables. The supplier of public (nonmarket) goods depends heavily upon surveys to obtain valid and accurate information about current levels of consumption (quantity demanded) for these goods, and then upon a variety of forecasting methods and techniques to predict how consumption levels can be expected to change under given conditions.

But what kinds of data are needed for forecasting? Cherry remarked, in 1978, that he "detected a considerable readiness among [Canadian] recreation researchers to shift their focus from activity research to studies concerned with the quality of the experiences obtained through participation in activities.." This, he noted, placed researchers firmly into a style "which emphasizes the place which a particular leisure activity has in a person's life, rather than on the activity itself" (Cherry 1979). What Cherry was suggesting, in effect, was that the kinds of recreation data that should be sought through surveys depends directly upon the types and quality of use that is to be made of these data. In the present context, what kinds of data are appropriately sought through outdoor recreation surveys depends upon the quality and utility of the forecasting techniques to which the data are to be applied. This leads directly to a discussion of the types and adequacy of current forecasting methods for outdoor recreation, specifically as these have been applied in North America.

There is a story told of a group of Americans travelling in Britain during the Second World War when all the road signs had been taken down in anticipation of a German invasion. They were trying to find their way to an American military base and were hopelessly lost in those winding roads that dot the British countryside. As they were about to give up in frustration, they saw an old country yokel leaning on a fence puffing his pipe. He was clearly a local resident (if not the oldest resident) and they were quite certain that he would be able to help them reach their destination. They went up to him and asked if he could tell them how to get to the American military base. The old man started to tell them what to do. He said: "If you go left down here, take the second right and then the fork by the Jones farm . . . No!! No!! that's not going to work!! Start again. Go right out of here, down about a mile, and you'll see a birch tree standing alone in the middle of a field on your right, and just after that there will be a turn to the left. Then you come to the Smith farm and you take the left fork. No!! That's not going to work either." He thought for a long while; scratched his head; and then he looked at them and said: "You know, you can't get there from here."

This story illustrates succinctly some major problems concerning present approaches to forecasting and attempts to predict the future of outdoor recreation demands in North America.

Approaches to Recreation Forecasting:
Positive and Normative Techniques

There has been considerable attention given in the past decade or so to outdoor recreation forecasting and to the development of outdoor recreation futures. A wide variety of techniques has emerged which have to do with predicting the future development of outdoor recreation. But, for all their variety, these techniques fall broadly into two classes.

On the one hand, there have been those techniques, such as extrapolation, projection, predictive modelling and the like, which are essentially <u>positive</u> in nature. That is to say, they are concerned with <u>what is, has been</u> or <u>will be</u>. The focus is upon the extension of the past into the future, albeit through sophisticated analyses of causal variables and their interactions. In their simplest form, these positive prognostications extend a single trend into the future. Thus, past trends and visits to National Parks have simply been extended into the future to indicate the probable number of visits at given future dates. Taken to their logical conclusion, such forecasts have been reduced to absurdity. Based upon changes in the number of visits to National Parks in Canada between 1967 and 1976, it can be shown that every man, woman, and child in Canada in the year 2000 will spend at least 250 days per year in a national park! At their most sophisticated, these techniques attempt to discover interrelationships between presumed causal variables, such as age, income, occupation, previous recreation experience, and so on, and, through a modelling approach, indicate what is expected to happen in the future. Given the uncertainty of present knowledge regarding relationships between variables, there has been considerable scope for the presentation of more than one future. That is, with changes in the assumptions about the nature of the interrelationships it has been possible to predict more than one future. These are generally called <u>alternative futures,</u> each of which has more or less probability of actually occurring.

The second approach has been <u>normative</u> in character. Instead of focussing exclusively upon what <u>will</u> happen, it attempts to imbue the forecasting exercise with attitudes and opinions by developing futures which it is thought <u>ought to happen</u>. In other words, it goes beyond predicting what is likely to happen and beyond the development of <u>alternative futures</u>, to posit <u>preferable</u> or <u>desirable futures</u>. These, however, have always been built upon exhaustive analysis of existing societal, technological, institutional, and economic conditions, so that preferable or desirable futures emerge out of alternative ones. In this sense, <u>normative</u> approaches to forecasting have been merely extensions or adaptations of <u>positive</u> approaches. Positive forecasts of what is likely to happen under given sets of circumstances have first been developed. These alternative (probable) futures have then been subjected to value judgments so as to develop a preferred (desirable) future. The purpose, of course, has been to understand the kinds of interventions that will be necessary if the preferred future is, in fact, to be obtained.

What is significant here, is that virtually all outdoor recreation forecasting to date in North America has been either <u>positive</u> or <u>normative</u> in character. Time series analyses, causal models, extrapolations, and scenarios have all set out to demonstrate what is expected to happen at given dates under given circumstances. Some of these have then gone on to suggest which of any given set of described futures is preferable and what it is necessary to do in order to obtain a particular preferred future. An excellent summary of these techniques was given in a report produced by the Canadian Outdoor Recreation Committee: "A wide variety of methods are (sic) available for forecasting the future. The simpler techniques which assume 'more of the same' are usually adequate for short-range projections. Mathematical models based upon causal relationships and correlations between variables permit more complex projections over extended periods of time. These models are based upon certain assumptions, and depend upon the quantitative relationships remaining static over time. Long-range forecasting techniques sacrifice precision and mathematical rigor in exchange for the ability to accommodate surprises or shocks. Although these methods are still being refined and evaluated, they are able to identify possible futures for which it may be necessary to prepare." (Canadian Outdoor Recreation Committee 1976). One cannot quarrel with this comment. On the contrary, it states succinctly, and with eloquence, what is the current state of outdoor recreation forecasting in North America.

Problems of Current Outdoor Recreation Forecasting

It is evident that one basic assumption underlies all (or almost all) present outdoor recreation forecasting techniques; namely, that the future is, in some way and to some degree, reflected in the past. Given the context of such forecasts, it is difficult to see how a general assumption of this nature can be avoided. These forecasts are based upon analyses of existing societal conditions—economics, technology, institutional organization, and the like. They posit changes in these conditions. The ability to perceive probable change is conditioned, in large measure, by experience of past change. Furthermore, there is no substantial evidence to suggest that such assumptions are wholly unrealistic or that they provide a picture of the future which is totally unrelated to what actually happens—at least in the short run. In the first place, it is clearly impossible for forecasters to foresee, very precisely, developments which arise from no obvious existing base. All technological forecasting, for example, is based upon a given existing technology. Forecasters may speculate about the likely effects of revolutionary discoveries arising out of known research; but they cannot be expected to take account of the effects of chance discoveries or genius. Secondly, experience and empirical inquiry have shown that many present conditions are, indeed, derived from clearly identifiable and consistent past trends and that, therefore, the future is, in some ways, reflected by the past. It is, therefore, not the assumption about a consistent relationship between the past and the future which provides a major problem for the forecaster, but, rather, the nature of that relationship. Herein lies the crux of the forecaster's problems. If there are factors existing in the past and the present which will significantly influence the future, what are these and how are they interrelated?

To date, outdoor recreation forecasters have concentrated upon what may be called descriptive and behavioral variables related to levels of participation in outdoor recreation activities or pursuits. Descriptive variables have been socio-demographic in character, covering such items as age, sex, marital status, occupation, education, income, and family structure. Behavioral variables have encompassed such items as the numbers of outdoor recreation activities undertaken in a given time period, the frequency of participation in these activities, their location, and the persons with whom they have been undertaken. Statistical relationships between the descriptive and behavioral variables have been plotted over time and these relationships then extended into the future to produce forecasts. The technique is, operationally, quite simple, especially for those with access to a computer, and is one which produces precise (and, hence, attractive) predictions. The descriptive or socio-demographic variables have been defined as independent ones. Changes in the behavioral variables - that is, in participation in outdoor recreation activities - then become dependent upon changes in the socio-demographic variables and upon the observed past changes in the relationships between these and levels of participation in the given activities.

The major difficulty with this approach lies in the assumption that the socio-demographic variables, are, in truth, independent ones. In reality, however, they are merely surrogates for other variables, such as preferences, attitudes, and values. The central problem of virtually all outdoor recreation forecasting to date is that it has failed to take account of, or to come to terms adequately with, the notions of individual and societal values, and changes in these. Western industrial and postindustrial societies have been fortunate in that values have changed only incrementally and relatively slowly over the past twenty years or so. As a consequence, the socio-demographic variables that have been employed in forecasting models as surrogates for, or indicators of, human values have served tolerably well.

Emery and Trist have suggested, however, that this pattern of relative stability is breaking down (Emery and Trist 1975). They maintain that urban-industrial people live today in an environment which is rapidly changing in radical and unexpected ways and which, thereby, exhibits great uncertainty. The socio-demographic characteristics of the population are no longer stable indicators of human values. If this is so, they can no longer be employed as independent or causal variables. Instead, forecasters must deal directly with values; for, in Emery's words, "only values have the necessary breadth and stretch in social time and space" to provide a stable base for forecasting and hence, planning (Emery 1975). But, even if one grants that outdoor recreation forecasting must attempt to deal directly with values and not seek to address them through easily measured surrogates, how is this to be done?

Incorporating Values in the Forecasting Process

Several approaches for incorporating alues in the forecasting process have been proposed and tested in recent years. The most well known of these is, perhaps, the Delphi Survey which is designed to provide a prognosis of future change based upon the opinions of individuals who are selected because of their expertise in a variety of fields, such as sociology, economics, politics, management, and so on. The task of these specialists is to form a concensus regarding probable future events and their timing. Employing more than one round of interviews (and, if necessary, bringing the participants together) the Delphi Survey seeks to develop concensus through interactions of a very specific kind among the participants in the process.

Trist and Emery have developed a technique called Searching (Trist and Emery 1975). It is a means of coming to grips with the "turbulent environment" which they identify as having emerged in the Western world during the 1960s. Central to the searching concept is the identification of the values and ideals of a community. Information retrieval and evaluation only come at a later stage in the process. Building on the view that only values provide a stable base for forecasting, Emery argues that they are also universal; that is, everyone in society has values and nobody is more or less of an expert in these values than anyone else (Emery 1976). Equally significant is the fact that there can be no single "correct value". In looking at the future, one must take cognizance of a variety of values, some of which may, indeed, be incompatible, but all of which have equal right to consideration. Thus, searching is a process which seeks to provide groups of people likely to be affected by future changes with an opportunity to identify and agree upon the values that may be affected by such changes.

The process is carried out by means of what is called a Search Conference, usually taking place over a three to five day period and involving from twenty to thirty people who are selected on the basis of having shown leadership and concern about issues pertinent to the search. Marriott has noted that it is usually carried out in "a social island," away from the usual working or living environments of the participants (Marriott 1979). This, he suggests, strengthens the formation of a community identity among the persons involved, as well as eliminating the disruptive influences of day-to-day living. A Search Conference is managed rather than led, the management team essentially functioning as facilitators and resource people whose role is to create and sustain the conditions in which the participants in the conference can explore changing values and ideals and, thereby, move to formulate workable guidelines for decision making.

The primary point to be made, however, is that, whether one uses a technique such as the Search Conference or the Delphi Survey, the focus of attention is not upon what participants think will happen in a given set of circumstances in the future; but, rather, upon what are the values of the people that make up a community and, hence, upon what people would like to happen. It is, in essence, a reversal of present approaches to forecasting, which stress, first, the identification of probable events in the future and, then, the choice from among these of a desired or preferred future. Through processes such as Searching, with their emphasis upon value identification, it is possible to determine what is the desirable or preferred future and, then, to examine present trends and conditions and their likely development to see if, in fact, there is any possibility that the preferred future will emerge from the present with little or no intervention. Alternatively, one is able to determine what kinds of intervention will be necessary to obtain the preferred future, if, in fact, it is deemed unlikely to emerge autonomously.

Few attempts have been made in North America to employ these kinds of approaches to forecasting. There have been one or two cases that stand out, which have tried, in part at least, to go beyond trend analysis and normative forecasting to this process of what may be called prescriptive forecasting. Perhaps the most significant of these for outdoor recreation was The Elora Prescription, which was developed by a group of concerned individuals and interpreted in a report prepared by Balmer for the Ontario Ministry of Culture and Recreation (Balmer 1978). This took a wide view of the future; but in this particular context, it attempted to look at changing values and their implications for the future of recreation in Canada. It examined, for example, the possible transformation of societal attitudes: from institutionalization towards individualism and humanism; from segmentalism towards holism; from professionalization towards participation and involvement; from a reactive to a proactive ethic; and from a consumptive to a conserver attitude in economic and social behavior.

Implications for Outdoor Recreation Research

There are several implications for outdoor recreation research which may be drawn from this discussion. First, a shift is required in the focus of research efforts. I have argued elsewhere that perhaps the most important step in the drive to maturity for the field of leisure research generally must be the development of an epistemology of leisure (Burton 1979). The establishment of a set of unifying concepts and codes for the field is essential if one is to be able to make any meaningful prescriptive forecasts about the future of recreation and leisure in North America. Until viable theories about the nature of leisure (and, hence, outdoor recreation) have been developed, the field of recreation and leisure studies cannot claim to be a mature one. More immediately, without a basic theory of the nature of leisure and recreation and their roles in North American industrial and postindustrial society, it will be impossible to fully comprehend the relationships between social and individual values, on the one hand, and leisure and recreation behaviour, on the other. Without a clear understanding of such relationships, one cannot provide reliable forecasts about the future. And, without reliable forecasts, planning and management will be, at best, hazardous.

It is important, also, that theories be tested. It is not enough to develop a set of Aristotelian or other concepts about the nature of leisure and recreation and their significance to society and the individual. Through studies designed specifically to test propositions and components of theories, a solid body of knowledge can be built up with empirical validity, about the relationships between values and leisure (and recreation).

Prescriptive Forecasting: A Value-Oriented Alternative

The crucial issue with respect to data collection, then, is not <u>how</u> to go about it, but <u>what</u> to encompass in it. Leisure research, and, more specifically, outdoor recreation research, was dominated in North America during the 1960s and 1970s by the activity survey. Emphasis was given to the collection of information about what people did in their free time, how often they did these things, with whom they did them, and where the activities were carried out. Such surveys, in themselves, were (and are) not necessarily illegitimate. They have often served, for example, as "benchmarks" (not unlike general population censuses) which provide leisure profiles of a population and illustrate the ways in which these changes. On the other hand, such surveys often have been of little or no use when their stated purpose has been to provide a base for forecasting and planning. The central question in all research which relies upon the collection of data is: how relevant are the data to the pursuit of the stated research problem? All too often this question has not been asked in leisure and outdoor recreation research. Reichmann noted more than two decades ago that "there are two widely divergent views of statistics currently popular among the general public. One view is that published statistics are themselves invested with some quality of meaning not unlike the qualities ascribed to numbers by the Pythagoreans, and that they enjoy such a degree of infallibility that they may be accepted without question. This, of course, is just as nonsensical as the other and yet more popular belief that statistics can be made to prove anything and, therefore, by implication, that in fact they can prove nothing" (Reichmann 1961). This latter view was put more colourfully by the British Prime Minister, Benjamin Disraeli, more than a century ago, when he declared that "there are three kinds of lies: lies, damned lies, and statistics."

It must always be remembered that the collection of data about leisure and recreation is not an end in itself, but a means to some other end, usually for purposes of forecasting, planning, and management in an age of ever more sophisticated computer technology, one can discern a growing tendency to consider the choice of data to be collected not on the basis of how well they address the stated research problem, but in terms of their suitability for computer programming and analysis. Data collection and analysis techniques must be seen in their proper role, as tools that assist or support studies aimed at understanding the values of leisure and recreation to North Americans and at explaining the roles that leisure and recreation play in individual self-fulfillment and societal development. What is important is not what the data <u>say</u>, but what they <u>mean</u>.

In conclusion, it is worth returning to the story told earlier. The kind of recreation future which reflects the values and preferences of individuals and society will not be identified through a continued emphasis upon <u>positive</u> or <u>normative</u> forecasting approaches. <u>Positive forecasting</u>, as defined, simply involves the extension of the past into the future, as though people are mere puppets whose destinies are already determined. It says: "here is what will happen." <u>Normative forecasting</u> permits a degree of choice over the future, but restricts this choice by, first, determining a set of probable futures based upon variations of past trends and their extension into the future. It says "here is what can happen; you may choose from within this." Prescriptive forecasting starts from values and seeks to determine the kinds of future that people want. It then asks how such futures can be achieved. It says "here is the future we want; let's create it." If one believes that the ultimate goal of individual and social activity is the betterment of man's lot through the expression of human values, then the only kind of recreation forecasting that makes sense is prescriptive forecasting. Or, to put it another way, employing positive and normative models, we really can't get there from here!

References

Balmer, K. *The Elora Prescription*. Toronto: Ontario Ministry of Culture and Recreation, 1978.

Burton, T. L. "The Development of Leisure Research in Canada: An Analogical Tale." *Society and Leisure*, 2, 1, April 1979, pp. 13-34.

Burton, T. L. "The State of Leisure Research in Canada." In *Contemporary Leisure Research, Proceedings of the Second Canadian Congress on Leisure Research*, edited by E. M. Avedon et. al. Toronto: Ontario Research Council on Leisure, 1979.

Canadian Outdoor Recreation Research Committee: *Park and Recreation Futures in Canada*. Ottawa: Federal-Provincial Parks Conference, 1976.

Cherry, G. E. "Observations and Comments." In *Contemporary Leisure Research, Proceedings of the Second Canadian Congress on Leisure Research*, edited by E. M. Avedon et. al. Toronto: Ontario Research Council on Leisure, 1979.

Emery, F. E. et. al. *Futures We're In*. Canberra: Australian National University, 1974.

Emery, M. "Searching: For New Directions." In *New Ways, For New Times*. Canberra: Australian National University, Occasional Papers in Continuing Education, no. 12, 1976.

Emery, F. E., and Trist, E. L. *Towards a Social Ecology*. London: Plemun/Rosetta, 1975.

Marriott, K. L. *The Provision and 'Effectiveness' Evaluation of Open Space in Australian Urban Areas*. Ph.D. dissertation, Monash University, Australia, 1979.

Reichmann, C. *The Use and Abuse of Statistics*. London: Penguin Books, 1961.

Section Four:
Planning and Policy Issues

1

Renewable Recreation Resources in the United States: The Resource Situation and Critical Policy Issues

H. Ken Cordell
John C. Hendee
J. Herbert Stevens, Jr.

Our country has had a long tradition of using forests, rangelands, and other open or green spaces for outdoor recreation. These traditions include picnics on town commons, hunting and fishing for sport as well as subsistence, and individual exploration of wild areas. The outdoor tradition in the United States has involved all segments of our society as a major expression of our national character.

Recently, we have begun to understand more about the benefits from outdoor recreation and their important role in our society. Kelly (1981) recognized three principal types of benefits from outdoor recreation: personal, societal, and economic.

Personal benefits are those directly experienced by individuals. These include many different satisfactions that may lead to an overall sense of enjoyment (Hendee and Bryan 1978). Societal benefits are those that accrue to large social groups. These include the improvement of communities, families, and friendship groups. Economic benefits include increased employment and income, both locally, for communities near recreation sites, and nationally.

Over the last eighty years, management and development of outdoor recreation opportunities on federal, state, and private lands and waters have centered on four major supply activities. These include: (1) preservation of natural, scenic, historic, and cultural resources; (2) provision of information, interpretation, and safety for visitors; (3) gaining access for public use of lands and waters by providing roads and trails; and (4) development of sites and facilities for such outdoor recreation activities as camping, snow skiing, and boating.

Accompanying these outdoor recreation supply activities have been increases in our standard of living and rapid growth of participation in outdoor recreation. However, trends indicate that increases in the standard of living have slowed ap-

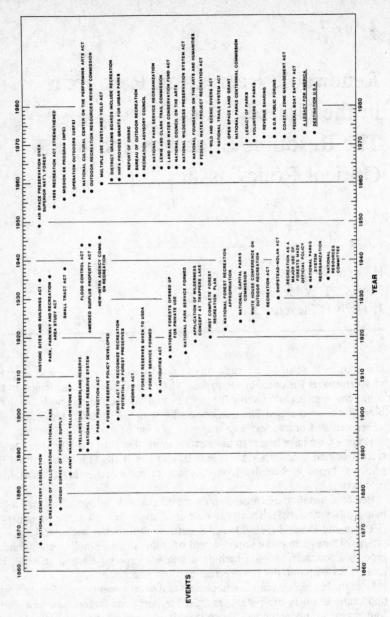

Figure 1

Chronicle of Federal Recreation and Parks Legislation in the United States,
1860-1975
SOURCE: Carleton S. Van Doren and Louis Hodges,
America's Park and Recreation Heritage - A Chronology.
Washington, D.C.: Government Printing Office, 1975.

preciably over the last ten years. It is difficult to predict whether this slowed rate of increase in the standard of living will continue, or what its impact on future recreation demands will be. Outdoor recreation is so deeply ingrained in our society's lifestyle that increasing constraints on some forms of participation may only change the activities and settings for outdoor recreation, not the overall amount of participation.

This chapter is an adaptation of an in-depth examination of the historical and current supply and use of outdoor recreation resources in the United States. The original analysis was developed as the resource paper on outdoor recreation in the United States for the Recreation Working Group of the National Conference on Renewable Natural Resources (Washington, D.C., December 1980). This resource paper was further elaborated upon to provide the base documentation for the Outdoor Recreation and Wilderness Assessment for the USDA Forest Service update in 1984 of the Resources Planning Act Assessment of the Forest and Rangeland Situation in the United States (Cordell and Hendee 1982). In these preceeding reports, and in a more abbreviated form in this chapter, we have analyzed social and economic factors related to future outdoor recreation supply and use, and from this analysis have briefly identified issues and needed actions.

THE RECREATION LEGACY IN THE UNITED STATES AND CURRENT PROBLEMS

Administrative and Legislative History

The history of outdoor recreation in the United States has been one of essentially free access to public lands. For over 100 years, legislation and major administrative actions have shaped federal and state outdoor recreation policy. A chronology of pertinent legislation from 1866 through 1975 appears in Figure 1 (Van Doren and Hodges 1975). Some of the more noteworthy actions that have impacted outdoor recreation since 1974 include the Forest and Rangeland Renewable Resources Planning Act of 1974, the National Forest Management Act of 1976, the Federal Land Policy and Management Act of 1976, and the Public Rangelands Improvement Act of 1978. These acts decreed that management of federal forests and rangelands would be based on detailed inventories of resources, careful planning, and public participation to achieve a balance among competing uses.

In 1975, the so-called "Eastern Wilderness Act" expanded the definition of wilderness to include more areas in the East. In 1977, the Clean Air Act required consideration of recreation benefits in all wastewater treatment projects and water quality management plans. In 1978, the Heritage Conservation and Recreation Service (HCRS) was established. HCRS was a consolidation of the previous functions of the Bureau of Outdoor Recreation and the heritage preservation functions of the National Park Service.

The National Parks and Recreation Act of 1978 mandated the study of unutilized, underutilized, and excess federal real property for possible wilderness, wildlife conservation, and recreation and park uses. Also in 1978, the Forest Service embarked on the second Roadless Area Review and Evaluation (RARE II) to identify lands for either wilderness classification, further planning, or non-wilderness use. In 1979, the "Alaska lands legislation" brought the total Wilderness System acreage in Alaska to more than 56 million acres and the total in the National Wilderness Preservation System to nearly 80 million acres. In 1981, the HCRS was abolished and its functions were transferred back to the National Park Service.

The above history helps one understand the current demand and supply situation and place some anticipated future trends into perspective. But times have changed and these past actions and policies, and the thinking they represented, may no longer be as appropriate or acceptable. We are currently entering a new era for outdoor recreation in the United States.

The Current Change in Direction

Up to the late 1970's legislative and administrative actions marked increasing support for the recreational and aesthetic values of natural resources. During the late 1970's, tightening economic conditions and an increasingly conservative mood lead to leveling off and some decline in proposals and appropriations for recreation management and acquisition and environmental protection. For example, real dollar appropriations for federal recreation management, which grew from about $85 million in 1960 to $718 million in 1978, fell to only $374 million in 1982 (Figure 2).

Smaller recreation budgets have forced federal agencies to reduce maintenance, development, and supervision at many developed sites. Some sites have been closed indefinitely due to a lack of operating funds. To help offset closures and restricted service, some agencies are looking for volunteers to provide area supervision, fee collection, and information. Local governments and private enterprises are being encouraged to manage some of the federal recreation sites. There is unprecedented withdrawal of federal involvement in recreation support and a shift toward a pay-as-you-go approach featuring higher fees on more areas and reliance on market and entrepreneurial forces to lower costs and increase recreation supply.

The move to involve the private sector and market forces in recreation management is a rapid and dramatic development. For example, the Tennessee Valley Authority, Forest Service, Corps of Engineers, and National Park Service have expanded the use of fees, the level of fees, and the concessionaire arrangements for operating facilities.

Currently, there is proposed legislation before the Congress to liberalize authorizations for charging fees for recreation on federal lands. Its intent is to broaden the range of recreation facilities and areas on which fees can be charged so that expected increased revenues can help cover rising operation and maintenance costs in the face of decreased levels of management appropriations.

Other cutbacks in federal support for outdoor recreation may not be so easily covered by the market place and increase entrepreneurial activity. For example, the nationwide planning and matching grants programs within the National Park Service have been drastically reduced and may be subject to discontinuation. Major programs that would be most directly affected include river and trail studies, land acquisition, the Urban Park and Recovery Program, nationwide planning, and technical services.

While the proposed reductions in federal support for outdoor recreation shock many administrators, they also represent both challenge and opportunity. Is there sufficient demand for outdoor recreation to stimulate a response by the private sector? Can private entrepreneurs provide recreation services on public lands at desired quality levels? Will increased reliance on the market to direct allocations among recreation programs compensate for reduced planning and study? Will market-allocated resources provide an equitable distribution of recreation opportunity among segments of our society? We don't have answers to all of these questions, but it is very possible that the shift toward deregulation of outdoor recreation could lead to greater efficiency in our nation's recreation delivery system.

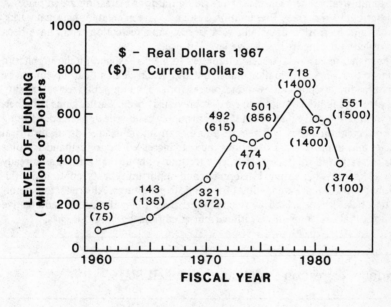

Figure 2

Estimated Federal Outlays for Recreation Resource Planning in 1967 Real Dollars.

SOURCES: Office of Management and Budget, the Budget of the United States Government: Fiscal Year(s) 1960, 1965, 1970, 1972, 1974, 1976, 1978, 1980, 1981, and 1982. Washington, D.C.: Government Printing Office and Bureau of Economic Statistics, Handbook of Basic Economic Statistics, Vol. 36, No. 1. Washington, D.C.: Economic Statistics Bureau of Washington, 1982, pp. 99-101.

Management Problems

Some of the more serious problems faced by land management agencies include crowding, traffic congestion, user conflicts, data availability, wilderness allocation, maintenance of visual quality, projecting future demands, maintaining and restoring heavily used sites, and understanding the satisfactions and benefits resulting from recreation experiences. Current efforts to address these problems and needs are being reduced in this era as philosophies about government's role in outdoor recreation change. In their broadest sense, current philosophies view government mostly as a provider of primitive and semiprivate opportunities, with much reduced regulation, service, and development. The private sector is viewed as the capital investor in intensive site development and services. Yet, in spite of these emerging philosophies, past acts by Congress and administrative events have clearly had enduring effects. Providing recreation opportunities is still a mandated government responsibility. Federal authority, facilities, coordination, and administrative mechanisms for providing outdoor recreation are in place. A vast National Wilderness Preservation System has been created; national parks, forests, and recreation areas and wild, scenic, and recreation rivers have been established and support impressive levels of use.

The mandate has always been interpreted to mean—expand public supplies in response to rising participation rates. But recreation demand can no longer be met so readily. Opportunities and resources for expanding public recreation supplies are more limited than they have ever previously been. Earlier gains from better coordination and expanded authority probably cannot be duplicated. Meeting future recreation needs will require more than linear extensions of historical policies and approaches. Projections indicate increased future demand for outdoor recreation in the face of greater uncertainty about that future, an already saturated supply, increasing development and opportunity costs, continued inflation, and more intense competition for public expenditures. All are factors pointing to a need for new, and more comprehensive, policy directions and creative solutions that are compatible with current conditions and philosophies.

Outdoor Recreation Supply in the United States

Outdoor recreation opportunities occur among a wide variety of resources including forests, rangelands, and specially designated areas such as national parks and wilderness areas. The kinds of opportunities provided are largely determined by the distribution of these land and water areas among various categories of public and private ownership and geographic distribution relative to population.

Ownership and Amount

The United States is comprised of about 2.265 billion acres of land and water surrounded by 84,200 miles of coastal shoreline. The water base contains 3.2 million miles of rivers and streams and 49,000 large and 2 million small reservoirs, lakes, and ponds which are especially important as outdoor recreation settings.

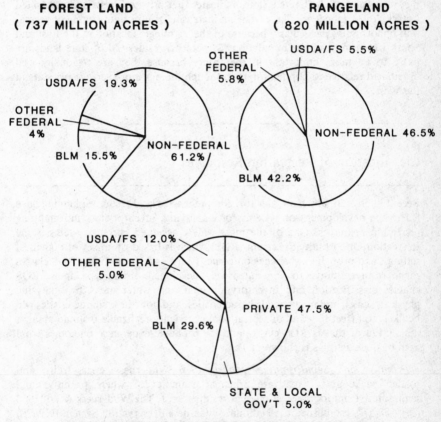

FOREST LAND
(737 MILLION ACRES)

USDA/FS 19.3%
OTHER FEDERAL 4%
BLM 15.5%
NON-FEDERAL 61.2%
OTHER FEDERAL 5.8%

RANGELAND
(820 MILLION ACRES)

USDA/FS 5.5%
NON-FEDERAL 46.5%
BLM 42.2%

USDA/FS 12.0%
OTHER FEDERAL 5.0%
BLM 29.6%
PRIVATE 47.5%
STATE & LOCAL GOV'T 5.0%

TOTAL FOR BOTH FOREST AND RANGELAND
(1,557 MILLION ACRES)

Figure 3

Percentage of Forest and Range Land Ownership in the United States, 1977
SOURCE: U.S. Dept. of Agriculture, Forest Service, An Assessment of the *Forest and Range Land Situation in the United States*. Washington, D.C.: Government Printing Office, 1980. pp. 34-35.

About 1.56 billion acres of the U.S. land base are classified as forest and rangeland and associated waters (Figure 3). Private ownerships hold approximately 47.5 percent of the total forest and rangeland acreage while the federal government owns 46.6 percent. The remaining forest and rangeland acreage (5.9 percent) is owned by state, county, and municipal governments. As Figure 3 also shows, 61.2 percent of the forested land is in non-federal ownerships, and most of this is in the eastern and southern regions of the United States. Similarly, 46.5 percent of the rangeland is in private ownership, and the bulk of it is located in the West.

This disproportionate distribution of forest and rangeland acreage relative to the population of the United States indicates that private forests and associated waters, for instance, are likely to be an increasingly important source of recreation opportunity, particularly because of their strategic location in the East and South where most of the population (78 percent) resides. Also, state lands are likely to be more important in the future because they are regionally well distributed relative to population, even though there is more acreage per state in the West.

Classification of Recreation Resources

Recent interest in, and mandates for, comprehensive land resource planning have led to the development of systems for classifying, inventorying, and mapping recreation resources. One of the most widely accepted current systems is the Recreation Opportunity Spectrum (ROS) which is based on mixes of activities, settings, and probable experience outcomes (Buist and Hoots 1982). ROS classes range from primitive to very intensively developed, urban-type areas. ROS enables classification and inventory of land and water areas by analyzing physical, social, and managerial characteristics, and how these characteristics will be likely to affect the kind of recreational experience realizable from an area. A description of the six ROS classes and the probable experience outcomes from each of these settings is shown in Table 1.

Primitive and SemiPrimitive Opportunities Wilderness areas, trails, and roaded backcountry areas are principal examples of where primitive and semiprimitive outdoor recreation opportunities exist. The Wilderness Act of 1964 (P.L. 88-577) established the National Wilderness Preservation System (NWPS) with an initial allocation of 9.1 million acres. As of January 1, 1981, the NWPS totaled 79.8 million acres with 56.5 million acres (70.8 percent) in Alaska and 23.3 million acres (29.2 percent) in the remaining states. Since 1964, visitor use of these areas has more than doubled with an average annual rate of growth in use of 4.3 percent (Peterson 1981).

Even though the NWPS has grown considerably since 1964 and provides a tremendous amount of primitive recreation opportunity, it should be noted that most of the areas within the NWPS have limited access and are distant from significant population concentrations. For example, only a little over 3 percent of the NWPS is located in the East where over three-fourths of the U.S. population

Table 1

Recreation Opportunity Spectrum (ROS) System for Resource Characterization Based on Setting and Experience Potential

		ROS			
Primitive	Semi-Primitive Non-Motorized	Semi-Primitive Motorized	Roaded Natural	Rural	Urban

Setting Characterization*

Primitive	Semi-Primitive Non-Motorized	Semi-Primitive Motorized	Roaded Natural	Rural	Urban
Area is characterized by essentially unmodified natural environment of fairly large size interaction between users is very low and evidence of other users is minimal. The area is managed to be essentially free from evidence of human-induced restrictions and controls. Motorized use within the area is not permitted.	Area is characterized by a predominantly natural or natural appearing environment of moderate-to-large size interaction between users is low but there is often evidence of other users. The area is aged in such a way that minimum on-site controls and restrictions may be present, but are subtle. Motorized use is not permitted.	Area is characterized by a predominantly natural or natural appearing environment of moderate-to-large size. Concentration of users is low., but there is often evidence of other users. The area managed in such a way that minimum on-site controls and restrictions may be present, but are subtle. Motorized use is permitted.	Area is characterized by predominantly natural-appearing environments with moderate evidences of the sights and sounds of man. Such evidences usually harmonize with the natural environment. Interaction between users may be low to moderate, but with evidence of other users prevalent. Resource modification and utilization practices are evident, but harmonize with the natural environment. Conventional motorized use is provided for in construction standards and design of facilities	Area is characterized by substantially modified natural environment. Resource modification and utilization practices are to enhance specific recreation activities and to maintain vegetative cover and soil. Sights and sounds of humans are readily evident, and the interaction between users is often moderate to high. A considerable number of facilities are designed for use by a large number of people. Facilities are often provided for special activities Moderate densities are provided far away from developed sites. Facilities for intensified motorized use and parking are available.	Area is characterized by a substantially urbanized environment, although the background may have natural-appearing elements. Renewable resource modification and utilization practices are to enhance specific recreation activities. Vegetative cover is often exotic and manicured. Sights and sounds of humans, on-site, are predominant. Large numbers of users can be expected, both on-site and in near-by areas. Facilities for highly intensified motor use and parking are available with forms of mass transit often available to carry people throughout the site.

Experience Characterization*

Primitive	Semi-Primitive Non-Motorized	Semi-Primitive Motorized	Roaded Natural	Rural	Urban
Extremely high probability of experiencing isolation from the sights and sounds of humans, independence closeness to nature, tranquility, and self-reliance through the application of woodsman and outdoor skills in an environment that offers a high degree of challenge and risk.	High, but not extremely high, probability of experiencing isolation from the sights and sounds of humans, independence closeness to nature tranquility, and self reliance through the application of woodsman and outdoor skills in an environment that offers challenge and risk.	Moderate probability of experiencing isolation from the sights and sounds of humans, independence, closeness to nature, tranquility and self-reliance through the application of woodsman and outdoor skills in an environment that offers challenge and risk. Opportunity to have a high degree of interaction with the natural environment. Opportunity to use motorized equipment while in the area	About equal probability to experience affiliation with other user groups and for isolation from sights and sound of humans. Opportunity to have a high degree of interaction with the natural environment Challenge and risk opportunities associated with more primitive type of recreation are not very important. Practice and testing of outdoor skills might be important. Opportunities for both motorized and non-motorized forms of recreation are possible	Probability for experiencing affiliation with individuals and groups is prevalent, as is the convenience of sites and opportunities These factors are generally more important than the selling of the physical environment Opportunities for wildland challenges risk-taking and testing of outdoor skills are generally unimportant except for specific activities like downhill skiing for which challenge and risk-taking are important elements	Probability for experiencing affiliation with individuals and groups is prevalent as is the convenience of sites and opportunities. Experiencing natural environments, having challenges and risks afforded by the natural environment, and the use of outdoor skills are relatively unimportant Opportunities for competitive and spectator sports and for passive uses of highly human-influenced parks and open spaces are common

SOURCE: U.S. Department of Agriculture, Forest Service, *ROS Users Guide* (Washington, DC: Government Printing Office, n.d.), pp. 7-8.

resides. The remainder of the NWPS is located in the West and in Alaska. Alaska alone contains over 70 percent of the NWPS acreage, further pointing out the remote proximity of most of these areas to population concentrations. This situation is also confounded because only modest increases in the NWPS seem possible in the future.

Just as proximity to populations and recreational access will be key issues for future debate over additions to the NWPS, some major wilderness management and policy issues are already in focus. The most heated of these centers on release for development of lands already under consideration, but not yet selected for NWPS designation. A core issue is the degree to which existing NWPS units should be opened to oil, gas, and mineral exploration and mining. Other current issues include establishing carrying capacities, dispersing visitors to combat "overuse in spots," increasing emphasis on "light-handed management" using minimum regulation to meet management objectives, and increasing the use of volunteers to accomplish wilderness management.

The extent of trail mileage is also a primary indicator of the availability of lands for recreation use in undeveloped settings. Of the more than 281,000 miles of trails nationally in 1977, 94,000 (33 percent) are on National Forest System lands, an additional 16,000 (6 percent) are on other federal lands, 55,000 (20 percent) are on state and local lands, and 116,000 miles (41 percent) are on private lands (Table 2). Most of this trail mileage falls under the ROS primitive and semiprimitive, non-motorized categories.

Table 2

Trail Mileage in the United States by Region and Ownership, 1977

| Region | Total | | Ownership | | |
		USFS	Other fed.	State & local government	Private
North	97,295 (35%)	4,404 (5%)[a]	708 (1%)	32,496 (33%)	59,686 (61%)
South	26,064 (9%)	4,649 (17%)	1,382 (5%)	7,711 (30%)	12,322 (48%)
RM&GP	94,923 (34%)	55,041 (58%)	5,078 (5%)	6,867 (7%)	27,937 (29%)
Pacific Coast	62,776 (22%)	29,538 (47%)	9,168 (15%)	7,931 (13%)	16,139 (26%)
Total U.S.	281,058 (100%)	93,633 (33%)	16,336 (6%)	55,005 (20%)	116,084 (41%)

SOURCES: U.S. Department of Agriculture, Forest Service, *An Assessment of the Forest and Range Land Situation in the United States* (Washington, D.C.: Government Printing Office, 1980), pp. 116-117 and National Association of Conservation Districts, Survey of Private Recreation Enterprises, 1975, (unpublished computer data file).

Regional differences in total trail mileage are evident in Table 2. The most striking difference is the low trail mileage in the South (9 percent) relative to the other three regions. Similarly, these data highlight the importance of the private sector and state and local governments in providing trails in the East, whereas in the West, the federal government, particularly the Forest Service, is the main supplier.

In addition to wilderness areas and established trails, forest roads ranging from paved to very primitive provide access to primitive and semiprimitive recreation opportunities. Roads are commonly the base from which many recreational activities occur, such as cross-country skiing, trail hiking, camping, fishing, and hunting.

Off-road vehicular use of forest and rangelands has increased steadily in the last fifteen years, both as an activity and as a means of gaining access to back-country areas. Policies allowing such use are usually liberal. In 1977, roughly one-fourth of the U.S. population, about 43.6 million persons, engaged in some form of motorized, off-road recreational activity (Seihl 1979). However, because it can damage resources, motorized use of some public lands is being restricted.

Nonprimitive Opportunities Nonprimitive opportunities (roaded natural, rural, and urban) often center on developed sites including campgrounds, visitor information centers, second-home developments, resorts, and other highly modified settings. On National Forests, for example, developed sites account for about one-third of total visitor days of recreation use. In addition to the sites provided on National Forests, the Bureau of Land Management, Tennessee Valley Authority, Corps of Engineers, the National Park Service, state parks, private lands, and others have traditionally provided numerous and varied developed facilities and sites.

In recent years it has become obvious that many government agencies are redefining their roles to provide less of the more developed opportunities. Many of the federal, state, and local government agencies, which previously have invested heavily in development, have either already begun or are expressing intentions to reduce the number and management of developed sites and facilities. General strategies often include closure of less used facilities, consolidation of smaller sites into larger ones for more efficient management, and transfer of operating responsibility to private or local government concerns.

Campgrounds seem to exemplify an emerging recreation supply dilemma. As shown in Table 3, the total number of campground facilities both public and private has decreased by 10 percent since 1973, and most of this decrease has been in the private sector. While the number seemed to remain stable between 1973 and 1977, from 1977 to 1981, there was a 23 percent decrease in the number of private campgrounds. This decrease occurred despite reported increases in the number of camping participants. A major issue in the immediate future will be whether reduced federal campgrounds and the stimulus of increased user fees will trigger more supply activity in the private sector.

Vacation homes provide another important form of developed site recreation, but they mostly occur on private lands. In 1970 (Ragatz 1978) there were 2.1 million vacation homes representing 3.1 percent of the total number of housing units in the United States. Of the 2.1 million vacation homes in 1970, 56.6 percent were in the North, 23.6 percent were in the South, 11.8 percent were in the Rocky

Table 3

Number and Percentage of Campgrounds in the United States by Region, Ownership, and Year, 1973, 1977, and 1981

Region	TOTAL						PUBLIC						PRIVATE					
	Number			Percent Change			Number			Percent Change			Number			Percent Change		
	1973	1977	1981	73-77	77-81	73-81	1973	1977	1981	73-77	77-81	73-81	1973	1977	1981	73-77	77-81	73-81
North	5,301 (34)[a]	5,579 (35)	4,969 (35)	+ 5	−11	− 6	1,809 (24)	1,827 (24)	1,801 (23)	+1	− 1	0	3,492 (42)	3,752 (45)	3,168 (50)	+ 7	−16	− 9
South	3,475 (22)	3,589 (23)	3,019 (21)	+ 3	−16	−13	1,355 (18)	1,447 (19)	1,437 (18)	+7	− 1	+ 6	2,120 (26)	2,142 (26)	1,582 (25)	+ 1	−26	−25
RM & GP	3,673 (23)	3,526 (22)	3,293 (23)	− 4	− 7	−10	2,228 (30)	2,230 (29)	2,388 (31)	0	+7	+7	1,445 (17)	1,296 (16)	905 (14)	−10	−30	−37
Pacific Coast	3,313 (21)	3,158 (20)	2,873 (20)	− 5	− 9	−13	2,103 (28)	2,065 (27)	2,143 (28)	−2	+4	+2	1,210 (15)	1,093 (13)	730 (11)	−10	−33	−40
TOTAL U.S.	15,762 (100)	15,852 (100)	14,154 (99)	+1	−11	−10	7,495 (100)	7,569 (99)	7,769 (100)	+1	+3	+4	8,267 (100)	8,283 (100)	6,385 (100)	0	− 23	−23

SOURCES: U.S. Department of Agriculture, Forest Service, *An Assessment of the Forest and Range Land Situation in the United States* (Washington, D.C.: Government Printing Office, 1980), p. 126, Table 3.8 (for 1973 and 1977 data) and Rand McNally and Company, *Campground and Trailer Park Guide*, (Skokie: Rand McNally and Company, 1982) (for 1981 data).

[a]Numbers in parentheses represent percentage of column totals.

Mountain and Great Plains region, and 8.0 percent were in the Pacific Coast region (Cordell et. al. 1980).[1]

Recent rises in mortgage interest rates and the limited availability of mortgage funds has had a depressing effect on the volume of sales of single-family vacation homes. A trend which may dominate the middle-income family vacation-home investments in the coming years is condominium "time-sharing." For a substantially lower price than that of owning a vacation home, a family can jointly own a condominium and have access to it for a few weeks each year. An added advantage to this arrangement is that use of "time-sharing units" can be traded worldwide so that the family is not geographically moored.

Other nonprimitive facilities in the United States in 1975 totaled 234,202 family picnic units, 832,546 acres of land in developed resorts, and 660,899 acres in vacation farms and ranches. The four main regions differ in per capita supply of these facilities. In general, the North has a much lower per capita supply of developed sites and facilities than the other regions.

Water Resource Opportunities   Water, as reported by the Outdoor Recreation Resources Review Commission in 1962, is usually a focal point for outdoor recreation. The United States has approximately 107 million surface acres of water of which 59 million acres are inland waters. There are nearly 2 million rivers and streams totaling 3.2 million linear miles. Other inland water resources include reservoirs, lakes, and ponds. As a result of inundating rivers to form reservoirs during the 1940's, 1950's, and 1960's, today over 99 percent of the United States' population lives within 50 miles and about 33 percent lives within 5 miles of a lake or reservoir. Also, construction of private farm ponds has created over 2.6 million acres of water opportunity nationwide (USDA SCS 1979).

In addition to inland waters, coastal waters comprise an important component of our water resources. Along the coast of the contiguous 48 states, there are almost 37,000 miles of shoreline. Along the Alaskan coast there are 47,300 miles (Table 4). Most (70 percent) of the shoreline in the lower 48 states is privately owned, and only 23 percent (8,500 miles) is owned by either federal, state, or local governments and is thus open for public recreational use. Of the 36,900 miles in the lower 48 states, only 9 percent of the total shoreline is developed or has purposely been made accessible by government for recreational use. Only 16 percent of the total has been made accessible by private owners. In total, only 25 percent of the U.S. coastal shoreline has been developed or otherwise designed as accessible for public recreational use.

Snow and Ice Opportunities   Snow and ice provide opportunities for downhill and cross-country skiing, sledding, skating, snowmobiling, and other activities. In late fall, winter, and early spring, virtually all forest and rangelands in the nor-

---

[1]According to the USDA Forest Service, the North includes the states of Minnesota, Iowa, Missouri, Wisconsin, Illinois, Michigan, Indiana, Ohio, West Virginia, Pennsylvania, New York, Maryland, Delaware, New Jersey, Rhode Island, Maine, Vermont, New Hampshire, Massachusetts, and Connecticut; the South includes the states of Texas, Oklahoma, Louisiana, Arkansas, Florida, Georgia, Alabama, Mississippi, South Carolina, North Carolina, Virginia, Tennessee, Puerto Rico, and Kentucky; the Rocky Mountains and Great Plains include the states of Montana, Idaho, Wyoming, Nevada, Utah, Colorado, Kansas, Arizona, New Mexico, North Dakota, South Dakota, and Nebraska; the Pacific Coast includes the states of Washington, Oregon, California, Alaska, and Hawaii.

Table 4

Ownership and Use of United States Coastal Shoreline, 1971

Ownership and use	U.S. (excluding Alaska)		Alaska	
	Miles	Percent	Miles	Percent
OWNERSHIP				
Federal	3,900	11	41,300	87
State and local	4,600	12	5,500	12
Private	25,800	70	500	1
Uncertain	2,600	7	0	0
	36,900	100	47,300	100
USE				
Recreational				
Public	3,400	9	0	0
Private	5,800	16	0	0
Nonrecreational	27,700	75	47,300	100
	36,900	100	47,300	100

SOURCE: U.S. Department of the Interior, Heritage, Conservation and Recreation Service, *The Third Nationwide Outdoor Recreation Plan: The Assessment* (Washington, D.C.: Government Printing Office, 1980), pp. 98-99, Tables IV-2 and IV-3.

thern states are potentially usable for winter activities. There is a growing concern, however, that problems caused by certain activities such as snowmobiling and the resulting conflicts with private landowners will cause acreage to be withdrawn from public access.

Private Sector Supply Role

Privately owned land and water resources should become an increasingly important source of outdoor recreation opportunities. Table 5 describes ownership of industrial and nonindustrial private forest and rangelands by region of the United States. About 91 percent of these private lands are owned by nonbusiness interests, such as individuals and families, in small tracts for a variety of reasons and thus are classified as nonindustrial.

The large amount of private ownership in the North and South, where 78 percent of the United States population lives, indicates how important it will be to re-

Table 5

Acreage of Industrial and Nonindustrial Private Forest and Range Land (1977) and Population (1980) in the United States by Region

| Region | Forest and Range Land (1977) | | | | Percent of population (1980) |
| | Industrial | | Nonindustrial | | |
	Thousands of acres	Percent of total	Thousands of acres	Percent of total	
North	17,522	26	110,142	16	48
South	36,009	53	248,249	37	30
RM & GP	2,095	3	262,436	39	8
Pacific Coast	12,349	18	50,950	8	14
United States	67,975	100	671,777	100	100

SOURCE: H. Ken Cordell, Michael H. Legg, and Robert W. McLellan, *The Third Nationwide Outdoor Recreation Plan,* Appendix IV, *The Private Outdoor Recreation Estate* (Washington, D.C.: Government Printing Office, 1980), p. 46, Table 1. and U.S. Department of Commerce, Bureau of the Census, *Current Population Reports: Population Estimates,* Ser. P-25, No. 909, *Estimates of the Population of the United States to January 1, 1982* (Washington, D.C.: Government Printing Office, 1982).

tain access to lands now open for public recreation and to stimulate the opening of more land. Usually, public use of private lands is in conflict with landowner objectives. Incentives, therefore, are needed to make it worthwhile for owners to open their lands. Possibilities include low-cost liability insurance, increased profit potentials from reduced public competition, and tax breaks. The shaping of policies and creating of conditions conducive to private recreation supply will be one of the major outdoor recreation resource management challenges in the future.

Table 6 shows the availability of private forest and rangeland for outdoor recreation as of 1977. Fifty-eight percent of the industrial and 31 percent of the nonindustrial land was available for use either without a permit or with a fee or verbal permission. An additional 42 percent of the nonindustrial, but only 15 percent of the industrial land, was available only to the owner's friends, employees, or special groups. The availability of an additional 27 percent of both industrial and nonindustrial land is not known.

Table 6

Percentage of Private Forest and Range Land in the United States Available for Public Recreation Use by Region, 1977

Region	Open without permission		Open only with fee, permit or verbal permission		Closed except for owner, special group or employee use		Not designated	
	Industrial	Nonindustrial	Industrial	Nonindustrial	Industrial	Nonindustrial	Industrial	Nonindustrial
North	62	10	1	24	1	40	36	26
South	39	3	19	15	22	16	20	15
RM & GP	73	12	1	41	1	25	27	23
Pacific Coast	33	1	24	17	12	34	31	49
United States	44	6	14	25	15	42	27	27

SOURCE: H. Ken Cordell, Robert McLellan, Herbert Stevens, Gary Tyre, and Michael Legg, *Existing and Potential Recreation Role of Privately Owned Forest and Range Lands in the United States: An Assessment*, (Clemson: U.S. Department of Agriculture, Forest Service, 1978), p. 6.

Aggravating the lack of private land availabilities is the increasing loss of forest and range to more intensive crop, pasture, urban, and industrial uses. Figure 4 projects a loss of approximately 75 million acres of forest and range to such uses over the next 50 years. These losses suggest that demands on public lands may be even greater than projections indicate.

OUTDOOR RECREATION PARTICIPATION

Continued growth of demand for virtually all outdoor recreation activities is projected. But the factors that influence demand growth are now moving in different directions than in the past. Major changes have already been implemented or proposed for recreation supply, especially reduced federal involvement and higher user fees. These changes in supply and projected changes in demand factors will be reflected in the kinds and amounts of future outdoor recreation participation. Unfortunately, the present information base for forecasting participation and for planning our Nation's recreation programs is generally inadequate and leaves a high level of uncertainty about actual future demand and participation patterns.

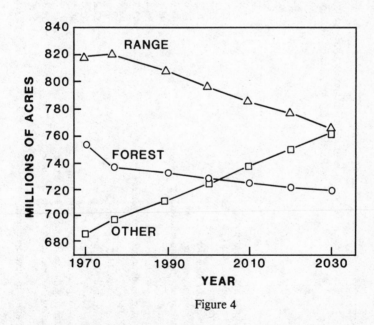

Figure 4

Land Area of the United States by 1970 Classification and Projections.
SOURCE: U.S. Dept. of Agriculture, Forest Service, *An Assessment of the Forest and Range Land Situation in the United States.* Washington, D.C.: Government Printing Office, 1980, p. 32.

Table 7

Number and Percentage of United States Population 12 Years and Older that Participated in Selected Outdoor Recreation Activities in 1977

	Participates at least once a year		Participates five or more times a year	
	(millions)	(percentage)	(millions)	(percentage)
Visits to amusement parks, zoos, aquariums, fairs, etc.	127.3	73	68.0	39
Picnicking	125.6	72	85.5	49
Driving for pleasure	120.3	69	99.4	57
Walking or jogging	118.6	68	99.4	57
Pool swimming and sunbathing	109.9	63	85.5	49
Sightseeing	108.1	62	62.8	36
Attending sports events	106.4	61	76.7	44
Playing outdoor sports or games	97.7	56	75.0	43
Fishing	92.4	53	62.8	36
Nature walks, bird-watching, or wildlife photography	87.2	50	62.8	36
Bicycling	82.0	47	68.0	39
Non-pool swimming and sunbathing	80.2	46	61.0	35
Attending dances, concerts, or plays	71.5	41	38.4	22
Boating (not including sailing or canoeing)	59.3	34	34.9	20
Tennis	57.6	33	41.9	24
Camping in developed areas	52.3	30	20.9	12

Hiking or backpacking	48.8	28	27.9	16
Use of off-road motor vehicles or motorcycles	45.3	26	34.9	20
Camping in primitive areas	36.6	21	15.7	9
Sledding	36.6	21	20.9	12
Hunting	33.1	19	24.4	14
Canoeing, kayaking, or river-running	27.9	16	8.7	5
Waterskiing	27.9	16	14.0	8
Golfing	27.9	16	19.2	11
Ice skating	27.9	16	15.7	9
Horseback riding	26.2	15	14.0	8
Sailing	19.2	11	8.7	5
Snowmobiling	14.0	8	8.7	5
Downhill skiing	12.2	7	7.0	4
Cross-country skiing or ski touring	3.5	2	1.7	1

SOURCE: U.S. Department of Interior, Heritage Conservation and Recreation Service, *The Third Nationwide Outdoor Recreation Plan The Assessment* (Washington, D.C.: Government Printing Office, 1979), p. 40, Tables II-12 and II-13.

The three national surveys investigating recreation participation discussed below yielded three quite different use estimates. Sampling procedures, the size of the sample, the clarity of questions, and the accuracy of respondent recall are some of the reasons for differences between these estimates. Wide differences from comparable surveys hamper accurate demand forecasting and recreation planning, and illustrate the need for further research in estimating recreational use.

The 1977 HCRS Recreation Participation Survey

The Heritage Conservation and Recreation Service (1979) reported percentages of the United States' population twelve years of age and older who participated in specific recreation activities at least once, and five or more times, during 1977 (Table 7). The most popular activities, with the possible exception of picnicking, do not depend heavily on a natural setting and are mostly within ROS classes

Table 8

Number and Percentage of Population, 16 Years and Older,
Participating in Fishing, Hunting, and Wildlife Associated
Recreation in the United States, 1980

Activity	Participation Number (million)	Percent
Fishing and/or hunting	46.7	27
Fishing	42.1	25
Freshwater	36.4	21
Saltwater	12.3	7
Hunting	17.4	10
Big game	11.8	7
Small game	12.4	7
Migratory birds	5.3	3
Other	2.6	2
Nonconsumptive[a]	83.2	49
Away from home	28.8	17
Near home	79.	47
Observe/identify	55.9	33
Photograph	12.4	7
Feed birds	62.5	37

SOURCE: U.S. Department of Interior, U.S. Fish and Wildlife Service, *Initial Findings Report on the 1980 National Survey of Fishing, Hunting, and Wildlife Associated Recreation,* 1982 (unpublished).

[a]Involves observation, photography, or feeding of wildlife.

"rural" and "urban." Among the traditional activities that depend on a natural setting, only fishing attracted participation by a majority of the United States' population (53 percent). Nevertheless, the numbers of participants in the traditional primitive and semiprimitive outdoor recreation activities are impressive; e.g., 52 million campers, 49 million hikers and back packers, 45 million off-road motorized vehicle users, and 33 million hunters.

The above participation estimates may change in the future as the American population continues to age. Hiking, primitive camping, hunting, whitewater boating, snowmobiling, and downhill and cross-country skiing are physically demanding. Participation in these activities, therefore, is generally lower among older persons. Aside from the influences of other social and economic changes, one might logically expect overall decreases in participation in these outdoor activities in the next few decades.

The 1980 National Survey of Fishing, Hunting, and Wildlife Associated Recreation

During January to May 1981, the Bureau of the Census conducted the National Survey of Fishing, Hunting, and Wildlife Associated Recreation for the U.S. Fish and Wildlife Service. The survey included 12,661 households reporting in general and more than 38,000 individuals 16 years and older who reported in detail on their fishing, hunting, and wildlife-related recreational activities during 1980. Major results of this survey are summarized in Table 8 and in Figure 5. Fishing and

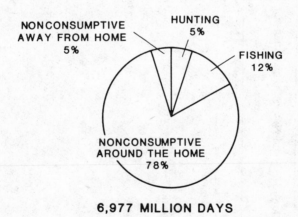

6,977 MILLION DAYS

Figure 5

Total Days of Wildlife Related Recreation in the United States by Type of Use - 1980.

SOURCE: U.S. Fish and Wildlife Service. *Initial Findings Report on the 1980 National Survey of Fishing, Hunting, and Wildlife Associated Recreation,* 1982, (unpublished).

Table 9

Visitation to Fee and Nonfee Management Units by Agency, 1979 and 1981 (Visitor Days in Thousands)

| | Year | | | | | |
| | 1979 | | | 1981 | | |
	Fee Unit Visitation	Nonfee Unit Visitation	Total Visitation	Fee Unit Visitation	Nonfee Unit Visitation	Total Visitation
Bureau of Land Management	6,538.5	37,205.3	43,743.8 (7.8)[d]	1,474.5	35,511.5	36,985.9 (6.8)
Bureau of Reclamation[a]	349.1	33,883.8	34,232.9 (6.1)	123.3	38,270.2	38,393.6 (7.1)
Corps of Engineers[b]	10,460.3	152,921.7	163,382.0 (29.2)	9,345.0	114,622.3	123,967.3 (22.8)
Fish and Wildlife Service[c]	47.2	2,072.2	2,119.4 (.4)	47.1	1,882.0	1,929.0 (.4)
Forest Service	26,749.0	193,416.6	220,165.6 (39.3)	28,104.6	207,604.6	235,709.2 (43.4)
National Park Service	73,495.4	11,203.6	88,865.7 (15.9)	78,826.5	21,033.3	99,859.8 (18.4)
Tennessee Valley Authority	558.3	6,762.3	7,320.7 (1.3)	591.9	6,084.4	6,676.3 (1.2)
TOTAL	118,197.8	437,465.6	555,663.4 (100)	118,512.8	425,008.3	543,521.1 (100)

SOURCE: U.S. Department of the Interior, National Park Service, Federal Recreation Fee Report 1981. p. 39, Exhibit C (Draft) and U.S. Department of the Interior, Heritage Conservation and Recreation Service, *Federal Recreation Fee Report 1979* and *Federal Recreation Fee Report 1977.*

[a]Preliminary estimates of expected visitation.

[b]An additional 57,094.5 visitor-days occur on project lands which are not designated as recreation areas.

[c]Includes the National Wildlife Refuge System, except fish hatcheries.

[d]Percent of column total.

nonconsumptive wildlife use attracted very large numbers of participants. In particular, observing and feeding urban wildlife near home has attracted large numbers.

Federal Recreation Use Reports

Table 9 shows recreation participation for 1979 and 1981 on the 755.4 million acres of federal lands. These lands received 543.5 million visitor-days of use in 1981, down from a total of 559.8 million in 1979. Most of this decrease occurred on non-fee units which include undeveloped primitive and semiprimitive areas where only essential maintenance and facilities occur.

The number of visitor-days of use and fees collected in designated federal fee areas are shown in Table 10. Receipts from fees at these sites have gone from $20.6 million in 1975 to $32.2 million in 1981. The average receipt on federal lands is substantially less than $1.00 per visitor-day, although this varies considerably by agency.

Traditionally, users of federal sites have been subsidized to the extent that only a small percentage of costs per visitor was actually recovered. Limited operating budgets, however, are forcing agencies to reexamine their fee policies. Obviously, total recreation revenues can be increased on federal lands, and there are definite initiatives underway to this end. Only 21.8 percent of the visitation in 1981 occurred in fee management units (Table 9) yielding $32.2 million in receipts for an average receipt per visitor-day of $.27 (Table 10). If all recreational visitors to federal lands in 1981 had been charged fees at that rate, $147.7 million would have been generated. The level of fees can be increased at presently designated fee units, plus, some of the current non-fee units could be redesignated as fee units. In 1981, 78.2 percent of visitation on federal lands occurred in nonfee areas.

Since the Forest Service hosts the largest number of visitors to federal lands (43 percent), participation data for the past three years for various outdoor recreation activities on National Forests are examined (Table 11). Over 60 percent of all land, water, and snow and ice-based activities on National Forests occurs in primitive or semiprimitive areas. From 1979 through 1981, participation in recreation on National Forests remained relatively stable or increased, except for winter sports. In particular, downhill skiing participation declined by nearly one-third. Both on-road and off-road mechanized travel, fishing, hunting, and hiking and climbing remain highly popular activities.

Indicators of Outdoor Recreation Participation

Expenditure and travel patterns associated with outdoor recreation can provide insights into current and near-future participation. The priorities individuals set for their discretionary income tend to signify priorities in recreational pursuits.

Personal Expenditures on Outdoor Recreation   In 1981, $1 of every $8 spent by persons in the United States was related to leisure pursuits. In 1965, Americans spent $58 billion for sports, outdoor recreation, and other entertainment. By 1981, spending in current dollars had increased 321 percent to $244 billion. In real

Table 10

Visitor Days' Use in Fee Areas and Fees Collected by Agency, 1975 - 1981

Agency	Use (Visitor Days in Thousands)				Recreation Receipts (Thousands)				Receipts Per Visitor-Day			
	1975	1977	1979	1981	1975	1977	1979	1981	1975	1977	1979	1981
Bureau of Land Management	7,542	7,039[a]	6,539	1,475	$208	$302	$388	$359	$0.03	$0.04	$0.06	$0.27
Bureau of Reclamation	167	146	349	123	299	286	559	582	1.79	1.96	1.60	4.73
Corps of Engineers	31,433	11,238	10,460	9,345	2,388	3,403	4,396	6,036	.08	.30	.42	.65
Fish and Wildlife Service	8	1,123	47	47	20	120	79	86	2.50	.11	1.68	1.83
Forest Service	25,667	25,646	26,749	28,105	4,611	5,528	6,097	8,518	.18	.22	.23	.30
National Park Service	115,417	79,596	73,495	78,827	12,884	16,404	14,980	16,138	.11	.21	.20	.20
Tennessee Valley Authority	275	542	558	592	146	188	207	502	.53	.35	.37	.85
TOTAL	180,509	125,330	118,197	118,514	$20,556	$26,231	$26,706	$32,221	$0.11[b]	$0.21	$0.23	$0.27

SOURCES: U.S. Department of the Interior, Heritage Conservation and Recreation Service, *Federal Recreation Fee Report 1975, Federal Recreation Fee Report 1977,* and *Federal Recreation Fee Report 1979,* (Washington, D.C.: Heritage Conservation and Recreation Service, 1976, 1978, 1980).

U.S. Department of the Interior, National Park Service, Federal Recreation Fee Report 1981, (Draft), p. 20, Table 17.

[a]Estimated because of questionable source data that reported 39,915 visitor days in BLM fee areas for 1977.

[b]Grand average.

Table 11

Estimated National Forest Recreation Use for 1979-1981

(Visitor Days[a] in Thousands)

Activity	1979	1980	1981
Camping	54,780.0	57,211.3	59,627.7
Picnicking	8,874.2	9,511.6	9,707.2
Recreation Travel (Mechanized)	49,536.5	54,998.1	55,198.0
Automobile	41,013.8	44,980.3	44,999.0
Scotter and Motorcycle	4,525.5	5,092.9	5,293.5
Ice and Snowcraft	3,408.4	3,448.2	3,141.3
Other	588.8	1,476.7	1,763.3
Water Travel	7,072.1	7,890.4	8,132.2
Boats, Power	4,029.3	3,925.6	4,084.0
Boats, Non-Power	3,042.8	1,651.0	1,724.0
Other Water Travel	---	2,313.8	2,319.2
Games and Team Sports	832.8	968.9	1,033.5
Waterskiing and Other Water Sports	888.0	995.0	983.4
Swimming and Diving	4,632.3	5,139.9	5,333.8
Winter Sports	14,485.0	13,864.2	11,262.5
Downhill Skiing	12,549.4	11,006.7	8,585.8
X-Country Ski/Snowshoe	---	1,204.2	1,349.2
Other Winter Sports	1,935.0	1,653.3	1,327.5
Fishing	16,776.0	17,117.1	16,972.8
Hunting	15,327.9	15,746.8	16,412.8
Hiking and Mountain Climbing	11,176.9	12,258.8	12,791.4
Horseback Riding	3,166.4	3,346.2	3,650.9
Resort Use	4,308.9	4,443.2	4,429.4
Organization Camp Use	4,086.8	4,112.4	3,935.8
Recreation Cabin Use	6,651.6	6,838.2	6,399.5
Gathering Forest Products	3,916.1	4,739.3	5,055.7
Nature Study	1,210.9	1,723.5	2,018.6
Viewing Scenery, Sports, Environment	8,321.1	8,003.4	8,525.3
Visitor Information (Exhibits, Talks, Etc.)	4,121.8	4,461.0	4,238.7
SERVICE-WIDE TOTAL	291,258.6	310,372.0	310,296.0

SOURCE: U.S. Department of Agriculture, Forest Service, *Annual National Forest Visitation Reports for 1979, 1980 and 1981.* (Unpublished)

[a]Recreational use of NF land and water which aggregates 12 person-hours. May entail 1 person for 12 hours, 12 persons for 1 hour, or any equivalent combination of individual or group use, either continuous or intermittent.

Table 12

Personal Consumption Expenditures for Outdoor Recreation and Percentage of Total Personal Expenditures, 1960-1979
(in billions of dollars)

Level and percentage	Year									
	1960	1965	1970	1973	1974	1975	1976	1977	1978	1979
Current Dollars	17.9	25.9	41.0	55.2	60.9	66.5	73.3	81.0	91.2	101.0
1970 Dollars	23.7	32.1	41.0	48.4	50.3	49.4	50.0	52.2	55.2	56.7
Percentage of total personal expenditures (current dollars)	5.5	6.0	6.6	6.8	6.8	6.8	6.7	6.7	6.8	6.7

SOURCE: U.S. Department of Commerce, Bureau of the Census, *Statistical Abstracts of the United States*, Sec. 14, (Washington, D.C.: Government Printing Office, 1980), p. 442.

dollars (adjusted for inflation), the actual percentage increase was 47 percent, still an increase of almost 6 percent annually.

For the period 1960 through 1979, expenditures in current dollars for outdoor recreation participation alone went from $17.9 to $101.0 billion, representing a 564 percent increase (Table 12). In real (1970) dollars, though, recreation participation expenditures have increased 239 percent from $23.7 billion in 1960 to $56.7 billion to 1979. The most significant information in these data is that the percentage of the average personal budget that is spent for recreation has remained stable at between 6 and 7 percent per year since the mid-1960s, regardless of recession, gasoline shortages, or other influences.

Fishing and Hunting Expenditures   Wildlife and fish-related expenditures are one of the largest categories of recreation expenditures according to the 1980 National Survey of Fishing, Hunting, and Wildlife Associated Recreation. For instance, fishermen spent, on the average, approximately $244 each during 1980, or about $12 for each day of activity. Fees, licenses, tags, and permits accounted for only 8.2 percent of these 1980 expenditures, estimated to total $10.2 billion nationally.

Hunters, on the other hand, spent an estimated $5.6 billion on hunting in 1980. Each hunter spent an average of $321 during 1980, or approximately $17 per day of activity. Finally, wildlife-related recreation expenditures were estimated to be $39.6 billion in 1980. Of this total amount an estimated 62 percent was for equipment (fishing, hunting, photographic, etc.), not including boats and vehicles; 18 percent was for food and lodging; 16 percent was for transportation; and 4 percent was for other related items.

Sporting Goods Sales   In 1980, the U.S. sporting goods industry recorded $8.6 billion in sales versus $8 billion in 1979. This represents a retail sales volume increase of 7 percent. Fishing gear and camping equipment were the greatest growth areas, whereas related goods, such as sleeping bags and hiking boots, were down 30 percent and 10 percent, respectively.

There were some other indications of declines in some activities. Downhill ski sales, for instance, dropped 16 percent and recreational transport sales (bicycles, pleasure boats, recreational vehicles, and snowmobiles) showed a sharp 27 percent drop between 1979 and 1980 sales. Overall, the 1981 sporting goods industry showed a slowdown in the previous rates of growth of retail sales.

Motorized Recreation Vehicles   Another indicator of outdoor recreation participation in the United States is number of motorized recreation vehicles. This number has grown rapidly over the last 20 years. In 1976, there were over one-half million camping and travel vehicles (including truck campers, camping trailers, travel trailers, and motor homes), almost 6.4 million motorcycles, 12.8 million recreational boats, and 1.6 million registered snowmobiles (Hogans 1979, and USDA Forest Service 1980).

The use of motorcycles and other motorized recreation vehicles on forest and rangelands has created the opportunity for new forms of recreation. It has, however, caused some problems. Noise, site disturbance, wildlife disturbance, and conflict with other recreation users are among the problems of greatest concern. Though gasoline is becoming increasingly expensive, the number of motorized recreation vehicles continues to grow as the demand for associated activities is stimulated by technology and design innovations.

Membership in Conservation Organizations   The organizations listed in Table 13 indicates the importance of conservation efforts to many Americans and their enduring interest in environmental and recreational activities. Most of these organizations have recorded a substantial growth in membership including the National Audubon Society, Sierra Club, Ducks Unlimited, and the National Rifle

Table 13

Memberships in Conservation Organizations, 1970-1981

Organization (Year founded)	Membership in thousands				
	1970	1975	1979	1980	1981
American Forestry Association (1975)	82	78	75	66	55
Appalachian Mountain Club (1876)	14	22	23.5	25	25
Ducks Unlimited (1937)	50	150	350	375	400
Environmental Defense Fund (1967)	9	57	46	46	46
Friends of the Earth (1969)	-	20	23	25	25
National Audubon Society (1905)	121	340	404	422	452
National Campers and Hikers Association (1954)	52	70	70	50	50
National Parks and Conservation Association (1919)	50	45	40	40	40
National Rifle Association (1871)	1053	1040	1100	1800	2000
National Wildlife Federation (1936)	-	3500	4100	4600	4600
Sierra Club (1892)	80	-	185	189	275
Wilderness Society (1935)	70	90	70	50	50
World Wildlife Fund (1961)	35	50	65	65	75
Zero Population Growth (1968)	20	10	6.5	6.5	11

SOURCE: This table has been compiled from membership lists provided by the above mentioned conservation organizations and National Wildlife Federation, Conservation Directory 1982 (Washington, D.C.: National Wildlife Federation, 1982), pp. 38-96.

Association. Although it is difficult to predict future trends, memberships in these organizations may grow in response to cutbacks in outdoor recreation and wilderness program budgets and to reduced environmental protection programs at the federal level.

Membership in these groups indicates a strong interest in the environment in general, and usually an interest in some aspect of natural resources in particular. The current high levels of membership point to a strong concern for the quality and general condition of our renewable resource base and support for maintenance of quality outdoor settings as recreation opportunities.

OUTDOOR RECREATION SUPPLY AND DEMAND PROJECTIONS

Projections of Recreation Participation

Figure 6 shows projections of the percentage of the United States population expected to participate in the three major categories of outdoor recreation activities—land, water, and snow and ice activities. The largest projected increases are for snow and ice activities including cross-country and downhill skiing, snowmobiling, sledding, and skating. The next largest percentage increases are in water activities, followed by land activities. Water activities include swimming outdoors, water skiing, canoeing, sailing, and other boating. Land activities include developed and primitive camping, operating off-road vehicles, hiking, horseback riding, nature study, picnicking, pleasure driving, and sightseeing.

In terms of the projected number of participants, land-based activities will be higher because of the much large current base of participants. Figure 7 illustrates this point by showing projected visitor-days of use of National Forests. As mentioned above, the largest growth in number of visitor-days is projected to be in land-based activities (105 million), even though the percentage increases are higher for snow and ice and water activities (Figure 6).

The implications of this are that greatly expanded facilities may be needed to accommodate the large increases in participation in snow and ice and water activities, should they become a reality. But, even larger increases in numbers of sites and facilities will be needed to accommodate land-based participation increases.

The best projections of recreation participation would logically be based on actual participation trends and an awareness of all the available survey-based projections. The overall patterns revealed by these data would probably give the most accurate idea of what to expect in the future. Problems with available projections, however, limit the conclusions about implications for resource allocations and management. During the past twenty-five years it was safe to assume increases in outdoor recreation as Americans exercised new found affluence, leisure time, and increased environmental awareness. There were also expanded opportunities resulting from government development and subsidized participation.

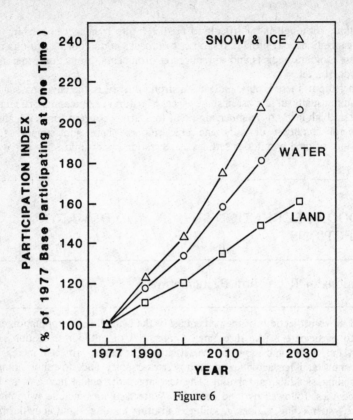

Figure 6

Medium Level Projections of Indices in National Participation in Land, Water, Snow and Ice Recreational Activities.

SOURCE: U.S. Dept. of Agriculture, Forest Service, *An Assessment of the Forest and Range Land Situation in the United States*. Washington, D.C.: Government Printing Office, 1980, p. 100-101.

Development of new technology and commercial production of equipment has also been important. But conditions are changing, and it is difficult to predict future outdoor recreation participation in light of these changing conditions. In an attempt to better understand where the future of outdoor recreation may lie, the next section of this chapter examines changes in social and economic factors that influence the consumption of outdoor recreation.

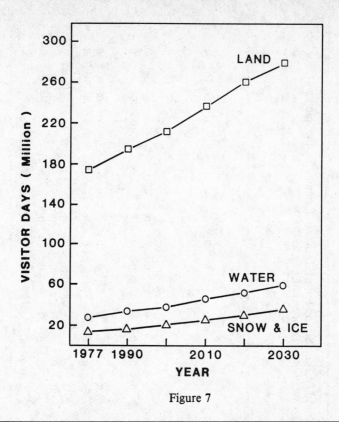

Figure 7

Medium Level Projections of Millions of Visitor Days of Participation in Land, Water, Snow and Ice Recreational Activities on National Forests - 1978 to 2030. SOURCE: U.S. Dept. of Agriculture, Forest Service, *An Assessment of the Forest and Range Land Situation in the United States*. Washington, D.C.: Government Printing Office, 1980, pp. 100-101, 113.

SOCIAL AND ECONOMIC INFLUENCES AFFECTING OUTDOOR RECREATION SUPPLY AND DEMAND

The following analysis of social and economic factors focuses on their likely effects on outdoor recreation supply and demand. Included in the analysis are trends in social and economic factors and a prediction of their effects on various forms of outdoor recreation.

The social-economic factors examined included: (1) inflation, (2) energy prices, (3) energy availability, (4) population growth, (5) interest rates, (6) non-work

Table 14

Influences of Selected Social, Economic and Political Factors (SE) on Future Trends in Demand for and Supply of Outdoor Recreation and Wilderness Opportunities, 1982-2000

Categories of Outdoor
Recreation and Wilderness
Opportunity[a]

SUPPLY[b]

Primitive wilderness[c]

Primitive and semi-primitive (non-motorized and motorized)
  Public
  Private

Roaded Natural and Rural
  Public
  Private

Rural and Urban
  Public
  Private

NOTES: Degree of influence of each factor on each element of outdoor recreation demand and supply is represented by a 5-point scale as follows: + + = major positive influence, + = moderate positive influence, 0 = little or no influence, - = moderately negative influence (decrease), and -- = major negative influence.

DEMAND															
Primitive wilderness	+	-	-	+	0	+	+	0	0	0	0	+	+	+	-	+
Primitive and semi-primitive																
Non-motor	0	-	-	+	+	0	0	0	0	0	-	0	+	+	-	+
Motor	-	-	-	+	+	-	0	-	0	0	-	0	+	-	-	0
Roaded natural and rural	-	-	-	+	+	0	+	+	0	0	0	+	-	+	0	++
Rural and urban	-	-	-	0	0	0	0	++	0	0	0	-	+	-	0	+
Importance and expected change in SE factor																
Importance[d]	C	C	C	C	C	C	I	C	I	I	I	C	I	I	I	I
Expected rate of change to 2000[e]	R	R	R	M	M	M	M	R	M	M	M	M	L	M	M	M

[a] Categories of opportunity are adapted from the ROS (Recreation Opportunity Spectrum) System Users Guide, USDA Forest Service, Washington, D.C.

[b] Supply refers to quantity available (e.g., acres, number of sites, number of miles) and does not refer to either social or physical capacity.

[c] Wilderness refers to areas established by Congressional mandate plus areas designated for study (Congressionally or Administratively) as candidate wilderness areas.

[d] C = critical, I = important

[e] R = rapid, greater than expected population growth; M = moderate, about the same as expected population growth; L = little, no growth or less than the rate of population growth.

time, (7) recreation information and technology, (8) national defense spending, (9) population geographic distribution, (10) population age, (11) personal income, (12) income distribution, (13) unemployment, (14) demand for raw materials, (15) political attitudes, (16) level of government spending, (17) government funding for recreation, (18) demographic characteristics of population, (19) urban/rural population distribution, and (20) legal restrictions on use and users. In Table 14, the influence of these factors on changes in demand and supply of outdoor recreation were expressed as follows:

> + + = major increase at a rate greater than projected population growth.
> + = moderate increase at a rate approximately equal to population growth
> 0 = no change or minor change
> − = moderate decrease at a rate approximately equal to population growth
> − − = major decrease at a rate greater than population growth.

No governmental or market intervention was assumed to ameliorate the supply and demand effects of changes in the twenty social-economic factors beyond that which currently exists. The analysis revealed that inflation will continue at an average rate of 8-10 percent; energy prices will rise more rapidly than will other prices and energy supplies will slowly become more scarce with potential severe short term shortages and rationing. Population growth will be more steady at about one percent per year reaching about 260 million in the year 2000 interest rates seem likely to remain at the same high levels of the past few years (14-18 percent) with perhaps some short-term fluctuations.

Nonwork time will be reduced slightly; recreation information and equipment technology development will continue; national defense spending will increase and consume federal monies that might otherwise be spent on public services, including recreation. Population geographic distribution will continue to shift toward the sunbelt states, and the age distribution will feature more elderly and more very young Americans. Personal (real) income will remain steady and the income distribution will see families with incomes above $10,000 gradually increasing; unemployment will remain high (6-8 percent), especially among unskilled workers and youth; demand for raw materials, including renewable and nonrenewable natural resources, will increase more rapidly than population; and political attitudes will favor reduced federal spending for services, lower taxes, and greater state and local control.

Levels of government spending will be reduced toward balanced budgets and government funding for recreation will decrease as public funds are directed toward higher priorities; population characteristics will feature more two-income families with more money but less time, a more highly educated population-at-large (at least in terms of years in school), smaller families and more single households; the urban-rural ratio of the population will increase and become more concentrated, with up to 75 percent of the people living in 29 distinct urban regions by the year 2000; and regulation of recreation use and public tolerance for it will increase.

The exact nature of the quantitative effects of each changing social and economic condition is uncertain. But in combination their general effects for the period 1982-2000 are more apparent and are summarized in Table 14.

Supply   The predicted trends in quantity of acres and sites by ROS class are as follows:

1. Wilderness (0): The National Wilderness Preservation System will grow slowly as the current allocation process is completed. The U.S. Forest Service and the Bureau of Land Management are completing their roadless area reviews and are submitting proposed additions through the Administration to Congress. There will be some additions to the System, but none of the magnitude resulting from the Alaska additions.

2. Public primitive and semiprimitive (−): A moderate decrease in public sector primitive and semiprimitive recreation opportunities will result from pressures for more intensive land uses and resource extraction.

3. Private primitive and semiprimitive (− −): Pressures for intensified management of private lands may lead to a major decrease in both non-roaded and roaded backcountry recreation opportunity. Economic factors have an even more dramatic effect on private land management than on public land management.

4. Public roaded natural and rural (−): Public roaded areas and less intensively developed sites which are heavily dependent on natural settings (campgrounds, picnic areas, and swimming beaches) are already beginning to decrease moderately relative to population growth.

5. Private roaded natural and rural (−): Overall, a small decrease in supply is projected which will result in less facility development, closure of some existing sites, and closure of some road and trail access requiring maintenance.

6. Public rural and urban (intensively developed) sites (− −): Intensively developed public sites, such as ski lifts, resorts, hut systems, and visitor centers will face serious downward pressures.

7. Private rural and urban (intensively developed) sites (−): Without governmental assistance and coordination, some decline of private, intensively developed sites is expected between 1980 and 2000.

Demand   Estimates of trends in demand for outdoor recreation between 1982 and 2000 are indicated below:

1. Primitive wilderness (+): A moderate increase in demand for wilderness opportunity, at a rate slightly greater than population growth, but less than the rates of the 70's, is predicted between now and 2000.

2. Primitive and semiprimitive nonmotor (+): Demand for primitive and semiprimitive nonmotorized recreation other than wilderness is expected to increase at a moderate rate.

3. Primitive and semiprimitive motor (0): Various positive and negative influences will collectively create growth in demand at about the same rate or less than the projected population growth.

4. Roaded natural and rural (+ +): Demand for roaded natural and rural recreation is predicted to increase faster than the rate of population growth between 1982 and 2000.

5. Rural and urban (intensively developed) sites (+): The net effect of positive and negative forces will be a moderate increase in demand between 1982 and 2000 at a rate approaching the projected population growth rate.

Major conclusions from the analysis of social and economic factor influence are that: (1) Without major policy changes, both public and private supply are predicted to decrease; (2) moderate rises in demand for all activity categories are expected, leading to potentially severe supply/demand imbalances due mainly to strong supply decreases; and (3) growth will not occur in private, nonprimitive opportunities and there will be a moderate decrease in private, intensively developed sites. This will all occur in the face of a needed increase in private sector supply of recreation opportunities to offset declining public sector involvement.

Conclusions and Recommendations

The data and analysis presented earlier in this chapter suggest that outdoor recreation participation rates will rise in response to increased demand. Expanding supply to meet the projected increase in numbers of users is expensive and resources for doing so are increasingly scarce, especially in the public sector. A plethora of social and economic factors influence recreation supply and demand. The complex effects and interactions of these factors make predictions risky, yet at the same time they are necessary. Generalized predictions are not adequate for total guidance of the heavy public investments in capital facilities and labor that characterize the existing outdoor recreation delivery system.

Recreation demand is going to increase, and, if recent history is any indication, perhaps to levels even greater than our predictions indicate and in directions we have not yet imagined. Because we do not yet know specific directions and amounts of demand increases and because of increasingly scarce resources, the broader and more lasting solution is to rely less on long-range planning and more on a system that is more responsive. We need a self-adjusting recreation delivery system that will quickly respond to unanticipated market fluctuations, as well as to more long-term growth or decline in recreation demand.

Flexible responsiveness will lead to more efficient delivery of outdoor recreation opportunities. Increasing the responsiveness of our delivery system will require some major policy changes, improved research and management technology, and perhaps new legislation. We feel that five major characteristics must be built into improvement of our delivery system:

1. It must explicitly acknowledge the increasingly important role of outdoor recreation. It should be assumed that shrinking public fiscal resources for development and management are an indication that outdoor recreation is fading as a part of the American lifestyle. Dwindling public fiscal resources are a problem throughout the range of traditional government programs and services. There is every indication that outdoor recreation is, in fact, rising in importance.

2. It must incorporate a much expanded knowledge base. Incomplete and inaccurate data, sometimes inadequate forecasting methods, and lack of compatibility and continuity of data bases often frustrate our efforts to make more efficient allocations.

3. It must decentralize to accommodate geographic and social imbalances in demand and supply. Many of the components of the existing delivery systems are cumbersome and simply cannot respond quickly. In addition, existing centralization of some allocating authorities must of necessity ignore imbalanced distributions of opportunities by geographic location and among social groups.

4. It must be fiscally solvent and equitable in the distribution of its financial burden. The era of heavily subsidized outdoor recreation is probably about over. A new era must incorporate sound business management and economic efficiency principles.

5. It must include expanded coordination, cooperation, and partnership among federal, state, local, and private sector entities. Overlapping and sometimes competing authorities and investments can no longer be afforded. Opportunities for economics of scale through consolidation, sharing of resources through cooperation, financial and technical assistance to provide stimulus, and partnerships in management and development must be explored and consumated.

References

Buist, L., and Hoots, T. A. "Recreational Opportunities Spectrum and Approach to Resource Planning." *Journal of Forestry* 80(1982):84-86.

Cordell, H. K. "Pricing for Allocating Low-Density Recreational Use Between Private and Commercial Users of Natural Areas." In *Proceedings of the National Conference on Recreation Use Allocation,* pp. 77-103. Reno, Nevada: 1981.

Cordell, H. K.; McLellan, R. W.; Stevens, H.; Tyre, G.; and Legg, M. H. "Existing and Potential Recreation Role of Privately Owned Forest and Range Lands in the United States: An Assessment." Report submitted to Resource Program and Assessment staff, Division of Programs and Legislation. Asheville, North Carolina: USDA Forest Service, Southeast Forest Experiment Station, 1978.

Cordell, H. K., and Hendee, J. C. "Renewable Resource Recreation in the United States: Supply, Demand, and Critical Policy Issues." Washington, D.C.: American Forestry Association, in press.

Hendee, J. C., and Bryan, H. "Social Benefits of Fish and Wildlife Conservation." Paper presented to the Western Association of Fish and Wildlife Commission Annual Meeting. San Diego, California: July 1978.

Hogans, M. L. "A Nationwide Assessment of Dispersed Motorized Recreation Opportunities and Participation: A Resources Planning Act (RPA) Report." Portland, Oregon: USDA Forest Service. Pacific Northwest Forest and Range Experiment Station, 1979.

Kelly, J. R. *Social Benefits of Outdoor Recreation.* Urbana, Illinois: Leisure Behavior Research Laboratory, University of Illinois at Urbana-Champaign, 1981.

Peterson, M. "Trends in Recreational Use of National Forest Wilderness." Missoula, Montana: USDA Forest Service Intermediate Forest and Range Experiment Station, USDA Forest Service Research note INT-319, 1981.

Ragatz, R. L., Associates, Inc. *Private Seasonal-Recreational Property Development and Its Relationship to Forest Management and Public Use of Forest Lands.* Eugene, Oregon: Richard L. Ragatz Associates, Inc., 1978.

Siehl, G. H. "Outdoor Recreation Considerations in River Basin Planning and Management with Possible Applications to the Potomoc." Congressional Research Service Report 79-243 ENR. Washington, D.C.: Congressional Research Service Library of Congress, 1979.

USDA, Forest Service. "An Assessment of the Forest and Range Land Situation in the United States." Washington, D.C.: USDA FS-345, 1980.

USDI, Heritage Conservation and Recreation Service. *The Third Nationwide Outdoor Recreation Plan,* the executive report, the assessment, and the appendices. Washington, D.C.: Government Printing Office, 1979.

Van Doren, C. S., and Hodges, L. *America's Park and Recreation heritage: A Chronology.* Washington, D.C.: Government Printing Office, 1975.

2

Recreation Resource Management for Visitor Satisfaction

Wilbur F. LaPage

QUALITY: OUTDOOR RECREATION'S CONCEPTUAL SAND CASTLE

Providing the environment for "a high quality outdoor recreation experience" is a goal of most recreation resource managers—public and private. As a useful goal, it is just clear enough to be professionally embraced and just fuzzy enough to go unchallenged as to its meaning. It is jargon, and a reasonably accurate translation would probably be something like: "experiences which are generally congruent with the ideals of the area's planners and managers." Unfortunately, there is a growing mountain of evidence that substantial differences exist between managerial and user perceptions of ideal locations, designs, facilities, supervision, and maintenance (Driver 1976, Hendee and Harris 1970, Lucas 1964, Peterson 1974).

Campground planners historically located their developments in wooded settings; and campers used them. Suddenly, in the 1950's, private enterprise started building campgrounds in fields, pastures, and other areas with minimal shade. Campers accepted them, used them, claimed to prefer them; and why not—they were sunny, dry, and superior for seeing other campers and being seen at a time when camping equipment was just becoming colorful, interesting, and expensive! Planners avoid developing stream-side and lake-side campsites for "environmental reasons". But many campers like waterfront sites and willingly pay more to use them, sometimes lots more; waterfront sites in some private areas rent for more than twenty dollars per night! Planners prefer rustic, unobtrusive facilities (like hidden toilet buildings), while visitors like to be able to find them, sometimes in a hurry!

Many managers sincerely believe that the least management is the best management—"be unobtrusive like the facilities!" Many of today's campers do not want an unobtrusive ranger; they expect to find someone who is "in charge" to provide security, information, and advice. Despite two decades of massive changes in the camping market and its needs for utility connections and modern facilities, most public campground systems have successfully resisted the markets' demands for hot showers and on-site electricity. Probably an equally long list of perceptual differences can be drawn for the planners, managers, and users of other types of outdoor recreation areas.

"Quality" seems to have become synonomous with "style" for a great many recreation resource managers. Primitive wilderness camping is no different from camping in a full-facility resort campground except for the style of participation. The quality of management, and the quality of the experience can be equally high (or low) at either location. The camper attacked by a bear in West Yellowstone did not have a higher quality experience than the camper attacked by hoodlums outside of Los Angeles. Campground management failed, in both instances, to provide a safe (high quality) environment.

Confusing quality with style, while not very professional, is at least understandable in light of the enormous arrays of style differences in most outdoor recreation activities, and the popular writer's penchant for idealizing the "purist onepercent" of most recreation markets. It is professionally inexcusable, however, to promote one's own style as the ideal model, and then to use that model as the excuse for not providing the services and facilities needed by those who prefer a different style:

"ONLY HIGH-QUALITY RECREATION PROVIDED BY THIS ESTABLISHMENT."

Finally, the quality sand castle completely collapses, when other "lesser" styles, inconsistent with facility design and capability, are allowed to co-exist with the quality-minded purists because it's politically inexpedient to discriminate. Twenty thousand dollar, utility-devouring camping vans parked on tent sites, "hot-dogging" on family ski slopes, trail bikes on hiking trails, and power boats on canoe streams, are some common examples of "quality" giving way to indecision.

MANAGEMENT STANDARDS: QUALITY SURROGATES

If quality is unrelated to style, what is it? Three basic assumptions may be helpful: (1) A high quality outdoor recreation experience is one which meets or exceeds each visitor's expectations; (2) the resource manager exerts a critical influence upon the quality of the visitor's experience; and (3) the manager's influence is both direct (inter-personal) and indirect through his influence on the recreation environment.

Given the extensive variability among visitor expectations, and the difficulty of measuring and monitoring those expectations, it is logical that some surrogate measure of experience quality would be developed by managers. Managerial standards have provided that surrogate. And, standards for every conceivable aspect of a recreation experience have been developed and used: "Restrooms will be checked and cleaned hourly." "Litter will be picked up daily." "Employees will wear clean uniforms at all times when meeting the public." "Pets are not allowed." "Playgrounds will receive a thorough safety inspection monthly."

Books of standards have been written for use by public agencies and private recreation enterprises to provide quality control from initial design to day-to-day management. The underlying assumption is that quality inputs will result in quality outputs.

Standards of operation are generally intended to insure that the manager's indirect influence on visitor experience quality is positive. However, providing the same assurance for the direct, inter-personal influence is more appropriately addressed through special training courses. Effective training programs in methods and techniques for greeting, serving, and hosting a diverse recreating public, are considerably harder to find than standards for cleaning a restroom! But they do exist, and in fairness, recreation area managers may be leaders in our so-called service economy in their sensitivity toward their clientele's needs. (In contrast with "service stations" that no longer offer services, grocery stores that no longer deliver groceries, and doctors who never make house calls.)

Whether recreation management is better in its public interaction than other segments of the economy is, however, less relevant than whether it is doing enough. Given the existence of limited research which indicates that staff-public interactions have a greater impact on perceived quality of park management than does the condition of facilities (Knopf and Barnes 1979), it may be that our emphasis on management standards needs to be duplicated for staff training. Certainly, a better balance between the two is called for, considering the prevalence of staffing the visitor reception function with individuals having the lowest pay, poorest training, and least stake in the outcome.

STANDARDS WITHOUT FEEDBACK: A THEATRE WITHOUT APPLAUSE

The combination of development standards, management standards, and training standards provides the concerned recreation resource manager with a substantial input arsenal for assuring a quality visitor experience. Most managers have been content to assume that those inputs are, in fact, delivering quality experiences. But standards aren't enough. Some feedback mechanism is usually necessary to ensure that the existing standards are relevant and uniformly applied by all employees who deal with the public. If input standards exist, in part, because of the difficulties in measuring recreation output, or experience quality, what kinds of feedback might be appropriate? Suggestion boxes and other visitor encouragements to comment are an obvious possibility. Though used, they are not effective in providing a reasonable cross-section evaluation of managements' performance. Occasional visitor surveys of attitudes, opinions, preferences, likes and dislikes, have been used, but in no systematic way that would efficiently monitor managerial performance.

Although research is both limited in scope and geographically scattered, it is clear that we can measure the perceived satisfaction of visitors to outdoor recreation areas. Although the measurement systems are still crude, we do know that satisfaction increases and decreases in response to a wide range of factors influenc-

Table 1

Average Satisfaction Scores on 14 Elements of a Camping Experience, Reported in 1978 by Visitors to Public and Private Campgrounds*

Factor	Public	Private
Your first impression	6.9	6.5
Cleanliness of campsites	7.0	7.0
Cleanliness of restrooms	6.0	6.4
Privacy of campsites	6.4	5.8
Good size of campsites	7.1	6.3
Good choice of campsites	6.5	6.3
Availability of firewood	5.7	5.9
Availability of supplies	5.3	6.3
Recreation opportunities	5.9	6.3
Ease of check-in	6.8	7.0
Safety and security	6.8	6.7
Good rules & regulations	6.8	6.7
Helpfulness of employees	7.1	7.1
Your recommendation of us	7.1	6.8
Mean Score	6.5	6.5
Number of campers	774	3045
Number of campgrounds	16	107

*From: *Satisfaction Monitoring for Quality Control in Campground Management.* USDA Forest Service Res. Paper NE-484. LaPage & Bevins, 1981. A perfect score of "A" = 8, "C" = average or 4, and "E" = poor or 0.

ed by management such as crowding, courtesy, and cleanliness (LaPage and Bevins 1981, Foster and Jackson 1979, Knopf and Barnes 1979). And, in turn, relative satisfaction affects the way in which recreators react toward management (LaPage 1962, 1968). In simplest terms, managements efforts to increase visitor satisfaction produce returns in the form of more business and fewer problems.

Given this knowledge, it would seem to be good business—public or private—for management to monitor visitor satisfaction as a means of assessing its own performance and avoiding potential losses. And the feedback provided by such monitoring, even if it is done on a very small sample basis, provides an excellent opportunity to evaluate the effectiveness of existing standards and investments in staff training.

Table 2

Summary of Satisfaction Changes Noted at
Nine New Hampshire State Park Campgrounds 1977-1980, and Frequency of
Manager's Recollection of a Change*

| | No. Parks | | Manager |
Change of at least 1.0 point	+	−	agreement
Cleanliness of sites	1	0	1
Cleanliness of restrooms	3	1	3
Availability of supplies	5	3	1
Availability of firewood	4	4	3
Privacy of campsites	1	0	
Recreation opportunities	2	0	
Rules and regulations	0	1	
Safety and security	1	0	1
Ease of check-in	1	1	
	—	—	
Totals	18	10	9

*From: *Satisfaction Monitoring for Quality Control in Campground Management.* USDA Forest Service Res. Paper NE-484. LaPage & Bevins, 1981.

VISITOR SATISFACTION: IMPLICATIONS FOR MANAGEMENT

A "report card" for assessing visitor satisfaction among campers, in use by the New Hampshire Division of State Parks from 1977-1980, appears to contain the essential elements of a practical, simple, economical, and sensitive feedback mechanism (LaPage and Bevins 1981). Using satisfaction levels of "A" through "E", the New Hampshire study assessed satisfaction for a composite of 15 different aspects of a camping visit, among more than 6,500 visitors to a wide variety of public and private campgrounds (Table 1). Using relatively small samples of voluntary responses, the researchers found that different campgrounds produced characteristic average satisfaction levels from year to year. But, when many campgrounds were average together, the composite satisfaction at both public and private campgrounds was remarkably similar. Element satisfaction, the average rating for individual elements on the report card, walso found to be sensitive to changes in management practices, increasing in response to improved security procedures, decreasing when budget cuts required less frequent clean-up operations (Table 2).

Since the New Hampshire satisfaction monitoring system is essentially an adaptation of the evaluation system commonly used by restaurants, hotels, and motels, further adaptations for other types of recreation areas are obviously possible. Because monitoring can be done with very small samples, it is not expensive. Possible, inexpensive, and an opportunity to improve business, while reducing problems, yet it is a decidedly uncommon practice among the nation's several thousand public and private outdoor recreation areas.

Visitor satisfaction should be considered both a goal and a tool of recreation management. The recreation manager who manages for satisfaction always stands apart from his competition, as does his staff. When the obvious goal is to produce satisfied customers, it takes a rare visitor to miss the varied signals that are evident. And, when that satisfaction is being measured and monitored, it becomes possible to target organizational goals on measured increases, along with commensurate employee incentives. Managing for satisfaction is good business from a marketing viewpoint as well. If "a picture is worth a thousand words," then one satisfied customer must be easily worth a thousand pictures. Knowing the importance of word-of-mouth advertising in this field, it is entirely appropriate to divert at least one-half of the advertising budget into visitor satisfaction monitoring and staff training.

IMPLICATIONS FOR RESEARCH: CEMENT FOR THE SAND CASTLE

While the major studies which have attempted to document that illusive concept, "quality of life," have failed to identify recreation as a significant component of the concept (Andrews and Withey 1976), the amount and quality of leisure must be a major contributor to each individual's satisfaction with life. The popularity of outdoor recreation experiences suggests that their role in the leisure component must also be significant. Recreation resource managers are therefore in the business of improving the quality of life of their visitors. If their visitors depart with feelings of dissatisfaction, disappointment, frustration, or even anger, the manager has failed, no matter how high quality its inputs have been.

This is not to say that input standards aren't necessary, or even that professional ideals about quality aren't useful. But, augmenting them with known levels and trends in visitor satisfaction seems to be a most logical method of testing their adequacy and relevance to those people for whom the resource is being managed. If, for example, a "high-quality" primitive camping facility is receiving low (lower than the average for similar facilities) camper satisfaction scores, presumably management would want to know why. And, if the average scores for similar facilities in a region are trending gradually downward, what are the implications for that segment of the market and that type of development? The possibilities for research into the causes for different satisfaction levels and trends are numerous, and the opportunities for immediate application of findings by managers and investors, makes this an attractive and useful field of study.

Finally, if theory-building with regard to outdoor recreation outputs is ever going to advance beyond its present inadequate state, it will be necessary to have some idea of the range in satisfaction distributions for different activities, resources, levels of management, and visitor inputs. Satisfaction is not just a surrogate for experience quality, it is quality in the minds of many visitors. Few visitors are so analytical (at least, the satisfied ones), or motivated, to identify, evaluate, and attempt to weigh the components of their experience. Just as an outstanding broadway musical can be ruined by a faulty sound system, or a gourmet dinner spoiled by a surly waitress, a high quality recreation experience can be destroyed by teh failure of any one of its parts. Minor flaws in technical excellence can often be compensated by that special extra "personal touch." By providing that extra personal touch, satisfaction monitoring is quality recreation management. And, to the extent that it is done jointly by management and research, it is also quality recreation research.

References

Andrews, F. M., and Withey, S. B. *Social Indicators of Well-Being: Americans Perceptions of Life Quality.* New York: Plenum Press, 1976.

Bultena, G. L., and Klessig, L. L. "Satisfaction in Camping, a Conceptualization and Guide to Social Research." *Journal of Leisure Research* 1(1969):348-354.

Driver, B. L., "Towards a Better Understanding of the Social Benefits of Outdoor Recreation Participation." Proceedings of the Southern States Research Applications Workshop, pp. 163-189. USDA Forest Service General Technical Reprt SE-9, 1974.

Foster, R. J., and Jackson, E. L. "Factors Associated with Camping Satisfaction in Alberta Provincial Park Campgrounds." *Journal of Leisure Research* 11(1979): 292-306.

Hendee, J. C., and Harris, R. W. "Foresters' Perceptions of Wilderness User Attitudes and Preferences." *Journal of Forestry* 68(1970):758-762.

Knopf, R. C., and Barnes, J. D. "Determinants of Satisfaction with a Tourism Reference: A Case Study of Visitors to Gettysburg National Military Park. In *Tourism Marketing and Management Issues,* pp. 217-237. Washington, D.C.: George Washington University Press, 1980.

LaPage, W. F. "The Measurement and Significance of Recreational Experience: A Case Study of Camper Satisfaction and its Significance to Recreation Resource Planning." Master's thesis, University of New Hampshire, Durham, 1962.

LaPage, W. F. "The Role of Customer Satisfaction in Managing Commercial Campgrounds." Upper Darby, Pennsylvania: USDA Forest Service Research Paper NE-105, Northeast Forest Experiment Station, 1968.

LaPage, W. F., and Bevins, M. I. 'Satisfaction Monitoring for Quality Control in Campground Management." Broomall, Pennsylvania: USDA Forest Service Research Paper NE-484, Northeast Forest Experiment Station, 1981.

Lucas, R. C. "Wilderness Perception and Use: The Example of the Boundary Waters Canoe Area." *Natural Resources Journal* 3(1964):395-411.

Peterson, G. L. "A Comparison of the Sentiments and Perceptions of Wilderness Managers and Canoeists in the Boundary Waters Canoe Area." *Journal of Leisure Research* 6(1974): 194-206.

3

Rationing and Redistribution of Recreational Use of Scarce Resources with Limited Carrying Capacity

George L. Peterson

Outdoor recreation opportunity in America is frequently dependent upon publicly owned wild land that is unique, scarce, and fragile. Scarcity of the resources and a tendency for them to be underpriced when they are publicly managed create the potential for overutilization that is inefficient and destructive. It is a "tragedy of the commons" (Hardin 1968) that is a perplexing management dilemma. The following chapter will review a background of concepts; the role of government in land management is first discussed, and this is followed by an explanation of managing scarce and highly demanded resources. This leads to the concept of recreational carrying capacity, which is briefly reviewed. Several important problems that generally clamor for management attention are then discussed. Choices must often be made among conflicting uses of the same resources; allocation may be required between private individuals and firms which provide complementary services such as outfitting and guiding. An attractive recreational resource that attracts large numbers of visitors may also lead to pressure for induced development and, ultimately, to conflict between local and national interests.

The various shapes and forms of overutilization are explored briefly. This is followed by a review of alternative management approaches to rationing and redistribution of use. The chapter concludes with an illustrative example from the Boundary Water Canoe Area Wilderness (BWCAW). The intent throughout is to keep the discussion nontechnical, with emphasis on concept and meaning rather than on theoretical logic. As with all such efforts, we may have leaped chasms for which the bridges are too short, climbed mountains which do not exist, or put the shoe on the wrong foot. Let the reader beware! The management accepts no liability for accidents caused by unmarked hazards.

THE ROLE OF GOVERNMENT IN RECREATION LAND MANAGEMENT

According to the theory of land economics, a competitive market allocates land efficiently by placing each parcel in the ownership of the highest bidder. The highest bidder is the party whose intended land-use yields the greatest net benefit, as defined and justified by the principle of consumer sovereignity. Government intervention in such a market would only tend to cause land to be utilized less productively, thereby reducing the overall wealth of society.

But, the assumptions required for land market efficiency are very rigid and not likely to hold perfectly true in real situations. It must be assumed, for example, that the most productive use for a given piece of land does not have the characteristics of a "public good." Nonrival and nonexcludable land-uses do not find themselves well represented by market transactions, although it may be inefficient not to allocate certain land parcels to their production.

The most productive use for each land parcel or aggregation thereof must be identified and protected in terms of clearly defined and exchangeable legal rights. There must be no external diseconomies such as might arise from attenuation of rights. It must not be possible for one person to reduce the productivity, health, or welfare of another except by voluntary exchange.

All land users must be perfectly informed. There must be no hidden costs or products of private decisions to which those decisions are insensitive. The required temporal and capital scale of the goods and services in question must not exceed the capacity of private suppliers. It is necessary to assume that the distribution of wealth, rights, abilities, and powers among the people is fair (including the endowments involved in intergenerational transactions).

The conditions leading to monopoly must be absent, and there must be an adequate framework for enforcing rights and contracts and for adjudicating disputes. Finally, there can be no rights of "public interest" which transcend individual rights, except by exchange in the free market or as specified in the accepted body of law.

Apparently we, the people, have decided through due process that the private land market is less than perfect. We have defined "public interests" and empowered agents at various levels of government to control and regulate land use, to deliver specific recreation goods and services through public ownership and management of specific parcels, and to transfer costs and benefits among individual members of society. Because of this, we enjoy the benefits of such phenomena as city, state, and national parks; urban forest preserves; state and national forests; and designated wilderness areas. It is generally agreed that such land uses would not be available in their most productive locations and forms if left to the private market. The principal difference derives from the conflict between the private quest for financial efficiency and revenue maximization on the one hand and the public quest for broader economic efficiency and social welfare maximization on the other hand. These conflicting quests occur in the presence of additional public objectives and market imperfection.

Of course, government agents are at least as capable of mistakes as private agents, but their perspective is different. They are charged with defending the "public interest," as defined through due process. Hopefully, that perspective, together with diligent pursuit of information on nonpriced and external value flows to which private decisions are not sensitive, results in overall improvement in the quality of life through selective government land management. The services provided by these public agencies include: 1) acquisition, retention, and sale of public land, 2) control of access to public land, 3) control of public land use, 4) provision of services and facilities on public land, and 5) regulation and taxation of private land use. It is clearly not efficient, however, to impose a remedy that is more costly than the illness it is intended to cure. The costs of intervention should be charged against the benefits thus obtained.

THE MANAGEMENT OF SCARCE AND HIGHLY DEMANDED RECREATION RESOURCES

Withdrawal of land by the government from the uses preferred by the private market has an associated cost. The cash value of the land is foregone, for example, which is a reflection of the net benefits that might be generated in alternative private use. The limitations and demands on public wealth and the pressures for alternative development by the private market restrict the amount of land that can be withdrawn. In concept, the withdrawal should be justified by net public benefits which at least equal the opportunity cost. Given the inherent difficulties in defining and defending those benefits and in view of the pressures (both inside and outside of government) toward financial efficiency based on cash flows, public land-uses are likely to be undersupplied.[1] In heavily developed regions such as major metropolitan areas, the opportunity costs will be extremely high. In undeveloped regions the opportunity costs will be much lower. In any case, the scarcity of public land-use will be aggravated if the service in question requires investments in addition to the withdrawal of land from the private market or if the nature of the service or the background of policy is such that the benefits created cannot be captured as revenue. Recreational land use also tends to focus on land attributes that are unique, rare, and difficult to maintain, and this contributes further to scarcity.

In a free market, scarcity of an excludable rival good (for which consumption by one person reduces the quantity available for consumption by others) drives up the market price. This regulates supply and rations the good among consumers according to willingness to pay. Given the usual microeconomic assumptions, the

---

[1]This assumes that undeveloped land is not in excess supply and that the recreational use in question is not simply free access to surplus land held in the public trust to preserve options for future development. It also assumes the existence of a reasonable pluralistic political economy of dispersed power which resists the growth of powerful self-justifying bureaucracies.

good then goes to those for whom it has the greatest net benefit and for whom the net benefit is positive. But, the use of public land tends to be underpriced, especially if the services being provided by the government are nontrivial and nonexcludable by nature. The fact that the government is the supplier (or a strong regulator of suppliers) deprives the market of the opportunity to set prices which will effectively control supply and demand. There may be public policies, such as social equity objectives, which forbid the extraction of efficient prices from the consumer. Supply costs are generally paid from general tax revenues, and this tends to disconnect benefits received by the consumer from costs incurred by the supplier.

Because of these factors, public lands are prime candidates for destructive overutilization by recreation unless the managing agencies ration their use. If use of the resource is underpriced, people will be inclined to consume the services at inefficiently high levels. This may divert their investments from more productive alternatives. It provides enticement to use observed levels of participation and congestion as naive justification for increasing supply. It may also have destructive consequences for the resource and for the quality of service it provides.

At some point the site becomes congested. A visit by one person begins to reduce the quantity and quality of satisfaction available to another person. This could be self-regulating. If all potential visitors are identical in tastes and preferences, the "price" imposed by congestion may tend to ration consumption.

However, if some visitors are more congestion-tolerant than others, those who are sensitive to congestion may be the first to go elsewhere. This may trigger a process of evolution which, if unchecked, leads to the production of very different services and experiences than those which motivated government involvement in the first place (Becker, Nieman, and Gates 1981; Anderson 1980). Because public lands may also be ecologically fragile, destructive consequences of overutilization may change the nature of the resource. This form of capital consumption can lead to "bankruptcy" of the resource and loss of the recreation opportunity. This successive modification of the resource base further encourages invasion and changes of types of land use.

The government which provides the recreation opportunities must decide how much of each type to provide. It must also contrive means to ration consumption in the absence of the missing market mechanism. This need to ration the resource requires someone to determine what the capacity is.

The Carrying Capacity Problem

Recreation opportunity supplied by the government on public land can generally be regarded as a congestible public good. Simply stated, consumption of opportunity by one individual does not reduce the amount of opportunity available to another until some critical level of use at which the area becomes congested. Obviously there is no magical discontinuity at which the appearance of one more user suddenly causes congestion. Over a range of use levels, it is possible to describe some higher levels as congested and other lower levels as uncongested.

This implies the existence of a point or interval which can be defined as recreational carrying capacity in terms of level of use (Lime and Stankey 1971, Frissell and Stankey 1972).

While this simple paradigm is useful in concept, the problem is much more complicated in application as demonstrated by Hendee, Stankey, and Lucas (1978, chapter 9) in their excellent overview of "Wilderness Carrying Capacity." Carrying capacity may be different for different types of activities and may depend on variations in the behavior of individuals, as well as on the relative mix of different types of use. Some activities will be in direct conflict with each other and will be rival in utilization of the resource. Other activities may be more compatible.

Carrying capacity has ecological and social dimensions. Recreation activity may have physical and biological impacts on the resource, thereby modifying attributes that are important to the production of recreation opportunity and/or other uses of the area. On the other hand, the mere presence of other people may be a negative factor in the process by which recreators receive satisfaction from the resource. For some, solitude may be a strong preference for its own sake. For others, the aversion may not be to the presence of people, per se, but to offensive behaviors exhibited by some people, such as littering, rowdiness, or a different sense of outdoor etiquette. An important component of social capacity is simply competition for limited facilities, such as preferred campsites. An interesting anomoly in social capacity is an observed tendency for some to prefer the presence of a few people over no people at all (Hendee, Stanke, and Lucas 1978, chapter 9). It is not clear whether this reflects an attraction to opportunity for social interaction or whether it is simply the product of concern for safety.

Too often ignored, but quite often decisive, is the political component of carrying capacity. The question ultimately boils down to one of rivalry over consumption of a scarce resource, and this implies a process of conflict resolution. A perfect market would resolve such conflicts through equilibrium in an exchange of excludable rights. Public recreation resources often find instead that they are the objects of intense political controversy among competing factions. Sometimes such controversy is resolved legislatively or by litigation. It often falls upon the local manager, however, to make administrative decisions in terms of available technical information, public concerns and pressures, and legal requirements and enablements. In any case, the determination of a resource's capacity for various recreation activities is an act of judgment with regard to what is and is not acceptable.

A relevant aspect of human behavior that is well developed in economic theory is that people are willing to make substitutions or tradeoffs. Apparently, this concept is not yet well developed in the literature or practice of recreational carrying capacity. For example, is social carrying capacity independent of the probability that a person will be denied access to a given resource? Other things being equal, are people willing to accept a higher likelihood of encountering other users in return for a higher likelihood of gaining access? This becomes a very important question when 1) social capacity is the limiting factor, 2) social capacity has been based on the preferences of persons in the act of using the resource (or conditional on the assumption of access), 3) demand exceeds capacity, and 4) access is rationed among applicants. Given a choice between higher congestion and exclusion, to what extent and in what situations will people choose higher congestion?

Research on social carrying capacity is based too often on direct questioning of people already on site. They are asked questions about their willingness to accept encounters. Results thus obtained are of questionable validity, because it is difficult to eliminate the incentive to give a wrong answer and next to impossible to provide incentive to give a correct answer. This requires careful and elaborate psychological design of the experiment. Answers obtained on site to direct questions about willingness to accept encounters may be very different than true preferences that would prevail under actual threat of denial of access.

The Problem of Conflicting Activities

A given recreation resource may be capable of producing several different kinds of recreation opportunity. Sometimes this results in the attraction of activities which interfere with each other. For example, satisfaction of wilderness paddle canoeists is degraded by the presence of motorized travel. Snowmobiling depreciates the quality of opportunity for cross-country skiing. Off-road vehicles and pack animals reduce the satisfaction of backpackers.

Where conflicting uses compete for the same resource, there may be the need to ration selectively or to separate the conflicts in space or time. Temporal zoning of a wilderness river might restrict use to paddlers only during designated periods, while allowing motorized travel at other times. Decisions to separate or selectively exclude conflicting uses should be based on comparison of the costs and benefits of the competing alternatives. Where only one of the conflicting uses can be served, the resource should be allocated to that use which generates the greatest net present value (other things being equal). In other words, the resource should go to the use which offers the highest "bid." It thus reduces to the problem of valuation of the costs and benefits of a congestible public good for which market facts and market mechanisms are unavailable.

If the state-of-the-art has allowed standard valuation methods to be developed, accredited, and canonized, and if the situation allows those methods to be applied, the matter can be resolved administratively. If not, a political resolution may be required. Values not represented through the market or delegated legislatively to administrative processes and accredited methods have to rely on political action.

Land managers who must make administrative allocations among conflicting uses of the resource first need to understand the conflicts. This requires an understanding of the experience preferences of those who might use the resource for various purposes (Driver 1976, Driver and Bassett 1975). Equally important, though, is the need to expose the process by which recreation experience is produced. The production function will show the input factors and output consequences required to produce the preferred recreation experiences. Exposure of this information for several activities competing for use of the resource will help to identify conflicts, as well as opportunities for joint production.

Once the conflicts are clearly understood, there are numerous methods available for measuring the relative economic benefits of competing activities.

The conflicts can occur at a very general level, such as between mining or timber harvest, on the one hand, and the production of water, livestock, or recreation opportunity, on the other. Or, it might be a matter of conflict among specific recreation activities. Which valuation methods are appropriate will depend on the nature of the conflicts to be resolved.

A detailed survey of valuation methods is not appropriate here and is available elsewhere (see, for example, Descousges, Smith, and McGivney 1982; Dwyer, Kelly, and Bowes 1977; Freeman 1979; Pearce 1978; Sinden and Worrell 1979.) The chapter by Dwyer in this book gives an excellent overview of benefit valuation for recreation. A state-of-the-art review in preparation by the U.S. Forest Service (Peterson and Randall 1982) provides a conceptual and methodological overview of the applications to timber, mining, water, range, wildlife, and recreation.

Unfortunately, some excellent methods that are available for valuation of non-market benefits are not universally understood or accepted and tend to be prohibitively expensive in specific applications. There are major challenges here for research and education. Methods need to be improved, validated, standardized, and certified. Misunderstandings need to be cleared up and applied capability improved. The expensive and complex methods need to be simplified and made more efficient, where possible. And, they need to be used in controlled experimental settings to produce generalized and routinized valuation models which can be applied inexpensively.

In summary, conflicts which must be resolved administratively require comparison of relative costs and benefits. Where choice is necessary, the resource should be allocated to the highest-valued use, other things being equal. The value of a resource in alternative uses will be sensitive to 1) the ability of the resource to support the activity in question; 2) the quality, quantity, and location of substitute sites; 3) the numbers and locations of individuals desiring to use the resource for the activity in question; and 4) the relative net value of the activity to its participants.

The Problem of Commercial/Private Allocation

When increasing demand collides with limited capacity, a conflict generally emerges between commercial and noncommercial users of the resource. The commercial users are individuals and firms which provide services to persons who come to the public land to engage in recreational activity. Any site which attracts visitors may also attract complementary commercial services. Many wilderness area visitors, for example, will desire peripheral food and lodging services and shops in which to purchase equipment and supplies. Outfitting and guide services may also spring up. Such complementary services stimulate the local economy by capturing income and providing jobs. They also enhance the attractiveness and value of the primary resource.

There is, however, a conflict of interest that tends to develop. The suppliers of complementary goods and services will want to stimulate demand for the resource in order to stimulate demand for their goods and services. This will further aggravate the carrying capacity problem and will put pressure on the managing agency to relax use limits. This is particularly troublesome when the carrying capacity-related restrictions move into the picture after the vendors of complementary goods and services have made large capital investments in anticipation of unregulated future growth.

Given that the resource supply has been limited by regulation to a specified number of visitors per time period, each of the commercial guide and outfitter firms will want to capture as many of those visitors as possible, up to their profit-maximizing level of activity. This creates competition between the commercial outfitters who provide complementary services and the private users of the resource who do not require those services. With restricted capacity of the resource, each private user who does not take outfitter services reduces the potential volume for the outfitter. One of the most perplexing decisions that must be made by public resource managers concerns allocation of resource capacity between commercially served visitors and visitors who are not commercially served and the allocation of commercial capacity among independent firms (Shelby and Danley 1979).

Assuming it can be accomplished, specifying and enforcing capacity restrictions and allocating commercial shares would appear on the surface to solve the problem. However, as with many regulatory "medicines," there are likely to be interesting, perhaps harmful, side effects. Recall that the restrictions and allocations are necessary because demand exceeds what has been judged to be the available supply. The imbalance occurs because the resource is scarce or fragile and underpriced. Under the circumstances, the natural economic pressures are the same as under monopoly, to drive up the price (Parent 1979).

Although the monopolstic situation is created by governmental restriction and not through action by the outfitters, it is quite unlikely the outfitters would be slow to refuse abnormal profits. Their natural tendency would be to raise the price of their services as high as the market will bear. In effect, their strong complimentarity with the resource that allows them to charge a fee for its use. If this happens, the commercial outfitter will be capturing some of the surplus that would otherwise go to the consumer. It can be argued that an effective market has been created which prices the resource more efficiently and also tend to ration the commercial use. But, it can also be argued that the effective fee is not consistent with the initial policy by which the opportunity was to be allocated among members of the public. Even if the fee itself is not objectionable, it certainly should go to the supplier of the resource, not to the supplier of complementary services. If a fee is to be extracted from some, why not from all users? This would effectively ration the resource, reduce the capacity regulation overhead, and, along the way, generate substantial revenue.

The Problem of Induced Development and Local versus National Conflict

When the recreation resource is highly attractive, intense economic development may be induced. Gattlinburg, North Carolina and The Wisconsin Dells are prime examples. Gattlinburg straddles the main route through the Great Smokey Mountains National Park. At the Wisconsin Dells, a scenic and regionally unique stretch of the Wisconsin River is relatively accessible to huge population centers (Chicago, Milwaukee, Madison, Minneapolis-St. Paul.)

In both locations, a unique natural area has been legally protected for preservation of its scenic attractions. Because of inherent recreational value and proximity to population, large numbers of people visit the areas. Complementary services have developed to serve the needs of the tourists in connection with their sightseeing. But, much of the economic development at these and similar locations bears little direct relationship to the natural feature. It is economic activity that has sprung up simply because people are there. The carnival rides, miniature golf, and specialty shops, for example, compete with the natural attractions for the attention of visitors. Indeed, the induced development has become a major attraction in its own right.

This kind of economic evolution creates a complicated environment for wildland management. Consumers, citizens, and firms with diverse interests invade the region. They may not value the designed functions of the primary resource. It may be to their financial advantage to exploit it in different ways. In fact, the costs and benefits of alternative uses of the resource may change as the local economy evolves. Local interests must be weighed against benefits which are regional or national in scope. If it is in the national interest to preserve the unique natural features of Yellowstone, the Grand Canyon, or the Boundary Waters Canoe Area Wilderness, control of the resource will have to be at the national level. The local political outcome of induced development may have rather different intentions. And, if the benefits accrue to residents of Illinois while the opportunity costs are suffered in Wyoming, Arizona, or Minnesota, local pressure to develop the resource should not be surprising.

If it is efficient by the criterion of national economic development (i.e., potential Pareto efficiency) to preserve the wildland, the aggregate national benefits will exceed the aggregate national costs. This means that the beneficiaries of preservation are willing to pay enough to compensate those who suffer the local costs. It is therefore the responsibility of the national government either to cause the compensation to take place or to overrule the local interests. The compensation could take place either through fees or through taxes and income transfers. Where intergenerational interests are involved, compensation is impossible. In any case, it is ultimately the responsibility of the federal Congress and the Supreme Court to decide what is and is not in the national interest.

Alternative Variations of Overutilization

Scarcity and excess demand may take several forms in public recreation areas. Seasonal variation in attractiveness of the area may cause temporal congestion. Fishing quality, climate, insects, etc., will vary as the seasons change. In the Boundary Waters Canoe Area Wilderness (BWCAW), for example, the lakes are generally frozen and snowbound from mid-November until May. During the winter, use is extremely tight. Fishing is best from mid-May through June, but June is the bug month when black flies and mosquitoes are very plentiful. In July and August the water warms up, swimming becomes more attractive, and the hazards of navigation on cold water disappear. The bugs decline to tolerable levels by mid-August, and the fishing begins to improve again in September. Such wide variations in recreation-relevant attributes of the environment selectively attract different kinds and varying numbers of visitors at different times.

However, the very attractive Fall colors, crisp nights, and Indian summer days of later September and early October are accompanied by a relative absence of people. This is because of variable factors in the life styles of those who use the area. Family vacations are severely curtailed by the fact that school resumes around Labor Day. Also, weekends and holidays are more crowded than weekdays because of work schedules. And, in places like the Boundary Waters where people take wilderness trips averaging five or six days in duration, the early part of the week tends to be more congested than the latter part. People generally travel to the area on the weekend; depending on how far they have to travel, they tend to enter the wilderness on Saturday, Sunday, or Monday. This causes a surge of congestion early in the week, with a waning toward the end as people diffuse into the wilderness or leave. Such environmental and cultural factors may combine to produce demand cycles which, at times, exceed carrying capacity.

If the recreation area is relatively large, has multiple features which vary in attractiveness, or has several points of entry, localized congestion may occur even though overall use does not exceed total capacity. In the Boundary Waters, there are eighty-four official points of entry to the million-acre wilderness. Because of the size and shape of the area and the pattern of access roads, some entry points are much closer to population centers. From Duluth, Minneapolis-St. Paul, or Chicago, the end of the Gunflint trail is about one and a half hours farther away (by automobile) than the popular Ely entrances. This translates to an increase of 60 percent from Duluth, 27 percent from Minneapolis-St. Paul, and 13 percent from Chicago. This is a price (travel cost) difference to which demand is quite sensitive. Using a constant elasticity form for the demand function, a recent study of BWCAW use (Peterson, Anderson, and Lime 1982) estimated the travel distance elasticity of demand to be -2.66 for paddle canoeists, -3.46 for motor boaters, and -5.04 for snowmobilers.

If the recreation area is large, there will also be internal travel cost differences which will encourage localized congestion. Differences in the inherent attractiveness of interior locations will have a similar effect. In places like Rocky Mountain National Park and Yellowstone, the roaded areas are more heavily visited than trailed areas, and trailed areas are more congested than untrailed areas.

Where roads and trails meet at popular trail-heads, congestion is intense. Picnic areas and campgrounds also attract congestion, as do popular scenic attractions. In the Boundary Waters, use is concentrated along the waterways. People seldom go ashore except at designated campsites, portages, and popular scenic locations, and use will be most concentrated in the more accessible areas.

The severity of these temporal and geographic concentrations of use will depend in part on the overall demand for the recreation area. This will be a function of its location relative to population centers, its location and attractiveness relative to competing opportunities, and the magnitudes of accessible populations. Thus, there are three basic congestion problems that may need to be managed: control of the overall level of demand for the area, control of the distribution of that demand over time, and, within the area, control of geographic distribution of use. This requires understanding of the demand process. The recreation area will be part of an external multiple origin, multiple destination, and multiple purpose regional demand process that needs to be understood. If the area is large and complex, there will be a similar multiple site process at work inside (Cesario and Knetsch 1976; Ewing 1980; Peterson, Anderson, and Lime 1982; Peterson, Dwyer, and Darragh 1983).

ALTERNATIVE METHODS FOR RATIONING AND REDISTRIBUTION

There are numerous approaches to rationing and redistribution of the use of recreation areas (Shelby and Danley 1979, Loomis 1980). In a competitive market, goods are rationed and distributed by prices which are established in equilibrium between supply and demand. If access to recreational land can be prevented, and if that access is restricted by regulation and enforcement to specified capacity levels, and if there is excess demand, use of the resource is, in effect, a "private" good. There will be competition among potential users for the right of entry. This creates "pressure" which can be captured and controlled through fees. Recreation expenditure is generally discretionary, not essential, and tends to be price-elastic. Raising prices may reduce demand and vice-versa. This has been clearly demonstrated for nonpriced recreation through travel cost analysis (Dwyer, Kelly, and Bowes 1977). Demand decays with increasing distance, even with highly unique and attractive sites, because of increasing travel costs.

In fact, travel cost can be viewed as a true supply cost, and, therefore, a true price, in those cases where the travel itself is a means of access to a desired destination, not a purpose of the trip and when the cost is correctly perceived. For any good that is produced at a location separated from the point of consumption, there will be shipment costs. The shipment cost is part of the supply cost and must be recovered through the price. In recreation, the consumer is shipped to the point of production, rather than shipping the good to the consumer. Thus viewing the shipment cost as the supply cost of a non-priced recreation resource, we have a discriminatory pricing system in which consumers at different locations pay different prices for use of the area. The decay of demand with increasing distance reveals the relationship between demand and price. Adding an entrance fee to the shipment cost simply increases the price, and the shift in demand can be predicted through travel cost analysis.

If the problem is to reduce overall demand, an appropriate general site fee may have this effect. If the problem is to redistribute demand over time or among specific entries or locations within an area, a system of variable fees may be effective. Higher prices at congested times and places may divert use to less congested times and places. Design of an effective fee structure requires detailed knowledge of the relevant demand processes. LaPage (1975) reports that variable campsite fees within a campground did not effectively redistribute use. This raises important questions about price-rationing and emphasizes the need for further study.

There may be institutional obstacles to a price-rationing approach. Public sector fees are generally justified under legal structures designed for the purpose of generating revenue, not for the control of demand. Innovative legislation may be required. Local public agencies tend to be reluctant to embark on legislative innovation because of uncertainty about the costs and outcomes of legal contests that may arise. There are concerns about constitutionality, political feasibility, and implied social welfare policy. Price rationing may require fees in excess of what can be justified by costs. It may also mean direct charges to the users for resources that have traditionally been considered free or tax supported. And, other things being equal, price rationing may discriminate against the poor. If the government agency is sensitive to questions of distribution of costs and benefits, or if there are "public interest" reasons for free access to the resource, price-rationing may not be acceptable. However, this is more likely to be a problem with local urban facilities than with remote regional or national resources. In the case of western national parks, for example, which are far removed from the urban populations of the east and midwest, travel cost is already a major discrimination against the poor. It is also noteworthy that society is not particularly squeemish about price discrimination in the private market.

If the legal enablement exists, if access to the resource is excludable, if demand is sufficiently price-elastic, and if the demand process is adequately understood, price-rationing can be efficient, effective, and lucrative. Some of the consumers' surplus can be captured to help support administration and improvement of the resource. Properly designed price structures will assure efficient allocation of the resource to those consumers who place the highest value on it. It may also cause more efficient allocation of consumer investment of time and money between outdoor recreation and alternative, perhaps more productive, activities. An interesting and potentially productive side effect may be the stimulation of a competitive private economy. For example, underpriced government campgrounds on public land may prevent private landowners from offering similar services. Pricing the public facilities at "true" value may allow more private suppliers to enter the market.

If price rationing is not feasible, a first-come-first-served system may be appropriate. Based on carrying capacity policy, quotas can be set for various locations, facilities, or time periods. People then would be allowed access as they arrive until capacity is filled. Subsequent arrivals would have to be turned away. Such a system has serious drawbacks when demand greatly exceeds supply. Extreme queuing costs can be imposed on the public. If long travel distances to the site are involved, uncertainty and risk may discourage use. Biases in favor of local users may be strong, because the cost of denial of access is lower for them. Problems of queue control and public dissatisfaction may impose high costs on the managing agency.

At the cost of additional administrative effort, first-come-first-served rationing can be made more convenient for some people by taking reservations in advance. This allows one to know in advance, before travel expense is incurred, whether the desired capacity will be available. While more fair and convenient for some, this approach is biased against people who cannot plan far enough in advance and eliminates the opportunity for spontaneity. It should also be noted that for every restrictive action taken by government, there will inevitably be a surprising counteraction from the people. People may respond to the convenience of advance reservations by making multiple reservations to preserve freedom of choice until a later date or to reduce congestion at the time and location of their intended use. To avoid such counter-moves reservation fees may have to be charged. Positive identification of the applicant may also be required to prevent abuse of the system.

When demand greatly exceeds supply, expensive queuing will occur at the time reservations are opened for the season, or reservations will have to be scheduled so far in advance as to render the system impractical. In such cases lottery rationing may be a useful option. In lottery rationing, advance applications are accepted up to a specified cutoff date, after which capacity is allocated among applicants randomly. The principal drawback with this approach is the heavy administrative cost of keeping the lottery fair. If the managing agency wants to allocate capacity without bias among potential users, extreme measures may be required to prevent cheating. Multiple applications and coalitions will occur unless prevented by personal identification and computerized cross-checking, application fees, etc. Whatever administrative rationing method is used, there is likely to be reactive strategizing by some applicants to find and exploit weaknesses in the system. With or without lottery assignment of permits, an advance reservation approach may stimulate the emergence of a "black market" where permits are exchanged for money. This, in effect, returns the resource full circle to price rationing, but with the revenue diverted from the public coffer. Avoidance of such exploitation requires careful and expensive strategizing and enforcement by the managing agency.

Although lottery rationing has the appearance of fairness when properly randomized and controlled, there may be serious questions about the efficiency of the resulting allocation among users (Loomis 1980). Assume all applicants are: 1) equal in ability to pay, 2) unequal in willingness to pay, and 3) willing to make the trip if a permit is won. In the blind lottery, there is no assurance that available opportunities will be assigned to those who value them most highly. The outcome is inefficient allocation. Some permit holders would be willing to sell their permits for less than what some "losers" in the lottery would be willing to pay. Of course, the applicants are not likely to be equal in ability to pay. Nonefficiency due to blindness to willingness to pay may be counterbalanced by gains in equity due to blindness to ability to pay. However, this is a subject for political value judgment.

Whatever mechanism is used for rationing a scarce resource, it will inevitably be found that "there is no such thing as a free lunch." Additional costs will inevitably be paid by someone. People diverted from more desirable times or places to less desirable times and places will pay additional costs in the form of increased travel, reduced convenience, and reduced satisfaction. First-come-first-served systems impose queuing and risk costs. Advance reservation approaches may also impose queuing and planning costs. They all impose strategy and effort costs which are various forms of willingness-to-pay for access to the resource. If effectively enforced, lottery systems eliminate the queuing costs but still will impose planning costs and add opportunity costs due to reduced efficiency of the resulting allocation. All methods impose administrative costs for operation and enforcement. Before any regulatory allocation scheme is adopted, its costs, benefits, and impacts should be explored carefully to be sure that it achieves the desired ends.

An Illustrative Case Study: The Boundary Waters Canoe Area Wilderness

The Boundary Waters Canoe Area Wilderness (BWCAW) in the Superior National Forest of northeastern Minnesota provides an interesting illustration of many of the concepts and problems discussed in the preceding pages. It is a wilderness area of more than a million acres, containing hundreds of lakes interconnected by short streams and portages. Being part of the Canadian Shield, it is rocky with sparse soil covering, of relatively low relief, and thickly forested. The water quality is generally high, but the water is soft and highly vulnerable to acid rain. Due to the sparce soil cover, the area is also vulnerable to pollution and damage from human use.

Throughout recorded history the BWCAW has been the object of virtually continuous political controversy (The Sierra Club 1970). In the seventeenth, eighteenth, and nineteenth centuries there were disagreements over tribal territories, trapping rights, and international boundaries. In the early twentieth century, struggles occurred among interests for logging, road building, and recreational development; hydroelectric power development; access by marine aviation; and preservation for wilderness recreation. Out of these controversies emerged the Boundary Waters Canoe Area Wilderness as designated by the Wilderness Act of 1964, and a sister area adjacent on the north in Canada, Quetico Provincial Park.

Still, the matter was not resolved. Conflicts continued over logging and motorized travel. Special provisions of The Wilderness Act allowed travel by snowmobiles and motorized watercraft along many routes in the wilderness, and restricted timber harvest was allowed to continue. Then, in 1970 a major crisis erupted. A mining syndicate moved heavy equipment into the heart of the wilderness to begin exploration for copper and nickel. The equipment was removed by the Forest Service, but the conflict went to court and remained there for several years.

In the mid seventies the local versus national controversy heated up when the Oberstar bill was submitted to the Congress. It called for reduction of the wilderness in size, relaxation of restrictions on certain kinds of use, and designation of much of what had been wilderness as a national recreation area. This stimulated a national debate which culminated in Public Law 95-495 of October 1978. The effect of the law was to enlarge the wilderness slightly, place further restrictions on motorized travel, eliminate logging from the wilderness, and, except in the case of national emergency, prohibit mining and mineral exploration.

Against the background of those controversies, recreational use of the BWCAW grew steadily until, in 1970, the Forest Service initiated research aimed at rationing and redistribution. The research was done cooperatively among the Superior National Forest, the North Central Forest Experiment Station, and Northwestern University. It resulted in the implementation, in 1976, of a quota and reservation system. (Hulbert and Higgins 1977, Peterson and Lime 1980, Peterson 1981). A parallel program of research produced a similar control system in Quetico Park in 1977 (Wilson 1977).

The basic problem to be solved was one of redistribution of use. People enter the BWCAW at any of eighty-four access points where roads end and wilderness begins. Some of these are more heavily used than others primarily because they are closer to population centers and because of relative ease of travel within the area. Complementary service development has occurred at the more heavily used entries. People who camp in the area spend an average of five or six days migrating through the lakes and portages. Camping occurs at water's edge in designated campsites restricted to no more than ten people. Congestion is much heavier in some areas than in others because some routes are more attractive and because of the uneven use among entry points. In the early twenties about two-thirds of the use entered through only seven of the eighty-four entry points, and two of those seven received 25 percent. There are also seasonal, weekly, and holiday cycles which further aggravate congestion. Carrying capacity was often exceeded in many parts of the wilderness. There was a clear need for administrative action to redistribute use.

It was decided that the redistribution should be achieved through daily quotas at the entry points. For this to be effective, it must be possible to predict average daily population at interior locations as a function of the quotas at the entries. Extensive research showed this could be done because of stable probabilistic patterns in the way people travel through the area (Wang 1976). A mathematical model was constructed which allowed optimal quotas to be derived for each critical entry point from carrying capacities specified for each of ninety-five interior zones. Linear programming was used to maximize the number of people allowed to enter the wilderness subject to the constraint that the average daily population of the interior zones must not exceed their respective carrying capacities. Management by entry point quotas was selected because it was the least obtrusive of available options. Once people crossed the boundary into the wilderness, they could be allowed complete freedom to travel where and when they please.

Given the quotas, a method was needed to ration the capacity of each entry point among potential users. Price rationing was considered, but not pursued because neither the needed information on sensitivity of demand to price nor the required enabling legislation were available. A first-come-first-served system with opportunity for advanced reservation was adopted. Much has been learned from the application of this redistribution program since 1976. Hopefully, some of that knowledge will be captured and published by the wilderness managers in coming years.

The reader should not get the impression that the quotas are decided by a computer. People make decisions; computers manage and display information. It is the person elected or appointed to manage the problem who must ultimately take responsibility for the outcome. To say "the computer made me do it" is a weak response to criticism. The current state-of-the-art is inadequate to allow incorporation in computer systems of all the diverse facts and multiple concerns that compete for attention in the "game" of allocation of scarce resources. Human judgment within a framework of established law, judicial review, and political conflict, aided by information systems, must ultimately be the decision method.

References

Anderson, D. H. "Displacement of Visitors Within the BWCAW." Fort Collins, Colorado: Department of Recreational Resources, Colorado State University, 1980.

Becker, R. H.; Niemann, B. J.; and Gates, W. A., "Displacement of Users Within a River System: Social and Environmental Tradeoff." In *Some Recent Products of River Recreation Research,* edited by D. W. Lime and D. R. Field, pp. 33-38. Saint Paul: USDA Forest Service, GTR-NC-63, 1981.

Cesario, F. J., and Knetsch, J. L. "A Recreation Site Demand and Benefit Estimation Model." *Regional Studies* 10(1976):97-104.

Descousges, W. H.; Smith, V. K.; and McGivney, M. P. "A Comparison of Alternative Approaches for Estimating Recreation and Related Benefits of Water Quality Improvements." (draft). Prepared for the Office of Policy Analysis, U.S. Environmental Protection Agency, by Research Triangle Institute, Research Triangle Park, North Carolina. July 1982.

Driver, B. L. "Quantification of Outdoor Recreationists Preferences." In *Research Camping and Environmental Education,* edited by B. van der Smissen and J. Meyers, pp. 165-187. Pennsylvania State HYPER Series 11, 1976.

Driver, B. L., and Bassett, J. R. "Defining Conflicts Among River Users: A Case Study of Michigan's Au Sable River." *Naturalist* 26, Spring. pp. 19-23.

Dwyer, J. F.; Kelly, J. R.; and Bowes, M. D. "Improved Procedures for Valuation of the Contribution of Recreation to National Economic Development." Research Report 128, University of Illinois, 1977.

Ewing, G. O., "Progress and Problems in the Development of Recreation Trip Generation and Trip Distribution Models." *Leisure Sciences* 3(1980):1-24.

Freeman, A. M. *The Benefits of Environmental Improvement: Theory and Practice.* Baltimore: The Johns Hopkins University Press (for RFF), 1979.

Frissell, S. S., and Stankey, G. H. "Wilderness Environmental Quality: Search for Social and Ecological Harmony." In *Proceedings, Society American Foresters Annual Meeting,* pp. 170-183. Hot Springs, Arkansas: 1972.

Hardin, G. "The Tragedy of the Commons." *Science* 162, December 1968, pp. 1243-1248.

Hendee, J. C.; Stankey, G. H.; and Lucas, R. C. "Wilderness Management." In USDA Forest Service Publication no. 1365, chapter 9, pp. 169-188, 1978.

Hulbert, J. H., and Higgins, J. F. "BWCA Visitor Distribution System." *Journal of Forestry,* June 1977.

LaPage, W. F.; Cormier, P. L.; Hamilton, G. T.; and Cormier, A. D. "Differential Campsite Pricing and Campground Attendance." Upper Darby, Pennsylvania: USDA Forest Service Research Paper NE-330, Northeast Forest Experiment Station, 1975.

Lime, D. W., and Stankey, G. H., "Carrying Capacity: Maintaining Outdoor Recreation Quality." In *Recreation: Symposium Proceedings,* pp. 174-184. Syracuse, New York: USDA Forest Service, Northwest Forest Experiment Station, 1971.

Loomis, J. B. "Monitorizing Benefits Under Alternative River Recreation Use Allocation Systems." *Water Resources Research,* vol. 16, no. 1, February 1980, pp. 28-32.

Parent, C. R. M., "Measuring Economic Performance of River Outfitters." In *Allocating River Use* by Shelby and M. Danley, pp. 116-131. Gorvallis, Oregon: Oregon State University, 1979.

Pearce, D. W., *The Valuation of Social Cost*. London: Allen and Unwin. 1978.

Peterson, G. L., and Randall, A. "Valuation of Wildland Resource Benefits: A State of the Art Review." (draft). Prepared for the Rocky Mountain Forest and Range Experiment Station, USDA Forest Service, Fort Collins, Colorado. 1982.

Peterson, G. L., "The BWCAW Visitor Distribution Model." Final Report to the Superior National Forest, Northwestern University, Evanston, Illinois, 1981.

Peterson, G. L.; Anderson, D. H.; and Lime, D. W. "Multiple-Use Site Demand Analysis: An Application to the Boundary Waters Canoe Area Wilderness." *Journal of Leisure Research* 14(1982):27-36.

Shelby, B., and Danley, M., "Allocating River Use." Corvallis, Oregon: Oregon State University School of Forestry, 1979.

Sinden, J. H., and Worrell, A. C. *Unpriced Values: Decisions Without Market Prices* New York: John Wiley, 1979.

The Sierra Club. "Wilderness in Crisis." 1970.

Wang, P. K., "Travel Behavior Analysis and User Management in the Boundary Waters Canoe Area (BWCA): An Application of Markov Theory and Linear Programming." Ph.D. Dissertation, Northwestern University, Evanston, Illinois, 1976.

Wilson, F. "Quetico Provincial Park." *Naturalist* 28(Winter 77):12-15.

4

Outdoor Recreation Management Planning: Contemporary Schools of Thought

Alan Jubenville
Robert H. Becker

THE NEED FOR AREA PLANNING: AN INTRODUCTION

There has always been a need for large area planning in providing for outdoor recreation interests. This would insure the continuity of particular recreation opportunities, plus the ability to integrate recreation with other land uses within the area. Gould (1961) stated:

> A major obstacle (to providing recreational outlets) has been the lack of a dynamic planning process... To eliminate later problems in recreation planning, it is best to begin with a comprehensive, clear-cut plan which would encompass the entire recreation complex of a forest sub-region. A concept is needed that will visualize the task of planning recreation facilities as a whole and not just in pieces and fragments.

We went on to suggest grouping related activities and developing facilities around those activities, and these groupings, or clusters, be considered as a recreation opportunity because of their social and resource capabilities. In some, Gould recognized the landscape setting as the key to wildland recreational opportunities. Burch (1964) offered a similar sentiment by suggesting that "activity aggregates" be the basis for recreation planning, rather than simply planning an individual site for an individual activity.

Although the need for this type of comprehensive planning has been continually stressed, most planning has continued to be fragmented and individual sites have tended to be developed in isolation of one another without concern for the effects of such planning or the total recreational opportunities within the area.

This chapter presents an overview and critique of various planning processes that have been directed toward managing recreation in natural areas. The authors trace the development of the carrying capacity concept, and raise questions regarding its past applications. Similarly, the Recreation Opportunity Spectrum

(ROS) is discussed in the context of its utility to natural area planners and managers.

The arguments presented are not intended to discard or dispose of any ideas of concept, but rather are presented to introduce an honest skepticism in the development of the outdoor recreation planning process.

HISTORICAL RESPONSE

Single-Site Planning

Typically, planners have responded to particular problems or situations by evaluating the situation in isolation from the greater area in which it was located — in essence, single-site planning. For example, suppose a small lake was suitable for boating and there was already a simple, but primitive, road to the lake and use was low. Then presume that the road (treated as an individual site) was upgraded. Visitor use increased, and need for day-use facilities (parking, picnic tables, boat ramp, etc.) became evident. The facilities were built and many people began to use these for overnight camping. Next, a campground was built further up the lake, with an appropriate road extension to separate the day and overnight use. Then one day, the planner recognized that the lake was crowded, the oldtimers were not returning, and there was a need for more intensive management of the new users of the area. This scenario may be a desirable one if the overall area were deliberately planned that way. Usually, that is not what the planner intended; the developments just evolved because of incremental planning — one feature at a time. In this case, the problems become evident in terms of the crowding of the lake, the conflict between day and overnight users, and the displacement of one user group with another. These are only the single-site concerns. What are the multiple-site concerns caused by attracting larger user groups and extending the road system into existing roadless area? Possibly, people used to backpack and camp around the lake, canoe to a distant shore and camp and hike, run a trap line, etc. Single-site planning usually does not account for these kinds of problems unless the actual site development (auto campground) is superimposed over an existing use-site (canoe camping area). Even then, there is no guarantee that the conflicts will be recognized.

Basically, single-site planning assumes that planning starts with the site and the goal is facility development. Once it is in place, it becomes the manager's job to manage all the problems. Further, it assumes that the manager is responsible for the recreational experience of the individual, and that the site, or the individual using the site, can be directly manipulated to produce a socially desired outcome.

What are the results of such planning? Typically, it produces a collection of unrelated (in terms of planning) sites that fail to account for the capability of the resource, existing patterns for use, the dynamics of recreational use beyond the individual site, and does not ensure diversity of recreational opportunities associated with the lake (the assumed primary attractor), or define the desired outcomes of the cumulative affect of the incremental planning decisions. The ultimate effect of incremental decision-making is change, an almost continuous change of your clientele group, moving from a compatibly potential heterogeneous user mix towards a larger but more homogeneous group. In our scenario, all diverse parts of the lake and surrounding area, even though visibly still intact, are becoming recreationally less diverse.

Unfortunately, in areas where there is a continuous change of managers, this change in the recreational opportunity is often very rapid and dramatic. New managers typically feel obligated to continue the course chartered by previous managers (even though there may be no real overall plan), or they feel obligated to do something (no one ever paid them to do nothing), or they simply add a touch that reflects their own interests (black-topping a road, foot bridges across a creek, boat dock/moorings, etc.). Wilderness areas, wild and scenic rivers, reservoirs, and even unique natural areas have suffered the effects of similar planning efforts. Access was improved, and more people came. Then one day the manager said, "We are overcrowded. Let's cut back to former levels of use." This problem seems universal and every manager is searching for a solution.

Carrying-Capacity Planning

To understand the direction of the search for a solution to the issues surrounding the "overcrowded" conditions at natural areas that has previously been taken, one needs to appreciate the training and background of most land managers and planners. Since planners and managers believed the issue of overuse in natural areas involved escalating demand for a finite resource base, they sought models that associate demand for recreation with the capacity and limitation of the resource base. While assuming a variety of forms, the models and approaches have become known as recreational carrying capacity.

Recreational carrying capacity, a term bastardized from range management, has become a widely accepted management concept (by both managers and researchers) in dealing with the problems of managing specific areas. Recreational carrying capacity has been defined as the character of use that can be supported over a specific time by an area and developed at a certain level without causing damage to either the physical environment or the experience for the visitor. Carrying capacity has also been used to express architectural or design limits. A parking lot may have a designed capacity of sixty cars. That parking lot's carrying capacity is determined by multiplying sixty spaces by an automobile turnover rate.

In outdoor recreational settings, capacity may be expressed in design units, such as camping spaces or picnic tables. When the recreational experience is separated from designed limitation, application of a design-capacity concept becomes less precise. Is the carrying capacity of a beach area the number of towels that can be placed next to each other? Probably not, very few people would tolerate such use levels.

The cause of the problems fostering the carrying capacity models — single-site planning — was not recognized, and so managers have continued with the same planning process while adopting a carrying capacity, management concept. It was an "odd-couple" marriage that was bound to work as long as the management output was measured in numbers of people, visitor-days, etc., and the on-site researcher found people satisfied with their particular experiences.

Wager's monograph (1964), *The Carrying Capacity of Wild Lands for Recreation,* described the essential paradox by stating:

> Thus, for purposes of determining recreational carrying capacity, the objective of managing wild lands may be stated as sustained production of the highest quality recreation that is possible at acceptable costs. On public lands, which provide most wildland recreation, decisions as to what costs are acceptable will have to be made by public servants striving to achieve the public good. Accepting limitation of use will mean fewer visits per person and is only one of the costs that can be paid for high-quality recreation.

Wagar showed that a manager can operate at any stated level for management objectives. If the manager achieves the desired level of use, then quality in terms of recreational oportunity has been achieved. However, resource managers familiar with the range management concept who were burdened by pressures for resource development and new at the recreation management game, often equated quality with related level of recreational use. Low use is high quality and high use is low quality. With that precept firmly grasped, the manager reached out with his other hand and grabbed the other precept in the summary statement — *limitation of use.*

Although expressed in many forms, the byword of both management and research became carrying capacity. Chubb (1964), Chubb and Ashton (1969), and Stankey (1973) did much to more fully develop the concept, identify the major components, and measure specific parameters, including a subdivision into social and biological capacities. Frissell and Stankey (1972) discussed two principles they felt necessary to implement a carrying capacity-based management program. The first was "acceptable limits to change," where the actual acceptable limits of change are defined as part of the management program. The second was the use of minimum value, where the most limiting factor, social or ecological, is identifiable and appropriate measures are taken to ensure that the effects of recreational use do not exceed the acceptable limits of change for the factor.[1]

Much of the social carrying capacity research has been based on the assumption that increasing numbers reduced the satisfaction of the visitor. This obsession with carrying capacity has tended to oversimplify the role of the manager. As stated by Heberlein and Shelby (1977), there is a need to ". . . help the manager with the most difficult problem — selecting a use figure." The research literature that constantly bombards the manager indicates that we, the researchers, are studying carrying capacity and gives the impression that there is some inherent

---

[1]Stankey and Lime (1973) published a comprehensive annotated bibliography on recreational carrying capacity for the land manager and recreation researcher, showing some of the complexity of the term and its management implications.

capacity of every river or facility, all we have to do is search for the magic number. The proposed management strategies reflect this posture with such terms as control of crowding (Lime 1977), mandatory permits (Hendee and Lucas 1973, Fazio and Gilbert 1974, Godin and Leonard 1977), allocating use (Utter 1977), allocation technique (Utter et. al. 1981), restricting recreational use of wildlands (Schreyer 1977), rationing (Stankey and Baden 1977, Stankey 1979), and so on. The management picture is evident — decide how much pie you have and divide it into shares. Use cannot exceed the capacity (shares) so one must ration this scarce resource. The manager's response to the research community (and misunderstanding of his/her own role in terms of establishment of objectives) was best summarized by Hartman (1977):

> The annual visitation limits on special use permits granted for the operation of float trips through Cataract Canyon in the Park (Canyonlands National Park) were reduced several years ago on an interim basis. The goal was to cut usage from a previous maximum of 10,000 visitors. It was reduced to 6,600 visitors. The purpose of the interim action was to stabilize use pending collection of hard data (by researchers) supporting a carrying capacity.

The carrying capacity model, then, fails to recognize cause-effect relationships. It assumes that all you have to do is work on the effect through number crunching. The relationships might be portrayed as follows:

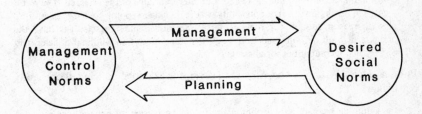

The social norms, in terms of numbers of people, can be achieved by direct management control. According to this model, when use exceeds carrying capacity, one can plan certain management control strategies. The actual management is the implementation of those strategies which achieve the desired social norms. Jubenville (1981) has pointed out the fallacy of such relationships since social succession may have taken place — the area may be supporting a different user population — one more tolerable to higher densitites/social contacts. Rationing then reverts use to former levels, not former users. This is the "wilderness country clubber" idea developed by Jubenville and Workman (1980). Since the actual cause-effect relationship is ignored in the carrying capacity model, the rationing technique is an artificial one for achieving the goal because it does not result in a reversion to former users. This will be discussed later under Jubenville's Law.

Burch (1981) reviewed the metaphors which have shaped recreational carrying capacity and concluded:

> ...data on non-human primates and higher social species demonstrate that the carrying capacity concept has limited empirical support. This uncertainty about the scientific and management utility of the concept is confirmed by mixed findings from a variety of studies on non-human and human social behavior. The paper concludes that the

transfer of concepts with limited empirical support to management realms of great ambiguity and controversy is a doubtful use of science and irresponsible management.

...the universal use of recreation carrying capacity standards may have more to do with coinciding lines of ideology held by the manager and the researcher than by the empirical data.

These conclusions are borne out by Hendee and Harris' (1970) study where they found that the foresters' perception of the typical wilderness user was more purist than was the typical wilderness user. Yet, case studies during the same period of time (Jubenville 1970) show the typical wilderness manager becoming more development-oriented (away from the perceived purist direction) by improving road access, upgrading trails, developing foot bridges, horse facilities, paved parking, latrines, and signs saying "Welcome to _____ Wilderness" or "Lake Solitude, Turn Left, 10 miles," etc.

Even the researcher has fallen prey to his own values. As indicated by Burch (1981):

One would expect the scientist to inventory elements and monitor processes of specific systems and to explore certain theoretical issues, while managers would use the available information to arrive at judgments whose consequences would remain their responsibility. Yet there seems a remarkable coincidence between the intuitive preference of bureaucrats to restrict public access and behavior to standardized and controllable dimensions and the results and interpretations of the research. The result seems to be organized irresponsibility where managers point to the "scientific" data as reason enough for their preferred decisions, and the scientists have the pleasure of both defining and "proving" the value of certain wildland policies held by personally compatible social strata.

Bultena, Field, Womble, and Albrecht (1981), for example, concluded one study by saying:

In examining recreational carrying capacity, it is necessary to have a wide range of contact levels among visitors so as to permit an effective test of the importance of increased contact levels for crowding reactions. The established use-levels at Mount McKinley Park, which were low to ensure solitude, presented a problem in effectively testing the hypotheses in that it would not be known how increased use beyond this minimal level might affect crowding and, in turn, trip satisfaction...

The average daily number of hikers in each of the experimental zones was 14.6, as compared with an average of only 2.7 hikers in each of the other zones. Use levels in the four experimental zones averaged 278 percent of their normal capacities, as compared with only 50 percent of capacities in the 28 control zones that had limits. Despite the fact that the experimental zones attracted more visitors than the control zones, the number of interparty contacts still were well below what was desired for effective tests of the hypotheses. The average number of daily interparty contacts was only 0.9 for parties in the experimental zones and 0.7 for parties in the control zones.

Yet, in another article dealing with the same data base in the same periodical, Bultena, Albrecht, and Womble (1981), speculated the following (even though their data did not bear this out):

The presence of a stringent rationing policy may be affecting the types of recreational clientele attracted to McKinley Park. Implementation of policies permitting relatively unconstrained access and complete freedom of camping activities in the Park would likely bring the displacement of some wilderness purists by persons seeking less density-sensitive values in their wilderness activities. Central to future decisions about rationing at McKinley Park is the issue of whether or not the experiential goals of wilderness purists should outweigh the benefits to be obtained from granting more persons access to this majestic and unique, natural environment. (emphasis added)

The best the authors could conclude is that the empirical data suggests that the assumptions used to determine the original capacity limits for the backcountry zones were not substantiated and that removing the capacity limits will not significantly increase visitor contacts. Beyond that the authors may have cast some suspicions on their own data, but they had no basis for concluding in the second article that the clientele would change, users would become more development-oriented, there would be a need for development to protect the resource against overuse, or that the benefits of capacity limits outweigh the costs.

This universal belief in the carrying capacity concept recently reached new heights when the National Parks and Conservation Association (NPCA) advertised nationally for contract proposals TO DEVELOP RECREATIONAL CARRYING CAPACITY ESTIMATION METHODOLOGY FOR USE IN THE NATIONAL PARK SYSTEM. The general requirements for the proposal were:

1. The methodology must specifically address the physical, environmental, and social aspects of recreational carrying capacity.

2. The methodology must incorporate scientific principles and natural resource management concepts.

3. The methodology must be applicable to any units of the National Park System containing natural resources, including historic and cultural units.

4. The methodology must be applicable to all types of natural resources and environments found within the national park system.

5. The methodology must be in a form readily usable by park managers.

The request for proposals stipulated that "this is not a request for research or field work proposals." The selected methodology will then be tested in some national park system units for "debugging."

Finally, the NPCA will seek system-wide adoption and rapid implementation of the methodology by the National Park Service. This can most readily be accomplished by involving the Service in all aspects of the project. Furthermore, we will launch an education campaign to inform the general public of the need to implement recreational carrying capacities and about the method that has been developed for the National Park System.

For the final solution in development of the carrying capacity concept, the NCPA was willing to pay the "tidy sum" of $10,000. The only thing missing was the requirement for the methodology to be placed on a user-friendly, menu-driven software package on a 5½" floppy disc that the park superintendent can drop into his personal computer and wait for the magic number (carrying capacity) to appear on the video monitor. The really important result and astonishing fact of all of this is that there will be many scientists who will submit the requisite prospectus without question!

While we're not asking that readers abandon their belief in the carrying capacity concept, one should be aware that it is both conceptually and empirically flawed as presently applied. What is needed is a planning system that is conceptually sound and theoretically based and the Recreation Opportunity Spectrum (ROS) provides that.

ROS: A RESPONSE THAT IS THEORETICALLY SOUND

While there are needed refinements in ROS, we hope to show that it is theoretically and operationally sound. The underlying recreation management theory, social succession, will be addressed as the foundation for ROS. Then ROS will be described as a concept, critiqued, and revised to reflect cause-effect relationships (dubbed Jubenville's Law).

Social Succession Theory

Jubenville (1981) and Becker and Jubenville (1981) presented a social or recreational succession theory as the framework for ROS and conceptualization of the roles of the manager, the visitor, and the researcher. Social succesion, where a group supplements or replaces another under changing environmental conditions, is not too dissimilar to ecological succession, except that the forces or agents of change are different and are often more subtle. A model of recreational succession is shown in Figure 1. Accordingly, the user seeks specific recreational opportunity settings to enjoy his own particular experience. He enjoys his particular experience, called Experience A22, and returns to areas as often as possible to find that experience. In sum, it is a positive experience.

Then some agent of change is introduced into the system incidently, such as the surfacing of a heretofore gravel road; accidently, such as chemical pollution of water; or purposefully, such as the introduction of a new management program such as a permit system, mass transportation, etc. These changes, even subtle ones, may have a significant effect on A types of user experiences (like A22).

If the A22 user does not recognize the changes, then essentially the change has had no effect on his experience. However, if he recognizes the changes and responds, his initial reaction is to ameliorate the effects of change. This means that Experience A22 is still a positive one, but some behavioral course of action must be taken to eliminate or avoid negative elements in a positive recreational experience. This is the process by which we maintain homostasis in the world around us. If you have a bad neighbor, you do not call the sheriff's office and ask

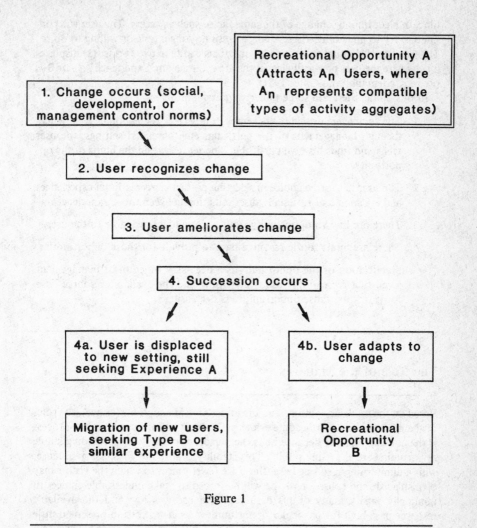

Figure 1

A Model of Recreational Succession

to have him removed, or sell out and move to another neighborhood. These are drastic steps. More than likely, you simply avoid him. You put up a fence, do your gardening on days he does not normally do his, avoid parties where he may be present, or some similar kind of behavioral response. People do the same thing in recreation. There are good examples of this: boating during early morning hours to avoid congestion on the lake, float-fishing the river during the middle of the week because most people float over a weekend, etc.

There may be several different types of changes that take place over a period of time, or a continuous change of the same factor such as access. The user will continue to try to ameliorate those changes until no longer able or willing to do so. This is when the actual succession begins. This can take two forms: (1) displacement where the user physically leaves the area still seeking Experience A_{22} or B_{19} (Becker, Niemann, and Gates 1981).

In this model there are some underlying assumptions:

1. The manager provides the opportunity for recreational experiences through management of the particular environmental settings; the user seeks and finds his own particular experiences within the limits of the opportunity.

2. The user has a free choice in selecting particular recreational experiences and is capable of rationally discriminating between those experiences.

3. There are known opportunity setting alternatives available to the user.

4. There are limits to the resource base to provide for those opportunities.

5. Stabilization of the opportunity is a necessary function of management given that recreational use is increasing and the available resource base for providing those opportunities is decreasing.

The Role of the Manager

Based on the model in Figure 1 and the underlying assumptions (above), the roles of the manager and user become evident. The most important role in the process is that of the manager because he is the person responsible for providing stable opportunities to the using public. This stability is absolutely necessary because, with a diminishing resource base, there are fewer places to which the visitor may be displaced; and subsequently he will be forced to make undesirable choices to minimally satisfy many of his desires. When use was low and the available resource base high for particular opportunities, social succession presented little problem to many users. Adaptation to the change was not necessary because a simple, geographic displacement would have been sufficient to find new stability in the old experience. This often is not true today. Thus, the most critical step in modern recreation management is stabilization of the opportunity setting. It is a guarantee to the using public that all precautionary steps have and will be taken to minmize the chance of introduction of agents of change that are not capable of being mitigated.

As indicated by Jubenville (1981), this places a burden on the manager to be able to describe in detail the opportunity to be offered. Without being able to describe in detail the recreational opportunity to be offered, the manager can neither plan nor manage recreation opportunities. The concept of the recreational opportunity spectrum (ROS) can help the manager describe the general opportunity (Clark and Stankey 1979); the additional descriptive details should reflect the unique aspects of the environmental setting in which the opportunity is available and those special services to be provided.

One end of the spectrum (opportunity A) is assumed to be a wilderness experience — the extreme undeveloped portion of the ROS. The use is nearly 100% by trail. As use increases, however, the manager has typically improved the road access, upgraded trails, and even established user facilities at the trail access. This slow, but continual, change of access and facilities has attracted a new type of user seeking a less physical and mental challenge, while many of the original users may not like the new situation and are simply displaced somewhere else. For the most part, they are probably not reacting to the change in development norms but the change in social norms caused by the change in the development norms, such as larger groups, higher densities of users, greater noise levels, etc. In sum, displacement has taken place and the manager is now offering Opportunity B in the roadless area. There is nothing wrong with offering Opportunity B, except his original mandate was to offer Opportunity A. Once displacement has occurred the manager usually recognizes that obvious social change has taken place (increased numbers of people) and responds with a change in management control norms to revert the social norms to former conditions. In wilderness, this has typically been a permit system to limit use to former numbers (densities) not former behaviors.

Becker and Jubenville (1981) suspect that "noise," in terms of feedback to the manager, comes at a point in the successional process where it is too late for the manager to respond because displacement is already taking place. For this type of feedback, Bultena et. al. (1981) reported: "...that persons opposed to regulations tend to be more aggressive in airing their grievances than are proponents in offering their support and can create a false impression that policies are unpopular. Our data, however, show that the backcountry policies at Mount McKinley National Park, despite being restrictive in nature, were endorsed by most visitors."

A plausible scenario for this argument is that, after management controls were placed on the backcountry users, many of them were displaced to other similar areas where their freedom was not restricted. The few hangers-on would tend to be hypercritical of the policy, but would still like the particular environmental setting and would adapt, but only to the degree necessary. Ironically, the threshold criterion used to establish the policy in the beginning was empirically shown to have rarely been obtained, making the policy itself unnecessary.

Furthermore, the researcher/manager must recognize that in ex post facto research designs, where an experimental variable (element of change) such as a new management program is introduced into the park/environmental setting and the effects of such are then studied at some future date, one will always produce positive results, i.e. the user agrees with the program. The social succession model, with its underlying assumptions, describes this phenomena: one would only expect those users who either agree or who are not upset by the program to remain, or users favoring the situation to be attracted, after implementation of the program. Jubenville and Workman (1980) and Jubenville (1981) titled the results of ex post facto studies the *Guaranteed Success Syndrome*. The manager must recognize that all changes, including policy (management control), may have a dramatic effect on the opportunity setting and experience clusters within the opportunity and must understand that the impacts of change are additive. Any single change may be ameliorated by the user, but the cumulative effects of several agents of change or periodic increments of the same agent of change may be disastrous to particular users.

The Role of the User

The basic role of the user is to seek out that type of opportunity setting that will allow him or her to fully develop his/her particular experience, and to try to ameliorate any change (negative impact) that would affect that experience. On public lands, the user typically assumes that the development norms (roads, trails, facilities, etc.) indicate the general type of available, stable opportunity. They must then participate in the particular setting to determine the unique aspects of the particular environmental setting and special services available to the user. Furthermore, the user assumes that, if they were to return, the experience would remain essentially the same. Thus, while participating, the user simply enjoys the positive experience that was enjoyed before or was described by others and tries to ameliorate any negative impact encountered. In sum, the user assumes the manager has stabilized the general opportunity setting and avoids the negative effects of change in that chosen opportunity setting through modification of their own behavior. This self-reliance seems even more imperative in recreation where one seeks intrinsic rewards from the experience itself and the choice of experiences is based on personal and free choice (Driver and Tocher 1970). It is important to recognize that the user is dependent on the manager as the primary stabilizer of the opportunity, and then the user assumes the responsibility as the secondary stabilizer of his/her own experiences. Succession then should never be allowed to continue to displacement or adaption to a new opportunity setting or experience cluster within a given setting unless the manager purposefully chooses to change the opportunity — requiring changes in the area management objectives.

RECREATION OPPORTUNITY SPECTRUM CONCEPT

As shown in the previous section, the critical axioms on the ROS are:

1. Managers provide opportunities through management opportunity settings.

2. Users provide their own experiences within those opportunities.

ROS is aimed at providing a defined continuum of recreational opportunities. While many earlier authors spoke of providing variety, it was not until the mid-seventies that this idea jelled into the spectrum concept (Brown, Driver, and Mc-

Connell 1978; Driver and Brown 1978; Clark and Stankey 1979; and McCool and Elmes 1975). Conceived as the link between recreational opportunities and experiences, ROS is described as a mix of six factors: access, nonrecreational resource uses, on-site management, social interaction, acceptability of visitor impacts, and acceptable regimentations; these factors combine together to form four recreational opportunity setting classes: modern, semi-modern, semi-primitive, and primitive. "The key is that the type of setting is determined by the combination of factors, rather than the name or number of categories." (Clark and Stankey 1979).

The importance of the spectrum concept is rooted in its ability to ensure variety of opportunities by providing a wide range of settings. Variety can be achieved because we now have the management criteria, as presented in the ROS, for describing, and thus being able to stabilize, particular recreational opportunity settings. This assurance of stability, plus the natural variation in the landscape, including existing man-made alterations of the landscape, should guarantee as much variety of opportunities as possible. Thus, the natural diversity of the great out-of-doors and the stability obtained by recognizing and managing within the criteria established under ROS should ultimately ensure the diversity of the system nationally, regionally, and locally.

As with the application of the carrying capacity model, ROS has not recognized the cause/effect relationship in producing a given social norm for a given recreational opportunity setting. There is still the belief that particular social norms (recreational behavior patterns) can simply be achieved through direct manipulation by the manager (or management control norms). As shown earlier under the section on carrying capacity, the attempt to maintain particular social norms through management assumes you are managing for experiences (not the manager's role) instead of opportunities. In the carrying capacity example, the end result was a movement toward sameness. Under ROS, the effect would not be as severe, only a decrease in variety within each opportunity class such that the continuum would appear as follows:

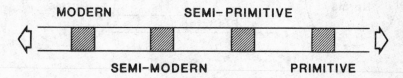

The dark areas represent the sameness within each class, sameness within variety. This sameness is a product of a limited definition of quality.

As in carrying capacity, quality is generalized to a few user types. Quality cannot be something that is dismissed because it is in the eye of the beholder or something one hopes to achieve by putting enough variety on the landscape to catch the eye of the beholder. Quality is something that is achievable along the entire spectrum of recreational opportunities. It simply refers to attracting the types of users compatible with the particular stabilized recreational opportunity settings. If you are managing an opportunity class having A_{1-14} possible recreational experiences then one would expect you to attract those type of users seeking A_{1-14} experiences. One would not expect all users to be Types A_{1-14}, but certainly the majority of them should be. The test of quality from a managerial perspective is how well you attracted the targeted clientele to the designated opportunity setting; for example, for type A area having A_{1-6} activity aggregates, did you attract A_{1-6} users? The level of quality achieved would be expressed as a percent or index based on the total number of users. We suspect that ascertaining the value of the quality index could be achieved through systematic observations (Clark 1977).

Jubenville's Law

Peterson and Lime (1979) recognized the potential for managing recreation areas through indirect attack on decision factors that affect behavior. However, they too have fallen prey to the idea of direct manipulation of the visitor through management control to achieve some social goal, without any exhaustive review of the indirect attack on decision factors, the real cause-effect relationships.

While managers have been interested in formal verbal communication with the recreators (Lucas 1981, Ross and Moeller 1974), managers are actually already communicating with the user — nonverbally (Jubenville and Workman 1980). As suggested by Peters (1973), humans respond cognitively to their environment. A manipulation of that environment may elicit a behavioral response in the individual as he receives, sorts, and responds to the various environmental stimuli.

In Jubenville's Law, social norms are driven by development norms.

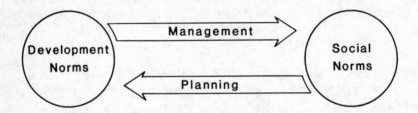

The underlying assumption is that there are specific attractors within a given area to attract particular user groups — a lake, whitewater river, a huntable wildlife population, scenic viewing, etc. The law then simply means that the social norms, e.g., types of users and levels of use, will be determined by the development norms — the type and level of access and associated facility development. One must also consider information as part of access. The cause-effect relationships are evident in the scenario developed by Clark and Stankey (1979). The message is clear; social norms are generally a product of the development norms. Consequently, one must carefully measure every management action to ensure that the right message is conveyed. One cannot ignore messages placed on the landscape and then at some future time expect to correct the problems through direct management intervention because of social succession.

Regardless of whether it was caused by management action or not, the message placed on the landscape is being read and responded to by the recreator. People are cognitively responding to their environment and managers must use the knowledge to achieve naturally what cannot be fully achieved through the use of artificial controls.

Our View

What needs to be done now is to rethink carrying capacity in terms of a natural equilibrium, where use comes into equilibrium with the environmental setting. This is the Wagar model (Wagar 1964). It has been reaffirmed by Frissell and Stankey (1972) where they described the equilibrium as a "limits to change" model, and by Clark and Stankey (1979). Becker and Jubenville (1982) concluded that a new equilibrium is established in response to change in the development norms (access and facilities) placed on the landscape, assuming there are some recreational attractors. These development norms are a result of direct action taken by the manager during the planning phase, or inaction during the management phase (i.e. allowng certain informal access and facilities to occur such as primitive roads, trails, etc.).

We need to take the lessons of Wagar (1964) and the warning of Gould (1961) and forge a future in recreational management that places the highest priority on comprehensive area planning, emphasizing the recreational opportunities associated within the particular environmental setting. But we must realize that the desired social norms for the opportunity setting are achieved through the message we place on the landscape, the development norms; and the regulation of social norms is intended only as a micrometer adjustment. That then is the equilibrium for the area, or carrying capacity. Thus, management success is not measured in cumulative satisfaction of the users of the area as some would suggest. Social succession theory would tell us that they are satisfied or they would have gone elsewhere (given sufficient time for a new equilibrium to be established). Management success, then, is measured as how well we achieved the desired social norms on the ground and the "thing" the manager can tinker with to adjust that equilibrium is the development norms. Managers must realize, however, that the equilibrium is often delicately balanced and they should therefore move slowly in adjusting an imbalance.

In sum, if you desired type A users (or use patterns) and you achieved this 80 percent of the time, Wagar would say "you are a success." We would say, "only if you know how you achieved it."

References

Becker, R. H., and Jubenville, A. "Forest Recreation Management." In *Forest Science* edited by R. Young. New York: John Wiley and Sons, 1982.

Becker, R. H.; Niemann, B. J.; and Gates, W. A. "Displacement of Users Within A River System: Social and Environmental Tradeoffs." In *Some Recent Products of River Recreation Research,* edited by D. W. Lime, and D. R. Field. USDA Forest Service General Technical Report 63, 1981.

Brown, P. J.; Driver, B. L.; and McConnell, C. "The Opportunity Spectrum Concept and Behavioral Information in Outdoor Recreation Resource Supply Inventories: Background and Application." In *Integrated Inventories of Renewal Natural Resources.* USFS General Technical Report RM-55, 1978.

Bultena, G.; Field, D.; Womble, P.; and Albrecht, D. "Freedom Versus Control: A Study of Backpackers' Preferences for Wilderness Management." *Leisure Sciences* 4(1981):297-310.

Bultena, G.; Field, D.; Womble, P.; and Albrecht, D. "Closing the Gates: A Study of Backcountry Use Limitation at Mount McKinley National Park." *Leisure Sciences* 4(1981):249-268.

Burch, W. R., Jr. "The Ecology of Metaphor — Spacing Regularities for Humans and Other Primates in Urban and Wildland Habitats." *Leisure Sciences* 4(1981):213-230.

Burch, W. R., Jr. "Two Concepts for Guiding Recreation Management Decision." *Journal of Forestry* 63(1964):707-712.

Chubb, M. "Outdoor Recreation Land Capacity: Concepts, Usage, and Definitions." M. S. thesis, Michigan State University, 1964.

Chubb, M., and Ashton, P. "Park and Recreation Standards Research: The Creation of Environmental Quality Controls for Recreation." Technical Report 5, Recreation Research and Planning Unit, Michigan State University, 1967.

Clark, R. N. "Alternative Strategies for Studying River Recreationists," *Proceedings: River Recreation Management and Research Symposium.* USDA Forest Service, General Technical Report PNW-98, 1977.

Clark, R. N., and Stankey, G. H. *The Recreation Opportunity Spectrum: A Framework for Planning, Management, and Research.* USDA Forest Service General Technical Report PNW-98, 1979.

Driver, B. L., and Brown, P. J. "The Opportunity Spectrum Concept and Behavioral Information in Outdoor Recreation Resource Supply Inventories: A Rationale." In *Integrated Inventories of Renewable Natural Resources: Proceedings of the Workshop,* pp. 24-31, 1978.

Driver, B. L., and Tocher, R. "Toward a Behavioral Interpretation of Recreational Engagements." In *Elements of Outdoor Recreation Planning,* edited by B. L. Driver. Ann Arbor, Michigan: University of Michigan, 1970.

Fazio, J. R., and Gilbert, D. L. "Mandatory Wilderness Permits: Some Indications of Success." *Journal of Forestry* 72(1974):753-756.

Frissell, S. S., Jr., and Stankey, G. H. "Wilderness Environmental Quality: Search for Social and Ecological Harmony." In *Proceedings, Society of American Foresters,* pp. 170-183, 1972.

Godin, K. V., and Leonard, R. "Permit Compliance in Eastern Wilderness: Preliminary Results." USDA Forest Service Research Note NE-238, 1977.

Gould, E. M., Jr. "Planning a Recreational Complex." *American Forests* 67(1961):30-35.

Hartman, T. L. "Perceptions of a National Park Service Manager of Whitewater River Recreation Management." In *Managing the Colorado River Whitewater: The Carrying Capacity Strategy.* Logan, Utah: Utah State University, 1977.

Heberlein, T. A., and Shelby, B. "Carrying Capacity Values, and the Satisfaction Model: A Reply to Grist." *Journal of Leisure Research* 9(1977):142-148.

Hendee, J. C., and Harris, R. W. "Foresters' Perception of Wilderness: User Attitudes and Preferences." *Journal of Forestry* 68 (1970):759-762.

Hendee, J. C., and Lucas, R. C. "Mandatory Wilderness Permits: A Necessary Management Tool." *Journal of Forestry* 71(1973):206-209.

Jubenville, A. "Role Segregation: A Conceptual Framework for Recreation Management Research." *Recreation Research Review* 2(1981):7-16.

Jubenville, A. "Travel Patterns of Wilderness Users in the Anaconda-Lintlar Wilderness." Ph.D. dissertation, University of Montana, 1970.

Jubenville, A., and Workman, W. G. "River Recreation Management and Research: The Guaranteed Success Syndrome." Seminar presented at University of Alaska, Fairbanks, 1980.

Lime, D. W. "When the Wilderness Gets Crowded...?" *Naturalist* 29(1977):1-7.

McCool, S. F., and Elmer, J. S. "Providing Recreational Opportunities Through State Park Systems." *Utah Tourism and Recreation Review* 4(1975):1-5.

National Parks and Conservation Association. "NPCA Project to Develop Recreational Carrying Capacity Estimation Methodology for Use in National Park System." Washington, D.C.: 1982.

Peters, R. "Cognitive Maps in Wolves and Men." In *Environmental Design Research.* vol 2, edited by W. F. Prieser. Stroudsburg, Pennsylvania: Hutchingson-Roth, 1973.

Peterson, G. L., and Lime, D. W. "People and Their Behavior: A Challenge for Recreation Management." *Journal of Forestry* 77(1979):343-346.

Schreyer, R. "Restricting Recreational Use of Wildlands." *Western Wildlands* 3(1977):45-52.

Stankey, G. H. "Use Rationing in Two Southern California Wildernesses." *Journal of Forestry* 77(1979):347-349.

Stankey, G. H. *Visitor Perception of Wilderness Carrying Capacity.* USDA Forest Service Research Paper INT-142, 1973.

Stankey, G. H., and Baden, J. *Rationing Wilderness Use: Methods, Problems, and Guidelines.* USDA Forest Service Research Paper INT-192, 1977.

Utter, J. "Allocating Use of Backcountry Rivers: Some Legal Issues." *Western Wildlands* 4(1977):53-58.

Utter, J.; Gleason, W.; and McCool, S. H. "User Perceptions of River Recreation Allocation Techniques." *Some Recent Products of River Recreation Research.* USDA Forest Service General Technical Report NC-63, 1981.

Wagar, J. A. *The Carrying Capacity of Wild Lands for Recreation: Forest Science Monograph* No. 7, 1964.

Section Five:
Recreation Planning Issues

1

Future Directions of Recreation Planning

Lisle S. Mitchell

How successful is your recreation planning? How detailed are plans for your use of today's leisure time? How specific are your plans for this weekend or for the next three-day weekends? Where will you spend your next vacation? When will you be going—the exact dates? What mode or modes of transportation will you use? Who will accompany you? Why are you taking a vacation and what is the purpose of the holiday? Can you afford to take a trip? These questions indicate the variety of considerations involved in recreation planning at a personal scale and in the extreme short term. It should be apparent that recreation planning at a corporate or government level is much more intricate, the time frame much longer, and includes land use and behavioral conflicts besides being subject to considerable fluctuation over time The probability of error, in predicting the future directions of recreation planning is, therefore, high.

The approach taken in this chapter, however, is conservative and presents an evaluation of the short, medium, and long-term prospects of recreation planning, and a number of alternative futures are introduced to place the analytical, evaluative, and synthesizing processes of recreation planning in an appropriate context. The purpose of this chapter is threefold. First, to explain the continuation of present planning practices into the near future. Second, to enumerate and discuss the factors and forces that make medium and long-range planning speculative. Third, to formulate and present pessimistic and optimistic perspectives of the medium and long-run future of recreation planning.

The rationale for the continuation of present planning practices into the near future will be considered after the characteristics of recreation planning and the differences between public and private recreation planning are put forward.

CHARACTERISTICS OF RECREATION PLANNING

There are three fundamental principles that underly the current set of planning practices: (1) planning is conceptually simple, (2) planning recreation is complex, and (3) planning implementation is difficult.

Some people believe that recreation planning is conceptually simple because the primary goal is to satisfy the needs and wants of a population. This view of recreation planning involves three concepts: demand, supply, and consumption. Demand is derived from heterogeneous individuals and groups with highly diverse desires. Supply is generated by individual entrepreneurs, private corporations, and public agencies that are engaged in providing recreation opportunities. The goal of equilibrium is achieved more complementarily between demand and supply occurs.

The principal problem of recreation planners may be to marshall the information necessary to attain the stability between demand and supply. For those who believe that planning is conceptually simple, this is accomplished by following relatively standard planning procedures (Table 1). These procedures result in a set of recommended, concrete steps (i.e., a plan) and encompass a methodology to evaluate the performance of the plan in terms of the formally stated goals and objectives.

The formulation of a plan is conceptually simple. If information and resources are garnered and used in relation to standard planning practices then a plan can be developed that will achieve the goal of satisfying the recreation needs and wants of a general population.

The creation of a plan may be viewed as complex for three reasons. First, a multitude of variables have to be considered in developing a plan. Overlapping and intermingled goals and objectives need to be sorted and organized into some logical pattern. A large volume of natural and social data must be collected and analyzed. An evaluation of the fit between demand and supply factors must be conducted and some theme or organizing principle must be formulated to integrate the various parts of the plan into a logical unit. A second reason for difficulty is the constant changing of variables over time. Planning takes place within a particular time period and the competent planner is constantly searching for the latest and most valid information sources. It is difficult, if not impossible at times, to have the latest data and even if that is possible, the data might become outmoded before a plan can be implemented. The third reason for planning complications is the many constituencies that have to be mollified. The largest and most complex group is made up of activity-specific recreators. The facilities, activities, and programs desired may range from the simple to the highly sophisticated and from the cheapest to the most expensive in terms of natural, as well as capital resources. A smaller but some times more influential group represents the administrators from the public and private sectors, such as a personnel director or land owners, who have vested interests to maintain and protect. Then there are the pressure groups with special causes to promote like the "preservationists" and those who espouse the "free-enterprise system." Finally, those who will be directly or indirectly impacted by the location of a site, a transportation network, or an access route must be considered.

Planning implementation is often difficult because it is hard to formulate a plan which is acceptable to those who are directly and indirectly affected, and who often have contrary concerns and viewpoints. A multitude of conflicting interests have to be overcome: consumers, suppliers, pressure groups, and landowners. Implementation requires time, financial and other resources, and is carried out in the context of other types of planning (i.e., land use, economic,

Table 1

Standard Planning Procedures

1. Statement of Goals and Objectives

2. Recreation Resource Inventory

3. Sociological and Geographic Features
   (Socioeconomic and Physical Variables)

4. Demand Analysis
   (Inventories and Survey)

5. Set Standards
   (Specific Region/Area)

6. Needs Analysis
   (Determine Future Needs)

7. Recreation Supply/Needs
   (Compare Demand Analysis and Needs Analysis)

8. Recreation Sponsorship
   (Levels of Government Responsibility)

9. Financial Resources

10. Graphic

11. Recommendations
    (Actions to be taken)

12. Evaluation
    (Measurement of goals and objectives against the implemented plan)

SOURCE: Modified from Sidney G. Lutzin, "The Comprehensive Leisure Services Plan," in Sidney G. Lutzin (ed.), *Managing Municipal Leisure Services*. Washington, D.C.: International City Management Association, 1980, p. 157.

political, etc.), both public and private. Overall, the difficulty of implementing a recreation plan is a function of the number of conflicting interests and the context in which planning takes place.

In summary, the idea behind the term planning is basically that of achieving a particular goal and following a detailed set of procedures. The formulation of a plan, however, is complex because of the large number of variables that need to be considered, the rapidity at which some variables change over time, and the many constituencies that have to be satisfied. Finally, the implementation of a plan is difficult due to a multitude of conflicting interests and because of the need to integrate recreation planning into a much more extensive resource planning context in which recreation competes with other public services, such as education and highways, for scarce financial support.

DIFFERENCES BETWEEN PUBLIC AND PRIVATE RECREATION PLANNING

Public and private recreation planning practices can be distinguished on the basis of the arena where the allocation process takes place. Planning in the public sector takes place in a political setting where a large number of individuals and groups have an opportunity to influence the decision-making process in a relatively open and free environment. Private sector planning, on the other hand, occurs in an economic setting where decisions are made within the limits of a corporate organization and in relation to competitive market considerations. As a result of these differences, three aspects of recreation planning need further consideration: responsibility, impact, and performance.

The responsibility or concern of public and private planning differs in terms of interest, the decision-making process, and accountability. Public planning is charged with the task of providing recreation goods and services to the general population at little or no cost. Private planning, on the other hand, attempts to furnish recreation experiences to various segments of the population for a fee or other economic or social consideration. In other words, private sector planning tends to be profit oriented, while public sector planning is nonprofit oriented. In terms of decision-making, public sector planning is not highly centralized because a multitude of individuals and groups may be involved. The private sector, however, tends to keep decision-making power concentrated in a relatively small group. Accountability in the public sector is indirect because the planner is first responsible to the executive and legislative branches of government and ultimately to the general public. Private sector planners, on the other hand, are directly accountable to a board of directors or an executive officer.

The impact of public and private planning differs because of the scope of the planning endeavor. The range of involvement of public planning is extensive: large areas are considered and board bands of public concerns are addressed. Private planning tends to impinge upon relatively small spaces and is limited to specific issues or concerns. Public planning, therefore, must consider the impact of its actions on a broad range of public issues like political, social, economic, and environmental situations that manifest themselves in the aspatial (i.e., organizational) and spatial (i.e., locational) structure of a neighborhood, community, district, city, county, state, or region. Private planning also must consider the various aspatial and spatial aspects of its efforts but, generally speaking, the range of consideration is relatively narrow, especially when compared with public planning.

The results or consequences of public and private planning may be contrasted in terms of performance. Evaluation is difficult due to the multiple purposes and constituencies which affect public planning and, as a result, public planning is generally seen as unsuccessful. Distrust of public sector planning is partially due to the multi-facted objectives of such planning, because of the extensive impact of such planning, and because of the degree of visibility and publicity surrounding public decision-making. Private planning efforts, on the other hand, are relatively easy to evaluate on the basis of profit or loss. Private planning is, therefore, generally seen as successful and this judgment is based on the relative ease of successfully attaining limited objectives. The success of private planning is also due to the fact that many private sector failures are not made public or publicized to the same extent as public errors.

The fundamental difference, therefore, between public and private planning are the differences between the political and economic arenas. Public planning operates in a political arena which is concerned with serving the public interest, utilizing a diffused decision-making process, and is accountable to the general public in hindsight. The impact of public decision-making is extensive in nature and its perspectives on organizational and locational aspects of the environment are extremely broad. Public planning is difficult to evaluate precisely because of its extensive purposes, responsibilities, impacts and performance; the result is a tendency to be evaluated as unsuccessful because of the absence of indicators of success (e.g., measure of benefits). On the other hand, private planning functions in an economic arena and is concerned with producing a profit, using a concentrated decision-making process, and being accountable to a limited constituency. Its impacts tend to be specific in nature and its considerations of the organizational and locational aspects of the physical-cultural ecology are narrow. Private planning is relatively easy to evaluate on the basis of economic indicators and its image as successful is beyond refutation because failures are seldom highly publicized.

CONTINUATION OF PRESENT PLANNING PRACTICES INTO THE FUTURE

In the relatively short term (i.e., approximately five years), I believe that planning practices will change slowly and the probability of a dramatic alteration is not likely. There are four reasons why planning procedures will evolve at a normal pace rather than accelerate. First, planning institutions, either public or private, are slow to change. Most human institutions are controlled by traditionalists and thus follow tried and true conservative policies of growth and development that attempt to minimize risk and to maintain the status quo. The negative perception of uncertainty, caused by rapid and possibly uncontrolled change, is abhorrent to a large majority of Americans and as a result most institutions are likely to change only slowly over time. Therefore, current planning philosophies and methodologies are likely to receive continued support into the future due to the stultifying effect of institutional inertia.

Second, no significant shift in the present planning paradigm is imminent. Planning theory and appropriate planning procedures are fairly well stabilized and sudden innovations are highly unlikely. Standardized planning processes, Delphi methodologies, alternative scenarios, and the computer have been in widespread use in planning for some time; there is no indication that revolutionary changes are about to occur that would alter the conduct of government agencies. General systems theory and cybernetics have been in existence for more than thirty years and, although they are extremely valuable and powerful tools, the software necessary to drastically alter their applicability to recreation planning does not yet exist.

Third, planning institutions, particularly in the public sector, have great difficulties in creating a consensus because they are fragmented and politized. Institutionalized planning is divided into a large number of different layers (i.e., city, county, special districts, state, regional, and federal) and no integrative mechanism or functional hierarchy exists which would foster cooperation among the various levels. Recreation problems, like most others, are not neatly contained within the jurisdictional limits of a particular planning authority. The solution to any planning problem, therefore, requires the cooperation and coordination of planning agencies, but this is difficult if not impossible to achieve because of the organizational structure of planning in the United States. In addition, the planning process is influenced greatly by political motives and maneuvering. Individuals and groups with political connections and/or political power are able to apply pressure on planning institutions and personnel in an attempt to influence the assumptions made, the interpretation of data, and the formulation of the final plan. The end result of political intervention is the creation of confusion and lack of direction in the planning process. Lack of direction slows down the entire process and tends to stabilize existing conditions.

Fourth, and last, planning deals with property and space and these resources, in many ways, are sacrosanct. Even when public officials are utililzing public property and public space, there are complaints because the siting and development of recreation facilities have a monetary effect on personal property and personal space. Positive and/or negative monetary or other impacts on individual property or space rights are accepted or rejected for a host of logical/rational or illogical/emotional reasons. Planning initiatives or final planning proposals, whether they are supported or castigated, tend to be slowed by any debate over individual and public rights; the end result of this conflict is to maintain the status quo.

THE FACTORS AND FORCES THAT MAKE MEDIUM AND LONG-RUN PLANNING SPECULATIVE

Any plan that extends or projects beyond a time period of three to five years is highly speculative because of the transformations that take place in political, social, and economic environments. In planning, as in almost any other aspect of life, the only constant is perpetual change. In this section nine factors or forces that have a significant influence over the operational planning of recreation sites, activities, programs, and facilities wil be discussed.

Population Growth and Distribution   Population in the United States is growing and even though the growth rate is decreasing, zero population growth rate is a long way off. In addition, the average age of the population is rising and the percentage of old people in the country is at an all time high. This growing population with an increasing average age in conjunction with the suburbanization and spread of the population from the central cities and the general tendency of people to migrate to the south and the west has a significant impact on recreation planning. Where should recreation sites be located? Which population segment should be catered to — the young or the not so young? What facilities should be constructed? Can facilities be built that can serve all age groups? When should the facilities be made operational? How will the programs and facilities be financed?

Multiple Goals and Objectives   The age of consensus and mass markets is probably a thing of the past due to the increasing diversity of the population. The United States is becoming more and more diversified. People can be differentiated on the basis of age, sex, ethnicity, social, political, economic, as well as ideological factors. All of these factors, and especially the latter because it tends not be correlated with the others, drastically influence the functioning of the recreation planner. How are priorities to be established? Who is to decide how to attempt to balance the conflicting objectives of these groups? What type of compromises concerning these goals can be reached? How does a planner develop his overall scheme in fact of a broad array of overlapping, conflicting, and contradictory recreation aims? Answers to these questions will be highly controversial as planners attempt to allocate public resources.

Economic Conditions   Evidence continues to accumulate that the economy of the United States is entering a postindustrial phase. A phase in which the primary and secondary sectors will decline in relative terms as a source of employment and gross national product, while the tertiary and quarternary sectors will increase. The decrease in jobs relating to physical production and the increase in positions providing personal, financial, and information services will have a definite effect on recreation planning. This is especially true as income generated by recreation and tourism related industries continues to grow. A postindustrial employment and income structure placed in the context of ordinary economic conditions (i.e., boom, good-times, recession, inflation, stagflation, depression) along with interest rates (i.e., high, medium, low) money supply (i.e., stable, expanding, contracting), and government regulations (i.e., conservative, progressive, liberal) create a host of problems for the planner attempting to create a vision of the future.

Diminishing Resources and Space   The prospects for resource availability in the future is bleak when viewed from a perspective of continued population growth and increased consumption of nonrenewable resources. Higher costs and potential shortages of basic fuels and metals support the validity of the "law of diminishing returns." The United States is increasingly dependent upon a supply of resources that are controlled and/or owned by foreign countries. All of these factors in conjunction with the extensive use of land for residential and industrial purposes near major urban centers, without provisions for open space, lead to serious planning problems. Recreation does not rank high on the priority list for the use of scarce resources and space, therefore, it is extremely difficult for a planner to envision a recreation future if resource availability is an issue.

Urbanization   Recreation planning is arduous under the best of conditions and it is even more frustrating when hampered by the processes related to urbanization. Dramatically increasing land values, fueled directly by demand and indirectly by inflation, make the selection of sites and procuring of land titles an extremely critical undertaking. Rapid evolution of existing spatial patterns of land utilization increase the difficulty of recreation planners. The lack of policy pertaining to open or green space makes the acquisition of land for leisure use an almost impossible task. Finally, the continuous expansion of central cities, suburbs, satellite cities, and even small, isolated towns and villages into the surrounding countryside produces a growing number of obstacles for recreation planners.

Political Fragmentation   Planning at its best and most efficient seems to take place in a centralized system such as in the private sector of the economy. The governmental sector, on the other hand, is fragmented into three levels: federal, state, and local; this separation results in conflicts over jurisdiction, scope of authority, and interpretation of law, just to name a few. Compounding these problems are a lack of viable communications between levels and the internal conflicts within each level. The mixed messages within each of the three divisions is a result of a lack of consensus; information transmitted from one agency to another lacks consistency and is often contradictory. Sound planning, obviously, can not take place in an environment of constantly changing and contradictory statements. Added to the serious communication problems within and between government levels is the proliferation of planning units that simply increase the complexity of the flow of information. Furthermore, the current attempt to decentralize programs from the federal to state and local governments is creating other types of problems for the recreation planner. Lastly, the widespread mistrust of governments at all levels has created a climate that makes it extremely difficult to project visions of recreation landscapes into the future.

Social Instability   Social instability is characterized by changing moral values, the breakup of the nuclear family, and differing life styles. In the past, social and behavioral norms were based on the widespread belief in the Protestant work eithic, but today adherence to this principle is limited. An illdefined, amorphous, poorly understood "leisure" or "non-work"/"non-productive" ethic seems to be the dominant factor influencing public morality and social conduct. The social control that appeared to flow down a hierarchy of authority based on age and experience has been lost. What remains is an apparent anarchy of life styles that seemingly have little or no philosophical or theological foundation, and thus the ability to predict behavior or comprehend social trends with some certainty is lacking. All of these conditions in and of themselves, and in relation to each other, lead to conditions of uncertainty that make recreation planning an intellectual nightmare.

Ethnic Tensions   The United States, a democratic society, has formally stated principles of ethnic or racial equality. In practice, however, there is anything but equality in the provision of the opportunity to recreate. Cultural differences based on wealth, religion, family background, or national origin also influence recreational opportunity, but the visual clues to these kinds of differences are not strong and are relatively easy to hide. Racial distinctions, on the other hand, are highly visible and almost impossible to camouflage. Therefore, recreation experience tends to be racially segregated although there are numerous exceptions to this generalization. The myth of racial integration and the reality of ethnic separation with regard to recreation makes planning a thankless endeavor. If the planner follows the law, controversy will probably develop over site selection, resource allocation, and integrative policies or programs because of difference in personal values. No matter what choice is made, the constantly changing pattern of race relations in the United States is a serious dilemma for the recreation planner.

Insufficient Knowledge of Recreation Process and Patterns Creating systematic plans to achieve formally stated recreation goals and objectives is simple when all of the necessary data are available and when all of the components that make up the recreation systems are known and comprehended. However, required data are seldom available in the quality or quantity that one would like and the various components that make up recreation systems are not all known and certainly not understood. Data sets have improved immensely over the past several decades, although they are far from perfect, but the comprehension of the processes and patterns that constitute recreation are only slightly known and even less well understood. Recreation research has increased fantastically since the end of the Second World War but no comprehensive, internally consistent, and logical set of generalizations, principles, or hypotheses have been produced. This lack of a general conceptual framework is one of the major blocks to improved recreation planning, and the designer is forced to rely on educated guesses, hunches, and intuition in the development of his or her plans. The absence of a logical, predictive doctrine is one of the primary reasons why planners have so much trouble in planning for the medium and long-run future.

Summary It should be apparent from the discussion of the nine factors or forces that any public planning endeavor that extends beyond five years is highly speculative. The matrix of information that is necessary to create images for the future is extremely complicated. Given political, social, and economic stability, however, complexity could be adequately dealt with and a sound plan formulated. In this era of perpetual transformation, however, the recreation planner has an almost impossible task because the intricate nature of life itself is developing at an accelerating rate. Planning, therefore, can no longer be viewed as an end in and of itself, rather it must be thought of as a continuous process that is capable of adjustment with the passage of time. Planning viewed in this manner becomes a methodology for constantly and continuously evaluating achievement of formally stated goals and objectives within the realistic context of changing factors and forces.

PESSIMISTIC AND OPTIMISTIC PERSPECTIVES OF THE FUTURE

The planner's task, as noted above, is conceptually simple: estimate recreation needs and wants; inventory existing supply and formulate a plan to bring into being the necessary sites, facilities, activities, and programs; monitor the complementarity between supply and demand to assure an acceptable level of satisfaction. In this sense, then, planning is a continuous process. Demand and supply data must be constantly collected, analyzed, and evaluated. The existing plan must be endlessly modified to fit current conditions. Consumption of recreation experience must be continuously monitored to insure an adequate level of satisfaction. If satisfaction is below standard then the plan must be readjusted to meet the design goal.

The remainder of this section of the chapter will be divided into two parts: pessimistic perspectives and optimistic perspectives. Each part will include a list of basic assumptions about the future and a discussion of the implications of those assumptions for the future directions of planning.

Pessimistic Perspectives

To predict a future that is less satisfactory than the present one requires at least three assumptions. First, the world population growth rate, now approximately two percent a year, will remain fairly stable in the short term but will increase to around three percent in the long run. The world's population would be approximately 11 billion in 2050 and over 22 billion by 2075. Second, the ratio of resources to population which is merely adequate in the 1980s, on a world scale, would be greatly reduced, possibly devastating in 2050, and probably catastrophic in 2075. Presently two-thirds of the earth's population is undernourished. This proportion would increase to more than four-fifths in 2050 and to more than 95 out of 100 in 2075. Third, technology would continue to grow, develop, and increase, but the rate of production of basic food and industrial raw materials will continuously decline in both a relative and absolute sense. The values of competition and material accumulation in an economy of scarcity will be held paramount. Economic, political, social, and racial differences will be magnified and the possibility of ideological consensus will become absurd. These assumptions about the future are bleak but certainly not out of the main stream of current pessimistic thinking. The implications for planning will be discussed in terms of the short, medium, and long run.

Short Run   As noted above, planning in the very short term will be a continuation of present and past practices. By the year 2000, however, the population to resource ratio will decline to a position where resources and space for recreation purposes will begin to be in short supply. Planners will have to make better use of their restricted financial and personnel resources as they carry out their tasks. They will be held more accountable for their production and their use of limited funds.

Planners, in the public sector, because they tend to provide recreation opportunities to the general population, will have to devise methods of substituting physicl and human resources for one another. For example, the operating hours of recreation facilities may be expanded as an attempt to use more, cheap human labor instead of using scarce natural resources to build additional facilities. Existing establishments that are user-oriented will have to be more intensively utilized by stricter scheduling and the application of the multiple-function concept. Other public facilities, such as school and public buildings and grounds, will be organized and structured to permit recreation activities. Increased use of public recreation and other buildings will result in maintenance and crowd control problems of major proportions. Strategies will have to be devised to care for the physical structure and to deal with congestion and increasing consumption even during off-peak hours and seasons. These tactics will probably include the involvement of the local community in repair and crowd control functions.

Private sector planners, because they tend to be responsible for relatively specialized recreation experiences that are equipment and/or facility oriented, will have to reduce marginal operations at both the corporate and industry levels. Due to the decreasing pool of individuals, families, and groups that can afford private recreation opportunities, planners will have to increase the technical efficiency of their operations. In addition, value will have to be added through the development of a better product or an improvement in service. The latter will be more likely due to the decreasing cost of labor. Other methods formulated to deal with decreasing consumption of their services will be to reduce prices and cut profit margins; to better determine the extent of the market by improved demand analysis; to restrict a particular market segment by increasing the degree of recreation specialization; on the other hand, some firms may find it advantageous to diversify their recreation offerings.

Medium Run   From the year 2000 to 2050, the balance between population and resources will tip more and more towards population and resource shortages will seriously affect large segments of the American population. Long distance travel for tourist purposes will be restricted to a relatively small group of individuals. Public planners' major task will be to communicate methods of constructive use of leisure time (i.e., time that might well be extremely limited—certainly for the masses by 2050) in the home or local community. Due to the scarcity of funds, planners will have to devise a method for deciding priorities to keep a public facility in operation, or in restricting use, or in ceasing operation. For those establishments that continue to operate a system of rationing use will have to be developed (i.e., a rotating basis, a fee system, a lottery, etc.)

Planners in the private sector will be concerned with providing recreation opportunities for a small elite group by 2050. Their major task will be to mask the recreation activities of the privileged few so that they will not be interrupted or disturbed by the masses. These recreation activities will probably be carried on in isolated places or in well concealed locations in population centers. These "underground" recreation establishments will be few in number, highly specialized, and operated with great secrecy.

Long Run   Based on the assumptions stated above there are no long-term implications for recreation planning because there will be no formal recreation to plan. There are two likely scenarios for the year 2050 and beyond. The first is analogous to the fall of the Roman Empire. The national state as we know it will cease to exist because of the lack of any resource or food surpluses; there will be no economic base to sustain a non-productive individual like a planner. The earth, therefore, will return to a state of anarchy and a subsistence economy and recreation will be confined to individual pleasures, family celebrations, and festivals or rituals of a productive or religious nature.

The second scenario is even more grim because it envisions a world racked by pollution resulting from a nuclear war. The total population or almost the total population will have been destroyed either directly or indirectly by atomic weapons. Thus, either human life ceases to exist as we know it, or man retreats to an early stage of development and begins the process of evolving on a planet that will be under the influence of nuclear pollution for thousands of years. In either case, recreation planning will have little role to play.

Optimistic Perspectives

The optimistic future forecast here assumes that world population growth rates that are now declining will continue to decrease until zero population growth is attained about 2050. Total world population at that time would be between seven and eight billion individuals. The ratio of population to resource would deteriorate slightly until 2000 when the proportion would improve due to significant technological breakthroughs in energy sources; recycling of metals and other materials; and the improvement in food production, storage, and distribution. The technical revolution lead by electronic-nuclear industries would remove the threat of Malthusian controls and replace them with a equilibrium between population size and basic raw materials. Within the ideological realm cooperation becomes the major mode of operation and a post-industrial age is ushered in with stable political, social, and ethnic conditions. The ideological conflicts between various "isms" is replaced by a spirit of cooperative competition and the fear of centralized planning becomes dormant.

These assumptions logically lead to the conclusion that all nations will have entered the high mass consumption stage by the year 2050. This kind of economic situation will free human kind from the thralldom of physical labor and result in an age of physical, educational, psychological, and spiritual growth unparalleled in human history. Everyone will be free to travel long distances at relatively low costs and the economy will be based on goods and services provided to tourists. The implications of this kind of a future on recreation planning will be viewed from four possibilities.

Back-To-Nature   Between the present and the year 2000, because of the short run imbalance between population and resources, a protectionist and preservationist attitude prevails. In this situation, it is the planners business to develop methods to wisely use recreation resources. For example, by setting aside selected wilderness areas and formulating a long-range, rotating system of recreation utilization and rejuvenation, the truly unique nature features of the United States could be treated as a renewable resource and placed into an inservice-fallow system. Additionally, planners could develop valid measures of carrying capacity for all types of recreation establishments and thus protect the integrity of resources by limiting use below saturation levels. For those areas where demand exceeds supply recreation opportunities could be rationed in some logical, just fashion.

Recreation Functions   Because of the almost complete lack of physical activity required to earn a living, everyone will be encouraged to adopt a physically active recreation lifestyle. Thus the wellness movement of the 1970s and 1980s will be expanded and walking, running, bicycling, swimming, dancing, body building, calisthenics, and other aerobic and static experiences will be of great significance. These recreation functions tend to be faddish and have unique and different space requirements. Planners may be challenged to change their emphasis from a facility approach to a functional approach. This may entail a concern for recreation function and its particular space and equipment requirements as opposed to the concern for constructing facilities and forcing the activity to fit the equipment. In this way planning may have to become more and more anthropocentric and place more emphasis upon the needs of the human and less on the problems and constraints posed by construction materials. This may mean a relative and absolute decline in the permanent recreation-sport complex, such as Madison Square Garden, and the increasing importance of semi-permanent structures with the internal ability to rapidly modify activity or programming modules.

Walking, running, and bicycling are linear activities that are extensive in total space demand but that can be contained within very narrow width limits. The planner may be forced to search for ways of interfacing these recreation functions with other transportation and land use modes. Swimming, dancing, body building, and calisthenics require relatively small spaces that can be intensively utilized, and that have relatively expensive equipment and or building requirements. The planner may have to create both permanent and semi-permanent facilities in locations accessible to large portions of the population.

Changing and Diverse Demand   An extremely diverse and rapidly changing population will create problems of semi-permanence in both activities and facilities. The planner will be faced with the problem of anticipating wildly fluctuating demands for recreation opportunity. Sophisticated procedures for securing information of on-site recreation trends, at-home recreation desires, and in-shop development of recreation pasttimes (i.e., recreational games and equipment) will have to be envisioned and produced. This type of continuous information flow will provide the data necessary for the planner to develop techniques of interfacing rapidly changing demands for recreation experiences with sudden shifts in the supply of recreation pasttimes.

Rapidly expanding electronic and computer technology may create unthought opportunities for the recreation planner to design new and different recreation experiences. Home computers for education, as well as recreation use, provide a host of interior building design problems. More and more sophisticated computer games may result in the formation of organized competition into a host of different ability/skill levels and could even evolve into spectator activities using gigantic electron display screens. This type of industrial development may provide the planner with a multitude of interesting design situations. The development of new modes of transport (i.e., individual flying packs or individual submarines), different types of athletic and sports equipment (i.e., super balls or people-proof rackets) and completely new games (i.e., air polo or water hurdles) may result in totally new and different recreational environments that may have to be designed by the competent planner.

Cybernetic Planning   The computer revolution that may occur in the medium and long-term future will probably first develop in the mathematical and engineering sciences but obviously could be available to the social sciences at a relatively early data. Computer hardware may develop at a rapid rate over the next century and, along with a very diverse and rapidly changing population, will create a need to better understand and control recreation pursuits. This need may fuel the development of accurate, reliable, operational symbolic models of recreation behavior. Such demand and consumption models used in conjunction with supply models will result in more efficient methods of using recreation resources, more effective ways of surveying recreation consumption, and more satisfaction by recreation demanders in spite of the rapid transformations taking place. The challenge to the planner and other social scientists interested in the topic of recreation may be to conduct the basic empirical research that is necessary to pro-produce the symbolic models.

Conclusion

The future directions of recreation planning are unknown, but some alternative courses have been identified. Certainly the extreme pessimistic and optimistic directions suggested above are unlikely to occur. Rather positions located somewhere between those two dichotomous perspectives are much more probable. Due to the ideological, institutional, and operational problems internal to the planning profession itself and due to the factors and forces external to the planning process, attention must be focussed on the near future.

It is realistically possible to accurately plan for the immediate future (e.g., one year). The longer the time frame of a projection, the greater the probability of serious error. Medium and long-range forecasts have value as a means of increasing awareness of future problems and anticipating major trends in demand, supply, and consumption patterns. However, planning, like life itself, takes place in the here and now. The planner must concentrate on the immediate past for viable information, must anticipate the near future with great caution, and must operate with the idea that planning is a continuous process and not an end in and of itself.

What specifically can be done to enable the practicing planner to better comprehend present recreation environments and to project recreation, sport, and tourist landscapes into the short-term future? First, communications between planners and academicans need to be improved. The planner-academic gap exists because the planner, who seeks to solve specific problems, and the academic, who attempts to formulate or discover generalizations, are working on two different levels: one specific and the other general. In order to bridge the gap, the planner needs to communicate the nature and scope of his problems and the researcher needs to adjust his agenda to address these issues. In other words, more research of a guided or applied character is required and/or some researchers must take on the task of translating so called "pure research" into information more useful to the planner. It is obvious that planning in the future will be greatly enhanced if the exchange of information between the two professions is improved.

Second, assuming the recreation researcher would like to make a contribution to improved planning practice, more narrowly focussed research efforts need to be conducted. The planner's list of wants and needs can provide an area of concentration. The analysis of plans that have partially or totally failed to meet stated goals is another area ripe with research possibilities. The funding of research for specific planning problems is a more direct method of producing useful generalizations. There are a large number of ways that the research efforts of social scientists can be made more directly applicable to the desires of the planner.

Third, and following logically from the second, is the need to generate a general theory that incorporates demand, supply, and consumption patterns and the concepts of purpose, structure, and distribution. Planners now operate without a comprehensive, internally consistent, and logical general doctrine of recreation that can be utilized to guide their planning decision pertaining to cost-benefit analysis, facilities development, site selections, resource use of program construction. Instead, a hodgepodge of unrelated hypotheses, generalizations, principles, models, and rules-of-thumb are available for the planner's use. In an area as complicated as recreation, however, such a collection of research tools does not adequately serve the planner. If the planner is to function at a level beyond that of an educated guess, hunch, or intuition then some better means of understanding recreation systems needs to be developed.

In 1962 the Outdoor Recreation Resources Review Commission (ORRRC) recommended that a Bureau of Outdoor Recreation (BOR), later the Heritage Conservation and Recreation Services (HCRS), be created to initiate a continuous survey of outdoor recreation supply and to encourage research efforts that would lead to a more comprehensive understanding of the components and processes that constitute the national recreation system. The failure of BOR/HCRS to accomplish these objectives, in part, explains why HCRS was dismantled in 1980 by an executive order from President Reagan. Nevertheless, those two objectives, if achieved by either the public or private sector or by cooperation between sectors, would go a long way towards establishing a strong foundation for the evolution of the future direction of recreation planning.

References

Bannon, J. J. *Leisure Resources: Its Comprehensive Planning.* Englewood Cliffs, New Jersey: Prentice-Hall, 1976.

Bucher, C. A. and Bucher, R. *Recreation for Today's Society.* Englewood Cliffs, New Jersey: Prentice-Hall, 1974.

Chapin, F. S., Jr. 2d ed. *Urban Land Use Planning.* Urbana-Champagne, Illinois: University of Illinois Press, 1964.

Chapin, F. S., Jr. *Human Activity Pattern in the City.* New York: John Wiley and Sons, 1974.

Chubb, M., and Chubb, H. *One-Third of Our Time.* New York: John Wiley and Sons, 1981.

Driver, B. L. *Elements of Outdoor Recreation Planning.* Ann Arbor, Michigan: The University of Michigan Press, 1970.

Gold, S. M *Urban Recreation Planning.* Philadelphia: Lea and Febiger, 1973.

Gold, S. M. *Recreation Planning and Design.* New York: McGraw-Hill, 1980.

Gunn, C. A. *Vacationscape*. College Station, Texas: Bureau of Business Research, The University of Texas at Austin, 1972.

Hall, P. *Urban and Regional Planning*. New York: John Wiley and Sons, 1975.

Hawkins, D.; Shafer, E.; Elwood, L.; and Ravelstad, J. M. eds. *Tourism Planning and Development Issues*. Washington, D.C.: George Washington University, 1979.

Jensen, C. R. *Outdoor Recreation in America*. Minneapolis: Burgess Publishing Company, 1970.

Jensen, C. R., and Thorstenson, C. R. *Issues in Outdoor Recreation*. Minneapolis: Burgess Publishing Co., 1972.

Jubenville, A. *Outdoor Recreation Planning*. Philadelphia: W. B. Saunders Co., 1976.

Kando, T. M. *Leisure and Popular Culture in Transition*. St. Louis: The C. V. Mosby Co., 1980.

Knudson, D. M. *Outdoor Recreation*. New York: MacMillan Publishing Co., 1980.

Lavery, P. *Recreation Geography*. New York: John Wiley and Sons, 1974.

Lutzin, S. G. *Managing Municipal Leisure Services*. Washington, D.C.: International City Management Association, 1980.

Mercer, D. *In Pursuit of Leisure*. Malvern, Australia: Sarrett Publishing Pty Ltd., 1981.

Napier, T. L. ed. *Outdoor Recreation Planning; Perspectives and Research*. Dubuque, Iowa: Kendall/Hunt Publishing Co., 1981.

Patmore, J. Allan *Land and Leisure*. London: David and Charles (publishers) Ltd., 1970.

Reynolds, J. A., and Hormachea, M. N. *Public Recreation Administration*. Reston, Virginia: Reston Publishing Co., 1976.

Shivers, J. S., and Hjelte, G. *Planning Recreation Places*. Cranbury, New Jersey: Associated University Presses, 1971.

Toffler, A. *Future Shock*. New York: Random House, 1970.

Toffler, A. *The Third Wave*. New York: William Morrow & Co., 1980.

2

On The Role of the Practicing Planner

Miles Logsdon

The profession of planning has roots in both the physical and behavioral sciences, and recreation planning is truly a specialty which utilizes both of these disciplines. Today's recreation agencies, whether federal, state, local, or private are placing increasing demands not only on the physical environment, but on economic and social systems as well.

The cliches, "increased leisure time" and "increased population," have become an overworked justification for recreation development and land acquisition. Planners are facing an increasing number of better educated decision-makers, councils, and commissions, who must consider social and political trends, as well as current budget and facility constraints. To better understand the research needs of the practicing recreation planner it is necessary first to understand his status, including his current constraints and his eventual responsibilities.

THE GROWTH OF RECREATION PLANNING

America's emphasis on planned recreation areas can be traced back to the early seventeenth century, with the development of the Boston Commons (Jubenville 1976). Many other villages informally established a "commons" as an open space and by the time our nation's capital was designed, lavish public gardens and green areas were an expected part of any city master plan. Washington, D.C., planned by Major L'Enfant, with the assistance of Presidents Washington and Jefferson, was as planned a community as could be found at that time.

The evaluation of recreation needs by city planners and designers brought about the evaluation of the professions of recreation. Perhaps the most heralded event in park planning came on September 11, 1857, when Frederick Law Olmsted was appointed superintendent of New York's Central Park, and on that same day a $2,000 first prize was announced for the park's design competition.

The outcome of that competition was one of the classic illustrations of the process of park planning and design. The process of planning and designing Central

Park focussed attention on the tenets of human and resource needs. More importantly though, it marked the beginning of an attitude toward the role of parks which would greatly influence the field of park planning in its infancy: the emphasis on environments that were pleasing to people.

Equally important during this time was the establishment of Yellowstone National Park in 1872, setting in motion the legislation which has since developed into our national park system of parks, recreation areas, and national monuments. In 1891, the Forest Reserve Act began the nationalization of major timber areas, but it was not until 1905 that these reserves were transferred to, and renamed national forests. Recreation, while important in the role of the national park, was not a stated policy until the Recreation and Public Purpose Act of 1926 (P.L. 69-386), when multiple-use management was recognized.

The philosophy underlying the planning and management of national park areas was strongly oriented to the preservation of resources. These areas were not thought of as "common" in the sense of Olmstead's philosophy; instead they were restrictive of people. The visitor was the exception in the landscape.

Recreation planning now engendered two opposing expectations which had to be made to complement each other. The planner had become a negotiator who considered the demands of social trends, while protecting the balance of nature. The planner's status grew from adapting the environment to people, through protection and preservation of the natural environment, into that of a mediator of viewpoints. Planners may be seen as implementors of goals by agencies, yet planners feel responsible for environmental impacts as well. Whatever the situation, the planner's status is that of advisor to either side, liaison between groups, and mediator of change.

THE RECREATION PLANNER

As an advisor, the planner's platform is often in front of a small select group of decision-makers. These groups may be called councils, committees, commissions, boards, or executive staff, but all have one thing in common; it is their vote which determines what will be done in the future.

Many organizational structures place planners in staff line position, outside the direct authority of either maintenance or operations. In this position the planner acts as an impartial advisor owing no loyalties to secondary staff goals. For most recreation agencies the planner is associated with development, and is closely aligned with recreation design and policy. His or her responsibility is to advise others regarding facility size, location, purpose, and use.

The planner is asked to gather, however he can, the information which decision-makers will need to formulate feasible goals and make logical decisions. A planner must rely on accurate, pertinent research in order to advise the decision-maker effectively and efficiently.

Problems which the planner faces most often in gathering and presenting information to the decision-maker can be divided into two types: problems of relevance and problems of predeterminism. Those constraints which deal with a lack of relevant data are most often a result of either inadequate time to prepare or a lack of basic data. Often the planner is forced to make an educated judgment, accepting findings from similar places and situations, and assuming they are applicable.

When the planner is fortunate enough to have something more than his own "gut feeling" to work on, he will most likely encounter research or plans that were developed with a predetermined solution or explanation in mind. While these base data may be unbiased, the methodology or priorities may be so specific as to lead to only one conclusion. This is often the case with feasibility studies or large scale futuristic master plans. In either case, the planner must overcome these constraints and prepare the decision-maker with the "best available" information and then provide the service which distinguishes his profession — that of offering recommendations, alternatives, and advice.

As a result of tradition, policy, trust, and workload, one of the planner's primary tools in effecting change is his/her advice and recommendation. It is his/her interpretation of the information which, when added to that of the decision-makers, results in change. If the decision-maker is also a direct manager of staff or individual facilities, the change may be immediate. If, instead, the decision-maker is an executive staff member, change may be expressed as a new policy or goal, which is often slow to show any actual results. However the results are measured, the planner must be knowledgeable enough and accepted enough to be believed, before he/she can be truly effective.

Classification of Research

Recreation research, as it is used by planners, may be divided into three basic types: (1) descriptive, (2) predictive, and (3) investigative. Descriptive recreational research encompasses two general areas. First, it describes the physical environment in terms of its application, classification, or change with regard to recreational impact or capability. Alternatively, it may describe the behavioral element of recreation, such as the types of users and their perceptions, needs, and actions. Predictive research most often begins with the results of descriptive research and seeks to further explain the physical and behavioral environments as they might be expected to react to changes in selected variables or general conditions. Again, studies of this type may address specific environments or individuals, or they may be directed towards a large grouping of users or behaviors. In either case, the goal of predictive research is to identify the possible reaction and alternatives to proposed actions or policies. Investigative research, on the other hand, is applicable to a specific location, time, and/or group of users in regards to supporting or rejecting a proposed alternative. All investigative research should be oriented toward providing simple, well understood short answers or solutions to specific well defined questions.

Ultimately, all research used by a planner has but one goal: practical solutions to real problems (Rutledge 1981). The task of transferring the findings of research into reality is one of the planner's major objectives when he faces new and unfamiliar projects. Too often we find that decisions have been made, budgets prepared, and constuction begun before complete and accurate research is even mentioned. Why is this true and what are the results of such actions?

The Problem, Practitioner, and Theorist

Different schools of thought exist in many fields of endeavor, and planning is no exception. The practitioner is concerned with problem solving, crisis intervention, and site development; whereas the recreation theorist's goal is to establish general principles which apply to all situations. Depending upon one's particular loyalties, the other group's attitudes are appreciated but not really understood or considered to be relevant. Individuals within the two groups often have similar backgrounds but rarely do they pursue similar futures. They come from two different schools of thought, representing different objectives, different approaches, different priorities. The essential difference is that the theorist strives to question, the practitioner to act. The practitioner asserts that the theorist is slow in recognizing changes and works in abstracts. The theorist begs the practitioner to read his/her crystal ball prediction and prepare for change. While they may appreciate each other's motives, neither fully understands why the other continues as he/she does.

Perhaps the reasons these differences exist can be best examined by looking at the expectations of each group. Both the theorist and the practitioner place demands and expectations on the other, and when the expectations are not met, or in some cases when they are fulfilled, it only serves to reaffirm their differences. The theorist expects the practitioner to know his or her problems, to be able to describe and anticipate them, and place priorities upon them. The practitioner should have basic information available, data, maps, and photographs which are accurate and useful in a variety of ways. Most of all, the practitioner is expected to proceed through a logical, well ordered process of implementation once the research is complete. The practitioner, on the other hand, expects the theorist to predict what problems will arise and to have strategies for their solution already in mind. The theorist, as an expert, is expected to call upon many more resources than the practitioner in gathering the necessary base information, and therefore remove this burden from the practitioner. The theorist should know, however, that when all is said and done, research was but one of many elements producing a given solution, and logic may give way to politics and competition for scarce public funds.

When all these elements come into play, the theorist often finds that a decision has been made before his research has been completed. Collection of base information costs the practitioner both time and money and the practitioner may often feel that he is well-off without the consuming element of research; on the other hand, the theorist may become frustrated by the impatience of the decision-maker pressured by politics, creditors, or the using public.

The planner, as a practitioner, is usually able to identify some very specific problems or questions, the answers to which would be useful. In choosing these problems, the planner develops his own methodology for research, performs his or her own tasks, and rarely discovers anything he didn't already know. To look to a theorist as a researcher for these seemingly simple tasks is often a waste of money and expertise. Therefore the planner continues to downplay the importance of the application of accurate research to real problems. The assignment of the theorist to basic research, which is applicable to any investigation regardless of individual circumstances, is not only grounded in a sense of special skills or resources, but often is a result of the territorialism that any profession tends to create. Unfortunately, the theorist has been too willing to accept this assignment, thus creating what many feel is a proliferation of duplicative research, updates of past studies and "cookbook" approaches to standard types of investigations. The practitioner, on the other hand, often shoulders his burden of responsibility for action with egotistical pride, confining himself to his own limited background and knowledge.

Many have suggested that through better communications and dialogue, planner and researcher will work together more effectively. In some situations, working together has been made mandatory by employment or by mutual agreement. Regardless of the reasons for which the planner and researcher become colleagues, for an investigation to be useful to the planner and fulfilling to the researcher, it must begin with a well-defined scope, include a reasonable time schedule, and produce a specific well understood answer.

Research Needs

In 1979, the Department of Interior, in cooperation with the National Recreation and Parks Association, prepared a national recreation research agenda for the 1980's. The study's concluding statement was: "The prevailing research need for recreation in the 1980's will be to document, with precision, the contribution of recreation to the physical, mental, emotional, social, economic, and political health and well-being of individuals in their homes, neighborhoods, cities, states and nation."

That statement in itself encompasses the entire scope of recreation research needs. Recreation is once again recognized as an important element in nearly all aspects of our society. Yet it is important to note that the underlying objective of that call for research was to "document the contribution of recreation," thereby justifying expenditures for recreation. This is certainly not a new objective of research, nor will it ever likely become a completed objective.

During the last twenty years, approximately twelve major conferences have been held concerning the future needs of recreation research. The latest Department of Interior study identified from over 500 research needs, 10 subject matter areas which would be the most significant to the greatest number and broadest range of research participants. They were, in order of priority:

1. fuel shortages and fuel cost

2. integrating recreation with other resource management activities

3. the value of resource use for recreation compared to other uses

4. comprehensive recreation plans

5. fostering cooperation among providers of recreation

6. increased recreation opportunities for the elderly

7. vandalism

8. media influence of recreation and leisure interests and choices between opportunities

9. estimating the economic value of outdoor recreation

10. survey of research techniques

While the majority of these topics are traditional areas for research, some very timely concerns are evident. Fuel shortages and fuel costs will continue to influence the recreation and leisure-time industry. For many managers, vandalism has become an expected operational cost, with no workable solution available. The potential influence and utility of the media has only begun to surface in the fields of recreation programming and marketing.

Research Inadequacies

Basic descriptive studies, such as national and statewide comprehensive outdoor recreation plans (SCORPs), have been available to the planner, but specific activity or site studies are less common. Funding more specific descriptive studies is difficult, but it may be justified if specific studies assist in development of a large scale project.

Recreation planners are, for the most part, still interested in updating traditional types of descriptive research. Participation rates, socio-economic indicators, willingness-to-travel or to pay, perceptions, and satisfaction levels as they relate to a wide array of activities: these areas will continue to be basic tools of the practicing planner. In most cases, the data collected in these studies is useful as a constantly available base to draw upon as different projects arise. The amount of detail in these studies is often criticized because of the time and expense required. Also, the expense of updating highly elaborate studies on a regular schedule often becomes prohibitive. The planner is primarily interested in documenting standard values for a few key variables to answer the basic "who, what, where, and how often" questions.

Many planners are facing difficult problems providing services in the areas of "risk sports" or challenging activities. Special interest groups which desire facilities for activities such as hang gliding, mountain climbing, or off-road vehicles continue to pressure recreation administrators for increased development. Other activities which require a large amount of space, such as wilderness hiking and cross-country skiing, while increasing in participation still require a disproportionate amount of space, money, and managerial time. While these activities have received some attention in both descriptive and predictive research, studies usually concentrate on either the user or the resource, rarely investigating both aspects of the activity together. The result is that the planner or decision-maker is given research pertaining to only half of the problem, and is left to make an educated guess or speculation as to the influence of the other half.

Predictive research, or research which foretells behavior or results of behavior, has generally not been useful to the planner. Most administrators believe that their properties or users are unique and that their problems are atypical, making the use of modeling to accurately predict specific behavior highly suspect.

Perhaps one of the most challenging problems facing the planner using predictive research is the political and financial climates in which decision-making takes place. The decision-maker has very few tools to assist him in predicting the success of projects or program development during differing periods of economic and social growth. The recreation industry, like any business, fluctuates in response to political and financial changes. Finally, predictive research must begin to concentrate upon the implications of major demographic shifts in the recreation public. Studies dealing with substitution of activities and areas, and longevity of participation in an activity will become increasingly important as the competition for recreation facilities and programs monies becomes more intense.

Investigative research is a very broad category that encompasses methodologies and objectives found in both descriptive and predictive research, differing primarily in scale and scope. This type of research offers the most direct benefit to the planner; and as you might expect, it is most often performed by the planner. The need to investigate the impacts of environmental or health hazards on recreation development has recently become an important concern. Environmental quality has always been an underlying element in recreation, yet recent years have seen a shift which has entrusted research on this subject to individuals or agencies which lack any recreational appreciation. Long-term research projects which can be on-going through years of park operation are especially needed in the area of environmental quality.

Future Needs

The categories of research which have been suggested: descriptive, predictive, and investigative are broad and very general, but they serve to focus on the purposes for which the planner uses research. It is these purposes which dictate the usefulness of the research and determine its acceptance. Recreation equipment, leisure counseling, and park interpretation and programming are the areas which have not been adequately addressed in today's research, and their investigation would help strengthen the bond between researcher and planner.

Recreation equipment is one key ingredient in designing and operating successful recreation facilities. Some balls bounce faster, some skis slide slower, some boats are wider. Many pieces of equipment are not standardized, making standard designs impossible. As an example, it is not enough to know how many recreation vehicles will come to a park. The planner must also know how many of them have electrical connections on the left side and how many on the right. This is a small detail, yet it affects thousands of dollars of installation, as well as the traffic design of an entire park. This is but one example of an instance where the planner, researcher, and designer must work as one. Many studies focus on the behavior of the user, but the design of his equipment may be even more of a problem than his behavior.

Another area for research which is growing in importance is the role that recreation programs and leisure time counseling will play in increasing measures of "quality of life." Leisure counseling is a profession which should become a major user of recreation research. The implications that leisure programs have on planning recreation services should not be underestimated. The importance of the individual is often overlooked in both research and planning but it is very important at the administrative and political level.

Certainly one of the most visible yet least researched aspects of park operation is interpretation and programming. Although interpretation and programming provide the threads which tie all of the elements of the recreation experience together, much of what is known about these areas has been borrowed from other disciplines, such as education and speech. To the planner, programming is the reason for park design and interpretation is its product. Research which can lead to adapting or instilling positive and productive interpretive programs will create a more effective and efficient park.

Summary

The recreation planner has evolved into a specialist drawn from many roots. The planner acts as the negotiator for both the user and the resource, seeking to strike the perfect balance.

Research, when accurate and timely, becomes the planner's best tool as he or she enters the arena with decision-makers, commissions, and executive staffs. Whether it is descriptive of people or spaces, predictive of behavior or results of behavior, investigative of one site or one day, research must seek attainable solutions to real problems. This will be facilitated by overcoming the language barriers between the planner and researcher; reducing the time lag from problem, to research, to solution; and eliminating the territorialism held by both sides.

The planner's research needs include many traditional areas, as well as some relatively new concerns. Basic participation, socio-economic indicators, willingness-to-travel or to pay, perceptions, and satisfaction level remain the basic tools of the planner. In addition, new areas such as substitution and longevity of participation, political and financial trends, and environmental hazards will become basic concerns in the future.

References

Jubenville, A. *Outdoor Recreation Planning*. W. B. Saunders Company, 1976.
Rutledge, A. J. *A Visual Approach to Park Design*. Garland STPM Press, 1981.

3

Agency Interaction: Meeting the Outdoor Recreational Needs of the Elderly

Richard V. Smith

This chapter focuses on the outdoor recreational needs of our elderly population. Recreation planning has most often had either a system-wide, site specific, or current problem/issue focus. Detailed study of the practices and needs of identifiable groups in the total population have usually been very narrowly focused in the context of a site or an issue. An example of a site orientation relative to the elderly would be the provision of leisure/recreation opportunities in an institutional or retirement setting. Similarly, the most familiar issue discussed with respect to the sixty-five and over population is that of therapeutic recreation. The purpose here is to look more generally at this group and to identify emerging trends and suggest possible approaches to both furthering our understanding of the elderly in the area of outdoor recreation and to list some of the ways the elderly might be better served.

There is little hard information on which to base an analytical study of the elderly and outdoor recreation. Very few comprehensive surveys have been conducted; nearly all of the available data used in considering this subject are drawn from surveys having far broader ends. Data adapted from such surveys rarely satisfies our needs. Therefore, this chapter is based on descriptive statistics drawn from Ohio surveys and on perspectives and observations offered by social service and recreational delivery agency officials. Complementing these information sources is a considerable amount of field observation carried out while preparing several parts of recent Ohio Statewide Comprehensive Outdoor Recreation Plans.

A significant number of eldely people (those sixty-five and above) are active in outdoor recreation. Still more wish to be active. For example, Ohio's elderly population has some participation in each of the outdoor recreation activities analyzed in the most recent statewide recreation plan. Survey data suggests that this age group expresses a particular preference for more picnic areas, fishing ponds and lakes, hiking trails (including nature trails), swimming pools, and developed campgrounds and indicates some interest in each of the other facility types suggested in the citizen user survey. Unfortunately, our knowledge of the elderly population's attitudes and practices relative to outdoor recreation is incomplete.

The lack of information about overall patterns may best be demonstrated by excerpting brief sections from two letters received from officials of the Ohio Area Agency on Aging. These comments typify the present situation among responsible Ohio administrators directly involved in bettering delivery systems to the elderly.

> ...Our needs assessments have not specifically asked about outdoor recreation but recreation opportunities in general, meet with enthusiasm. As far as time use is concerned, it is our experience that senior citizens manage their time in about the same way they always have. If they always had a lot of leisure time they still do, and if they kept busy they still do... We realize this reply is vague and we apologize...One factor that may have a bearing on the use of outdoor recreation is available transportation. No matter how attractive the opportunity if one cannot get there it means very little... Hope this helps some.[1]

And from a second agency:

> ... I wish I could be of help but our Area Agency has absolutely no information for you. I would venture a guess that what you are able to collect in this field would be extremely limited. I started dreaming a couple of years ago about developing a total outdoor program for the elderly, but never have gotten it off the ground because of time constraints. I would be most appreciative receiving the findings after you are finished. I would hope your efforts would be in nature study, nature walks, nature crafts, bird watching, bicycling, hiking, picnicking, badminton, croquet, boating, swimming, golf, fishing, horseshoes, tennis, lawn tennis, volleyball, fitness, day camping, short-term camping, recreational vehicle camping, week long or longer resident camping.[2]

Clearly, there is a felt need to look toward a better outdoor recreation program for this age group.

A REVIEW OF THE LITERATURE

The need for additional information about the elderly was recognized in the first national outdoor recreation plan published in 1973 under the title *Outdoor Recreation — A Legacy for America*. One section dealing with the groups of people whose needs require consideration centered on "older Americans" and said:

> A large elderly population is a phenomenon new to this century. Since 1900, the 65 years and over population has grown much faster than the rest of the population, and the 75 and over segment has grown even faster. At the turn of the century, there were 3 million older persons, every 25th American; today, there are 20 million, every tenth American; the 65 and over group is six and a half times as large as in 1900; the under-65 group is only two and one-half times as large. Over 95 percent of older Americans depend to a large extent on community resources and services. The availability of neighborhood recreation facilities is important for the eldely, since transportation is one of their greatest problems. The older person has all the interests and much of the outlook of his lifetime. If he has enjoyed hiking, tennis, hunting,

---

[1]Letter from official of Area Agency on Aging - Number 9 (Ohio), August 8, 1979.

[2]Letter from official of Central Ohio Area Agency on Aging, August 3, 1979.

fishing, swimming, camping, or sightseeing, these interests continue. The difference lies in the energy available to participate in these activities, and in the time required to accomplish them.[3]

Other sections of this national plan deal with the need to remember particular needs of the elderly in site planning and in the establishment of fee schedules.

Smith provided an overview of planning for the elderly during the preparation of Ohio's 1975-80 Statewide Comprehensive Outdoor Recreation Plan and noted that there were just two questions on the survey questionnaires dealing with the needs of the elderly or the handicapped. This data along with the results of interviews with public officials in parks and recreation agencies across the state led to the conclusion: ". . . that there is an extreme dearth of recreation planning and programming for the handicapped and aged throughout the state. Furthermore, there appear to be no programs forthcoming in the near future for these groups for various reasons including: lack of money, trained personnel, time, insurance complications, etc. The planning and programming that do exist are localized and therefore limited in scope and magnitude."[4]

A typical large Ohio city might summarize the status of recreation for the elderly: 'The city does have senior citizen centers, but these provide for mainly indoor recreation. Little is currently done in terms of detailed planning and programming of outdoor recreation facilitiies for the aged and disadvantaged. A nature trail and organizations of senior citizens which allows lower fees for the use of golf courses and similar facilities are examples of what is done. It is evident that more indoor recreation, crafts, and interest group programs are operated than is true in the case of outdoor activities.' Smith (1979) summarized the problem asserting that "the recency of major advances in both gerontological and leisure studies is clearly a contributing factor to this dearth of material."

Nevertheless, the Older Americans Act of 1965 listed ten major service objectives; three of these had clear and significant implications for the recreation/leisure area (an optimum environment and the development of sound physical and mental health; meaningful activity within the widest possible range of civic, cultural and recreational opportunities; and efficient use of community resources to provide social assistance in a coordinated and accessible manner)[5]. In that same year the Bureau of Outdoor Recreation (BOR) released a study dealing with the participation of different groups within the population in the several outdoor recreation activities (BOR 1965). Picnicking, walking for pleasure, and sightseeing ranked highest for the sixty-five and over population. A preference for the less strenuous activities also emerged. The BOR study noted that the

---

[3]*Outdoor Recreation: A Legacy for America* (Washington, D.C.: Bureau of Outdoor Recreation, 1973), p. 9.

[4]Memorandum to John Bradley, Ohio Department of Natural Resources, undated.

[5]The Older Americans Act of 1965 created the Administration on Aging and provided the stimulus for much of the growth in programming for and improved understandings of the elderly population. The Act has been modified on several occasions since its passage; the points noted here were taken from S. G. Lutzin and E. H. Storey, *Managing Municipal Leisure Services* (Washington, D.C.: International City Management Association, 1973), p. 140.

relatively low level of outdoor recreation activity seemed to be a product of a lack of specialized facilities for the elderly, inadequate financial resources for participation in certain more expensive activities, and a feeling of inadequacy as to ability to participate successfully. The combination of these important 1965 events laid the base for in-depth types of analyses.

Today, studies with a focus on wilderness users, or the handicapped, or youth, or water oriented activities users, or the elderly are emerging.

Although relatively little has been published in the past decade having a direct focus on outdoor recreation and the elderly, some research has been published in both the gerontology and recreation literature with indirect relevance to outdoor recreation as the generalized leisure needs and concerns of the elderly are addressed or as the total population is analyzed for improved understandings about recreation participation and non-participation. Generally, the literature can be divided into five categories: (1) case studies of particular communities or settings, (2) treatments of the basic importance of active involvement in leisure, (3) analysis of what keeps people from participation, (4) participation rate studies, and (5) needs analyses. Some examples of this literature are given at the end of this chapter. Similarly, the majority of the standard texts dealing with either outdoor recreation or social gerontology contain relatively little on the subject. Most references deal either with general statements about the apparent need to do more in meeting the outdoor recreation needs of elderly Americans or refer to needed site modifications. The scarcity of published material is attested to in a brief bibliography (Dearden and Lum 1981).

Other scholars have argued for in-depth analyses of the elderly population's needs and desires relative to outdoor recreation. Lawton (1978) described the role of leisure in considering the needs of the elderly and concluded "... Improvement in the quality of life of the elderly of the future will come only by providing opportunities for older people to express their diversity of needs and preferences and to exercise more fully their remarkable capacity to match their choices of meaningful activities to their own needs and capabilities." McAvoy (1979) examined the leisure preferences, problems, and needs of the elderly in Minnesota. He concluded his paper by stating: "While progress has been made in the study of leisure preferences, participation rates, problems, and needs of the elderly, much remains to be done to effectively plan with and for this growing segment of the population." Increasing interest in the needs of elderly Americans was reiterated through the selection of "Leisure and Old Age" as the theme for the December 1981 issue of *Parks and Recreation*.

A STUDY OF THE ELDERLY IN OHIO

A major study on the elderly and outdoor recreation was included as part of the 1980-85 Ohio Statewide Comprehensive Outdoor Recreation Plan. The full study conducted by Smith (1980) is on file in the Office of Outdoor Recreation Services, Ohio Department of Natural Resources, Columbus, Ohio. What follows are excerpts from the summary report.

Table 1

Percent of Households with Participants

	Elderly	All Households
Picnicking	52	55
Hiking/Walking	44	35
Fishing	16	36
Swimming	14	45
Golf	9	18
Boating	7	18
Camping	6	26

SOURCE: 1978 Ohio Citizen User's Survey of 5,078 Households Including 448 "Elderly" Households.

Participation in Outdoor Recreation   Members of households with an elderly head do participate in all outdoor activities analyzed in the Ohio study. However, seven activities are of primary importance (see Table 1); the level of participation in the other activities is too low to permit meaningful comment. Table 1 also compares participation by the elderly in selected activities with participation by all surveyed households. In every case, the proportion of elderly households participating in each activity is clearly below that for all surveyed households. The decline is most abrupt in those activities that generally require a high level of physical exertion. Although emphasis on vigorous outdoor activities may not be appropriate for senior citizens, the data indicate some physically demanding activities (e.g., swimming, golf) are popular for this group.

Factors Influencing Participation   A variety of economic, social, and attitudinal factors influence participation in outdoor recreation activities by the elderly. In light of the available information, the elderly population can be divided into two broad categories in terms of outdoor recreation participation. One group is characterized by middle to upper middle incomes, a reasonable average of years of schooling completed, access to transportation, and long-term involvement in one or more outdoor recreation activities. This group is comfortable in what they do. They are experienced and generally able to maintain a level of participation that is directly in line with their wishes. The participation rates for this group just after retirement normally remain at levels similar to or slightly above participation rates for those just prior to retirement. At approximately age seventy, these rates commence to decline rather sharply; this rate of decline appears to be very high after the mid-seventies. This is an advantaged group. Its needs are satisfied by a wide range of public and private service-providing agencies. The facilities they wish to use are available and their relatively flexible time budget permits them access during non-peak periods. This group is relatively patient and is willing to take their turn during peak period times. Detailed data are not available to sustain these impressions, but a variety of observers agree that this generalization is reasonably accurate.

The second group is not as fortunate. The elderly in this group tend to be concentrated in central cities and are characterized by a lack of experience in outdoor activities, little income, and restricted mobility. This is a sizable group which has had few options. To many social gerontologists, it seems to be an extremely eager group, characterized by a desire to experience the outdoors. These elderly people often have no specific activity in mind, they simply wish to be presented with an opportunity. It is in this group's needs that most of the unsatisfied recreation demand among the elderly is found.

Each of these two major components of the elderly population could be divided into numerous subgroups. However, the existing situation (in terms of public policy impact) can be adequately summarized through an understanding of these two groups, with special emphasis on the second, which is lacking in both options and experience.

Changing Habits   A common belief among many recreation professionals is that various changes in life circumstances can influence recreational behavior. One question in the survey asked adults whether there has been a meaningful change in their recreational activity in passing from youth to adulthood. Of the households with an elderly head, just over one-half said that their current recreational activities were similar to those engaged in during their younger years. Table 2 illustrates that more than half of the elderly in all community types, except central cities, indicate that they still participate in similar activities. Only 38 percent of those living in central cities indicated that they participate in similar activities. Whether this is a function of socioeconomic factors or a product of central cities' limited and/or alternative recreation opportunities is unclear. Nevertheless, recreation professionals must help dispel some of the common myths about the elderly: that senior citizens are incapable of learning new activities; that they are set in their ways and activities; and, that they have left their best years behind them. Of those who responded that they still engage in similar activities, an exceedingly small percentage described their volume of activity as having increased. Evidence suggests that the majority of elderly people experience a decline in outdoor recreational activity as a result of many intervening factors.

Attitudinal Barriers   Attitudes also play an important role in influencing participation in recreation activities. The 1980-1985 Ohio Statewide Comprehensive Outdoor Recreation Plan (SCORP) identifies attitudinal barriers as significant deterrents to participation in outdoor recreation by the elderly. Table 3 provides a breakdown by political unit of various factors that limit visits to outdoor recreation areas for households with a head sixty-five or over. The elderly respondents indicated that crowded conditions, a lack of clean areas, travel distance factors, and a general lack of facilities for the aged are the most important factors limiting visitation to outdoor recreation areas. A lack of interest and of information about available facilities and programs are also significant deterrents. For the most part, these factors are also indicative of typical attitudes among the total population surveyed in the Comprehensive User Survey (CUS). Fortunately,

Table 2

Recreation Activity Changes from Youth to Adult Years for Households with Head Older than 65, by Political Unit
(Percent Distribution)

		Total −65 Population	Central City	Suburb of C.C.	City 10,000-50,000	City under 10,000	Rural non-Farm	Rural Farm
Are your recreation activities now similar to those in youth?	Yes	51	38	55	54	62	37	62
	No	49	62	45	46	39	43	38
If yes:								
Do you do more now, or less,	More	8	7	11	8	9	6	7
	Less	28	20	33	23	46	32	19
or about the	Same	17	14	10	24	7	22	37
same?	No opinion	47	59	45	45	38	40	37

SOURCE: 1978 Ohio Citizen User's Survey (CUS) of 5,078 Households Including 708 With a Household Head of 65 or More.

Table 3

Importance of Various Factors Limiting Visits to Outdoor Recreation Areas For Households with Head Older than 65, by Political Unit (Percent Responding "Yes")

	Total − 65 Population	Central City	Suburb of C.C.	City 10,000-50,000	City under 10,000	Rural non-Farm	Rural Farm
Lack of time	29	23	16	41	45	31	35
Too far away	44	47	36	41	38	55	32
Too crowded	31	45	52	58	54	56	40
Lack of money	30	34	23	27	23	36	28
Lack of interest	38	30	42	45	45	31	61
Lack of information	38	34	48	38	39	38	31
Lack of transportation	7	25	15	7	10	19	19
Lack of interesting facilities	29	25	32	26	28	28	50
Lack of orderly clean areas	47	47	56	38	50	47	33
Lack of park sponsored activities	21	19	26	22	11	28	11
Lack of facilities for aged	39	40	39	21	44	41	65

SOURCE: 1978 Ohio Citizen User's Survey (CUS) of 5,078 Households Including 708 With a Household Head of 65 or More.

many of these barriers can be alleviated through better recreation planning and management efforts.

A mixed response pattern is evident when attitudinal factors are analyzed by community type. Rural farm people have the least interest in recreation, those in small cities feel they have the least time, the rural non-farm population is most concerned with the distances to outdoor recreation areas, and a lack of clean, orderly areas is of major importance to the elderly in the central cities, suburbs, and smaller towns.

Social Services Available to the Elderly A multitude of federal, state, regional, local, and private agencies specialize in the provision of various social services, including recreation, for the elderly in Ohio. Generally, these agencies provide comprehensive programs oriented toward the multi-faceted needs of the elderly. Some typical programs/services that these agencies provide include coordination with other public and private agencies; educational programs and activities; nutrition and meal programs; transportation, escort, and outreach programs; health related programs; information and referral, and other supportive services.

For the most part, the development of programs for senior citizens by park and recreation agencies did not begin until after 1965. Since that time, the recreational needs of the elderly have rarely been high priority development and programming concerns (although there are examples of agencies at all levels of government that have implemented positive programs and policies). Today, many more public park and recreation agencies have become actively involved in programming for the elderly. Reduced user fees, special programs, and senior citizen centers are familiar responses designed to help satisfy the elderly's recreation needs. Some agencies have even conducted surveys to identify preferences and special recreation needs of the elderly. Other agencies have developed special facilities and/or hired professional staff to plan and coordinate activities for the elderly.

Summary To summarize the data obtained through the survey of Ohio households, the elderly participate to varying degrees in all activities analyzed. They seem less likely than the general population to make adjustments in their recreation behavior as a consequence of tighter financial constraints. Approximately one-half of the elderly participate in activities similar to those they engaged in as youths. Finally, the elderly desire more facilities of all types and would like existing facilities to be managed to minimize crowding and various forms of depreciative behavior.

The information obtained during this study points to the growing importance of the elderly population as a group in need of recreation services. It indicates their interest and participation in a wide variety of outdoor recreation pursuits, and the need for planners and managers to become more sensitive to the special needs of the older participant.

The survey data and the opinions of the many experts consulted not only confirm the significance of the recreation needs of Ohio's elderly citizens, but are also indicative of our ability to meet most of these needs using existing resources. For those with well-developed recreation preferences and the means necessary to enjoy them, it seems that little needs to be done save allow them the opportunity to pursue leisure activities in safe, accessible, and useable environments. Program design and management should reflect the special needs of the elderly; such accommodations, however, are often easily made.

For those less fortunate older Ohioans, an active outreach program is needed statewide. The removal of physical, economic, and attitudinal barriers must be accompanied by an active campaign to make these people aware of the opportunities that are available to them. As many of the elderly in this second group do not participate because they have <u>never</u> engaged in outdoor recreation pursuits, outreach programs must also assume an educational, "how to" approach.

OTHER PERSPECTIVES ON THE ELDERLY AND OUTDOOR RECREATION

A number of additional generalizations have emerged from our research in considering the topic of the elderly and outdoor recreation. The great bulk of the sixty-five and over population can physically use existing facilities and have the freedom of time to use them at off-peak periods. Relatively few among the elderly require major facility modifications for the practice of the most popular activities, but most elderly are appreciative of and can more easily use facilities that have simple modifications which make the experience just a little easier. It should be remembered that a significant proportion of the elderly are potential occasional users of recreation facilities and that the number of possible users will increase in relative terms more rapidly than the population as a whole and sharply above the rates for the most youthful age categories.

The elderly, as perhaps is true of many other age groups in the total population, need advocates to push their causes. All evidence points to the importance of outdoor recreation as a valuable ingredient in successful aging. The desirability of extending opportunities for satisfying aging to more and more of the population has evident merit. The great need is to create a situation within which funding permits the offering of programs with trained leadership and the means (e.g., transportation) to take advantage of the many opportunities and resources that exist. Thus, cooperative efforts between groups and agencies concerned with the aged and those having recreational facilities and programs makes sense. So also does a linking together in formal or informal associations of those numerous groups (governmental, social service, church, neighborhood) which have an interest in the productive use of leisure time and the well-being of the elderly.

A further look at comments by officials in agencies serving the elderly (obtained in interviews with the author) is appropriate because aging agencies acknowledge the importance of leisure and recreation and the desirability of extending opportunities. They also tend to emphasize that: (1) their agency can put little money, if any, into recreational services for the aged because of limited funds; (2) most efforts are focused on home care services; (3) the trend for federal dollars for the elderly is to put those monies into hard core services; (4) a governmental problem in improving recreational services is the stereotype that the elderly are too old for recreation; (5) most elderly in our major cities will not use facilities because of fear of children and disturbances; (6) there are too few trained aging agency employees with knowledge in the area of recreation other than therapeutic recreation specialists and craft leaders; and (7) aging agency officials may often feel that churches and other social service agencies are already serving this need.[6]

Most aging agencies have no policy on recreation except to urge that recreational agencies recognize the diversity within the elderly population. Agency workers are among those who tend to emphasize that the elderly may be divided into two major groups: first, those with the means and the past experiences to keep active in some recreational pursuits and secondly, those who may be described as disadvantaged, having had few experiences or advantages and consequently few options and opportunities. The first group is likely to express greater and greater demands in the future since their numbers will be bolstered by those now younger who are more active in recreation. And the second group wants a chance to participate and presents a major challenge to providing agencies.

Other aging agency employees comment succinctly:

> What good does the facility do (any facility) unless it is used? How can we use these facilities more effectively for the disadvantaged elderly in the down time of these resources? Things are available for other age groups - but not for the elderly. The example of school buses is a frequently used example - their availability for children, but the lack of a comparable vehicle or access to school vehicles for most elderly around the state.[7]

Some senior citizens groups have developed innovative programs that make effective use of their area's potentials. Sensitive programming filled with options, the opportunity to try many different things along with many others seeking the same type of experiences, and sound publicity about available offerings have drawn significant numbers of area citizens. The need there and elsewhere is for transportation assistance, programming funding and staffing, some slight modification of facilities, and an encouragement of cooperative use of facilities among groups.[8]

Many city recreation-parks agencies have become involved in programming for the elderly in recent years. Reduced fee concepts are familiar, as is an increasing effort to develop special programs and senior citizens centers. Some agencies have made surveys to identify the felt needs of the elderly, while others have made no efforts of note. Some suggest that they have had no expression of interest or demand as an explanation for minimal present offerings. Some communities have moved in the past few years to create a park and a coordinator of activities for the elderly with a variety of special programs and fee schedules. In general, there is a feeling that the demands from the elderly group will become more and more pronounced in the years immediately ahead. In many cases the success or failure of programs serving the elderly is a product of a person who provides leadership. The role of the individual appears to be of great importance in community after community.

---

[6]Compiled from interviews with officials in Council's on Aging in Cincinnati, Columbus, and elsewhere, summer 1979.

[7]Compiled from interviews with officials at Senior Citizens Centers in various cities, but especially Cincinnati, summer 1979.

[8]Interview with representative of the Hancock County Senior Citizen's Inc., July 1979.

Suggestions for Future Research

As the foregoing indicates, the elderly are likely to be increasingly involved in outdoor recreation, but our understandings of the practices, attitudes, needs, and limitations of this rapidly increasing group is very slight. The data base is inadequate. Some descriptive statistics have been generated and have a limited utility. Few meaningful analytical studies have been completed because of inadequate data sets or our inability to ask the right questions which, in turn, provide explanations in which confidence can be placed. Current efforts focus on analyses designed to identify relationships and explain recreational behavior and to lay a sturdier base for the development of predictive models. This work will continue, but the central need is for a much larger research effort by far more researchers who will in time develop better ways of examining current and emerging questions. Examples of research topics needing investigation to help lay the base for an improvement in delivering outdoor recreation opportunities to the elderly include:

1. Identifying the barriers to greater participation in outdoor recreation among groups within this population

2. Identifying whether or not more elderly would engage in outdoor recreational pursuits if barriers were modified and opportunities made evident.

3. Uncovering the attitudes of recreation and park managers toward seeking increased use by elderly groups during non-peak periods

4. Delineating the several groups of elderly people within a population and developing an understanding of their recreational needs, wishes, and problems

5. Because a much larger proportion of the future elderly will have had early recreational experiences when compared to the present elderly population, we should identify the implications for recreational facility management and expansion

6. Specify the effect of retirement upon outdoor recreational practices. Can better pre-retirement planning encourage a "better" or more continuous involvement in active recreation?

This list could be greatly expanded. The point is, quite simply, that we are essentially ignorant of the many realities that relate to a consideration of the elderly and outdoor recreation.

Possible Policy Options

The preceding discussion suggests that many questions and options are likely to confront the decision-makers in both recreation and social service delivery agencies. The possibilities which follow are intended to be suggestive of the kinds of issues that may well confront agency directors as they look for ways to improve the outdoor recreation situation for their elderly citizens.

Local agencies should attempt to counter two primary problems characteristic of the elderly's recreational information base: (1) Many simply do not know what is available to them; the improvement of public dissemination of such information would be a great benefit. Perhaps the enlargement of a specific section of the local daily newspaper(s) detailing activities and locations would suffice. (2) Many elderly have had little opportunity to experience the outdoors or to participate in a recreational activity. Local recreation agencies should greatly expand their demonstration and instruction offerings to help in overcoming this block.

For example, local communities, through local parks and recreation departments, could conduct a periodic needs assessment or make certain that data pertinent to the needs of the elderly are included in community (area) wide surveys carried out by planning or other agencies. Second, recreation programming for the elderly population can be concentrated in off-peak time periods (from Labor Day through Memorial Day or on summer weekdays). Local providing agencies for services to the elderly and community recreation departments might develop formalized arrangements to utilize community resources (sections of parks, tennis courts, campgrounds, school buses) during these periods. Formalized arrangements do, however, require the proper sharing of costs and responsibility. Third, every effort could be made to expand joint program offerings. Ventures jointly sponsored by, for example, city recreation agencies and senior citizen centers or churches can provide a healthy base for larger and more responsive programming. In larger cities there may well be a remarkable potential for improvement in the recreational experiences of the elderly. There is some evidence to support the notion that large group programs may prove attractive where individually oriented or quite small group programs fail. A formal link could be established between city and county park systems and city and county aging agencies and senior citizens centers.

Beyond administrative charge is the concern of the elderly in all parks, but especially in urban parks, for their feeling of insecurity. Many fear the types of users found in most parks and often are concerned with a feeling of conspicuousness and vulnerability among crowds of youth. Better patrolling is a clear need to ensure that the elderly may use park facilities and have peace of mind.

Beyond these suggestions, a formal link should be established between the State Parks and area Aging Agencies as well as major Senior Citizen's Centers. Many of the elderly's needs can be satisfied through the use of present state park facilities in their off-peak periods. If simpler communications can be introduced and if the park staff and facilities can be oriented to such groups in non-peak periods, a major step will have been taken. Perhaps groups of parks in specified geographic areas can be linked to the several district agencies and to the senior citizen center systems of major cities in the regions of each state.

Lastly, facility modification needs are modest for the elderly, but it would be helpful if its present efforts were accelerated. That is, modifying the grade of selected trails, altering rest room facilities, placing steps on slight inclines, reserving parking in close-in areas of parking lots, locating camp sites on essentially flat terrain, and providing numerous benches will assist in putting the non-experienced elderly user at his/her ease. The data in this chapter have shown that there is little if any need for new facilities for the elderly; modest changes will suffice in terms of facility development.

Conclusion

How can communities proceed to deal with these concerns? It is to be hoped that basic research will add to our understanding of the elderly/outdoor recreation relationship. In the meantime, any city (or county or other governmental unit) might consider the following issues in planning for the elderly in their local area:

I. The identification of the target population. The essential characteristics that should be measured include:
   a. Develop summary data on basic population characteristics - numbers of people by age and sex.
   b. Map and analyze the distribution of the elderly in the community.
   c. Attempt to develop a composite perspective on the income patterns of the elderly; total income is useful, but some idea of the proportion (if any) of total income that may be considered discretionary for leisure time spending purposes is of particular importance.
   d. Identify health levels in the context of limitations on involvement in specific outdoor recreation activities.
   e. Determine what transportation is available to the individual and/or the household. Cars, public transportation, senior citizen "help" vans all may be of significance in some communities.
   f. Attempt to assess cultural and educational background characteristics -an increasing amount of evidence suggests that an understanding of these considerations may be of major importance in adapting opportunities for specific groups in the population.
   g. Determine what kind of housing and residential units do the elderly occupy.
   h. Using the variables developed in the listing above, develop a classification of household types appropriate to the particular community.

II. Recreational practices, desires, and needs. Specifically:
   a. How much leisure time is available and when do blocks of time tend to be available?
   b. How is leisure time presently used - time budget studies?
   c. How much, if any, of leisure time is spent on outdoor recreation? For those who do engage in outdoor recreation, how does their time allocation for this purpose compare with other leisure time uses.
   d. Compile information on outdoor recreation participation - rates, location, means of access, and satisfaction with experiences.
   e. Study nonparticipation in outdoor recreation - reasons, identification of wishes, and identification of barriers to attainment of desires.

f. What are the effects of retirement on recreation behavior?

g. Classify the elderly population into categories of outdoor recreation involvement and noninvolvement; develop correlation of recreational patterns and wishes with socio-economic attributes developed in I. above.

h. Analyze spatial variations of need (e.g., central city-suburbia; neighborhood A versus neighborhood B).

i. Identify neighborhoods (case study areas) to be the target areas for further study and experimental program development.

j. Study the relationship between recreational competence and successful aging.

III. Facilities, programs, and delivery agencies.

a. Inventory and evaluate all existing facilities and programs.

b. Identify the facilities/programs specially designed for the elderly and identify facilities/programs available to the elderly under the same conditions as the total population.

c. Review policies of state and local governments on recreation for the elderly, past, present, and future plans.

d. Determine trends in legislation and funding.

e. Examine the role of private groups and agencies.

f. Evaluate and compare the roles of the public and private sectors in serving the elderly.

Program and Facility Development for the Elderly   The preceding sections of a community study provide the basis for future program and facility development. Needs will have been determined; the roles and policies of the several levels of government will have been reviewed and, presumably, the probable future policies of those governmental units that affect any local government will have been identified and considered.

The product of such a community study should be the development of clear guidelines for action plans that respond to the program and facility needs of the elderly within the context of the community's financial abilities and policy objectives. Another desirable outcome of such a study might be the design and offering of experimental programs in order to more fully understand the factors which motivate or limit the participation of elderly people. If successful aging can be aided by providing diverse options for leisure time use, such efforts will have a measurable benefit that will add to the evidence concerning the value of leisure and recreation throughout one's life.

References

Dearden, P., and Lum, E. "Senior Citizens and Outdoor Recreation: A Guide to the Literature." *Vance Bibliographies,* 1981, p. 845.

Francken, D. A., and van Raaij, W. F. "Satisfaction with Leisure Time Activities." *Journal of Leisure Research* 13(1981):337-352.

Kelly, J. R. "Outdoor Recreation Participation: A Comparative Analysis." *Leisure Science* 3(1980):129-154.

Lawton, M. P. "Leisure Activities for the Aged." *Annals of the American Academy of Political and Social Science* 438(1978):71-80.

Lutzin, S. G., and Storey, E. H. *Managing Municipal Leisure Services.* Washington, D.C.: International City Management Association, 1973.

McAvoy, L. H. "The Leisure Preferences, Problems, and Needs of the Elderly." *Journal of Leisure Research* 11(1979):40-47.

Ohio Department of Natural Resources. *1980-85 Ohio Statewide Comprehensive Outdoor Recreation Plan*. Columbus, Ohio: Ohio Department of Natural Resources, 1981.

Outdoor Recreation: A Legacy for America. Washington, D.C.: Government Printing Office, 1973.

Palmore, E. "Predictors of Successful Aging." *The Gerontologist* 19(1979):427-431.

Pippin, R. N. "Assessing the Needs of the Elderly with Existing Data." *The Gerontologist* 20(1980):65-70.

Smith, R. V. "The Elderly and the Geography of Recreation." *East Lakes Geographer* 14(1979):26-36.

Smith, R. V. *Outdoor Recreation and the Elderly*. A technical report to the Ohio Department of Natural Resources, 1980.

Yoesting, D. R., and Christensen, J. E. "Reexamining the Significance of Childhood Recreation Patterns on Adult Leisure Behavior." *Leisure Science* 1(1977):219-230.

4

Planning and Policy-Making: The View from Within the Agency

Richard D. Westfall
Edward L. Hoffman

Within a government outdoor recreation management agency, research, planning, and policy-making and the relationships among these activities are often not what they might be assumed to be based upon articles such as those contained in this and other texts. This is not intended to be an attack on the theoretical sophistication, scientific validity, or good intentions of the efforts which are documented in this literature. Rather, there are certain aspects of research, planning, and policy-making within an outdoor recreation management agency that can only be fully appreciated by "being there."

Once "there" for a sufficient period of time, one begins to recognize that some of the familiar beliefs, assumptions, and paradigms so readily embraced by the student and academician are less than fully accurate. In fact, some take on the quality of "myths" when viewed from the "firing line."

This chapter first discusses some of these myths about research, planning, and policy-making in terms of the realities of the managing agency. Some suggestions are then offered to those involved and interested in these activities to hopefully improve the results of research, planning, and policy-making. Finally, some concluding comments concerning the roles of researchers, planners and policy analysts within agencies are made.

While we do not claim to be familiar with all agencies providing outdoor recreation, we do have fifteen years combined experience working as members and supervisors of research and planning staffs in an outdoor recreation agency and are in contact with others in similar positions across the country. The ideas presented in this chapter are very much our own, and are intended to provide a background for, and at times a perspective to, the other chapters in this text.

MYTHS ABOUT RESEARCH, PLANNING, AND POLICY-MAKING

Myth #1: Research, planning, and policy-making are carried out in a systematic, logical sequence.

In a well ordered world, (1) issues and problems are identified which generate hypotheses and define information needs, (2) research is conducted to test these hypotheses and fill information gaps, and then (3) planning and policy-making are carried out based explicitly on these research findings. In reality, agencies more often function in a reactive mode, responding to issues and problems when they become crises, rather than anticipating problems. Often policy is made first without the benefit of relevant information. Plans are then initiated to implement the policy and research may or may not be done on underlying issues. The research, when completed, may then provide information on the validity of the initial policy.

Policy-making and planning cannot always wait for relevant research. Funding cycles, changes in administrations, public pressure, and many other factors may dictate that policy be made and planning occur without an adequate information base. This does not mean that the researcher, planner, or policy analyst is irrelevant. By scoping the research or planning project to the available time frame (see suggestion #3), budget, and staff, they can bring as much technical expertise and rationality to decision-making as the circumstances permit without impeding the necessity for a rapid agency response.

Myth #2: Comprehensive, quantitative, long-range planning is the ideal or ultimate planning model.

The interest in forecasting "demand" in this text and in the literature (i.e., Yu 1981) implies that data-based, mathematical models are superior to less formal planning methods. The history of Statewide Comprehensive Outdoor Recreation Plans (SCORP's) with their requirements for "supply-demand-needs" analyses illustrates this belief. There is an inherent appeal to this approach. If we could just predict the number of activity days of camping and relate them to the number of existing campsites, then we could feel comfortable about doing our job of providing camping experiences.

Ross (1978, pp. 38-39) has commented on the dangers in placing too much faith in comprehensive planning. He identified four types of problems: (1) simple problems, with a specified number of calculable variables, (2) compound problems, with an unspecified number of calculable variables, (3) complex problems, with a specified number of incalculable variables, and (4) meta problems, with an unspecified number of incalculable variables. He goes on to say,

> Comprehensive planning can only be done on simple problems, or on compound problems that are composed of more than one simple problem. This is due to the

fact that comprehensive planning is a rational process requiring a closed system. Planners often make assumptions to reduce the variety and number of variables to enable closure of the system. There is no point in defining a problem or stating a goal such as 'improving the quality of life' as this problem definition lies outside the strategies available for solution.

In other words, Ross is arguing that planning based on such often-heard objectives as "providing quality outdoor recreation experiences," cannot currently be based on a comprehensive planning model. More specific objectives can be identified; however, as the specificity of objectives increase, the amount of agreement among agency policy and decision-makers on these objectives is likely to decrease. This makes the task of the comprehensive planner, who is often considering many different activities at once, even more difficult.

Among the general problems with SCORP's that have been identified previously (National Academy of Sciences 1975), the major methodological problem has been associated with "needs determination." In general, little thought is given to the joint analysis of supply and demand data. Supply and demand data collection are often done by different investigators using different activity definitions for different time frames. Theoretical, as well as methodological, development in joint supply-demand analysis has been minimal. Such potentially useful concepts as "substitutability" (Hendee and Burdge 1974) have seldom been incorporated into these analyses.

Existing needs-determination methods are often simplistic. Usually some arbitrary design or population-based standard is applied to supply figures resulting in an indication of "capacity". Then demand is compared to capacity and a "need" identified where demand exceeds capacity. Temporal considerations, including peaking; the effects of site and facility quality; the extent to which supply "creates" demand; and other variables, such as changes in recreation-related technology, are generally ignored. As the National Academy of Sciences found (1975, p. 20):

> Using population-based standards as a measure of the relative demand for a resource ignores many of the crucial factors affecting demand for recreational opportunities... this approach assumes that the individual characteristics and social relationships that affect the desire of individuals to participate in recreation... are distributed similarly across all areas to which the standards are applied. It also ignores the differences in geographic character of the same kind of recreation areas...as well as the evidence that different groups respond differently to recreation opportunities. Although standards could be developed to account for variations in population characteristics and the nature of recreation sites, the standards that have been used in most recreation planning have not done so.

The need to generate numbers appears to have outweighed sound methodological development in this major area of SCORP data collection and analysis. In examining most SCORP's, it is evident that the ratio of effort expended on data analysis to data collection has been low, and the ratio of data interpretation to data collection has been even lower. In most cases, the data produced has been of little value for many planning purposes. It is typically too general to answer questions relating to specific sites, activities, or programs. The data tends to provide little more than background information for most, more specific functional planning at the state level. From a national standpoint, these research efforts seldom result in data comparable from state to state. As the National Academy of Sciences (1975, p. 7) has concluded: "Reliance on a comprehensive planning model has led to a set of analytic techniques and data collection activities that are not appropriate for the decisions that are actually made."

Comprehensive planning, in the sense of considering all aspects of a problem and evaluating all solutions, is valid. As Farrell (1979, p. 74) has put it: "The most commonly asked question [of the researcher]...is: 'Did you consider...?' A negative reply to this question casts doubt on the reliability of the research product as a background product. Particularly important is the investigator's recognition of all the alternative courses of action open to the [decision-makers].

In summary, the comprehensive model, its use for Land and Water Conservation Fund eligibility requirements and especially the methodological difficulties with supply-demand-needs analyses, suggest that other, less ambitious approaches may be of more use to the management agency. Addressing specific, more narrowly defined issues of interest to the agency from an integrated policy and research-based planning framework may prove to be more useful and marketable.

Myth #3: Political considerations invariably decrease the quality of decisions about outdoor recreation provision.

"Politics," both external, partisan, and internal to the agency, can enter research, planning, and policy-making when: (1) the sheer number of major decisions to be made outstrips the agency's ability to conduct research, planning, and policy-making with respect to each decision; (2) events, such as changes in leadership, loss of funds, and staff turnovers occur; (3) the process takes too long, for example, year-long data collection to cover all four uses seasons, along with lengthly analyses, often presents a staggering time frame within which to address "immediate" problems; (4) the objectives of research, planning and policy-maker do not have agency-wide concurrence; (5) external public pressure is sufficiently great to increase agency anxiety over some aspect of research, planning, and policy-making; and (6) research, planning, or policy-making addresses some issues linked to the politically-related values of agency policy-makers.

Political decision-making does resolve issues, at least temporarily, although not always to everyone's liking. For many issues, particularly those "with an unspecified number of incalculable variables" as Ross (1978) would put it, there is not enough staff, time, resources, or faith in a comprehensive approach to justify anything other than a primarily "political" resolution. Political decision-makers can draw on the results of research, planning, and policy-making along with information from other sources (e.g., managers, other politicians, lobbyists, journalists, and their constituencies) to make their decisions (Shelby 1981). Virtually every major decision regarding public outdoor recreation provision will be "political" in some sense. The more surprising finding is that research, planning, and policy-making often has a significant bearing on the outcome of the decision.

Finally, government does not exist independently of political institutions, processes, and forces. To act otherwise as a member of a government agency, e.g., to try to plan or make policy without explicitly considering the political implications of your activities and recommendations, is naive and is tantamount to buying a one-way ticket to disaster. Good planning and policy-making must consider all relevant factors, whether or not one's personal or perceived professional inclination is to do otherwise.

<u>Myth #4</u>: Research, planning and policy-making models based on "optimization" are the most effective models for agencies.

The belief in "optimization" is consistent with the interest in comprehensive planning. Related maxims such as "agencies should maximize the satisfaction of their clients," "meet deficits," and "provide high quality experiences" are frequently voiced in the literature.

However, agencies operate on the basis of compromise, not optimization. Competing interests <u>within</u> agencies, which usually reflect competing external constituencies (e.g., between natural resource protection and provision of outdoor recreation opportunities) often can, at best, only result in plans and policies that are <u>acceptable</u> to the various interests within the agency. These plans and policies seldom maximize the interests of any single group, although they do usually result in agency movement toward meeting mandated responsibilities. As one source (Fairfax 1981, p. 200) puts it, "(g)iven the finite resource base and escalating user pressures, no group's demands will be fully met."

The assumption associated with the mathematical technique, linear programming, viz., optimization under various constraints, may be more realistic. Linear programming may prove to be a more promising model for many decision processes, although its precise data requirements have probably limited its applications to date.

At a minimum, understanding how tenacious competing interests within and external to an agency, as well as other involved government agencies, will be regarding their position on a specific project, program, plan, or policy, is crucial in all cases. Otherwise the compromise necessary to achieve some problem resolution will be difficult, if not impossible, to achieve.

<u>Myth #5</u>: Managers can conceptualize their problems, communicate them to researchers and planners and, in turn, will implement research findings or plan recommendations at a specific location or for a specific program.

Managers seldom have time to ponder the "big picture." The crush of day-to-day decisions is formidable. Little time is left to sit back, introspect, and shift from a concern with the specific to the general, e.g., to abstract researchable problems from the mass of activities with which they are <u>daily</u> involved. "Problems" are generally seen and discussed in terms of "too few dollars" and "too few staff," rather than in terms of underlying factors and their interrelationships.

Researchers and planners attempting to "directly" and conversationally determine the problems of managers, sometimes skeptically view the managers as having too much "spare time." This perception inhibits communication between managers and researchers and planners. Other, more effective and acceptable diagnostic methods are needed. In general, the busy person finds it easier to react to suggestions, especially in evaluative "like-dislike" terms, than to propose problem definitions, alternative solutions, etc. Often the vehemence of the manager's reaction is an indicator that something of importance has been tapped. This sort of back-and-forth approach to "teasing out" problems is time consuming, awkward, and is most effectively employed by someone with agency experience. The option of waiting for direction, definition, and structure from "above" is usually not a viable alternative ... it may never come. The initiative usually lies with the researcher, planner, or policy analyst.

Similarly, expecting the manager to seek out and apply research results, for example, expressed as implications in a typical journal article, or the recommendations of a comprehensive plan, such as a SCORP, especially at the site level, will require an effort on the researcher or planner's part beyond completing the plan. (See myth #7)

Myth #6: Basic research, with hypotheses generated from theoretical models and tested by sophisticated analytical techniques, is needed by the agency more than straightforward data gathering efforts.

Researchers, not surprisingly, usually have a strong interest in basic research and tend to believe that such research is what agencies really need. In addition, the details and time involved with large-scale, often tedious, data collection "studies" or inventories are not typically associated with the rewards researchers in most academic institutions receive.

Agencies, however, generally badly need the extensive data from such mundane studies to make decisions. Agencies often have responsibilities that require detailed information about specific locations, populations, resources, facilities, etc. Site, regional, statewide, and national information is necessary to make and support decisions within the agency, before the executive or legislature branch, and in courts of law. Without such extensive knowledge, those who disagree with a particular decision will usually claim it is based on opinion, not fact.

Extensive data on an issue, however, may eventually legitimize more basic research on the issue. Simply documenting the degree and extent of a problem may provide the "critical mass" needed to justify more careful and analytic investigations of underlying relationships, which, in turn, may better indicate resolutions of problems.

Myth #7: Researchers study phenomena and document their findings; planners produce plans with recommendations to guide agency activities; managers are responsible for implementing findings and following recommendations.

Researchers and planners are hesitant to become involved in the implementation of their findings, sometimes to the extent of not even making specific recommendations for managers. This separation of responsibilities is neat and clean and allows researchers and planners to easily determine when they are finished with an issue. However, within an agency, plans and studies typically will not be implemented without effort, sometimes considerable, by the researcher and planner. In some cases, the researcher or planner who is employed by the agency and does not make this effort may soon find himself working in another setting, leaving behind a shelf full of dusty documents.

Managers, on their own, will not automatically implement studies or plans. They are frequently left out of the research, planning, or policy-making process, and therefore, feel little concern about implementing what is to them an alien product. Unforeseen events may invalidate some study findings or plan recommendations and so, rather than salvage the still relevant results, the "baby is thrown out with the bathwater." On a more basic level, change may be threatening to managers. In order to improve the chances for implementation, managers need to be involved in the study, plan, or analysis from the beginning. They need to have substantive input into the why, what, where, how, and when of the effort. The direction of a study or plan may have to be altered after it commences if necessary to maximize its chances of being applicable to "new" agency realities (e.g., lower funding levels). Without this intimate association between the researcher, planner or analyst, and the manager, "on-the-ground" results of studies and plans may not occur.

When implementation does not occur, it reinforces opinions that research, planning, and policy analysis do not result in anything concrete and are unnecessary for the agency to support, either as a staff function or contractually. This perception over time makes it increasingly difficult for research, planning, and policy analysis to be funded, carried out, implemented, and ultimately play a useful role in the agency. The broader implications of a lack of interest and follow-through in implementation on the part of the researcher, planner, and policy analyst on the general image of and regard for their professions is also worthy of consideration.

Myth #8: Agency decision-makers look to planners for major policy guidance e.g., to "chart the course" of the agency over the next five, ten, etc. years.

Although the role of the planner within agencies, when viewed from the outside, is often idealized, the reality is that in many instances, planning and planners occur within agencies because of legislative mandates and the availability of associated federal or state funds. States in particular have encountered planning requirements tied to federal programs. SCORPs, State Comprehensive Fish and Wildlife Plans, and State Forest Plans are now, or have been, required to obtain federal funds. In these cases, planning occurs to maintain eligibility, as much as to provide direction to the agency. In many states, maintenance of eligibility is actually the overriding concern, as evidenced by the demise of many SCORP programs when state Land and Water Conservation Fund grants were terminated in 1982 by the Reagan administration.

However, staff identified as "planners" are often seen in agencies as the resolvers of "messes." When something goes wrong (i.e., a major controversy arises) planners are typically given the assignment. When the issue is particularly complex and may involve extensive public participation, planners are usually called on. Planners are seen as useful in these situations because: (1) they have specialized analytic skills and experience, (2) they are removed from day-to-day management and may be less biased, (3) they know how to get information, (4) they can synthesize a wide variety of information and points of view and achieve at least a reluctant consensus, and (5) they often write well.

Thus, planners can play a pivotal role in agencies, particularly in connection with controversial issues, even though they are not formally regarded as agency policy-makers.

SUGGESTIONS

There have been many suggestions made to improve the "researcher-manager relationship" (for example, Yoesting 1981). There have even been entire conferences devoted to this subject (U. S. Forest Service 1976). The following suggestions for outdoor recreation researchers, planners, and policy analysts interested in their work having an impact on government's management of outdoor recreation are related to the discussion in the preceding section and, as such, may be somewhat more basic.

Suggestion #1: Knowledge of the management agency is important; real understanding of the agency is half the battle.

We cannot emphasize enough the necessity of learning the organization. Research, planning, and policy analysis to improve outdooor recreation management has a much greater chance of success when it reflects the formal and informal goals, resources, and structure of the agency. The agency's mission and formal organization can be obtained from statutes, policy statements, and other public documents. Informal goals, less tangible resources (such as staff expertise), and structures are much more difficult to observe, infer, and understand, but well worth the effort in the long run.

Organizations can have "personalities" independent of the individuals staffing the organization. Understanding the history of an agency, the forces which have and are currently influencing its actions, its attitudes, and typical responses to situations can make the difference between successful research, planning, and policy-making and an exercise in frustration. For the student, courses in organizational behavior are recommended. For the academician, an open mind and patience are necessary. For the staff planner and researcher, flexibility and pragmatism are essential.

Suggestion #2: Researchers should be less reluctant to get involved in simple data collection efforts.

The collection, storage, management, and retrieval of information usually is of more immediate, if not long-term, interest to outdoor recreation management agencies than basic, or even theory-based applied research. Spending the time and effort to complete less glamorous research projects can allow the researcher to eventually pursue more specific research objectives after he or she has gained the trust and respect of managers. Furthermore, once a close relationship is established, the results of research may begin to have a bearing on the agency.

Although academic reward systems have often considered projects such as statewide resource inventories as theoretically trivial, perceptions of the worth of these efforts can be improved under certain circumstances. Often the inventory of a natural resource is associated with citizen efforts to protect the resource (e.g., natural areas). Similarly, citizen surveys and facility inventories may be used to partially guide new capital improvement initiatives. Under these circumstances, the data collection effort becomes part of a larger movement with attendant publicity, recognition, and broader opportunities for involvement by the researcher sensitive to these possibilities.

Suggestion #3: Researchers, planners, and policy analysts should focus their efforts on intermediate-range problems.

Farrell (1979, p. 74) states that research that focuses on immediate problems will generally not interest decision-makers since they are usually forced to make their decisions within a short time frame. Research related to long-range problems also will usually be of little interest to decision-makers, particularly elected officials. Their "horizon" is typically the next term or session and long-range direction, even though it may be of value, simply is not within their perceived sphere of control. In order to be a basis for government decision-making, research, planning and policy analysis efforts are most productively spent on intermediate-range problems.

Suggestion #4: Long-term involvement between researchers, planners, and policy analysts and the manager, as implied by both of the previous suggestions, will have a positive effect on agency decision making.

Long-term involvement leads to better understanding of the agency on the part of researchers and to better understanding of the value of research by managers. The involvement is not likely, however, to be gained by annual conferences or semi-annual meetings designed to pay lip-service to this often repeated suggestion.

Real understanding will only occur through long-term, sincere, and sensitive attempts to really know the managers and the agency. This will not be easy, but it is possible. For the researcher, planner, and policy analyst who is sincerely interested in making a real contribution to the public provision of outdoor recreation, mutual understanding and respect is crucial to attaining this satisfaction.

Conclusions

It is often difficult for the student and the academician who emerge from an environment where research, planning, and policy-making are generally highly valued activities to accept the realities of life in most outdoor recreation management agencies. In the agency, the terms "research," "planning," and "analysis" may, in fact, have basically negative connotations and policy-making, at least in its explicit forms, may be a carefully guarded perogative of the few and powerful.

In many states, the legislature views research as a function of "research agencies" or universities, but definitely not of management agencies. However, the management agency's ability to influence a research agency or university to do the type of research it needs is often limited because of small budgets for research, reflecting the legislature's views, and, more recently, difficult economic times, which have resulted both in an inability to pay for needed research and increased difficulty in influencing the research agencies' and universities' priorities. These priorities are often more sensitive to the interests of individual researchers and the need to spread resources across many areas, instead of investing in the expensive collecting of the massive amounts of data often needed by the management agency. In addition, attitudes within the management agency itself often uncritically reflect the attitudes of the legislature, and sometimes the executive branch budget agency. That is, the manager may come to believe that if research has so much trouble obtaining funds in the budgetary process, it must not be all that important.

Similarly, planning is less than unanimously popular in management agencies. Good planning is usually specific enough to place contraints on decision-makers. Often these decision-makers are powerful, independent-minded agency personnel who resent having their actions dictated by a document. If this document was prepared to satisfy requirements for federal funds, its legitimacy is that much easier to question.

Similarly, policy-making abstracted from daily problems and specific instances related to a policy concern is seen by most policy-makers as a low priority activity. However, policy made under crisis circumstances for single instances is often confounded enough by the unique characteristics of the specific instance that it is inadequate for the next application of the policy. Further, in all cases policy-making is viewed as an important prerequisite for power and even the suggestion of an explicit policy-making process based upon planning is often enough of a threat to be viewed with suspicion.

Therefore, research, planning, and policy-making do not always occur within a supportive agency atmosphere. The life of the agency researcher, planner, or policy analyst, whether permanent staff or consultant, may be difficult and, for some intolerable. However, for those who have left their naivete behind, the management agency can be a vigorous, challenging, and exciting environment which provides a real opportunity for public service.

Planners, researchers, and policy analysts do have a role to play, if they can master the subtle rules of the game. Although their chosen fields of endeavor may never be regarded with the same esteem in the agency as they are elsewhere, to the extent that the researcher can provide information and answers to problems which make the manager's job easier; to the extent that the planner becomes a problem solver, especially when the agency is in a difficult situation; and to the extent that an exercise in policy-making results in consensus among acrimonious, competing interests within the agency, the researcher, planner, or policy analyst may be regarded as truly a member of the management team.

References

Fairfax, S. K. "RPA and the Forest Service." In *A Citizen's Guide to the Forest and Rangeland Renewable Resources Planning Act,* edited by E. Shands. Washington, D.C.: U.S. Forest Service, 1981.

Farrell, W. J. "Advising State Legislators on Environmental Issues." *The Environmental Professional* 1(1979):71-77.

Hendee, J. C., and Burdge, R. J. "The Substitutibility Concept: Implications for Recreation Research and Management." *Journal of Leisure Research* 6(1974):155-162.

National Academy of Sciences. *Assessing Demand for Outdoor Recreation.* Prepared for the USDI Bureau of Outdoor Recreation, 1975.

Ross, J. D. "Comprehensive Provincial and Regional Planning for Outdoor Recreation." *Recreation Research Review* 6(1978):39-45.

Shelby, B. "Research, Politics, and Resource Management Decisions: A Case Study of River Research in Grand Canyon." *Leisure Sciences* 4(1981):281-296.

U.S. Forest Service. *Proceedings of the Southern States Recreation Research Applications Workshop.* Asheville, North Carolina: Southeastern Forest Experiment Station, 1976.

Yoesting, D. R. "Research Utilization in Decision-Making." In *Outdoor Recreation Planning, Perspectives and Research,* edited by T. L. Napier. Debuque, Iowa: Kendall/Hunt.

Yu, J. "A Leisure Demand Projection Model." *Leisure Sciences* 4(1981): 127-142.

5

Planning and Research: Forging a Partnership for Recreation's Future

Wilbur F. LaPage

Two decades ago, Morton Grodzins alluded to the "chaos of confusion" that is public outdoor recreation with its numerous agencies, missions, and jurisdictions. Over the years, that chaos has doubled and redoubled as a result of new agencies, new laws, and new conflicts. By 1976, public outdoor recreation was being labelled a "policy wasteland," characterized by conflicting public policies, an almost complete lack of agreed-upon professional direction, intense fragmentation, and a disturbing habit of allowing itself to become the pawn of other "more important" public policies. The millions we spent on research and planning in the sixties failed to produce the slightest doubt about recreation's expendibility in the energy-short seventies. Our mad dash to buy more and more land for public parks succeeded only in producing a net loss of more than one-half acre per person between 1960 and 1980! Perhaps if a fraction of those billions of dollars had gone into a fund to encourage private land development, we would not have the lack of growth that now characterizes nearly all outdoor recreation industries! And, perhaps if another fraction had gone into maintenance of existing facilities, we would not have the deteriorated public recreation estate that exists today! Such failures can not be attributed to a lack of planning. We had a plan; but it was a plan preoccupied with the long range at the expense of the immediate future!

Beginning with the third Nationwide Outdoor Recreation Plan, we began to join the real world of incremental decision-making. With the initiation of a system of annual assessments and updates, we recognized that outdoor recreation in America does not lend itself to rational comprehensive analysis and long-range planning. But, we are still a long way from implementing an alternative system of planning where a variety of periodic indicators provides us with: (1) measures of how well we are performing as a profession to meet society's needs, and (2) an opportunity to make needed "mid-course" adjustments.

FROM MASTER PLANNING TO "MUDDLING THROUGH"

A pattern of philosophical evolution in both the planning and research arms of the recreation profession is apparent. The concept of an emerging crisis of demand outstripping supply had a powerful influence throughout the 1950's and the 1960's. The response of planners tended to be one of documenting the extent of the supply deficiency, while many researchers focused on better methods to predict the recreational demands for the use of our public lands. Neither discipline seemed eager to embrace the idea of attacking the issue head-on. Thoughts about expanding supply by using the private sector, or that demand might be reduced to noncrisis levels by increasing fees were unrealistic. Eventually, both concepts caught fire (private sector expansion first, and cost-based fees more recently), but in neither case were the efforts of public sector planners and researchers particularly influential.

Not surprisingly, the crisis mentality also encouraged researchers with a natural resources background to invest heavily in the concept of resource carrying capacity as a tool for limiting use in advance of the crisis. While a complex set of natural, social, and managerial variables ultimately served to limit the usefulness of carrying capacity as a tool for planners, planning was evolving from predicting growth to controlling growth! Eventually, carrying capacity, as a research thrust, would give way to studies of recreation experience quality: what is quality and what influences it? Since most planners tend to be advocates for whatever it is they are planning for, it will be interesting to see whether a concern for "quality of experiences" will strongly influence research and planning in the future.

The crisis concerns of the fifties and sixties dimmed noticeably throughout the 1970's as a combined result of enormous private sector growth and a massive federally-supported expansion of public resources at the state and local level. And, our planning philosophies further evolved in the direction of strong goal orientation. What can each sector of an agency do best? How can we share the load and avoid competition? What do people want as opposed to what have they been doing? Research responded to the changing times with studies designed to answer or help answer some of these questions: What are the various recreation market trends? What substitutions will people make between activities, destinations, and sectors? How can we best encourage citizen participation in the planning process? For both researchers and planners, recreation in the 1970's was increasingly being viewed in subjective ways; the search for hard answers was giving way to soft, temporary, dynamic solutions.

The 1980's seem to be starting out as the decade of decision for recreation planning and research. Strong currents for a "national assessment" of the role of recreation in America, though much in evidence, are being diluted by a tide of enormous reductions in federal support for data gathering, research, and planning. However, the needs for information and the mandates for planning still exist. The growth in numbers of private recreation planning consultants and research firms specializing in recreation market trend data is clearly evident and destined to continue. And, the trend should be considered a natural and very healthy development for both the planning and research disciplines! The idea of a market, and a profit potential, for recreation research might have been scoffed at two decades ago. In a free enterprise economy, this change can only be interpreted as having "arrived," and those pioneering public sector planners and researchers who helped bring it about should feel a sense of satisfaction.

The customary objectives of research — the visitor and the resource — so common in the past two decades, are now shifting in the direction of management and policy-making processes. If this decade is to continue with its initial promise of being one of decision, we will need to have vastly improved data and monitoring systems in place to: (1) document the costs of producing all kinds of recreational experiences, (2) assess the relative performance of various management strategies, and (3) estimate the social and economic impacts of changing recreation programs and policies. Planning and research must work together to meet the challenge of providing responsive data systems and imaginative program alternatives. And, the impetus for planners and researchers to work together can only come from a new sense of professional self-interest. Political activism is a professional imperative, but it can not be effective if it lacks carefully researched facts and logical alternative plans.

THE PROFESSIONAL FOUNDATION

Three essential elements, competency, dedication, and dignity, are the hallmarks of any professional activity. In a free, pluralistic, society like ours, criticism can be considered the "grease" that makes our political machinery work to accomplish social goals. As such, becoming "political," in the sense of providing constructive criticism, is a professional as well as a personal responsibility; it is not something to be avoided or apologetic about! But criticism, to be professional and constructive, must pass the tests of competency, dedication, and dignity. Failure to do so can only diminish a profession's credibility and usefulness to the community it serves.

Competency is the lifeblood and the primary marketable commodity of any professional. It is that combination of skill, training, and experience that allows surgeons to operate, educators to teach, and lawyers to represent their clients. If there is a common thread binding the diversity of disciplines that make up the park and recreation profession it is the ability to provide recreation programs, facilities, and resources to meet the specialized needs of all segments of society. How the professional accomplishes that task is a function of individual skill and organizational purpose. It is not (and must not be allowed to be) a variable level of performance responding to peaks and dips in public recognition and support. To state, as Gray and Greben have, that "1974-1978...was a brief period when we could enjoy the luxury of being creative, of dreaming about what 'is possible', and then using our intellect and problem-solving abilities..." does a serious disservice to a profession which puts its creativity, intellect, and problem-solving abilities on the line for society each and every day. And to further state that "the intense period of ...concern for the quality of life was short," seems to make some prejudgments about both our professional goals and our federal administration's motives which are patently absurd!

Competency without dedication is as useless as a stamp without glue. If competency is our lifeblood, then dedication is the heart that pumps it. Dedication is what drives some among us to demand reinstatement of federal grant-in-aid programs for parks and recreation. Such dedication is professional if goal oriented, and self-serving if it is simply an attempt to perpetuate a means of achieving goals. As a means, federal grant programs do employ a lot of professionals; but are they the only, or even the best, way to deliver recreation services to the American public? There are, obviously, many ways of delivering needed recreation services. Technical competency isn't tied to a single method. In fact, new technologies, new and better ways of doing the job, often borne of necessity, characterize most socially responsive professions.

Of course locally designed and developed systems will result in varied standards among fifty states, but is that really undesirable? Won't that produce even greater professional challenge and opportunity for growth? The Land and Water Conservation Fund was a direct result of a sound recommendation by the Outdoor Recreation Resources Review Commission. That recommendation, clearly recognizing the states' dominant public responsibility and the importance of their retaining the "pivotal role," saw the fund only as a federal "stimulus." Nearly two decades of federal encouragement ought to be ample by any standards.

Examples of misplaced dedication, dedication to what we believe is best instead of what the public wants, seem to abound in our profession. Right now, for example, three of the four major federal agencies that provide camping opportunities are "experimenting" with concession management on a few of their campgrounds. And, in every case, the concessionaire is constrained from providing a camp store. Dedication to perpetuating the status quo, in this case, is directly in opposition to dedication to serving the recreating public, or even dedication to an established national goal of energy conservation. The federal perception of an "appropriate recreation experience" must be maintained even at the cost of sending millions of campers several miles to the nearest store, draining away millions of leisure hours from their recreation experiences, and wasting millions of gallons of gasoline, rather than allowing a few delivery trucks to do the same job! Without the supplemental store income, the campground "experiment" will likely fail; and another threat to our professional supremacy will have been neatly countered.

As essential as they are, technical competence and dedication usually need the "packaging" of professional pride, salesmanship, and dignity to be effective. This is not the false dignity of superiority, but rather that which flows from self-confidence in ones' ability to serve, and the assurance of knowing ones' facts and plans are sound.

Dignity, for individuals and professions alike, means above all else self-sufficiency. For too many years, heavily subsidized public recreation has offered a puzzling contradiction to the claims of recreation and parks professionals that their services contribute to human dignity. How exactly does a $100,000/year dentist from Boston find dignity by letting the taxpayers pay for his two-week stay in the Bob Marshall Wilderness Area? Unfair example you say? Perhaps, but have you taken a hard look lately at who is using your grant-in-aid developed tennis courts, bike paths, jogging trails, and campgrounds? While you're doing that, take a look at how much of your operating budget is covered by user fees! A consistently ignored finding from twenty years of outdoor recreation research is that the people who are using our public parks and recreation areas can usually afford to pay the costs. It should be obvious that across-the-board subsidies will always fail to provide assistance to the truly disadvantaged by artificially inflating demand and crowding them out, while simultaneously reducing the availability of public capital for special programs. Available research which fails to influence our policies, our plans, and our hopes to better serve America seems to suggest that further research is a poor investment!

Subsidies are not generally regarded as a hallmark of dignity. Similarly, endowments for parks may be a good short-run investment, but only if they contribute to helping the profession walk alone at some realistic point in the future. Has our historic record of across-the-board subsidies really served to strengthen a single benefit argument, develop a constituency, or foster individual and professional dignity?

Both the parks user and the recreation profession have been subsidized for years. Rather than being thankful for the investment, we seem to be acting churlish to our benefactors and suggesting that we aren't ready to stand on our own. If ever a time of professional challenge existed for parks and recreation, it is now. The practice of professionalism demands that we come forward with soundly researched alternative plans, not simple criticisms.

TODAY: THE FUTURE WE FORGOT TO PLAN FOR

Plans are primarily tools to implement policy. And, policy is, or should be, a logical extension of philosophy. Where are our recreation policies! Do they reflect recreation philosophy? Lacking coherent, logical, broadly-supported policies, recreation planning becomes little more than an exercise in writing wish lists. If we can not convincingly support today's programs with documented facts about their costs and benefits, don't blame the budget cutters; the fault lies in our own professional weakness! If twenty years of research and planning haven't improved our competitive standing, we obviously need to take a hard look at our professional leadership.

The record of the past two decades is clearly one of data-deficient planning. In the absence of available and reliable data, planning tends to be long-range. The poorer the data, the longer the range! Had we recognized the need for a few reliable data series to monitor the condition and trend of recreation in America, we would, today, be engaged in extremely short-range planning soundly based on readily available situation assessments.

A number of future scenarios about the research-planning relationship are possible. Most probable, however, are those which recognize the realities of shrinking federal support for research which is not keyed to the goals of: (1) strengthening the public-private partnership, (2) limiting the role of government, and (3) increasing the cost-benefit ratio of public investments. The goals, for the present at least, are clear. Recreational planning must ultimately chart the course for moving us, as a society, toward achievement of those goals. And, research must take responsibility for identifying the barriers, and monitoring our progress. The luxury of researchers and planners "doing their own thing" was an interesting, perhaps necessary, era; but it belongs in the past. Today's planner must be the catalyst for developing continuous data series to monitor recreation's social contributions, and for finding ways to ensure that those current and relevant measures of merit get attention in the political arena. Real professional expertise will usually do well in that area.

References

Gray, D. E., and Greben, S. "Future Perspectives II: The 1980's and Beyond." *Parks and Recreation* vol. 17, no. 5, NRPA, Alexandria, Virginia, 1982.

Grodzins, M. "The Many American Governments and Outdoor Recreation." In *Trends in American Living and Outdoor Recreation,* pp. 62-68. Washington, D.C.: Government Printing Office, 1962.

Braybrooke, D., and Lindbloom, C. *A Strategy for Decision: Policy Evaluation as a Social Process.* Glen Cove, New York: The Free Press, 1963.

LaPage, W. F. "Public Outdoor Recreation: A Policy Wasteland." In *Critical Conservation Choices: A Bicentennial Look,* pp. 183-188. Soil Conservation Society of America, 1976.

USDI, National Park Service. "Public Recreation Acreage Growth and Distribution in the Past 20 Years." (mimeo) Washington, D.C.: USDI, 1982.

6

Managing the Research Function for More Effective Policy Formulation and Decision-Making

Jay Beaman
Scott Meis

It has become fairly commonplace in the applied social science research field, in general, and in tourism and recreation research specifically, to lament the lack of relevant information relating to planning and implementation decisions regarding facility development, services, and other policy. On the other hand, it is also usual to lament the lack of sufficient resources or time for sophisticated and elaborate studies concerning such matters as social carrying capacity, social and economic impacts, etc. Indeed, several recent reviews have argued that most (Driver and Knopf 1981, Rossi 1974, Dimaggio 1980) research and information generated in the field is relatively ineffective or irrelevant to applied decision-making processes. We contend that this state of affairs arises as a result of either an inappropriate organizational environment for applied research, or insufficient or inappropriate management of the applied research and information exchange processes. A corollary is that the effective utilization of applied social research in policy formulation and decision-making depends upon a careful management of the interface between the research and the decision-making functions.

In recent years, the most crucial advance in both applied social research and management information systems (MIS) has been an understanding of the need for active and careful management of the research and information systems processes (Schwarzhart 1979, Rossi 1974). Experience has made it clear that most applied research and MIS projects have had gross overestimates of their expected benefits and their relevance and impact. There has also been a gross underestimate of associated costs, labour, and time requirements for such projects. This has led to frustration, broken promises, eroded confidence, and bad feelings between management and their research and systems development groups. It has meant that much research was ineffective. Even where researchers have strived to be relevant, work has often been of low professional quality.

While the judgments just made are leveled at the social and information sciences in general, it doesn't take much literature review or thoughtful reflection to realize that they are also equally applicable to research in the specific field of tourism. However, with the benefit of hindsight, or from the position of a detached observer of the field, it is much easier to identify weaknesses than it is to suggest possible corrective measures. Applied research by its very definition involves practical problem solving. The processes by which research projects are defined, initiated, and carried out and by which resulting information is successfully integrated into decision-making and policy formation, are not well developed. Based on our experience and reviews of the rather considerable literature, there appear to be a series of prescriptions that are essential for success. This chapter makes many of these clear as we see them.

ORGANIZATIONAL PREREQUISITES FOR EFFECTIVE RESEARCH

Often there is a failure to adequately recognize organizational factors that are outside a researcher's control as critical to effective research. A supportive organizational environment is such a prerequisite. An appropriate organizational situation is essential if most of what we suggest is to be relevant to a research manager, much less useful. Actually, there are several important organizational prerequisites relating to senior management's use of applied research as a decision-making aid.

Senior management support is necessary in setting the tone, style, and criteria used in research. Ultimately, it is senior management who are accountable for whether or not organizational structure and processes are in place to facilitate research and its use. Senior management responsible for research will not in general, and need not, have special research skills. However, they must understand and to some degree approve "research." At the least, certain critical seniors managers must recognize and be able to explain the limits of research to organizational equals and superiors. If research is to be effective, the senior manager to whom the tourism research function reports must certainly play a powerful role in decision-making. Playing a powerful role means having the organizational power to see that important issues that should be researched are usually researched. The preceding is meant to imply that senior management has a reasonable commitment to taking action based on research findings, along with other decision inputs and to supporting some general research, as part of the necessary conditions for having an effective research function. In other words, senior managers must make decisions as if there were a genuine commitment to both informed decision-making and specific and general research to support this. This is rather than just creating the appearance of such a commitment.

Following from the point just raised, the research function must have a high reporting level in the organization; and there must be direct, albeit informal, channels of communication between the research function and organization decision-makers at all levels. In the nonsupportive organization, the reporting level of the research function is frequently low. As a consequence, the results of a unit's work have no symbolic authority. Research can thus be automatically designed as noninfluential. Quite apart from its vertical orientation, formal communication paths between researchers and other functional decision-makers are characteristically nonexistent or of dubious value. If research results are to be relevant and timely, multiple informal direct and open channels of communication must exist between the research function and research users involved in the decision-making processes.

One other important organizational prerequisite for effectiveness of tourism research, is the designation of a person who is functionally accountable for the quality and effectiveness of tourism research. In other words, a position within the organization needs to be identified as "tourism research," with functional responsibility for managing the research activity, including its interface with other functions, professional quality, and effectiveness. When we speak here of research management, we use the term management in the sense of a very direct concern with the rational (i.e., ends-means) allocation of resources but not to imply a superior to subordinate authority over most researchers. In the case of the applied research game, the concept of functional responsibility is further specified as playing a lead role in the rational and efficient allocation of resources toward research activities leading to the achievement of organization decision-making goals and objectives.

In this context, it is our contention that effective senior research managers must spend much of their time engaging in two main general activities: research planning, and research and information coupling.

By research planning we mean the specific activities of: (1) identifying potential areas for research support and establishing needs, rationales, and priorities for supporting these; (2) selecting appropriate research to support given finite resources; (3) selecting the modes and resource levels for supporting such research; (4) reviewing research activities to see that they are well planned and that they remain "on track" throughout all stages of their execution; and (5) assessing the successes and failures of research and appropriately modifying project selection, priority criteria, resourcing, etc.

The term "research coupling activity" is used to describe the communication and organizational structuring activities directed towards dialogue between researchers and user groups. It should be noted that these communication processes should be two-way. They involve communicating needs to researchers and involve researchers working with uses to make effective applications of research results (Price 1959).

PLANNING AND RESOURCING PRESCRIPTIONS FOR THE RESEARCH MANAGER

For both planning and coupling activities, it is possible to present a number of prescriptions for success. Obviously, in research management, substantial attention and importance must be given to the research planning process (Price 1969,

p. 46; Price 1965, p. 19). The selection of the research problems that make up the research program of a private firm or mission oriented agency is a difficult matter. It is characterized by few guidelines, many choices, high costs, high risks, and slow and uncertain results (Price 1969; Brooks 1967; Weinberg 1966). The success stories are far less numerous than the failures. Careful planning is essential to minimize the risks and reap some of the potential benefits involved. Having a good program is very different from recognizing a number of "user requirements" and responding to these according to some priority plan.

Identification and Specification of Research Problems   The single most important part of the overall planning process is the identification and specification of research problems. Users are often not the appropriate people to define research needs, at least not with sufficient specificity to provide an adequate basis for research. Nevertheless, their input is critical in defining problems! Particular care and attention must be given to identifying how the product from the proposed research is to be used by the tourism policy-maker or decision-maker (Caplan 1975b; Berg 1978). Relevant research is research that answers the real questions of persons participating in decisions. The pivotal phase in developing relevant research is framing questions. An obvious concern is deciding whose questions! The importance of this aspect of relevancy was specifically identified by Beaman (1976) as a weakness in Parks Canada's early work in tourism research. He also has identified a requirement in education for tourism research to educate researchers to define problems, not to (a) meet information requests, (b) investigate in vogue hypotheses, or (c) fit all problems to a "PET" method, etc.

Elaborate front-end research planning and review processes have been introduced by government for almost all surveys of people or businesses when these are carried out by or for a Canadian or U.S. government department. Yet the major weakness in such "government control processes" is that they focus on sophisticated data collection, not on real needs. Whether valid analyses to achieve applied (e.g., decision) objectives are part of a research plan is not easily subject to external review. Client's statements that they need data and do or will use them to plan or "evaluate" X are usually not challenged or adequately verified! Actually, it is questionable if any bureaucracy can, on a continuous basis, cope with such management decision related formal critique across organizational units. We feel such matters must be handled internally through planning and coupling and review or by periodic functional audit.

Setting Priorities   Setting priorities for research is certainly the next most critical matter when problems are well defined. However, setting priorities and determining if a priority system is giving good results is not a simple exercise. This is not to say that many simplistic and/or arbitrary approaches are being used! The following sections of this chapter provide "soft" criteria variables to consider in prioritizing, organizing (putting various needs into one project), and selecting research. The critical prescription is that a unidimensional or additive scale is not the way to select a research program. An obvious critical step is acknowledging work that must be done one way or another, as well as expected continuing research or data generation. An examination of such a research program to see if numbers of projects, their types, and dollars meet some of the balances cited below, as well as meeting user needs, is good prioritizing. Keeping such judgmental material to review in assessing achievement and modifying the resourcing approach is also important.

Searching For Standard Response Modes To Structured Problems   The efficient research manager is constantly searching for ways to attain more leverage on his work load by identifying standard problems and converting their solutions from expensive, one-time research to more cost efficient activities using administrative routines or data, using automated systems, or using other management science tools. The important consideration in managing the research work load in terms of this objective is the extent to which decision-making needs are highly structured (Keen and Scott-Morton 1979). Simon (1965) used the terms <u>programmed</u> and <u>non-programmed tasks</u> to describe activities that could be prespecified by a set of rules or decision procedures from those decisions that are one-time or recurring but based on changing criteria. The point they all make is that highly structured problems can be routinized or automated. Semistructured problems, on the other hand, are not so amenable to routine research solutions. Unstructured or judgmental problems can only be partially supported by research and information systems (Keen and Scott-Morton 1978). Given an analysis of various decision-support systems (DSS), the appropriate research response can vary from developing clerical processes (Keen and Scott-Morton 1978) to developing a data base and associated analysis systems. Such analysis may lead to systematic questions and definition of alternatives to present research methods and related allocation of resources. Certainly if it shows that structured decision-making can be supported by cost effective developments, these will probably have high developmental priority. Still the most common research in the tourism business tends to be the one-time research study.

At the same time as he constantly attempts to convert decision support responses from costly one-time research projects to routine information systems, the research manager must never forget that even routinized and automated "research" or misfunctions must be subject to occasional review for cost effectiveness. Their continued value must be assessed, since, in so far as it is part of structured decision-making, one makes virtually fixed commitments of resources to such "structured research." The relevance of such work and the percent of a budget committed to such activity should always be questioned!

Tailoring Research Scale and Scope to Users' Decision Requirements   In addition to considering the mode of research, the research manager must frequently judge the appropriate scope and scale of the research activity required to adequately satisfy the decision-makers needs. The successful tourism research and information system manager has no shortage of problems. In fact, he often finds himself besieged with requests, problems, and proposals. In order to make the most of his resources, the research manager must be conscious of, and skilled at (1) determining the scale scope and precision of projects and (2) selecting the appropriate mode of response to each request. This involves considerations of level of aggregation, and scope and degree of accuracy required. The users budget alone should not be the criterion dictating accuracy or elaborateness of methodology! The variables, appropriate aggregation and scope and degree of accuracy needed, are themselves a function of the level of decision-making being addressed and the stage of the decision process of the users concerned (Ritchie 1980).

The size of an organization is important. In general, big tourism organizations can affect and collect much more extensive and expensive data and get included in more grandiose analysis endeavors than small ones (Ritchie 1980). Governments collect and hopefully use more data than individual operators of tourist enterprises. Hotels, lodges, golf courses, etc., most often must bond together regionally to participate in major data collection and to carry out elaborate analyses.

The level of management of the user is also a significant consideration. Ritchie (1980) and Antony (1965) have clearly pointed out that within an organization the level of management influences the level of decision-making processes and the nature of the research or information systems responses required. In this regard, top management in large organizations generally has a strong interest in strategic planning that involves setting organizational objectives and formulating overall policies. Management control and tactical planning, largely carried out by middle management, is concerned with issues such as facility location, new product development, and budget preparation. Operational planning and control focuses on the effective use of existing facilities and resources to carry out activities (Ritchie 1980). Information requirements differ at each of these levels of activity. These differences are cited by Ritchie (1980, p. 341) as follows: "In general, strategic planning requires more outside information, less accuracy, and more summarization than tactical planning. Management control and planning tends to require more accurate (reliable), precise (valid), current time series data than strategic planning. Operations activities tend to use data in a less aggregate form than management control." These are only some of the more striking differences in the characteristics of information required by the different decision-making levels. Somewhat similarly, the stage of the client in their decision-making process affects the degree of rigour and precision required of the research response. For example, Ritchie (1980), in discussing the development of tourism information systems, cites an elaboration (Davis 1974) of Simon's (1960) three stage decision-making model. The different information service responses appropriate to each stage of the decision-making process are claimed to be: (1) intelligence (problem recognition), (2) design (solution identification and analysis), and (3) and choice (choice, implementation, feedback).

Without careful management of this aspect of the research process, waste of research resources or failure to communicate to management occurs. Most often, either data are collected to a level of detail not needed by the management involved; or data are reported to management in so much detail that they are unused because they would require further analysis by management themselves to discern the relevant from the trivial. One extreme is when data are obtained at a level of statistical accuracy that is irrelevant for their intended use as a basis for long-range forecasts or market estimates. When guesses on the future are made using the data based on high sampling accuracy, resources are wasted. Information + 25%, + 50% or even + 100% are acceptable. There are many more ineffective, inefficient, and inept practices, but the key to avoiding them all involves intelligently tailoring research to the client's needs.

Maintaining Project Flexibility   While it is crucial for the reasons noted above to target research projects to satisfy specific decision-makers requirements, it is nevertheless also desirable to strike a balance between obtaining information of specific relevance and obtaining that which is likely to be generally useful or useful in the longer run. In this way the manager builds a broader base of support for a project, thus protecting it from changes in the specific focus of the clients interest or changes in the decision-makers during the life cycle of the project.

Such a balance can be struck. First, one designs and rationalizes studies in terms of certain primary objectives relating to the specific needs of specific organizational clients. At the same time, however, one plans and designs the studies to also satisfy certain secondary information objectives relating to less specific, less clearly defined, or possible future needs. By thus mixing specific research objectives with general objectives, the work is relevant to some needs even after the research is completed and the client or the decision problem has changed.

Maintaining a Work Load Mix of Both Broad and Narrow Scope Projects   In addition to taking project-specific planning actions, such as those described previously, the effective research manager exercises care and judgment in planning his or her overall program of research activities. As a part of this planning process, special consideration must often be given to the mix between studies of broad phenomena, such as mass leisure trends, and studies of specific focal points within those fields. While an agency's research program should have a "centre of gravity of interest" (Price 1966) which meets the needs of the agency it supports, the distribution of projects must, at the same time, not be restricted by too narrow a definition of relevance. It should be recognized that areas of research such as tourism and outdoor recreation behaviour may have special importance to several mission-oriented organizations and that support of these areas by more than one agency can be important, not only to assure adequate research support in these vital areas, but also to provide an added basis for communication between the agencies within the field (Price 1966). A mix of work, both of broad, and narrow scope, is also justifiable given the uncertainties in our knowledge of tourism phenomena. Providing a mix of broad and narrow projects ensures that results of any particular study, or even the relevance and use of new findings to an agency such as Parks Canada or any industry in the tourism sector can occur even when new alternatives for projects are being considered or needs have changed in other ways.

Maintaining a Mix of Both Basic and Applied Research   To be effective in the long run, it is very important for the tourism research manager to understand and to successfully manage the interface between applied and basic research in the social science (Price 1966, Rossi 1978). While the dividing line is by no means always clear, the distinguishing criterion between the two types of research is the purpose for which the research is primarily conducted. Applied research is conducted to aid in the solution of some real world problems, while basic research, in contrast, is conducted to enhance our knowledge of a phenomena. In Coleman's (1973) words, applied research is "decision oriented" while basic research is "phenomena" or "discipline" oriented. In other words, one is technology, the other is science.

The common conceptual model assumes a linear relationship between these two areas of science and technology. On the other hand, a number of recent studies have shown that the relationship between these two areas of endeavor is fundamentally interactive: each field facilitates but does not produce developments in the other. More specifically, new science sustains further scientific development in the context of a permissive ambient technology. Similarly, technological developments lead to still further technology in the context of a permissive ambient science. In other words, research indicates that one does not usually find a phenomena-oriented research result producing a new and unexpected opportunity which then stimulates a new technological opportunity and vice versa. In summary then, studies of the relation between science and technology do not support the conventional model of science and technology, as a process in which unique scientific events are followed in an orderly manner by applied research developments (Price 1968). Instead, each fosters development in the other. For this reason, it is important to maintain staff involvement in a mix of the two different types of research.

It would, for example, be a mistake in designing a tourist agency's research program, to allocate virtually all of the research budget to projects that support very specific applied technological goals. Such a commitment would not be fully successful since it assumes a direct and simple relationship between the general research program and the technology development. For example, if Parks Canada and all tourist organizations and agencies were to do primarily statistical analysis, survey design, and demand model research, they would end up with more applied technology but very little general knowledge and conceptual development. This, in fact, is very much the state of affairs that some feel most characterizes tourism and outdoor recreation studies in general (Coleman 1980, Stankey 1981). The weaknesses of such an approach are threefold. First, there is an absence of a broad continuous flow of information. Second, there is little opportunity to develop a general field-wide trend toward increasing sophistication in handling technological problems. Third, there is no development and elaboration of organizing conceptual frameworks that integrate research findings across applications (Stankey 1981).

The Decision to Make or Buy Research   The successful and efficient tourism research manager also strategically controls the mix between work conducted in-house and that contracted out-of-house to university or private industry consultants. He/she not only allocates resources to projects based on priorities, he/she makes rational decisions on resources to hire and those to buy. Problems frequently crop up that demand skills or expertise that are unavailable or that one cannot afford to maintain.

Appropriate decisions in this realm are important in several respects. Appropriately chosen and judiciously applied contract researchers extend the manager's leverage on his work load. They can also reduce the risk associated with particularly tricky projects. When the experienced research manager encounters some of the following conditions associated with a particular research project, out-of-house contracting is frequently his best approach:

1. There are short-term needs for specialized knowledge and skill that are outside in-house capabilities.

2. There is a need for objectivity and a fresh view to concentrate attention on problem identification and specification of research.

3. A project or assignment has to be performed promptly and on schedule to

be relevant to the management decision-making process, but the size of the internal staff or previous commitment limit the internal capability to respond in a timely fashion.

4. An independent researcher is needed to say something that members of the agency cannot say because of policy, credibility, or political considerations.

5. Cost-saving advantages are possible in buying into syndicated research programs. (Heit 1978).

6. There is a need to expand and contract frequently to deal with field work and analysis activity at peak and slack work periods and prevent project backlogs from developing (Foreman and Bailey 1969).

7. There is need or desire to shift the financial responsibility for the research over to the user and away from the in-house research unit (Foreman and Bailey 1969). This may be to see if the client really thinks the research is worth what it costs!

8. Research requires contract staff to compensate for their inability to recruit competent in-house researchers because of some larger organizational problem, such as a nonresponsive staffing function (Foreman and Bailey 1969) or simply due to pay scale and lack of availability of persons at the rates paid to in-house staff.

9. There is a need for theoretical, conceptual, or methodological development work that cannot be justified as a priority item on the workload of an in-house applied research unit but can be funded (resourced) at a low level by contract (e.g., with universities).

While the research manager gains certain strategic or political advantages from contract research, it too has its limitations. Principle among them are the following:

1. The particular problem at hand may require an extensive period of in-house education and orientation which makes it unamenable to external approaches (Foreman and Bailey 1969).

2. The problem may be relatively unstructured and subject to many changes over the course of the project life cycle which is not easily accommodated under an agency's relatively rigid contracting procedures (Foreman and Bailey 1969).

3. The problem may be sufficiently amenable to the development of programmed solutions so that the tourism agency prefers to conduct the work themselves and to make the mistakes so as to gain the educational benefits themselves and in doing so develop an in-house expertise or standard solution to the problem. (Foreman and Bailey 1969).

4. Buying research involves a different set of skills and a different allocation of effort than is required for conducting research oneself. Both the skills and resources for this mode of operation may be unavailable within the research unit at any given time (Heit 1978).

RESEARCH COUPLING PRESCRIPTIONS

As mentioned earlier, when we speak of research coupling activities we are talking about the activities of the research manager to bridge the gap between the researcher and the client. A fairly considerable general scientific literature now exists on this subject alone. Siedel (1982), in a recent review of this literature, observed that most of the prescriptions in this area can be subsumed under three different theories for effective information and technology transfer activities. He refers to these as (1) the communication theories, (2) the linkage theories, and (3) the collaboration theories (Siedel 1982).

Communication Theories   Training for employee presentations, language use, and other communications aids are frequently mentioned as appropriate to improved communication of research information. Quite a number of writers including Glaser et. al. (NMIH 1971), Caplan and Barton (1976), Berg (1978), Glaser and Taylor (1973), Paisley (1968), and Rosenblatt (1968) have commented on particular aspects of the report packaging problem as a means of increasing the effectiveness of research results. Such matters recognized as important include simple language (NMIH 1976), good graphics (NMIH 1971), effective translation (Caplan and Barton 1976), targeting (Glaser et. al. NMIH 1971; Rosenblatt 1968; Paisely 1968), and personal contact (Glaser and Taylor 1973). In the final analysis, however, despite many stylistic prescriptions, authors reviewing "packaging" or formating of social science presentation usually conclude that it is not really the critical factor in effective research use (Korobkin 1975).

Linkage Using Special Communication Strategies   While the general literature in applied science suggests that collaborative approaches are best for coupling with the research user, other linkage strategies appear most effective in maintaining productive relations with the academic scientific community. One sees, in the field of tourism research and management, that there are researchers, users, and managers that largely separate into different communities or cultures. Nevertheless, one can pass information back and forth if one creates the appropriate linkage structures. Such linkage structures include middlemen, advisory committees, opinion leaders, information transfer specialists, conferences and travel symposia, and other information exchange transfer events. Some of these structures, namely, special events, symposia, advisory committees, and opinion leaders seem partially successful in bringing phenomena information problems to the attention of potential researchers. They do not, however, seem particularly successful with applied users (Siedel 1982). For these groups, the linkage theorists suggest the use of information transfer specialists. It has been noted by several commentators, however, that there are problems in finding people who are able to bridge the gap but who are still neither producers nor users themselves (Dior 1981; Frankel 1959).

The Collaborative Model   In terms of coupling activities, the literature suggests that the single most important key to effectiveness in the application of research and technical information to decision processes remains a collaborative approach (Siedel 1982, Driver and Knopf 1981). A collaborative approach involves structuring problem solving situations such that the research and information producers work together at producing appropriate information plans, decisions, and actions. Siedel (1982) quotes Caplan as providing a particularly succinct statement of the need for a collaborative approach (1975b). The policymaker has to know what he needs to know; he or she must understand that the formulation of a problem is at least as essential as its solution or how one defines or determines what is done about it. Also, both the policy-maker and the problem researcher must share a mutual understanding of policy issues and knowledge that is needed. Finally, the researcher, in particular, must contribute an understanding on the basis of "science" or data-based knowledge, as well as determining what must be pursued on the basis of nonresearch knowledge.

A collaborative approach is important in achieving such a mutual understanding because it has frequently been observed that managers and researchers do not initially share the basis for such an understanding. For a start, Duncan (1974) has commented that they often possess different values. Both researchers and managers place considerable importance on practicality, usefulness, and applicability to specific problems. Researchers often display concern for empirical validity, while managers place importance on profitability or the likelihood of payoffs.

Furthermore, Driver and Knopf (1981) suggest that the two professions attract different personality types: individuals who are attracted to the managerial professions have different characteristic personalities, styles of thought, and orientations than individuals who are attracted to the research professions. Individuals attracted to research tend to be stimulated by mental games, like to work with abstract things, have a high degree of tolerance for uncertainty (unpredictability and ambiquity), and are not bothered considerably by waiting to get closure on a problem. Research reports often reflect these characteristics. Individuals attracted to the managerial profession, on the other hand, tend to be less abstract or more "down to earth," they like to deal with more tangible things. As a rule, they have less interest in things that are uncertain, unpredictable, and abstract. They need an environment that is clearcut and familiar. For them, the solution to problems must usually be evident, and they tend to seek immediate results from their efforts. Managers are often described by researchers as not liking to read research reports or hear what researchers have to say. While this might be the case in some instances, it might be that what they read and hear needs to be more understandable. Certainly, managers don't want "iffy" statements or the conditional "maybe" and "perhaps" of many researchers. They don't want things that are heavily qualified. And, they don't want discussions of things that are beyond their control or vision, given everyday operating budgets, pressures, and staff limitations. Instead, managers seek clearcut answers or specific, tangible steps that they can take to resolve the problems they face on a daily basis. And ever so gently, we will suggest that managers, under the press of time and everyday pressures, frequently do not have the time or resources to step aside sufficiently to really understand their problems. Much of the understanding is intuitively sound, but it is frequently quite difficult for them to articulate clearly what their managerial objectives are in a specific problem situation (Driver and

Knopf 1981). In this regard, managers and researchers respond to quite different professional recognition reward structures (Driver and Knopf 1981).

Collaboration breaks down barriers. It also allows researchers and user to clarify together their responsibilities and goals. It has been proven to work. Siedel comments as follows: "Examining the results of over twenty studies, supporting the collaboration theories; Glaser et. al. (NINH 1971, p. 17) noted increased relevance of information, mutual trust and education, and greater commitment to research and the user. But what then, are the keys to good collaboration? These appear to be four fold: commitment, involvement, competence and recognition of the other parties requirements (Siedel 1982, p. 23). Both parties must share the first three requirements while in the case of the fourth one must recognize the importance of freezing and specifying the problem in a researchable form and the researcher must recognize that the user must make a decision with or without his help. In the end the Tourism manager must draw conclusions or take a position with respect to the decision problems in question. The researcher will rarely have the luxury of waiting until all the evidence is in before he speaks.

Summary and Conclusion

The basic premise of this chapter has been that the major reason why tourism research has not been effectively applied is that appropriate conditions are usually not present to warrant such an outcome. Organizational preconditions that we feel are essential if research is to be effectively applied in tourism decisions were stated. Essentially, we maintain that senior management support, sufficient reporting levels, direct channels of communication, and defined functional accountability are prerequisite conditions for successful research operations. Given these preconditions, we believe that a research manager has to successfully master and manipulate two areas of activity: research planning and research coupling. In each of these areas, in turn, there are a series of further specific prescriptions to follow in managing the research function. For research planning, eight of these were commented on in detail. In the area of research coupling, we emphasized the need for attention to three coupling activities.

Possibly the one point that has not been adequately stressed is that provision of information should not be equated with research. Doing scientific research and making it available to the "impure" civil servant or private sector person as "relevant" to their problem is not doing applied research. We have been careful to focus attention on managing research, not on an information brokerage or haven for would-be or has-been academics! Confidence in his or her art, professional competence in dealing with practitioners as well as colleagues must be charcteristic of senior researchers. By endeavoring to satisfy conditions such as the ones just cited, we believe that the goal of improved research for more effective policy formulation and decision-making in tourism can be achieved.

References

Anthony, R. N. *Planning and Control Systems: A Framework for Analysis.* Cambridge, Massachusetts: Harvard University Press, 1965.

Barton, E. *Social Indicators 1973: A Study of the Relationship Between the Power of Information and Utilization by Federal Executives.* Ann Arbor: Center for Research on Utilization of Scientific Knowledge, University of Michigan, 1976.

Beaman, J. "Education for Tourism Research for the 1980's."

Beaman, J. "Leisure Research and Its Lack of Relevance to Planning Management and Policy Formulation: A Problem of Major Proportions." *Recreation Research Review,* October 1978.

Brooks, H. "Science and the Allocation of Resources." *American Psychologist* 22(March 1967):3 Paper delivered at 1966 annual meeting of American Political Science Association New York, September 1966.

Brooks, H."Applied Research: Definitions, Concept, Themes." In *Applied Science and Technological Progress: A Report to the Committee on Science and Astronautics,* pp. 21-55, U.S. House of Representatives by National Academy of Sciences. Washington, D.C.: Government Printing Office, June 1967.

Caplan, N. et. al. *The Use of Social Science Knowledge in Policy Decisions at the National Level.* Ann Arbor: Center for Research on Utilization of Scientific Knowledge, Institute for Social Research, University of Michigan, 1975a.

Caplan, N. et. al. "A Minimal Set of Conditions Necessary for the Utilization of Social Science Knowledge in Policy Formulation at the National Level." Prepared for the Conference on Social Values and Social Engineering. International Sociological Association, April 1975. Ann Arbor: Center for Research on Utilization of Scientific Knowledge, Institute for Social Research, University of Michigan. 1975b.

Coleman, E. "Rethinking the Sociology of Tourism." *Journal of Tourism Research.* vol. 6, no. 1. January/March 1979, pp. 18-35.

David, G. B. *Management Information Systems: Conceptual Foundations, Structures and Development.* New York: McGraw-Hill, 1974.

Dimaggio, P., and Useem, M. "Small-Scale Policy Research in the Arts." In *Policy Analysis,* pp. 187-210. Sage Publications, 1980.

Driver, B. L., and Knopf, R. C. "Some thoughts on the Quality of Outdoor Recreation Research and Other Constraints on its Application." In *Social Research in National Parks and Wilderness Areas.* USDI, National Park Service. Southeast Regional Office. Atlanta, Ga. 1981. pp. 85-99.

Dior, Y. "Applied Social Science and Systems Analysis." In *The Use and Abuse of Social Science,* edited by I. L. Horowitz. New Brunswick, New Jersey: Transaction, 1971.

Duncan, J. W. "Research and the Manager: A Comparative View of the Need for Mutual Understanding." *Management Science* 2018(April 1974):1157-1163.

Forman, L. W., and Bailey, E. L. *The Role and Organization of Marketing Research: A Survey.* New York, New York: The Conference Board, 1969.

Frankel, C. "Being In and Being Out." *The Public Interest* 17(1969): 44-59.

Glaser, E. M., and Taylor, S. H. "Factors Influencing the Success of Applied Research." *American Psychologist,* February 1973, pp. 140-146.

Heit, M. J., and Farrell, R. P. "The Consultant - Client Process: Toward More Effective Research." October 1978.

Keen, P. G. W., and Scott-Morton, M. S. *Decision Support Systems.* Reading, Massachusetts: Addison Wesley, 1978.

Korobkin, B. *Images for Design: Communicating Social Science to Architects.* Washington, D.C.: American Institute of Architects, 1975.

Kotler, P. *Marketing Management Analysis: Planning and Control.* Englewood Cliffs, New Jersey: Prentice-Hall, 1976.

McFarlan, W. F.; Nolan, R. L.; and Norton, D. P. *Information Systems Administration.* New York: Holt, Rinehart and Winston, 1973.

Morton, J. A. "A Model of the Innovation Process". In *Proceedings of a Conference on Technology Transfer and Innovation.* NSF 67-5. May 1965, pp. 15-17.

Myers, S. "Technology Transfer and Industrial Innovation." NFS Contract C321. February 1967.

National Institute of Mental Health (NIMH). *Planning for Creative Change in Mental Health Services: A Distillation of Principles on Research Utilization.* vols. 1 and 2. Washington, D.C.: Department of Health, Education, and Welfare (DHEW) and NIMH. DHEW Publication no. (HMS). 73-9148, 1971.

Paisley, W. J. "Information Needs and Uses." In C. A. *Annual Review of Information Science and Technology.* vol. 3, edited by Cuadra. New York: Wiley Interscience, 1968.

Piore, E. R. "Science and Technology in Industry." pp. 1-8 of this volume.

Price, D. "Is Technology Historically Independent of Science? A Study in Statistical Historiography." *Technology and Culture* 6, no. 4, Fall 1965, pp. 553-68.

Price, W. J. "Concerning the Interaction Between Science and Technology." *OAR Research Review* vol. 10. December 1966; also published in *Cryogenic Technology* 3, no. 4. July-August 1967, pp. 141-43.

Price. W. J. "Planning Phenomena-Oriented Research in AFOSR." In *Planning Phenomena-Oriented Research in a Mission Oriented Organization.* 12th Institute on Research Administration, the American University Center for Technology and Administration. Washington, D.C. 234-27 April 1967.

Price, W. J. "The Key Role of a Mission-Oriented Agency's Scientific Research Activities." In *The Interaction of Science and Technology,* edited by W. D. Comption, pp. 32-67. Urbana, Illinois: University of Illinois Press, 1969.

Quinn, J. B., and Cavanaugh, R. M. "Fundamental Research Can be Planned." *Harvard Business Review,* no. 1. January-February 1964, pp. 111-23.

Ritchie, J. R. B. "Marketing and Marketing Research in Tourism Management." In *Management Problems in the Sphere of Tourism* Proceedings 26th Congress of AIEST. Bern, Switzerland, 1976.

Ritchie, J. R. B. "Tourism Management Information Systems - Conceptual and Operational Issues." In *Tourism Marketing and Management Issues,* edited by D. E. Hawkins, et. al., pp. 337-354, Washington, D.C.: George Washington University, 1980.

Hawkins, et. al., pp. 337-354, Washington, D.C.: George Washington University, 1980.

Rossi, P. H. et. al. "The Theory and Practice of Applied Social Research." *Evaluation Quarterly.* 2(1978):171-191.

Rubenstine, A. A., and Haberstrah, C. J. eds. *Some Theories of Organization.* Homewood, Illinois: Richard D. Irwin, Inc., 1965.

Schwarzbart, G. "Recent Advances and Trends in the Design and Implementation of Management Information Systems." In *Proceedings of the International Symposium of I.U.F.R.O. Subject Group 6.03 Information Systems and Terminology,* edited by S. Shrader. 1979.

Sherwin, C. W., and Isenson, R. S. "Project Hindsight." *Science 156,* no. 3782. June 23 1967, pp. 1571-77. "First Interim Report on Project Hindsight." Summary, June 30, 1966, revised October 13, 1966. AD 642-400. Springfield, Virginia: Clearinghouse for Federal Scientific and Technical Information, pp. 87-94.

Siedel, A. D. "Usable EBR: What Can We Learn From Other Fields?" In *Knowledge for Design,* edited by Bart et. al., pp. 16-25. College Park: Maryland: Environmental Design Research Association, 1982.

Simon, H. A. *The New Science of Management Decisions.* New York: Harper & Brothers, 1960.

Stankey, G. H. "Integrating Wildland Recreation Research Into Decision Making: Pitfalls and Promises." Symposium

CONTRIBUTORS

David J. Allton
Planning and Management Consultants,
  Ltd.
Carbondale, IL

Jay Beaman
Parks Canada
Ottawa, Ontario

Robert H. Becker
Department of Recreation and Park
  Administration
Clemson University
Clemson, SC

Thomas L. Burton
Department of Recreation Administration
University of Alberta
Edmonton, Alberta

Kenneth C. Chilman
Department of Forestry
Southern Illinois University
Carbondale, IL

Neil J. Dikeman, Jr.
Center for Economic and Management
  Research
University of Oklahoma
Norman, OK

John F. Dwyer
United States Department of Agriculture
North Center Forest Experiment Station
Chicago, IL

Gordon Ewing
Department of Geography
McGill University
Montreal, Quebec

Daniel R. Fesenmaier
Department of Recreation and Parks
Texas A & M University
College Station, TX

John C. Hendee
United States Department of Agriculture
Southeast Forest Experiment Station
Asheville, NC

Edward L. Hoffman
Illinois Department of Conservation
Springfield, IL

Alan Jubenville
School of Agriculture and
  Resource Management
University of Alaska
Fairbanks, AL

John R. Kelly
Leisure Research Laboratory
University of Illinois
Champaign, IL

Wilbur F. La Page
United States Department of Agriculture
Northeast Forest Experiment Station
Durham, NH

Ralph L. Levine
Department of Psychology
Michigan State University
East Lansing, MI

Stanley R. Lieber
Department of Geography
Southern Illinois University
Carbondale, IL

Weldon Lodwick
Department of Mathematics
University of Colorado
Boulder, CO

Miles Logsdon
Oklahoma Department of Tourism and
  Recreation
Oklahoma City, OK

Scott Meis
Parks Canada
Ottawa, Ontario

Lisle S. Mitchell
Department of Geography
University of South Carolina
Columbia, SC

George H. Moeller
United States Department of Agriculture--
    Forest Service
Washington, DC

George L. Peterson
Department of Civil Engineering
Northwestern University
Evanston, IL

and

United States Department of
    Agriculture
Rocky Mountain Forest and
    Range Experiment Station
Fort Collins, CO

Herbert W. Schroeder
United States Department of Agriculture
North Central Forest Experiment Station
Chicago, IL

Timothy Schroeder
Department of Recreation
University of Oklahoma
Norman, OK

Elwood L. Shafer
United States Department of Agriculture--
    Forest Service
Washington, DC

Richard V. Smith
Department of Geography
Miami University
Oxford, OH

Stephen L. J. Smith
Department of Recreation
University of Waterloo
Waterloo, Ontario

Herbert Stevens
Department of Forestry
Clemson University
Clemson, SC

Daniel J. Stynes
Department of Park and Recreation
    Resources
Michigan State University
East Lansing, MI

D. Christopher Thomas
Department of Recreation
University of Waterloo
Waterloo, Ontario

Geoffrey Wall
Department of Geography
University of Waterloo
Waterloo, Ontario

Richard D. Westfall
Illinois Department of Conservation
Springfield, IL